T0114448

ELAINE FEINSTEIN

Anna of All the Russias

Elaine Feinstein is a prizewinning poet and novelist and
the author of highly praised biographies of Pushkin,
Marina Tsvetayeva, and Ted Hughes. She lives in London.

Anna

of

All the Russias

THE LIFE OF ANNA AKHMATOVA

Elaine Feinstein

VINTAGE BOOKS

A DIVISION OF RANDOM HOUSE, INC.

NEW YORK

FIRST VINTAGE BOOKS EDITION, APRIL 2007

The Library of Congress has cataloged the Knopf edition as follows:
Feinstein, Elaine.
Anna of all the Russias : the life of Anna Akhmatova / Elaine Feinstein.
p. cm.
Includes bibliographical references and index.
1. Akhmatova, Anna Andreevna, 1889–1966. 2. Poets, Russian—
20th century—Biography. I. Title.
PG3476.A324Z665 2006
891.71'42—dc22
[B] 2005044542

Vintage ISBN: 978-1-4000-3378-2

Book design by Iris Weinstein
Author photograph © Tim Bishop, The Times

www.vintagebooks.com

147468846

In memory of my husband,
Arnold Feinstein

CONTENTS

ILLUSTRATIONS

First insert:

Anna Andreevna Akhmatova, 1922[1]

Andrey Antonovich Gorenko, Akhmatova's father, St. Petersburg, 1882[1]

Inna Erazmova Stogova, Akhmatova's mother, circa 1870[1]

Anna with her brother, circa 1905[4]

Akhmatova as a young girl, Sebastopol, Ukraine, 1899[1]

Nude (Anna Akhmatova), circa 1911, pencil on paper by Amedeo Modigliani[7]

Portrait of Akhmatova by Nathan Altman, oil on canvas, 1914[3]

Nikolay Stepanovich Gumilyov[1]

Nikolay Vladimirovich Nedobrovo, St. Petersburg, 1914[1]

Osip Mandelstam, circa 1938[5]

Nadezhda Mandelstam at her dacha near Moscow, 1979[6]

Nikolai Gumilyov with Alexander Blok, 1924[1]

Boris Anrep in his workshop in Paris, 1908[1]

Olga Sudeikina with a doll in her hand, 1920[1]

Second insert:

Nikolay Nikolaevich Punin[1]

Artur Sergeevich Lurye, Paris, 1931[1]

Akhmatova, Leningrad, 1924 (N. A. Nolli)[1]

Nikolay Punin, 1950[1]

Punin in his student days, 1919[1]

Lydia Korneevna Chukovskaya, 1928[1]

Faina Grigorievna Ranevskaya, 1940[1]

Vladimir Georgevich Garshin, Moscow, 1948[1]

Isaiah Berlin, 1940s

Lev in 1932; 1934; 1949; 1953; 1956

Boris Pasternak, 1930[7]

Joseph Brodsky, 1988[4]

Akhmatova receives Oxford degree, 1965[7]
Anna Kaminskaya, St. Petersburg, 2003[2]
Anatoly Nayman, Frankfurt, 2003[2]
Yevgeny Rein, Moscow, 2003[2]
Akhmatova, Leningrad, 1959[1]

[1] Anna Akhmatova Museum
[2] Courtesy of the author
[3] The State Russian Museum
[4] Private collection
[5] Novosti Photo Library
[6] Magnum Photos
[7] Getty Images

ACKNOWLEDGEMENTS

All the translations of Akhmatova's poems in this book are my own. For many of the prose passages translated in this volume I worked from literal versions. For these, I am indebted to Alla Gallich, Emily Finer, Irina Kostyrina, Daisy Cockburn and Nigar Hasan Zade. Prose from published books is acknowledged in the Notes.

I am aware that Russians find the use of first names without patronymics discourteous. However, an English readership is uncomfortable with patronymics. Hence, after the childhood of the people in this story, I have generally used surnames alone—Akhmatova, Gumilyov, Punin—which seems acceptable to both groups.

I should like to thank Yevgeny Rein, Mikhail Ardov and Anatoly Nayman, who knew Akhmatova well and were kind enough to speak to me at length in 2003; also Nadya Rein, who answered questions by email, and Anna Kaminskaya, granddaughter of Nikolay Punin, who spoke to me at some length in St. Petersburg in 2003. I am grateful to Dmitry Bobyshev, who responded to my emails, and to Mikhail Meylach, who spoke to me in St. Petersburg.

I am grateful to Richard McKane, who generously shared his wide knowledge of Akhmatova on many occasions, and also helped me trace source notes; to Jana Howlett for useful conversations and her network of Russian friends; and to Elena Riumina and Valerie Paikova, whose help in Russia went far beyond the duties of an interpreter in 2003.

I gratefully acknowledge the following sources from which I have drawn and quoted: FTM Agency Ltd. for 684 lines of Anna Akhmatova's poetry; Anna Akhmatova, *My Half Century: Selected Prose*, trans. Ronald Meyer (Ann Arbor, 1992); V. I. Chernykh, *Letopis, zhizni, i tvorchestva Anny Akhmatovoi* (Moscow, 2003); Sergey Lavrov, *Sudba i idei* (Moscow, 2003); Orlando Figes, *A People's Tragedy* (London, 1996); Konstantin Polivanov, *Anna Akhmatova and Her Circle* (Fayetteville, 1994); Frances Laird, *Swansongs* (First Books Library, 2002); J. Marin King, *A Captive Spirit* (Ann Arbor, 1980); Amanda Haight, *Anna Akhma-*

tova, A Poetic Pilgrimage (New York and London, 1976); Solomon Volkov, *Conversations with Joseph Brodsky* (New York and London, 1998); Solomon Volkov, *St. Petersburg* (London, 1996); Lydia Chukovskaya, *Entretiens avec Anna Akhmatova* (Paris, 1980); Nadezhda Mandelstam, *Hope Against Hope* and *Hope Abandoned* (London, 1975, 1989); Emma Gerstein, *Moscow Memoirs* (London, 2004); Irma Kudrova, *The Death of a Poet*, trans. Mary Ann Szpozrluk (London, 2004); Simon Sebag Montefiore, *Stalin* (London, 2003); Lydia Chukovskaya, *The Akhmatova Journals* (London, 1994); Maria Enzensberger, *Listen!* (London, 1991); *Selected Poems of Alexander Blok*, trans. Jon Stallworthy and Peter France (Oxford, 1970); Lois Oliver, *Boris Anrep: The National Gallery Mosaics* (London, 2004); S. Monas and J. Green Krupala, *Diaries of Nikolay Punin* (Harry Ransom Humanities Research Center, University of Texas Press, 1999); Vera Inber, *A Leningrad Diary* (London, 1971); Georgy Dalos, *The Guest from the Future* (London, 2000); Sophie Ostrovskaya, *Memoirs of Anna Akhmatova's Years, 1944–50* (Liverpool, 1988); Anatoly Nayman, *Remembering Anna Akhmatova* (London, 1991); Faina Ranevskaya, *Dnevnik na klochkakh*, ed. Dmitry Sheglov (St. Petersburg, 2002); *F. Ranevskaya Monolog* (Smolensk, 1998); and Faina Ranevskaya, *Sudba shlokha* (Moscow, 2003).

I should particularly like to thank Veronique Lossky, who thought through some of the problems with me; Professor Valentina Polukhina, who gave me advice and introductions to people who could help me; and Pamela Davidson. I am grateful to Lady Berlin, who spoke to me in Oxford in 2004. Particular thanks are also due to Nina Popova and her assistants at the Akhmatova Museum in St. Petersburg. I should like to thank Simon Sebag Montefiore, who introduced me to several notable archivists, and Jennifer Anderson and Anne Wollheim for help in relation to Boris Anrep. I am indebted to Roberta Reeder, not only for her scrupulous scholarship in *Anna Akhmatova: Poet & Prophet* (1994), but also for her help and personal friendliness when she visited me in London in 2004 and for giving me a list of publications which have appeared since her book came out. There has indeed been much important new material in recent years which throws fresh light on Akhmatova's life, for instance the work of Vadim Chernykh, *Letopis, zhizni i tvorchestva*, Vol. I (1996) to Vol. 4 (2003); S. Monas and J. Green Krupala, and Leonid Zykov's editions of the journals of Nikolay Punin (2000);[1] the work of Sergey Lavrov, *Sudba i idei* (2003), which includes Lev Gumilyov's autobiography; and Emma Gerstein's *Moscow Memoirs*, first published in 1998 in Moscow and now available in John Crowfoot's English translation from Harvill Press (2004), along with other publications listed in the Select Bibliography.

I should like to thank my editor, Ion Trewin, and his assistant editor, Anna

Hervé, for all their help, and Linden Lawson, Margaret Body and Ilsa Yardley for their meticulous attention to detail. I am very grateful for a grant from the Society of Authors, made in 1998, which helped to launch me on this project; and for a Wingate Scholarship, which enabled me to return to Russia, travel to Germany and spend the necessary time on this book. As always, I am deeply grateful to my patient secretary, Jane Wynborne.

NOTES ON THE TEXT

All translations are by Elaine Feinstein unless otherwise indicated.

In February 1918 Russia changed from the old Julian calendar to the Gregorian calendar already used in the rest of Europe. The gap between the two had widened from ten days (in the seventeenth century) to twelve (in the nineteenth century) and thirteen (in the twentieth). Thus February 1, 1918 (Old Style) became February 14, 1918 (New Style). As a result the Bolshevik Revolution was from then on celebrated on November 7 (New Style) instead of October 25 (Old Style) when under the Julian calendar it actually took place.

For ease in reading the narrative, all dates are given in the New Style except where otherwise noted.

PREFACE

Anna Akhmatova is one of the greatest poets of Russian literature. Her work has a classical elegance drawn from Pushkin, and a passionate voice rising directly out of the drama of her own life. Many men fell in love with her beauty, yet all three of her marriages were miserably unhappy. She began writing at a time when "to think of a woman as a poet was absurd," as she remarked ironically. Her genius soared above any such category; yet she paid for that triumph as a wife and mother.

All the momentous events of the twentieth century touched Akhmatova's life directly and she became the voice of a whole people's suffering under Stalin. She needed exceptional courage in the quarter of a century when she was not allowed to publish, especially in the years when her son and her third husband were held in the Gulag. An iconic figure for all those whom the Soviet regime repressed, she sustained that heroic role through illness, poverty and a lifelong conflict between womanly affections and the demands of her art.

Akhmatova endured all her unhappiness with a dignity and composure which led Marina Tsvetaeva, the only woman poet of comparable genius, to call her "Anna of all the Russias" as if she were a tsarina.

Anna of All the Russias

St. Petersburg · 1913

The whole mournful city was drifting
Towards a destination nobody guessed.[1]

—AKHMATOVA

*L*et me begin in 1913. The dark and glittering verses which open Akhmatova's *Poem Without a Hero* circle about her memories of that year, the final moments of a corrupt and glamorous world. In the poem, Akhmatova is waiting for guests to celebrate New Year 1941. Candles have been lit, wine and crystal set out when, instead of her expected visitors, a sinister phantasmagoria of dead friends crowd in upon her, dressed as mummers. Their presence calls up St. Petersburg as it once was, when Akhmatova was twenty-four, a fashionable young woman already famous as a poet, with the violent upheavals of the twentieth century not yet under way.

In 1913 St. Petersburg was an Imperial capital, with a black and yellow flag flying over the Winter Palace, private carriages pulled by thoroughbred horses with footmen in uniform who rode on the running-boards. There were trams and trolleys and occasional motor cars. Enticing shop windows on the Nevsky Prospekt had oysters from Paris, lobsters from Ostend and "fruitcakes, smelling salts, Pears soap, playing cards, picture puzzles, striped blazers . . . and football jerseys in the colours of Oxford and Cambridge."[2] On the sunny side of Nevsky Prospekt bookstores sold the latest poetry.

Built below sea level, at the edge of the Baltic, St. Petersburg was always an unnatural city. Thousands of slave labourers died of disease and hunger to realise Peter the Great's grand design of a window on the West. Even after he had declared St. Petersburg his new capital, wolves boldly entered the city at night as late as 1712, and occasionally devoured their prey in broad daylight. Floods constantly overwhelmed the islands, and in 1721 Peter himself was nearly drowned on Nevsky Prospekt. It is the city of Pushkin's "Bronze Horseman," where a poor clerk's lover is carried away by the waters and Falconet's grand statue of Peter pursues him when he dares to protest. It was Gogol's city of shadows and phantoms. The poverty and squalor of the streets and squares still remained much as in Dostoevsky's nightmare vision.

Akhmatova called St. Petersburg her cradle, even though she was not born there. In her autobiographical jottings, she describes childhood streets filled with organ-grinders, Tatar ragmen and tinsmiths, the houses painted different shades of red, front entrances scented with the perfume of ladies and the cigarettes of passing gentlemen, back staircases smelling of coffee, *bliny*, mushrooms and, frequently, cats.

The year 1913 was the Jubilee of three hundred years of the Romanov dynasty, and in February all the main streets of the city were decorated, statues garlanded and portraits of a long line of tsars pasted to the front of buildings. Everything was done to impress foreign and provincial visitors. Electricity illuminated the Winter Palace, the golden spire of the Admiralty arch, other columns, arches and double-headed eagles. The rich dressed with flamboyance. At one opera house, in 1913, for a performance of Glinka's patriotic *A Life for the Tsar*, the boxes blazed with jewels and tiaras. For the nobility, most of whom lived on or near the Nevsky Prospekt, there were balls and banquets. Everywhere military music celebrated the absolute rule of Nicholas II, and the magnificence of his empire.

On the February day which inaugurated the Jubilee celebrations, the Imperial family drove in an open carriage towards Kazan Cathedral. To protect the Tsar on his first public appearance since the revolution in 1905, one battalion of horse guards rode in front of his carriage and another behind. Imperial Guards lined the route. Tourists from all over the empire, and foreign dignitaries from the rest of Europe, were staggered by the splendour of the occasion.

Behind these central areas, St. Petersburg remained a city of filth and disease. Many factories were allowed to discharge their waste into the rivers and canals. With a cholera outbreak on average once every three years, the death rate was the highest of any capital city in Europe. Water had to be fetched in buckets and boiled before it was safe, but thirsty workers gave little attention to this and the general domestic water supply was a breeding-ground for typhus as well as cholera. London had eradicated similar problems in the nineteenth century by building a new system of sewers. No attempt was made to improve the situation in St. Petersburg until 1917.

Nicholas thought of himself as divinely appointed and the many peasants who still wrote directly to him for help saw him as a father who felt compassion for their difficulties. Over Nicholas' vast empire, however, the memory of 1905 remained raw. Reprisals had included executions of suspected radicals and mass violence against ethnic minorities, particularly Jews, incited by the Tsar's Prime Minister, Stolypin. The ruling authorities remained suspicious of Poles and Jews, who were always regarded as likely revolutionaries, and indeed 1913 was the year of the Beilis trial, with its medieval trumped-up charge of child murder against a totally innocent Jew. Nevertheless, in 1913 Nicholas was confirmed in his delusion that his people loved him.

Of the skills required to run a country in pre-revolutionary ferment, it has to be said Nicholas had none. He was a shy man and had always been treated like a child by his family. He danced gracefully, rode well and spoke good English but his agonised cry when his father died at forty-nine was entirely appropriate: "What is going to happen to me and all of Russia? I was not prepared to be a Tsar. I never wanted to become one."[3] Nor was his Empress a popular figure. She did not enjoy public occasions, and found the Jubilee celebrations a strain, even withdrawing from a gala performance at the Maryinsky Theatre. She had acceded to the Russian throne at twenty-two and, although regarded as German by the Russians, she was in fact English. She ordered factory-produced furniture from the London department store Maples for the Winter Palace, where it looked out of place alongside the classic Empire style. She and

Nicholas used domestic English endearments for one another such as "lovey" and "wifey."

The Empress wanted desperately to give Russia a son, but she had four daughters before producing the Tsarevich Alex, who was soon discovered to suffer from haemophilia. This is what brought the strange figure of Rasputin into her life, since he did seem to possess some unexplained powers to stop the child bleeding—even, in one well-attested case, through the power of a telegram, the so-called "Spala miracle." As an influential presence at court, Rasputin enjoyed gifts, bribes and sexual favours. Though it was said he had shrivelled private parts, he spent days in bathhouses and brothels with prostitutes. Rumours about his behaviour widely increased the unpopularity of the royal family. Nicholas, however, would not remove him from court while the Empress continued to put her faith in him as the only healer for her son.

No visitor would have recognised that "the moon was growing cold over the silver age."[4] It was a year of extraordinary cultural ferment. Nineteen-thirteen saw the serialisation of the first parts of Andrey Bely's *St. Petersburg*, Russia's most significant modernist novel, and the publication of Maxim Gorky's celebrated autobiographical trilogy. There were three opera companies, and at the Maryinsky it was virtually impossible to get tickets when Fyodor Chaliapin was singing. On Wednesdays and Sundays there were performances of ballet, where Anna Pavlova and Vaclav Nijinsky could be seen, sometimes in the modernist choreography of Fokine. St. Petersburg enjoyed a great range of theatre, from the Imperially subsidised and traditional Alexandrinsky to the modernist experiments of Vsevolod Meyerhold. Numerous foreign films could be seen in cinemas all over St. Petersburg, while the most popular Russian film actress of the time was Vera Kholodnaya, adored in films that usually took the theme of love unrequited or humiliated.

All the avant-garde movements which were to make themselves felt in the arts took their shape between 1908 and 1913. Futurism drew on street theatre, performance poetry and bizarre costume, and was powerful in the visual arts.[5] Whether poets used classical forms or not, they were instinctively opposed to the values of the society around them. Few of them were committed to political ways of changing that society, but Russian poets before 1913 felt that poetry might make anything happen.

Below street level on Mikhailovskaya Square, at the corner of Italyanskaya Street, lay the legendary cellar of "The Stray Dog," owned by the actor Boris Pronin. To reach the Stray Dog you had to descend a narrow stone staircase and enter a doorway so low that a man had to take off his top hat. All the windows of the café were blocked up, as if to keep out the everyday world, and the walls and ceilings of low, curving plaster were painted with flowers and birds in brilliant colours by the artist Sergey Sudeikin. A group of bohemian artists gathered there after the theatres closed and often stayed talking until dawn. The clientele took pleasure in chilled Chablis, and anglophiles among them preferred the taste of white *bulka* to black Russian *khleb*.* It was a crowded room—very stuffy and not always merry, a society turned in on itself, almost as if unaware of what was happening in the streets above.

In 1913, the Stray Dog was one of the few places in the nightlife of St. Petersburg where literary and artistic people, often with little money, could find themselves welcome. Unlike La Coupole or Les Deux Magots, the Stray Dog did not function as an ordinary café: it was more like a club, with serious lectures, art exhibits and musical evenings. Guests had to sign in a thick volume bound in pigskin. Among the regulars were composers, painters, scholars and occasional foreign visitors such as Richard Strauss and the Italian Futurist Filippo Marinetti. Writers and artists were admitted free of charge, while ordinary punters, dismissively nicknamed "pharmacists," had to pay a hefty 25 roubles a head.

> They were glad to pay. Where else could they see the prima ballerina Tamara Karsavina on a giant mirror performing numbers choreographed by Fokine, or watch Vladimir Mayakovsky in the pose of a wounded gladiator lying in his famous striped shirt on a huge Turkish drum and triumphantly striking it at the appearance of each bizarrely arrayed comrade in futurism![6]

By 4 a.m. at the Stray Dog there would be tobacco fumes, empty bottles and only a few tables at the side still occupied. In an early poem, Akhmatova described the heady yet oppressive atmosphere:

* Two kinds of bread.

> *We are all boozers here, and sleep around.*
> *Together we make up a desolate crowd.*
> *Even the painted birds and flowers on the walls*
> *Seem to be longing for the clouds.*[7]

It was a world of every kind of experiment, especially sexual. Love between women or between men and *ménages à trois* were easily accepted among the intelligentsia. Anna Akhmatova, too, was part of this sexually promiscuous society, though she had married Nikolay Gumilyov on 25 April 1910. In old age, she spoke of their life together as "a marriage of strangers," while Gumilyov described his own unhappiness at being married to "a witch, not a wife."

Musicians like Artur Lurye, then thought of as a rising young composer, played the piano[8] and Ilya Sats, who was famous for his plays at the Stanislavsky Arts Theatre in Moscow, sometimes experimented with a "prepared" piano in the manner of the much later American composer John Cage. Sats had thick black hair and a walrus moustache and wrote his most important work—*The Goat-Legged Nymph*—while sitting in the Stray Dog. Symbolists, Futurists, Acmeists, for all the differences that separated their aesthetic theories, were crammed together there at crowded little tables. Above all there were the poets. Vladimir Mayakovsky in his yellow tunic, Mikhail Kuzmin and Osip Mandelstam—a thin boy with long, dark eyelashes, sometimes remembered with a lily of the valley in his buttonhole. Akhmatova often sat smoking a cigarette at a side table, dressed in a tight skirt, with a scarf round her shoulders and a necklace of black agate. She was always surrounded by a group of admirers. Alexander Blok, the great poet of the preceding generation, found Akhmatova's beauty strangely terrifying. Mandelstam described her as "a black angel" with the mark of God upon her.

Akhmatova's whole bearing changed when she stood to read her poems. She became pale and intense, almost as if hypnotising her listeners. One reason for her charm lay in her voice. The artist Yury Annenkov wrote: "I do not recall anyone else among the other poets who could read their poems so musically." Georgy Adamovich remembers: "When people recall her today, they sometimes say she was beautiful. She was not, but she was more than beautiful, she was better than beautiful. I have never seen a woman . . . whose expressiveness, genuine unworldliness and inexplicable sudden appeal set her apart anywhere and among beautiful women everywhere."[9] Many artists tried to catch her poise in their portraits, notably Natan Altman. Akhmatova was always ambivalent about his celebrated portrait, which shows her in a silken blue dress, its folds almost Cubist in their emphasis, and a bright yellow shawl. Instead, she preferred a portrait by Alexander Tyshler.

The central figure of the cabaret at the Stray Dog was the actress Olga Glebova-Sudeikina. Olga had danced in the Maly Theatre and played Columbine in Meyerhold's *Columbine's Scarf*. Her performance in Sats' *The Goat-Legged Nymph* was highly erotic. She also played the role of the Virgin in *The Flight of the Virgin and Child to Egypt*, with a script by Mikhail Kuzmin and music by Sats.

Olga's apparition hovers over Akhmatova in *Poem Without a Hero*, a fluttering black and white fan in her hand, whispering of springtime, and evoking a dream of their lost youth together. Akhmatova called Olga her "double" but the two women did not much resemble each other physically. Olga had long golden braids, "like Melisande," as Artur Lurye put it. Whatever Olga's charms, Akhmatova's beauty was of another kind. She was elegantly slender to the point of angularity, with a straight back and haughty bearing. Her face had high cheekbones, huge grey eyes and a soft mouth. Her black hair was caught back severely at her neck and cut into a fringe over her forehead. Her features had a classical perfection, though seen from the side her aquiline nose would not be admired today. "Her face and her entire physical appearance was striking. When she stood on the stage, with her shawl falling off her shoulders, she had a strange poised nobility which blended harmoniously with her image."[10]

Even her jewellery took on an iconic quality. Akhmatova's grandmother had bequeathed her a black ring, a band of even width covered with gold enamel. In the centre was a small diamond. Anna was superstitious about its powers to protect the wearer.

In Akhmatova's "A Petersburg Tale," the figure of "Confusion Psyche" lives in an apartment furnished in the style of Olga's home:

> *Your house was flashier than a circus wagon.*
> *Dilapidated Cupids stood on guard*
> *There at the side of Venus' altar.*
> *Your song birds were uncaged,*
> *Your bedroom decorated like an arbour.*[11]

Olga was passionately interested in Italian *commedia dell'arte*, masks and puppets. Rather surprisingly, she came from the province of Pskov where her great-grandfather had been a serf, while her father was one of the poor functionaries described by Dostoevsky. Not everyone found her interesting. Nadezhda Mandelstam, Osip's wife, wrote of her with some unkindness as one of the "dolls" of St. Petersburg, and comments on her faded, tired look, even while admitting she was a "nice, light-headed, flighty creature."[12] Vera de Bosset—in later life the wife of Igor Stravinsky—married Sudeikin after taking him away from Olga; she claimed "basically she was a rather empty-headed little thing whose only interest was suitors."[13] Artur Lurye, however, who lived with her for a time, observed that she was exceptionally musical and had an enchanting laugh and a playful manner. She enjoyed making dolls, and kept her treasures—Don Juan, the Queen of the Night and Desdemona—in special boxes, only taking them out when guests came to visit her. She liked to walk to the Alexandrovsky market, where she bought old china and knick-knacks such as snuff boxes and miniatures. "She loved to entertain in the famous Ozarovsky 'theatre house.' This exquisite little house contained Elizabethan furniture made of Kerelian birch, harpsichords, Venetian mirrors, Russian glass . . . She had a wonderful ear, and an extraordinary memory for music. She could sing anything at a moment's notice."[14]

Osip Mandelstam, one of the giants of Russian twentieth-century poetry, often sat at Akhmatova's table. He was a wonderful reader of his own poems. Akhmatova, who could be bored by listening to poetry, remarked to Anatoly Nayman, a friend from her last years, "All of us were reading poems, and then Mandelstam starts to read and it's as if a white swan glides up."[15] Mandelstam always regarded himself as a *raznochinetz*—that is, an upstart intellectual who belonged to no particular class of society. He was born in Warsaw in 1891. His father Emil was a Jewish leather merchant.* As a *raznochinetz*, Mandelstam fitted easily into the society of the Stray Dog and fell in love often, though Akhmatova teased him out of falling in love with her,

---

* Emil spoke German as his first language and had Goethe and Schiller on his bookcase as well as a "Judaic chaos of books in Hebrew." His wife spoke excellent Russian and it was she who arranged for her sons, including Osip, to have an education at the Tenishev School, one of the best secondary schools in St. Petersburg.

since she wanted him as a friend. She became a close confidante through his infatuations with the beautiful artist Anna Mikhailovna Zelmanova, the great poet Marina Tsvetaeva and Princess Salomea Andronikova, who was one of Akhmatova's intimate circle.*

For all her many admirers, however, Akhmatova's first two books of laconic, intimate lyrics speak most poignantly of unrequited love. Her first book of poems, *Evening* (1912), "accompanied the next two or three generations of Russians whenever they fell in love," as the eminent critic and translator Korney Chukovsky put it. It is never entirely clear for whom she feels such intensity of longing. Unhappiness left no mark on her cool bearing.

In the cellars of the Stray Dog, Akhmatova was already the undisputed queen when Tsvetaeva wrote of her in 1913,

> *Your narrow, foreign shape*
> *   is bent over written papers,*
> *and a Turkish shawl is dropped*
> *   around you like a cloak.*
>
> *You make a single line, which*
> *   is broken and black at once.*
> *You are equally cool—in flirtatious*
> *   gaiety—or unhappiness.*[16]

Tsvetaeva was so overwhelmed by the experience of listening to Akhmatova that in later life she dedicated a whole cycle of poems to her. In 1913 she wondered more simply:

> *who on earth is she*
> *with her cloudy, dark face?*[17]

---

* Professor Valentina Polukhina once asked Salomea how she could have resisted Mandelstam, and reports her as replying, "But, Valentina—he was so *ugly*."

TWO

Becoming Akhmatova

On his fingers there is no ring of mine
Nor will I ever give my ring to anyone.[1]

—AKHMATOVA

In many ways Anna Akhmatova invented herself. She took the pseudonym Akhmatova from a Tatar princess among her maternal ancestors when her father objected to her writing poems which he feared might bring shame on him. Joseph Brodsky called that choice of a name "her first poem."

She was born Anna Andreevna Gorenko on 23 June, St. John's Eve 1889, in Bolshoy Fontan, close to Odessa on the Black Sea coast. Tradition has it that powers of both good and evil are so strong on St. John's Eve that purification rituals—such as jumping over bonfires—were instituted by the Orthodox Church. These superstitions retained their force even among the intelligentsia, and Anna always relished the thought of having dangerous powers.

She was the third child of Andrey Gorenko, a naval engineer, and his second wife, Inna. In 1887 Gorenko was ordered to resign from the Naval Academy in St. Petersburg because of his acquaintance with Lieutenant Niketenko, whose enthusiasm for political change led him to work on designing a bomb. Niketenko's bomb was passed to revolutionaries, who used it to kill a minor member of the Imperial family, and Niketenko was hanged for this act of treason. Gorenko cannot have been much involved himself in either the design or the use to which it was put, since he was only dismissed from his post, a surprisingly light punishment.

After retiring with the rank of Captain, Gorenko was offered a modest Civil Service post, which he took up in 1890. The family moved first to Pavlovsk, close to St. Petersburg, and then to the little town of Tsarskoye Selo, where the Tsar's family spent their summers. This had developed as a summer resort for the aristocracy, and remained a training-ground for regiments of Tsar Nicholas' Imperial Guards throughout Anna's childhood. The Imperial Palace, designed by Rastrelli in 1752 for Tsarina Elizabeth, was only used by Nicholas II and his wife for formal receptions and banquets.

Both Anna's parents had been married before, and Gorenko had two children by his first marriage. He belonged to the aristocracy, though his family had only acquired hereditary nobility a generation earlier, when his own father was rewarded for service in the navy. The Gorenkos had six children: Andrey and Inna, who were older than Anna; Irina, born in 1892; Iya, born in 1894; and Viktor, Inna's last child, in 1896. Serious illness ran through the whole family. Inna's health was frail, and Irina, nicknamed Rika, died aged four in the summer of 1896. Later in life Akhmatova confided to Amanda Haight, her first biographer, that this death threw a shadow over her whole childhood.

Anna spoke sadly of her sisters and particularly of her older sister, Inna, whose death at twenty-seven in 1906 she was always to remember vividly: "Inna was very special, severe, stern . . . She was the way readers always imagined me to be, but I never was."[2] Inna never liked Anna's poetry, which she considered frivolous. Anna's mother responded with greater sensitivity. When her mother read some of Akhmatova's poems she burst into tears and said, "I don't know, I only see that my little daughter is in a bad way."[3]

During the winter of 1900, while the family were living in Tsarskoye Selo, Anna herself was taken gravely ill, probably with smallpox. She wrote her first poem then, at the age of eleven, and always linked beginning to write poetry with that illness: "But even before that my father for some reason called me a decadent poetess."[4] All her life Akhmatova denied that her childhood had any

influence on her stoical personality, shrugging off the whole question of whether it had been an unhappy one by remarking, "Children have nothing with which to compare and they simply do not
know whether they are unhappy or not."[5] Nevertheless, an inner
melancholy seems manifest by her adolescence.

The household was not an harmonious one. Gorenko, always a
handsome man, dressed beautifully with a tall hat worn slightly to
one side. Anna's mother, Inna, came from the Stogov family, once
rich and powerful landowners, now only of modest means. Inna's
first marriage had been to a much older man named Zmunchilla,
who shot himself soon after the wedding. Inna fell in love with
Gorenko as a dashing young man and lived happily with him for a
time until she began to realise that her new husband was, in the
words of her younger son Viktor, "a great chaser after good-looking
ladies and an even greater squanderer of money."[6]

Anna's mother was a beautiful woman. All her life Anna spoke of
her with love, and Anatoly Nayman, who knew Akhmatova in her
old age, remembers that her face changed and softened whenever
she mentioned her.[7] In the first of Akhmatova's *Northern Elegies*, she
wrote about her mother's kindness. Inna was a woman

> *whose clear eyes were so deep a blue that*
> *looking into them was to think of the sea.*
> *She had an uncommon name, white hands*
> *and a kindness that has come down to me:*
> *though it has been a useless inheritance*
> *in this harsh life of mine.*[8]

However, Yevgeny Rein, who also knew Akhmatova well towards
the end of her life, remarked: "Akhmatova always described her
mother as a warm, kind woman—but as I understand it she did not
have a very close relationship with her once she left home."[9]

Her school friend Valeria Tulpanova (later Sreznevskaya) remembered Inna's superb complexion, her pince-nez which was always
falling down and her inability to do anything whatsoever in the
house. She was hopelessly impractical. Although employing many
servants, she could not organise her household. Even lighting a
stove was beyond her skill. Akhmatova's own inability to manage
the simplest domestic task in later life came from her childhood

acceptance of this household confusion. Her father, on the other hand, hated the disorder, and had a spiteful tongue when he criticised it.

The Gorenkos were not a literary household, though an aunt of Anna's Stogov grandfather had been the first woman Russian poet, Anna Bunina. Gorenko and Inna shared some liberal views, however, and knew by heart several of the poems of Nikolay Nekrasov, which were filled with sympathy for the troubles of the Russian poor. Even that book of Nekrasov's poetry—which Anna remembered as the only book of poems in the house—was a present from Inna's first husband.* Both Gorenko and Inna admired the heroism of the wives of the Decembrists in the early nineteenth century. (These women, after the failure of the revolt against the Tsar in 1825, had followed their husbands to Siberia and inspired generations of writers thereafter.) They both sympathised with the aims of "People's Will," which was not simply a party with liberal aspirations for Russia, but a Socialist revolutionary group responsible for several political assassinations.

Inna remained a simple, believing Christian whatever her political sympathies. Anna remembered her mother on Palm Sunday going into the kitchens, bowing to the servants and saying, "Forgive me, sinner that I am." The servants also bowed, and responded with grave ceremony and an acknowledgement of their own need for forgiveness.

The Gorenko family were never part of the Petersburg elite, who lived in the fashionable residential streets around the Nevsky and Liteiny Prospekts. They settled in Tsarskoye Selo. While Anna had no access to the Tsar's palaces, she loved to explore the magnificent parks around them, and even as a schoolgirl relished the thought that the young Alexander Pushkin had explored the gardens before her:

> *For more than a century we've cherished*
> *The sound of a step we can still hear.*[10]

For Anna, Tsarskoye Selo was inseparable from Pushkin, who had gone to school at the Lycée there, and she liked the way the inhabi-

* Or so Akhmatova told Lydia Chukovskaya on 9 June 1940.

tants were never extravagantly dressed but left such displays to the wives of lawyers and doctors. Since Pushkin's time, many other poets, from Lermontov to Innokenty Annensky, found inspiration in the small town.

On market days in Tsarskoye Selo rough wooden tables in the marketplace were piled high with ironware and bolts of fabric; farmers' carts were heaped with potatoes, onions and cabbages. Further from the town centre were streets of wooden houses, usually only one storey, each surrounded by a wooden fence. The Gorenko family lived at a distance from the solemn palaces, in a dark green wooden house with its front on Shirokaya Street. This had once been a tavern and still smelled of milk stored in its cellar, or so Akhmatova remembered it. Opposite their house on Bezymyanny Street was a bootmaker's shop.

Anna's room had an iron bed, a stand for her books, an icon and a brass candlestick, and looked over a lane, which was covered with snow in winter and overgrown with weeds in summer. Remembering her childhood, Akhmatova speaks of herself as a "monster," nicknamed "the wild girl" by neighbours. She was a tomboy who could swim like a fish and climb like a cat. On the shores of the Black Sea, where the family usually spent their summers, Anna walked around without a hat, swam with no more than a thin dress over her naked body and went barefoot. Other young girls used to wear a corset with a bodice top and two petticoats, one of them starched, as well as a silk dress when they went to the beach. They would put on rubber shoes and a special cap and splash themselves with the sea. Anna jumped right in and would swim for about two hours. She describes sitting on a rock like a mermaid, her dress becoming stiff as a board as it dried because of the salt in it.

Akhmatova's poem *At the Edge of the Sea*, written much later, in 1914, uses recollections of her own adolescence, her longing for the love of a prince and her unhappiness at discovering herself tied to an ordinary mate. What gives the poem light and colour is the memory of a childhood which is at once carefree and touched by intimations of being specially gifted, a dreamer on the shores of the Black Sea. She conjures up a landscape of seas, gulls and sails, and remembers picking up fragments of shells and shrapnel from earlier wars as if they were mushrooms or blackberries. She imagines an infatuated grey-eyed boy whom she mocks when he brings her roses. Interestingly, his offer of marriage includes the chance of leaving the provincial world:

> *"I'll grow up soon," he said,*
> *"And take you with me to the North."*[11]

A gypsy prophesies a prince for her, but those words are fulfilled sadly. When her prince finally arrives, he is the captain of a yacht and he drowns when his boat overturns.

Observers were troubled by her habit, even as a young child, of walking in her sleep, sometimes dangerously along the roof of her house. Once her father found her and carried her home in his arms. Like most people who become aware they are regarded as *strange*, Anna began to think of herself as *special*, and once horrified her mother by declaring that the *dacha* they sometimes occupied in the Ukraine would one day bear a plaque with her name. It does indeed do so now, but her mother was shocked at her remark, which she found immodest and dismissed as an example of bad manners.

Anna seized on incidents that seemed to suggest a remarkable destiny was waiting for her. Her nannies and governesses played a large part in fostering this, particularly a peasant woman from Kaluga. When Anna was only five, she came upon a rare type of mushroom, called a "tsar mushroom," in the Estonian spa town of Gungerburg, where the family were staying. Her superstitious nanny found many portents of good fortune in the discovery. As a child in Kiev, Anna found a pin in the form of a lyre in a park called the Tsar's Garden, and her governess told her this meant she would become a poet.[12]

Her mother took little hand in Anna's upbringing. Anna, with none of the hothouse precocity that marked Tsvetaeva's childhood,[13] learned to read at seven from Leo Tolstoy's ABC book and was sent at the age of ten to school in Tsarskoye Selo. By thirteen, she was already infatuated with poetry, particularly that of Alexander Blok.

From 1900 Anna attended the Maryinsky Gymnasium in St. Petersburg. Poetry was not much loved by the pupils there, and for the most part her classmates found Anna too introspective. Her friend Valeria thought her quiet and reserved in contrast to her own mischievous and outgoing personality.[14] The two girls, however, formed a close and long-lasting relationship once their families began to share the same house in Tsarskoye Selo. There they were able to play in a wonderful, large garden and Valeria soon discovered that Anna was far more remarkable than she had guessed, not only writing poetry but reading banned books. By the time Anna was thirteen, she already knew all the French *poètes maudits,* including Verlaine and Baudelaire.

Photographs of Anna at six or seven show a girl with a plump face and short hair. By fourteen, the pudginess of her childhood face had altogether disappeared, and Anna had become a beauty, with chiselled features, huge grey eyes and long, black, straight hair. She had a dancer's body. As an adolescent she was five foot eleven inches tall, and so lithe and supple that "she could easily touch the nape of her neck with her heels when she lay prone."[15] Valeria observed that Anna had begun to take a new interest in her appearance.

At the Maryinsky Gymnasium not all the pupils were rich. Those who were had their lunch carried to them on silver trays at noon by their valets. Although not among those privileged creatures, Anna was learning how to behave like an aristocratic young girl nevertheless. She had already acquired an immense poise, even if her sleepwalking suggests some inner disturbance, to which the general disorder in the household and the frailty of her siblings may have contributed. Lydia Chukovskaya, who became Akhmatova's closest friend in later years, traced the vulnerability, helplessness and fecklessness in Akhmatova to the loneliness of her childhood. In this, Anna's growing comprehension of the troubles in her parents' marriage must have played a part.

In 1902 Anna was enrolled by her father as a full boarder at the Imperial Educational Society at the Smolny Institute in St. Petersburg, which had a reputation for severe discipline. After only a few weeks, Anna had to be withdrawn from it, probably because she was found sleepwalking down the school corridors.

Anna saw much less of her father than of her mother, though it was he who sometimes took her to St. Petersburg to visit the Opera House and the Hermitage. But her father's infidelities were current gossip, and in Tsarskoye Selo people recognised a certain Leonid Galakhov as his illegitimate son.

In autumn 1904 Anna's older sister Inna married Sergey von Stein, a philologist and a scholar of Pushkin. The poet Annensky, who was related to von Stein through his own daughter-in-law, remarked: "In his place, I would have married the younger daughter." It was a compliment Anna was to treasure all her life; and indeed in the manuscript of Sreznevskaya's memoirs this sentence is written in Akhmatova's own hand.[16]

Her longing for love is evident in a poem of 1904, dedicated to "A.M.F.," probably Alexander Fedorov—an Odessa man of letters—of whom she wrote unromantically to von Stein that when he kissed her he "smelled of dinner." In her poem, however, that kiss is recalled as tender and trembling. Her longing for a poetic mentor was equally intense. Later, she would find in Annensky a simple, direct voice which conveyed subtle psychological insights through objects observed in everyday life. Akhmatova and her friend Valeria first read him as school children and always remembered the speech Annensky gave in 1899 at the inauguration of Pushkin's monument.

It was 1905 that Anna spoke of as a watershed and an awakening, though she usually connects the horror of it to the Russian fleet destroyed by the Japanese at Tsushima. More generally, it was a year of revolt and reprisal, and in that winter Anna heard real gunshot for the first time. However, she was only aware of the Revolution of 1905 at a distance.[17] Nor did she know anything about life in the workers' districts of St. Petersburg, where there was no water, and excrement had to be piled into backyards until it was collected by lorry. Though Anna would have seen little of these horrors, she could not fail to be aware of the Peter and Paul Fortress, across the River Neva from the Winter Palace, where prisoners of the Tsar were held and sometimes kept in cells so small that they could neither stand nor lie down.[18]

On 9 January 1905—which came to be known as Bloody Sunday—150,000 unarmed workers, led by a priest called Father Gapon, marched, singing hymns and carrying crosses and icons, to present a humble plea to the Tsar in the Winter Palace. The Tsar was not there at the time, but playing dominoes in Tsarskoye Selo. Those who were guarding the Winter Palace were alarmed by the column of demonstrators and the petition was not even received, let alone examined. Instead, rifles were fired directly into the crowd.

Then the cavalry charged, which resulted in many injuries and perhaps 1,000 dead. Country-wide risings followed as news of the mas-
sacre spread; these were put down with vicious brutality.

Yevpatoria on the Black Sea, where Anna was living with her
mother in that year, was far from the epicentre of the events of 1905.
All the Gorenko family, however, would certainly have known of
many brutalities in the countryside. Provincial Russia was a place of
poverty, cruelty and disease. Even in the twentieth century, eighty
percent of the population was classified as peasantry. Women in the
villages suffered particularly barbaric treatment. Wives could be
stripped naked and beaten by their husbands, and peasant proverbs
stressed the likely benefits of such beatings: "The more you beat
your wife, the tastier the soup will be." There were crueller punish-
ments. Erring wives were sometimes tied to the end of a wagon and
dragged through the village streets. Women were not the only
group to suffer. Other transgressors were punished by castration,
hacking to death by sickles, or stakes driven down the throat.[19] The
Tsar had for many years watched the growth of nationalism in his
vast empire with distrust, which was particularly heartfelt against his
Jewish subjects, who were mistakenly held to be responsible for the
assassination of Alexander II.

The Revolution of 1905 was a crisis that had been brewing since a
decade of crop failures brought famine from the Ural Mountains to
the Black Sea. Alongside calamitous struggles, vicious reprisals and
pogroms which the Tsar made no attempt to punish, a series of disasters befell the Gorenko household. In spring 1905, following a dis-
pute with his employer, the Grand Duke Alexander Mikhailovich,
Anna's father decided to retire from his Civil Service post. In September 1905 her sister Inna went into a sanatorium for tuberculosis
patients and was dead less than a year later, on 15 July 1906. It was
the second death of a sister in Anna's short life and it affected her
profoundly. In a letter to her brother-in-law, von Stein, she confessed to a depression so extreme that—if we are to believe her
account—she tried to hang herself and might have succeeded if the
nail had not popped out of the limestone wall. It is unclear which
particular event drove her to such an extremity. This was also the
year of her parents' separation.

The immediate occasion for Andrey Gorenko's break-up with his wife was his affair with Yelena, the widow of Rear-Admiral Stran-nolyubsky.[20] It was she who persuaded him to send his family off to the Crimea, saying the climate was better there. Andrey moved in with Yelena Strannolyubskaya, and his wife and children left for the south. Anna must have guessed at her mother's pain, however proudly she bore herself. Some of Akhmatova's strange willingness to accept the unhappiness of her several marriages in later years may spring from witnessing the way her mother adopted the role of abandoned wife so meekly. Akhmatova always referred to her father's mistress as "practically a hunchback." This was altogether unfair. In fact Yelena was an unusual woman, a graduate of Oxford University, who had decided that Anna's father should become her exclusive property. For the rest of her life, Anna was usually dismissive of the wives of men with whom she had affairs, so it is unsurprising that she had no good words to say of her father's mistress.

Anna's remarks suggest a sense of personal hurt that went deep, and she was angered enough by her father's desertion to write of him later: "I cannot respect my father, I never loved him, why should I obey him?" She had often declared how much she hated her father's shouting. Now she remembered him as grudging and mean, even refusing her the money for a new coat.

Perhaps the most momentous event of 1905 in Anna's personal development, however, was the loss of her virginity. In spring 1905 she fell in love with Vladimir Viktorovich Gulinishev-Kutuzov,[21] a student at the University of St. Petersburg and ten years older than she was. She allowed him to seduce her, and longed for him miserably when he returned to his University. In the winter of 1905 Anna was in Yevpatoria, and only moved to Kiev in 1906 to take examinations. There, she lived in an apartment with her aunt, and attended the Fundukleyevskaya Gymnasium. Since her sister Inna's death, as she wrote to von Stein, she felt lonely, far from her family and friends in Tsarskoye Selo, and was always crying or silent.

In the south of Russia, when Anna was a child of little more than thirteen, the poet Nikolay Gumilyov recognised he had fallen deeply in love with her. It was not their first meeting. He and his elder brother had already met her with Valeria Tulpanova on their way home from school, and Gumilyov was overwhelmed by the serious young girl and often arranged to encounter her as if by chance. Occasionally, they had met at receptions given by Inna and von Stein. Anna was not particularly interested in the boy, who was awkward, with a slight lisp and a wandering eye.

Gumilyov, often referred to by the diminutive "Kolya," was not handsome, but he had an original mind, and was dedicated to both literature and a life of adventure. He shared many of Anna's enthusiasms, particularly for Symbolist poetry and Alexander Blok. Akhmatova was to love other men more passionately than Gumilyov, but the course of his life and death were fundamentally to mark her own, and he was to be the father of her only child.

Gumilyov was born on 3 April 1886 at the naval base of Kronstadt, which guarded the approaches to St. Petersburg. His father was a ship's doctor, eighteen years older than his wife. After his father retired, Tsarskoye Selo became as much Nikolay's childhood home as it was Anna's. He, too, did not live among the palaces and pavilions, but in a staid backwater favoured by retired military personnel.

As a child he was very close to his mother, and learned through her to enjoy reading. Indeed, his poor health led him to be educated at home until the age of ten, when the whole family moved to St. Petersburg and he was enrolled at the Gurevich Gymnasium. He had very wide-ranging interests, including astronomy, and by thirteen was familiar with Milton, Coleridge and Ariosto in translation as well as the Russian classics.

At fourteen, his family moved to Tbilisi, Georgia, at the edge of the Caucasus, surrounded by the spectacular scenery which had so aroused Russian poets of the nineteenth century. A precocious child, Gumilyov had discovered Nietzsche by 1903 and determined to dedicate his life to poetry. His first poems were published at his own expense in October 1905.

As a schoolboy, attending the gymnasium, Gumilyov dressed flamboyantly in a uniform with a white lining, and fellow students already gossiped about his arrogance and wilful transgressions. It was an interesting ostentation in a boy who thought himself ugly and had not yet won any reputation as a poet. One person who took Gumilyov's wish to become a poet seriously was the headmaster of his gymnasium, a teacher of classics and a poet himself: the very same Innokenty Annensky whose poems were to delight the young Akhmatova a few years later. Annensky was not a very impressive head teacher: the school lacked all discipline and he seemed not to mind if most of his pupils loafed about. He was, however, a talented translator, and his own poetry was poignant and lyrical. He made time to encourage Gumilyov.

Gumilyov's first declaration of love for Anna, at Easter 1905, was serious enough for him to fall into a depression when she rejected him. He threatened to take his own life. Anna was so appalled by the unwanted responsibility this placed on her that she quarrelled with him and they stopped meeting for a time, only making up in the spring of 1906. All through that autumn Akhmatova lived in Kiev and, although she was no longer seeing Kutuzov, who had returned to St. Petersburg, she was, as she confessed in a letter to von Stein, still in love with him. She begged her brother-in-law to procure a photograph of him. At length, and perhaps reluctantly, he acceded to her request.

When on 11 February 1907 Anna wrote to thank von Stein for the photograph of Kutuzov, her description of his coldness and stylish indifference gives the very pattern not only of figures who would appear in her poems but also of many of the men she was to find sexually attractive in later life: "In this photograph he is exactly as I knew him, loved him, and was horribly afraid of him. Here he is so elegant, so unconcerned and so cold."[22] In the same letter, she reported: "I can't tear my soul away from him. I'm poisoned for life." Perhaps the notion of "poisoning" seems overdramatic, of a piece with anxious descriptions of her state of health. Yet to lose a first love so soon after her mother had been deserted by her father may indeed have altered her mindset. For the rest of her life she expected to be abandoned, and that expectation coloured her poetry.

Pavel Luknitsky records that it was in Sebastopol at the *dacha* of their friends the Schmidts that Gumilyov was told by Anna that she was no longer a virgin.[23] It may have been the pain of this discovery that led him to make a serious attempt at suicide in August 1907 after he returned to Paris.[24]

Gumilyov was only twenty-one years old. His awkwardness in company was due to shyness, not timidity. He was as passionate about exploration as he was about literature. In 1907 he made his first trip to Istanbul, using money he had saved from his monthly allowance from his parents. On his way back home, filled with the excitement of his trip, he stopped in Kiev, staying in a cheap hotel near the station, in order to see Anna again. This time they discovered more rapport: they spoke about poetry and the mysteries of an occult world.

Yet he already had a life of alternative excitement. In a letter to the Symbolist poet Valery Bryusov, Gumilyov described with some bravado an affair he had had with a Greek woman in Smyrna, and a fight with gangsters in Marseilles. He continued to have affairs with other women, even as he pursued Anna. At Vyacheslav Ivanov's Tower, a salon held at the poet's large apartment, Gumilyov met the poetess Elizaveta Dmitryeva, with whom he was to begin a love affair in 1909. Travelling with her to visit the poet Max Voloshin at Koktebel in the Crimea, he went so far as to propose marriage but was rejected, to his chagrin. When he returned to visit Anna in a resort town near Odessa, she sensed something insincere in his renewed protestations of love. After an attempt to start a journal, *Ostrov (Island)*, with Alexey Tolstoy, which lasted only one issue, Gumilyov joined with Sergey Makovsky and others to launch *Apollon*, which soon gathered an important group of literary contributors and became one of the most influential journals of the period.

However, Dmitryeva and Voloshin joined forces to concoct a poetic hoax. Together they invented a fictitious poet, Cherubina de Gabriac, and sent poems supposedly by her to the editorial offices of *Apollon*. Makovsky was taken in by them and intrigued by the fact that the poet would not consent to a meeting. Dmitryeva was soon exposed as the author, but this joke may have had serious consequences. Makovsky chose to publish the verses of Cherubina de Gabriac rather than those of Annensky, and Akhmatova always believed that this insulting substitution so depressed Annensky that it led to his death from a heart attack a month later. Gumilyov, too, was outraged to discover that Dmitryeva had combined with Voloshin to make a fool of him.

When Gumilyov published his own first volume of poetry, he sent his poems to Bryusov, whom he continued to ask for literary advice even when he was enrolled in the Sorbonne for a course in French literature. He remained socially awkward in Paris, and perhaps lonely, though Anna's brother Andrey was there and he had a good friend in Alexey Tolstoy, who later became a leading novelist. However, he smarted from several snubs. Konstantin Balmont, an eminent Russian poet who lived close by Gumilyov's lodgings, did not bother to reply to a letter that Gumilyov sent him. And he was humiliated by Zinaida Gippius. Gumilyov was carrying with him a letter of introduction from Bryusov to Gippius and her husband Dmitry Merezhkovsky, both of whom had been exiled for their opposition to the Tsarist government at the time of the 1905 Revolution.

Zinaida Gippius had a mass of copper hair, green eyes and a heavily powdered face. She was an exotic figure, acknowledged as a poet and someone who prided herself on the distinguished celebrities she drew to her salon. When Gumilyov presented himself awkwardly at her Paris address with Bryusov's letter, she behaved so rudely that he never forgot the humiliation. Gippius gave Bryusov her own unkind account of meeting the nervous boy: "Have you actually seen him? We absolutely died. Boris had enough strength to make fun of him, but I felt absolutely paralysed. Twenty years old, sickly and pale, full of clichés. . . . He then put on his top hat and left . . . I found some issues of *Vesy* with his poems, wishing at least to justify your interest in the brilliance of his verse, but could not."[25]

Anna's own correspondence with von Stein continued throughout 1907. It must have come as something of a surprise to her brother-in-law when, on 2 February 1907, she suddenly announced to him: "I am going to marry my childhood friend, Nikolay Stepanovich Gumilyov. He has loved me for three years now, and I believe that it is my fate to be his wife. Whether or not I love him, I do not know, but it seems to me that I do."[26] A few days later, on 11 February 1907, she was once again writing unhappily to von Stein of her unrequited love for Kutuzov, though in an earlier letter she had declared: "But Gumilyov is my Fate, and I obediently submit to it."[27]

Her life was far from easy. From Anna's letters to her brother-in-law, we gather how much her mother's finances had suffered as a result of her father's departure. When her great wish was to go to St. Petersburg for Christmas, lack of funds put the journey in doubt. Yet her father had not withdrawn his paternal authority, and still felt within his rights to forbid his daughter to do as she wanted.

When Anna returned to the gymnasium to complete her last year, she wrote to tell von Stein,[28] without any admission of pleasure, that a poem of hers—"On his hand are many shiny rings"—had appeared in the second issue of Gumilyov's magazine *Sirius*. In fact, *Sirius* only ran to three issues, and most of the poems in it were written by

Gumilyov under various pseudonyms. Probably Akhmatova was right not to value this early verse highly, but the peculiar mixture of sadness and defiance has something of the tone of later poems:

> *On his hand are many shiny rings—*
> *from tender hearted and submissive girls.*
>
> *The diamond triumphs, and the opal*
> *dreams, the ruby glows like a miracle.*
>
> *On his fingers there is no ring of mine.*
> *Nor will I ever give my ring to anyone.*
>
> *The golden rays of the new moon made it for me*
> *and slipped it on my finger in my sleep, whispering:*
>
> *"Keep this gift and be proud of your dream."*
> *I will never give my ring away,* never.

Perhaps uneasy about von Stein's reaction, Anna told him, "I am not writing poetry any more. Everything has gone out of my soul, along with the only bright and tender feelings that illuminated it."[29] In the same letter, she inquired about the date Kutuzov's examinations would come to an end. On 28 May 1907 Anna herself graduated from her Kiev gymnasium with good grades.

She was now nearly eighteen. Her health was not good, though there may be an element of hypochondria in her description of it. She complains in the letters to von Stein of fevers, headaches, insomnia and those heart palpitations which were to afflict her all her life. In Kiev, where the family were living on Meringovskaya Street, she told von Stein that she fainted when no one was in the apartment. She was homesick for St. Petersburg. She admits that she feels this in part because she knew that Kutuzov lived there. The tone of the letters is now less sad than flirtatious, however. She seems to be trying to impress the older man with her romantic condition.

At the end of April 1907 she changed her mind once again about Gumilyov's proposal of marriage and they stood in silence together, looking at the shore while he absorbed the disappointment. Gumilyov wrote of this moment in "Rejection":

> *A princess—or maybe nothing but a sad child—*
> *She leant over the sleepy sighing sea*
> *And her lithe and graceful body seemed as slight*
> *As if straining to meet the dawn in secrecy.*[30]

In the last quatrain of this poem she comes vividly to life, as "a tired child with a look of helpless sorrow."

When Anna spent the summer of 1907 with her mother, Gumilyov took a room next to them and begged Anna to come away with him. She continued to refuse. That autumn she began to study law at Kiev University, though she found Latin and history the only interesting parts of the course. In December 1907 Gumilyov returned to Paris and tried again to poison himself. He was found unconscious in the Bois de Boulogne. Nevertheless, he dedicated his second book of poems to Anna. Four months later he returned to Sebastopol to propose marriage once more, but Anna repeated her refusal. In August 1908 Anna travelled to St. Petersburg on her own and stayed there for ten days. What might have looked like a gesture of unusual social temerity was rendered respectable by the fact that she stayed at her father's house.

Anna continued to refuse to marry Gumilyov, saying she did not love him though she admired him as an outstanding man. In the autumn of 1909, however, Anna suddenly allowed herself to be persuaded. She claimed that what convinced her was a single sentence in his letter: "I realised that only one thing in the world is interesting to me. And that is everything that concerns you."[31] This was a boundless assurance of *centrality* which it seemed she desperately needed. In one of Anna's most dispirited letters to von Stein, probably in 1906,[32] she had written, "No one will ever need me." Gumilyov's long pursuit seemed to guarantee she would at least always be necessary to him.

Akhmatova, who was to write of herself in the fifth part of *Northern Elegies* as someone who found her shape as if "in someone else's" dream, or "in a mirror not my own,"[33] saw herself in Gumilyov's early lyrics as a mermaid with a sinful ruby necklace at her throat (1904), a princess or a capricious child (1907) and as Eve, a young tigress, at once whore and saint in his poem "Adam's Dream" in 1909.

On 29 November 1909, after watching Gumilyov and a few other authors working for *Apollon*, who were giving a poetry reading in

Kiev, she responded to his new proposal of marriage with unexpected consent. Gumilyov nevertheless set off to explore east Africa, visiting Alexandria and Cairo, the Nile and the Sphinx in search of inspiration for his poetry.

In February 1910 Anna travelled to St. Petersburg, once again staying with her father, and saw her friend Valeria. She did not discuss her forthcoming marriage. But by the end of the same month, in a letter to Valeria, she wrote with unexplained foreboding: "My bird, I am going to Kiev now. Pray for me. Things cannot get worse. I want to die. You know everything. My unique, beloved, tender Valya. If I were able to cry. Anna."[34]

Why did Anna marry Gumilyov in 1910? Her school friend Valeria was convinced she was never in love with him but that he represented a literary world which she passionately wished to join. He was always a poet with a highly original mind; Osip Mandelstam was to declare him one of the few people he found worthy of conversation. Yet Anna never thrilled to his poetry as she did to that of Annensky, or, later, listening to Mandelstam.[35]

Still, in love or not, she writes humorously to von Stein of her excitement at receiving letters from Paris from her fiancé: "Then there is usually a fainting spell, cold compresses and general bewilderment. This is due to my passionate nature, nothing else. He loves me so much that it is positively terrifying."[36] In the same letter she begs von Stein not to abandon her when she goes to live in St. Petersburg, and adds, "I hate and scorn myself; I cannot bear the lie which entangles me." What is the lie? Is all this an adolescent affectation? Anna, it must be remembered, had only recently finished school.

In worldly terms, her acceptance of Gumilyov was entirely sensible. Provincial society was dull, and it would be quite understandable if Anna wanted to marry only to escape the likely course of her life. Anna was unusually poor for someone of her rank. "We live in terrible poverty," she wrote.[37] "We have to scrub floors and do our own washing." She now lived with an uncle who shouted words of abuse at her. Conventions still oppressed unmarried women, and Gumilyov offered her the chance to leave the provinces and enter the exciting literary world of St. Petersburg, in which he was already a figure. Anatoly Nayman thought her dislike of Chekhov's plays—which she expressed throughout her life—came from a recognition that "he wrote about girls like Anna Gorenko."[38] She disliked Chekhov's description of situations which offer no escape, and perhaps feared some such destiny could be her own. At length, for whatever combination of reasons, she agreed. It is possible to imagine that she might never have become Akhmatova if she had remained in the provincial south.

THREE

Marriage to Gumilyov

Since I can't have love, and I have no peace,
Allow me a bitter glory.

—AKHMATOVA

khmatova and Gumilyov were married on 25 April
1910 in the Nikolayevsky Church in Nikolska Slo-
bodka, on the River Dnieper near Kiev. None of
Akhmatova's family attended the wedding, which is all the stranger
as her mother lived in that very town.[1] Neither husband nor wife
was in the least suited to matrimony or an ordinary domestic life.

They stayed in Kiev until the end of April, and then set off for
their honeymoon in Paris. Makovsky was also travelling on the same
train. He claims to have asked Akhmatova how she was "enjoying
marital relations and were they giving her satisfaction?" She stalked
out of the compartment without replying.[2] Even if this tale is true—
and Irina Odoevtseva, though a student of Gumilyov, was less close
to him than she suggests in her memoirs—the interpretation of it is
far from straightforward. Makovsky would like us to imagine that
Akhmatova and Gumilyov were sexually incompatible but it seems
likely Anna was simply offended at such an intimate inquiry. Her
own insight into what went wrong between Gumilyov and herself is

far more persuasive. It is from Akhmatova's own lips we hear the suggestion that Gumilyov's desire for her had diminished early. She
thought they had been engaged for too long and by the time they
married in 1910 he had "already lost his passion" for her.[3]

To judge from the poetry he wrote in 1910, Gumilyov was barely
married before he began to chafe at the constraints of matrimony.
Perhaps his infidelities were no more than the conventional behaviour of an aristocratic young man, yet he had been obsessed with
Akhmatova for seven years and had pursued her until he wore her
down. Now he possessed the flesh-and-blood woman, his passion
had cooled.

However, Paris was there to be enjoyed. It was the first time
Akhmatova had seen the city which is such an important part of the
Russian cultural landscape, or heard the language whose poetry she
had loved from childhood, spoken casually by Frenchmen. She and
Gumilyov strolled together to admire the Eiffel Tower, elegantly
dressed women and a Paris of green squares and narrow cobbled
streets lined with wine shops, sweet-smelling bakeries and stalls
piled with lettuces and radishes. They took a room at number 10
Rue Bonaparte, and were soon visiting museums, the medieval city
of Cluny and the Latin Quarter which Gumilyov so much enjoyed.
It was there Akhmatova first encountered the Italian artist Amedeo
Modigliani, who wrote many letters to her when she returned to
Russia. On this visit she listened to Ida Rubenstein performing *Salome*
and watched Diaghilev's *Ballets Russes.*

At the end of June the couple returned to Russia, once again on
the same train as Makovsky. They shared their excitement over
Diaghilev's productions, and seemed happy enough together,
though Makovsky feared their marriage would soon be troubled by
Gumilyov's restlessness, which went along with an unusual need for
emotional support. For her part, Akhmatova found Tsarskoye Selo
"completely dead" after Paris.

Gumilyov was financially generous to his new wife, according to
Irina Odoevtseva, though it is far from clear where he found the
money to be so: "When I married Anna I . . . put 2,000 roubles in the
bank in her name. I wanted her to feel independent and completely
provided for."[4] On their first Christmas together he bought her a
box covered with floral material and filled to the brim with silk
stockings, a bottle of Coty perfume, two pounds of Kraft chocolate,

a tortoiseshell comb and Tristan Corbière's *Les Amours jaunes.* "How thrilled she was. She danced round the room with delight."[5]

Some of Gumilyov's poems suggest a love that rapidly became a battle of wills. Eschewing the magical imagery he often uses to evoke an African landscape, one particularly fierce lyric baldly describes a sexual struggle. The lover has learned to understand that a quarrelsome woman may reject him one day, and be ready enough to submit the next. Gumilyov warns that taking pleasure in such a game is dangerous and threatens that she should not be surprised:

> *If the moaning of love turns to moans of torment*
> *And our kisses are stained with blood.*[6]

A biographer must acknowledge that this poem could well refer to one of Gumilyov's other love affairs. In spring 1911, however, Gumilyov writes less violently of a domestic evening reading and talking about the poems of Leconte de Lisle, which seems likely to have been spent with Akhmatova. Together, they conjure up the spirit of Leconte de Lisle himself:

> *Through the twilight of evening, thrown back in his armchair*
> *The sharp profile of the Creole with the soul of a swan.*[7]

The predominance of the first person in Akhmatova's own lyrics makes it very tempting to read her early poems as a kind of diary, and many of the poems in her first book, *Evening,* suggest the same isolated and solitary girl who confessed her unhappiness in correspondence with von Stein. The reader feels addressed directly by someone exposing her most intimate feelings of unrequited love, oddly flavoured with a bitter-sweet pleasure. Later, when she writes about a love affair in which the heroine has been rejected, it is clear that the heroine is herself a poet:

> *And if I die, then who*
> *Will write my poems to you?*[8]

However, her heroines have none of the laconic wit of her conversation recorded in the memoirs of friends.

It is particularly difficult to be sure which of Akhmatova's poems were written with her husband in mind, though one dating from 1910 seems to go to the heart of their swift estrangement:

> *He loved three things in this world:*
> *White peacocks, evensong*
> *And faded maps of America.*
> *He hated it when children cried.*
> *He hated tea with raspberry jam, and*
> *Any female hysteria in his life.*
> *Now imagine it: I was his wife.*[9]

Any problems in their relationship were aggravated by a spell in the countryside that summer on Gumilyov's family estate. In Slepnyovo, neighbours such as the Nevedomskys compared Akhmatova's face to that of a stern novice from an Old Believer convent. Far from finding her beautiful, they thought her features too angular and described her great eyes as unsmiling. The household in general found her too exotic. Old family servants spoke of her as a Frenchwoman, and the chief of the district council thought she must be Egyptian. Though she may have been able to ignore such comments, Akhmatova was bored by the country. While Gumilyov enjoyed horse-riding, she did not, and otherwise there were only amateur dramatics to divert them.

Vera Nevedomskaya recalled that Akhmatova was always silent at table. Akhmatova had a significantly different memory of mealtimes. She saw that Vera was flirting with her husband and guessed that their relationship was probably already intimate: "I remember I found a letter from her addressed to Nikolay which could only be interpreted one way."[10]

By early autumn, Akhmatova was very ready to return to Tsarskoye Selo, and to live in the town house there that belonged to Gumilyov's mother. This had two storeys and, though the plaster was flaking, the rooms were warm and comfortable, and included a library with wide divans, heaps of cushions and bookcases up to the ceiling. Anna brightened up at the prospect of literary St. Petersburg. Gumilyov, however, was already planning a new trip to Africa, this time Abyssinia. He left on 25 September 1910 and did not return until March 1911. Alone in the Gumilyov family house, Akhmatova began to visit St. Petersburg on her own, to see her school friend Valeria Tulpanova. Later, she went to her mother in Kiev, and there she read Annensky's "Cyprus Chest" with exhilaration and found it generated poems of her own which now began to "arrive in a continuous wave."[11] During the six months Gumilyov was in Africa, Akhmatova worked on the poems that were to go into *Evening*.

On 21 October, only a few weeks after Gumilyov's departure, Akhmatova wrote the following poem while briefly in Kiev. It is tempting to read it as a memory of saying goodbye to her husband, though it seems unlikely that she offered him such an intense expression of her earlier passion for him:

> *You want to know how it was?*
> *A clock in the dining room struck three.*
> *She had to hold on to the banister*
> *until she managed to speak. "Goodbye.*
> *That's all. Ah, no, I forgot.*
> *I love you. I always loved you.*
> *Even then." And he said, "I know."*[12]

There was no other man in her life at this point, though she may have been remembering Kutuzov. It is as if she has infused the poem with her own disappointment, and given it fictional intensity.

Part of the following poem, dated 17 February 1911 and written in Tsarskoye Selo, also suggests Akhmatova might have Gumilyov's departure in mind:

> *Through a half open door*
> *The linden trees smell sweetly,*
> *Forgotten on the table lie*
> *A riding crop and a glove.*
>
> *Inside the yellow lamplight*
> *I listen to the murmurs.*
> *Why did you go away?*
> *I still don't understand . . .*[13]

This next poem, however, also written in 1911, seems far more likely to be fired by an adulterous passion for a lover, at once calculating and controlling, to whose will she can only submit:

You are drinking my soul through a straw.
An astringent, heady flavour.
I won't interfere with the torture.
For weeks now I've been at peace.

When you are finished, tell me.
I'm not sad without a soul today.
I'll walk down a road close by here
And watch young children at play.

The gooseberries are in bloom now.
Workers haul bricks over there.
Are you a brother or lover?
I don't need to remember.

It is bright here. There is no shelter.
My exhausted body can rest,
While those who pass by me wonder:
"Was she widowed yesterday?"[14]

Gumilyov was neither a model nor a mentor for the young Akhmatova and he was not at first an admirer of her poetry, even though he had published the early poem in *Sirius*. According to Akhmatova in later life, as Chukovskaya reports, Gumilyov "couldn't stand" her adolescent verse:

He'd agree to listen and pay close attention because it was me but he was very critical; he suggested I occupy myself with something else . . . And then it was like this: in April we married . . . And in September he left for Africa and spent a few months there. During that time I wrote a lot and had my first taste of fame: all around . . . He came back. I didn't tell him anything. Then he asked: "Have you written any poetry?"—"I have." And I read it to him . . . He gasped. From that time onwards, he always loved my poetry very much.[15]

One of the stories which most annoyed Akhmatova, and which she went to some trouble to rebut in later life, was that Gumilyov was jealous of her success and discouraged publication of her poems in *Apollon*. Makovsky writes that when he suggested publishing some of her poems, she replied: "What is Nikolay Stepanovich going to say on his return?" In fact, Gumilyov was not against her being an author and Akhmatova herself indignantly denied Makovsky's story that he had offered to pretend he had stolen poems from her album without her consent. However, even though Gumilyov was not envious of her success, he was jealous of her passion for poetry, which he felt unnaturally exceeded anything she felt for him.

Soon Akhmatova began to make a significant mark upon members of the artistic community, not only with her beauty and her poetic gifts but also with a presence of majestic sadness. In March 1911, she was invited to read at Ivanov's Tower. Ilya Ehrenburg recalled Ivanov as looking like a pastor out of Ibsen in old-fashioned clothes and gold-rimmed spectacles. At the Tower, candles were lit in chandeliers, red wine flowed and an evening usually began with a paper read on some religious or mystical topic. The atmosphere was heady: "He [Ivanov] invited her to his table and offered her a place to the right of himself which had been occupied by Annensky when he was alive. When he introduced Akhmatova, he described her as 'a new poet who reveals to us everything that was left unrevealed in the secret places of Annensky's soul.' "[16]

"The Grey-Eyed King," one of Akhmatova's most celebrated poems, dated 11 December 1910 and written in Tsarskoye Selo, packs something of the punch of one of the *Border Ballads*. It begins with a husband casually telling his wife that the king is dead but, as we move through the poem, his wife's distress and the grey eyes of his daughter hint that the king has fathered the child the husband thinks is his own:

> *Welcome to you, everlasting pain!*
> *The grey-eyed king died yesterday.*
>
> *The autumn evening was scarlet and humid.*
> *When my husband returned he told me calmly*

"They brought him back from the hunt, you know.
They found his body lying by an oak.

You must be sorry for the young queen. They say
In a single night her hair has gone grey."

Then my husband found his pipe near the fire
And went out promptly for his night's work.

Now I shall wake up my little daughter
And look deeply into her grey eyes.

Outside poplars are sighing in the wind.
"He is no longer alive, your king."[17]

The poem contains personal resonances, even if the central situation is invented: an ideal love has been lost, a husband is disappointingly offhand. But perhaps Gumilyov is at once the husband and the grey-eyed king. The young Nikolay who had promised to be an ardent lover is dead. Akhmatova is left with a distant husband who seems only too eager to escape from her presence.[18]

In May 1911, Akhmatova returned to Paris. Nadezhda Chulkova, who met Akhmatova for the first time on this trip, remembers going for walks with her and sometimes venturing into little cafés. Akhmatova could not fail to be aware of the immense interest she aroused. "She was very beautiful. Nobody in the streets could tear their eyes away from her."[19] It was on this trip, as Akhmatova spent several weeks alone in Paris, that she formed a close friendship with Modigliani, whom she had met briefly in 1910. She sat with him in the rain on a bench in the Jardins du Luxembourg under an enormous black umbrella, while they recited Verlaine to each other, or wandered about the old parts of Paris in the moonlight with him.

Amedeo Modigliani was born in Livorno in July 1884, the fourth and youngest child of Sephardic Jewish parents. His father was an unsuccessful entrepreneur, his more enterprising mother ran a school. It was an unconventional household. Indeed, Amedeo's eldest brother, Emmanuele, was sentenced to six months in gaol as an anarchist when Amedeo was eighteen.

After studying under Giovanni Fattori, an Italian Impressionist, he moved to Venice where he met some of the artists who were among the leaders of the Futurist movement, then to Paris in 1906. His mother was able to give him a small allowance. When Akhmatova first met him, he was without the least reputation as an artist and had almost no money. Such fame as he enjoyed was as a drinker and someone who experimented with drugs; and the year before Akhmatova got to know him he had been forced to retire to Livorno for a time, sick and exhausted. He was in his early twenties, however, and very handsome. Not for nothing was he known as "Modi," an affectionate pun on the French *maudit*, or accursed. Indeed he believed that artists were an altogether different species of human being, for whom ordinary rules of morality did not apply.

Modigliani was living at Impasse Falguière when Akhmatova returned to Paris and they became more intimate friends, though Akhmatova never spoke of him as her lover. He was so poor that, when they sat together in the Luxembourg gardens to eat lunch, he was unable to pay for the customary chairs and they used a bench. She recollected that he seemed to know none of the friends she had in the Latin Quarter.

Perhaps because of French anti-Semitism, then unknown in Italy, Modigliani discovered a much stronger sense of his Jewish identity in Paris and made friends with several important Jewish artists working there, including the painter Chaim Soutine, who sat for him when Soutine was a very young man, and the poet Max Jacob. Akhmatova remembered him telling her, "J'ai oublié de vous dire je suis Juif." She was not affected by the discovery, and indeed always denied that she could see any difference between those of her friends who were Jews and those who were not. Several of her later lovers were Jews, but her lack of prejudice was not shared by many Russians. The only Jews allowed to live in St. Petersburg at all were wealthy merchants, people with higher education, certified craftsmen or men who had served in the army. These numbered about 35,000 in the Russian capital in 1913 nevertheless and, though they made up less than two per cent of the population, they were often talented artists, musicians and writers.

Modigliani made several drawings of Akhmatova; one in which she is scantily dressed on a bed, and another nude, certainly suggest intimacy;[20] she sometimes called on him without arrangement, which underlines their familiarity. Once, finding he was not there, she threw a bunch of roses in at his window. Whether or not they were lovers, their friendship was an important one, and helped to open her heart to other loves when she returned to Russia.

~

The inner circle of the Symbolist movement continued to gather at the Tower on Zubovsky Boulevard. Symbolism was an attempt to grasp at some "higher reality." In contrast, Acmeism set itself the task of understanding individual human experience. Rather like the Imagists in America, the Acmeists demanded sharpness and clarity above all, and wrote about objects in the real world. As early as 1910 leading members of the Symbolist movement were beginning to reject the idea of poet as priest. An article in *Apollon* by Mikhail Kuzmin, "About Beautiful Clarity," though mainly about prose, was a harbinger of the changes to come as the Acmeist movement began to break away from the old tenets connecting poetry to mystery. Akhmatova, Gumilyov and Osip Mandelstam were the key figures in the new movement and Akhmatova's lucid verses the purest expression of it. The Poets' Guild of Acmeist poets met sometimes in Tsarskoye Selo at the Gumilyovs', or in the home of the poet and critic Georgy Adamovich. At these meetings Akhmatova said little and became animated chiefly when Mandelstam read his poems.

When *Evening* came out from Gumilyov's Poets' Workshop in an edition of 300 copies in 1912, the book proved so popular that it had to be reprinted several times. It contained forty-six poems and an intelligent introduction by Mikhail Kuzmin. Gumilyov wrote wonderfully about the poems, particularly praising the way "a series of beings, mute until now, had acquired a voice . . . women in love, cunning and rapturous, at last speak in their own genuine and at the same time artistically convincing language."[21] Akhmatova was almost embarrassed by her sudden fame: "I considered it indecent, as if I had left a stocking or a brassière on the table."[22] She wanted the poems to be read as fictions rather than confessions. But, although she cleverly hides which man her poems were written about and may well have collapsed several figures into one, all the lyrics expose undignified emotions. Mandelstam saw Akhmatova's poetry as introducing "all the enormous complexity and wealth of the nineteenth-century novel into the Russian lyric."[23]

Gumilyov's enthusiasm for poetry was heartfelt, but his insatiable curiosity and love of adventure marked him out from his fellow writers. The exhilaration of travel to exotic parts of the globe was far more interesting to him than the literary salons of St. Petersburg. His first hazardous trip through Egypt and east Africa had been undertaken by mule train, and he returned from it with his skin burnt and his clothes in tatters, bearing the hides of several animals he had hunted. On his second trip, to Abyssinia and the Somali peninsula, he received modest support from the Academy of Sciences, and made a fascinating photographic record of the expedition. He met Haile Selassie, the future emperor, crossed a crocodile-infested river and endured a summer heat too intense for travel by day. He found the whole experience intoxicating and began to hate even more intensely being pent up in domestic life. Marriage had been a mistake, he now believed, however eagerly he had pressed for it. Perhaps the reasons he gave for feeling as much were disingenuous. Irina Odoevtseva reports in her memoirs that Gumilyov had dreamed of a happy home and wanted not only a wife but a friend and cheerful companion, while Akhmatova preferred to make jealous scenes followed by stormy reconciliations.

One of Akhmatova's most celebrated poems, written in 1911, may have been composed after a marital quarrel:

> Beneath my veil, I clutch my own hands.
> "Why do you look so pale today?" they ask.
> "Because I made him drunk with misery
> And desperate grief," I say.
>
> How to forget that? He staggered out,
> His mouth twisted into a line of pain
> And I ran after him down the steps
> Only catching up with him at the gate.
>
> Panting, I cried, "It was all a joke.
> Don't leave me. If you do, I'll die."
> His smile was grim and cool as he replied,
> "It's windy now. Don't stand outside."[24]

Whoever occasioned the poem, the image resembles other figures in her early poems. And in this lyric at least there is little irony, though the newspaper *Utro Rossii*, reviewing *Apollon*, which contained some of Akhmatova's poems, on 3 December 1911, identified the secret poison of irony which infused almost every one of them. If Gumilyov objected to the confessional tone of her poetry, he made no issue of it, though he admitted to disliking the subject matter of some of her poems, notably lyrics such as the following:

> *Yesterday my husband beat me*
> *With his woven belt folded double.*
> *I've been at the window all night*
> *Waiting for you by a candle.*
>
> *Dawn breaks. A puff of smoke*
> *Rises over the forge. Once*
> *Again, you couldn't be here*
> *To visit this sad prisoner.*
>
> *For you, I have accepted a wretched*
> *Life of misery and torture.*
> *Is it a blonde you love?*
> *Or does she have red hair?*
>
> *How can I not cry out? My*
> *Heart is dark. I'm stifled.*
> *And only a few thin sunbeams lie*
> *On my unrumpled bed.*[25]

This is a realistic attempt to imagine the life of a Russian peasant girl waiting for her lover. It could, of course, be read to imply quite unfairly that Gumilyov was himself a sadist. The source of Akhmatova's fantasy has been debated, since any cruelty she had suffered herself was never physical. No doubt she had an element of masochism in her own makeup,[26] but the popularity of her poems among women all over Russia confirms this as a common enough phenomenon.

If Gumilyov disliked Akhmatova's "fictions," he disliked even more the rumour that he could not resign himself to the role of prince consort once her fame had grown wider than his own. Akhmatova, too, was always indignant at the accusation. Long after Gumilyov's death, when his verse remained out of print and disregarded, she threw much of her energy into setting that record straight.

He does not seem to have been physically jealous of her admirers. He readily accorded his wife the same freedom he took himself, yet, despite his infidelities, Anna Akhmatova probably remained the great love of his life. He had no idea of divorcing her, for all his involvement with other women. Yevgeny Rein, however, finds his account of Akhmatova's jealousy peculiarly unlikely. She was never passionately in love with Gumilyov and since "he was sleeping with any woman who would have him, she regarded him less with jealousy than disdain."[27]

It may be so. Her school friend Valeria remarks that she found few images of Gumilyov in Akhmatova's poems, whereas his "were full of her until the end of his life." Akhmatova's disappointment in her marriage, however, was far more profound than her husband realised. There is no doubt that she felt betrayed and humiliated by the role of cheated wife. Her younger brother Viktor observed in 1973, some years after his sister's death, that the adolescent experience of her father's abandonment of her mother made it hard for her to resign herself to having a young husband who was behaving in much the same way. Nadezhda Mandelstam speculates that if there had been no Revolution, Akhmatova might have been content with an open marriage to Gumilyov and would not have divorced him. She found it difficult, though, to imagine Akhmatova presiding over a salon in a wing of his house.

In Gumilyov's "In Foreign Skies," Akhmatova recognised herself as Margarita in love not with Faust but Mephistopheles, and found his description of a relationship which is a battle to the death similar to their own. But she had dreamed of a tsarevich, and the tsarevich was dead. Her own sense of desolation could only be eased by discovering another source of strength in poetry, and perhaps the fame that went with it. Hence Gumilyov's complaint that Akhmatova did not find his love her greatest treasure:

> *Her soul is open greedily*
> *Only to Poetry's bronze song.*

Nevertheless, Gumilyov continued to value what she wrote. In a letter to her from Odessa on 9 April 1913 he said: "All day I've been remembering your lines about the girl by the sea. It's not just that I like them. They intoxicate me. . . ."[28]

Fidelity aside, Akhmatova was always loyal to Gumilyov. When she heard how Zinaida Gippius and Dmitry Merezhkovsky had once been hurtfully dismissive of Gumilyov's appearance at their Parisian salon, she determined never to enter their circle, however powerful. It was a decision she held to even when courted by Gippius.

Akhmatova was three months pregnant when she and Gumilyov left for Italy together on 3 April 1912, travelling on the way to Berlin, Lausanne and San Remo before taking a boat to Genoa. Gumilyov took a week on his own to explore Rome while Akhmatova remained in Florence. On the way back they went through Bologna, Padua and Venice, staying in Venice for about ten days. Akhmatova was fired by this experience of Italian art to speak of the paintings entering her imagination as vividly as a dream.

Akhmatova spent the summer of 1912 with her mother at her cousin Nanichka Zmunchilla's estate near the Austrian border. But she was back in Tsarskoye Selo when she went into labour. She felt the first pains early, and she and Gumilyov set out for the hospital on foot because he was too confused to suggest taking a cab or even a tram. They arrived at the maternity hospital on Vasilievsky Island at 10 a.m., but in the evening Gumilyov disappeared and did not return all night. He reappeared the next day when everyone was visiting Akhmatova to congratulate her on the birth of a son, a little embarrassed because he had not spent the night in his own home.[29] Their son Lev (a name often made more affectionate as "Lyova" or "Lyovushka") was born on 1 October 1912. Some time after his birth, the couple agreed to give each other complete freedom to do whatever they wanted sexually, and "stopped being interested in each other's intimate life."[30]

The accounts of Akhmatova's feelings for her new baby are contradictory, some suggesting that she found the responsibility burdensome. Nevertheless, Akhmatova breast-fed the child herself, and for a time did not leave the house, until she agreed that Gumilyov's mother, who enjoyed the daily task of looking after her grandchild, should care for Lev in Slepnyovo. It was far from uncommon for women of Akhmatova's class to have others bring up their children, but in later life Lev came to see her decision as a kind of desertion.

When she was able to return to the Stray Dog, she found life going on much as usual. In her poem describing an evening there, Akhmatova suggests a whole society longing to escape, and ends:

> You are puffing a black pipe
> Into smoke with a strange shape.
> I've put on my tightest skirt
> To look even more svelte.
>
> The weather outside is unknown to us.
> The windows are sealed shut.
> You look around with the eyes
> Of a very cautious cat.
>
> My heart is sick with longing—
> Is it death I am waiting for? Well,
> I know that woman, dancing,
> Over there, will end up in hell.[31]

The woman dancing was surely Olga Sudeikina, already a close friend of Akhmatova, and altogether amoral sexually. On 29 March 1913, her lover Vsevolod Knyazev shot himself in the chest and died from the wound on 5 April. When, in later years, Akhmatova came to write about this period of her life in *Poem Without a Hero*, his suicide and Sudeikina's callous behaviour became an image for a whole group who thought themselves above conventional morality. There are hints that Akhmatova felt responsible for a similar death. Over a period of twenty years assessing the history of events in her own life, and wishing to believe in a just God, Akhmatova came to think that this childish selfishness which she shared with Olga had led to the terrible years of war and terror.

The most vivid impression we have of Vsevolod Gabrielovich Knyazev comes from the poems and diaries of Mikhail Kuzmin, a composer as well as a poet, who was for a time a lover of Sergey Sudeikin. Kuzmin was characterised as Mephistopheles when Akhmatova came to write *Poem Without a Hero*, but at the time of the Stray Dog she inscribed a book to him as her "wondrous teacher."[32]

Knyazev was a strikingly handsome Cornet of the dragoons, who wrote poetry and at nineteen had attached himself to the actress Palladiya Starynkevich. Kuzmin, then thirty-eight, met Knyazev on Sunday, 2 May 1910, at Pavlovsk, and was immediately attracted to his good looks. Throughout 1911, they had a passionate sexual relationship and Kuzmin wrote a number of explicitly erotic love poems to the young man.

In the summer of that year, Kuzmin and Knyazev lived with Sudeikin and his wife Olga, because Sudeikin wanted to paint a picture of the two men together. Sudeikin and his wife enjoyed an open marriage, which allowed them both to pursue their own proclivities, and it soon became apparent that Knyazev was much taken with the pretty Olga. His affair with Kuzmin came to an abrupt end, though there was a brief emotional reconciliation. This is the background to Knyazev's jealous attachment to Sudeikina which led to him shooting himself when he watched her returning home with another lover. Looking back at that suicide across the murderous century that was to follow, Knyazev's gesture must have seemed absurd as much as tragic.

A year after his son's birth, on 1 October 1913 Gumilyov once again set off for Africa, as a director of an expedition to Somalia. Pavel Luknitsky recollects that Akhmatova told him how, when Gumilyov departed, his mother asked her to sort out the drawers of his writing desk. There Anna found letters from one of his lovers. It was the first she knew about this particular affair, and one cannot help wondering whether her mother-in-law wanted her to make that discovery. Although she and Gumilyov had already agreed to give each other complete sexual freedom and Akhmatova proudly denied feeling any jealousy, she didn't write a single letter to Gumilyov while he was abroad. When they met on his return, she gave him the love letters she had found in his desk with a queenly gesture. However bravely she bore herself, the intimate details of his betrayal hurt her. Yevgeny Rein's insistence that Akhmatova could not have been jealous because she did not love Gumilyov ignores her personal humiliation.[33]

On 13 October 1913, Gumilyov had a son, called Orest, by Olga Nikolaevna Vysotskaya, an actress in Meyerhold's theatre. Akhmatova recorded the event in her notebook but added that it had absolutely nothing to do with herself. Akhmatova and Gumilyov continued to appear together at the Stray Dog. Gumilyov did not feel tied to Olga and moved on to his next affair, with Tatyana Adamovicha, the sister of the poet and critic Georgy Adamovich.

In the autumn of 1913, Akhmatova wrote a key poem that has to be read in autobiographical terms because of the last verse, which is central to an understanding of her life and the strength that poetry had begun to give her. It opens:

> A woman loved can ask whatever she wants.
> One who is loved no longer can ask for nothing.[34]

She goes on to recommend that her lover should save her letters, if only to throw light on his own biography. Her consolation lies in the thought that school children will read her poems after her death:

> And learning my unhappy story
> Let them smile at it, however slyly.
> Since I can't have love, and I have no peace,
> Allow me a bitter glory.[35]

As 1913 wound down, Akhmatova pursued her separate life. On 15 December, she visited Alexander Blok with books for his inscription. In two of them he simply wrote "To Akhmatova from Blok." In the third volume he wrote out a madrigal dedicated to her. Akhmatova described the madrigal with some amusement as a way of keeping her at a distance, holding out the palms of his hands in a warding-off gesture, which seemed to say "Don't touch me." For all Blok's reputation as a lover of women, Akhmatova hinted to Chukovskaya that even *femmes fatales* who tried to seduce him were unsuccessful since "he pushed them away at the last moment."[36]

At the beginning of January 1914 Akhmatova wrote her own poem for him. Blok's beauty and fame attracted many admirers, who bought picture postcards of his romantic features.

> I visited the poet on Sunday,
> precisely at noon. It was quiet
> inside his enormous room.
> There was frost outside the windows,

and a sun as red as raspberry
above a straggle of blue smoke . . .
how intensely my silent host
now looked at me.

He had the kind of eyes
that everyone can recall.
For me it was better
not to look at them at all;

what we said, I still remember:
that Sunday, and a smoky noon
inside his tall, grey house,
by the sea gate of the Neva.[37]

Blok's wife was the beautiful actress Lyuba Mendeleyeva, the daughter of the great chemist Dmitry Mendeleyev, and the woman to whom he had written many hundreds of poems in *Verses to a Beautiful Lady*. However, they lived separate lives.

Akhmatova's and Blok's poems for one another were published side by side on 13 February 1914 in a magazine called *Lyubov k tryom apelsinam*, edited by Meyerhold. Romantic Russians liked to believe that Blok and Akhmatova were lovers, but there seems no evidence for this and Akhmatova herself always denied it. Such a relationship would have pleased Blok's mother, who observed that Akhmatova "was stretching out her arms to her son and would be ready to love him" but he "turns away from her even though she is beautiful and talented."[38] She suspected her son did not like Akhmatova's habitual air of sadness. When *Rosary* came out, however, Akhmatova inscribed a copy for Blok: "From you I learnt all the pain and the craft of writing poetry."

On 6 January 1914, Pavel Luknitsky questioned Akhmatova about the year she broke physically with Gumilyov and records her sharp reply: "We were intimate for a very short time, until 1914 approximately."[39] Although four years is not such a short time—and indeed it is rather surprising to discover their sexual relationship went on two years after they had given one another complete freedom— Gumilyov had been away for many months of their marriage.

Some time in 1914 she wrote a lyric which alludes to Gumilyov's latest infatuation, and promises not to pursue him with jealous letters. The poem hints at unhappiness but asserts, "I don't ask for your love," and advises him with some irony to:

> *Give her my poems to read,*
> *Give her portraits of me.*[40]

Akhmatova seems to draw herself up to her full height as she recommends him not to come back to her when his desire is surfeited:

> *What help could I give you?*
> *I don't set out to cure happiness.*[41]

One lyric, dated January 1914, was clearly not written for her husband:

> *We met for the last time,*
> *as always, on the embankment.*
> *The waters of the Neva were high,*
> *In the city, they feared floods.*
>
> *He spoke of Summer, and said the idea*
> *Of a woman as poet was ridiculous.*
> *I still remember the tall palace of the Tsar*
> *and the Peter and Paul fortress.*
>
> *I knew the air did not belong to us*
> *but was a miraculous gift from God.*
> *And exactly at that moment, the last*
> *of my sad songs was given to me.*[42]

Even if we cannot put a name to this man, we recognise his whole being from a significant poem, to which she gave the title "The Guest" and dated January 1914:

> *Everything is as it was. Against the windows*
> *A fine snowstorm was beating. Even I*

Had not changed very much.
And then a man approached me.

I asked him: "What do you want?"
He said: "To be with you in Hell."
I laughed at that: "You prophesy
Disaster for both of us."

But raising his dry hand
He lightly brushed the flowers:
"Tell me, how do men kiss you,
Tell me how you kiss."

Then he stared at my ring
With fixed and weary eyes
And not one muscle moved
In his vicious, radiant face.

I know what comforts him.
He understands precisely:
That he needs nothing from me
While I can refuse him nothing.[43]

On 15 March 1914, Akhmatova published her second book of poems, called *Chetki*, which can be translated simply as *Beads*, though it is more commonly translated as *Rosary*. There is some religious imagery in the book but most of the poems are secular and, as the epigraph from Baratynsky suggests,* the dominant theme continues to be the parting of lovers, though there is now more overt sensuality, notably "In the Evening," which describes with relish "oysters in ice, smelling of the sea," even as a lover touches her dress "as someone might stroke a cat or a bird." Most reviews were enthusiastic, including that of Gumilyov.

By 1914 Akhmatova had met several figures who would be important in her emotional life. In February 1914 she made the acquain-

---

* "Then let us say goodbye forever. But understand that two names of the guilty ones, not one, will be found in my poems. . . ." Baratynsky is a contemporary of Pushkin.

tance of Artur Lurye and the art historian Nikolay Nikolaevich Punin.[44] Nikolay Nedobrovo, the poet and critic, was already in love with her, and letters from Nedobrovo's close friend, Boris Anrep, filled with praise for her lyrics, were already exciting her interest. All these men became her lovers.

Akhmatova was to give Luknitsky an account of how, in the first half of June 1914, Tatyana Adamovicha had begun pressing Gumilyov to get a divorce. In her notebook Akhmatova claims proudly that the only reflection of Gumilyov and Tatyana Adamovicha in her poetry were the lines written in May 1914:

> *I don't want a bit of happiness*
> *I'll see off my husband to his sweetheart.*[45]

These are, however, startling lines. The man she is writing about cannot be mistaken, and the sense of unhappiness his betrayal has caused her is not disguised. Akhmatova at once agreed to a divorce, stipulating only that her son Lev must remain with her. Gumilyov's mother was furious when she heard of this, and told her son: "I'll tell you the truth. I love Lyova more than Anna and more than yourself." Her passion for Lev is far more frequently described than Akhmatova's, whose attachment to her little son was deep nevertheless.

On 13 July 1914, Akhmatova went to visit Lev at Slepnyovo and wrote to Gumilyov that she found him healthy and happy and very sweet. A few days later she wrote to him again, confessing herself already bored with the neighbours there. She wonders, rather wistfully, whether Gumilyov might be coming back to Slepnyovo after his visit to Tatyana Adamovicha in Vilnius. She also shows an unexpected concern about their joint financial situation, since she had no money herself, and suspected he had none either. She implored him to remember to redeem a number of things they had pawned. This kind of poverty was relative: they continued to eat well enough and employ servants to look after them.

She spent the rest of the summer of 1914 with her mother near Kiev with Nedobrovo living nearby. Rumours of war reached Tver province faintly. Nevertheless, Akhmatova wrote her prophetic "July 1914" with a true apprehension of events to come:

There's a charred smell. They have been burning
dry peat in the marshland for weeks.
Now even the birds have stopped singing
And the aspen no longer trembles.

The sunshine shows God's displeasure.
There's been no rain since Easter.
Into my yard came a stranger
with only one leg, and he said to me:

"Frightening times are approaching. Soon
fresh graves will cover the land:
there'll be earthquakes, plague and famine;
eclipses and signs in the heavens."

And yet our enemies will not
rip up our lands at their pleasure,
for the mother of God herself will spread
a white cloth over our sorrows.[46]

In the second part of this poem, moans of wives and widows have begun to rise to the heavens, and earlier prayers for rain on parched fields have been answered cruelly with a drenching of red blood. Akhmatova has taken on the robes of Cassandra. She will continue to write love poems, but from now on her range has widened.

FOUR

Petrograd

We grew a hundred years older in an hour.[1]

—AKHMATOVA

The sense of an impending war in Europe had been present for some time. Often felt in Russia as a clash between Teutons and Slavs, it roused atavistic memories of medieval heroism. As such, this called up popular loyalties, and by the time of the Balkan Wars in 1912–13 several major Russian cities witnessed huge demonstrations in support of Slavs. There was a mood of belligerence in the higher echelons of the army. The reality was a struggle between two power groups. On 1 August 1914, Germany declared war on Russia. In her notebook, Akhmatova wrote, "In the morning, there are still quiet poems about other things. But in the evening the whole world is smashed to smithereens."[2]

The Tsar called for general mobilisation on 30 July 1914, and when he announced hostilities, on Sunday, 2 August, from the balcony of the Winter Palace, the whole crowd before him knelt and sang the national anthem. This swell of patriotism may have been brief, but a xenophobic response lasted longer, and was strong enough to provoke an attack on the German Embassy and led many to change their German-sounding names precipitately. In the same spirit, the name of the city of St. Petersburg was changed by the government to the more Slavic-sounding Petrograd.

Akhmatova visited her father in Petrograd and her mother in Kiev, before returning to join Gumilyov and Lev again in Slepnyovo. On 5 August at Tsarskoye Selo railway station, with Gumilyov already in soldier's uniform, the couple met Alexander Blok. Akhmatova recollected that Gumilyov was shocked to think of him being sent to the front line and muttered: "It is like roasting nightingales."[3] Akhmatova returned to Slepnyovo. She was very ill with tuberculosis the first summer of the war, and on doctor's orders was only allowed out of bed for a few hours a day.

The intelligentsia, always looking for signs of spiritual renewal, hoped the war would provide a reason for individuals to sacrifice themselves for the good of the country. This patriotism was not much in evidence among the millions of peasants and workers who set off for the front, but few expected a long war, still less the bloody stalemate of the early campaigns from autumn onwards.

Gumilyov joined the cavalry with enthusiasm the day war was declared, looking for a chance to prove his own physical bravery and much influenced by Nietzsche's aphorism that war and courage do greater good than charity. He left for the front a month after war was declared, and wrote vividly of the adrenalin of going into battle. Several poems reflect the excitement he drew from the danger. His exhilaration, so different from the experience of most front-line English war poets, is argued for convincingly in a letter:

> I did not sleep the whole night. The attacks were so strong that I felt in good spirits. I think that at the dawn of humanity, people also lived anxiously, created a lot and died early. It is difficult for me to believe that someone who eats lunch every day and sleeps every night can introduce something into the treasure house of the culture of the spirit.[4]

He reassures his wife that she must not worry if she does not hear from him for weeks at a time, because it might be impossible to post letters from the front and he had instructed several of his friends behind the lines to write if anything happened to him. To a friend, he continued to confess his euphoria: "standing watch at night, drank myself sick with plum brandy, stuffed myself with chicken, goose and pig meat . . . Generally speaking, I can say that this is the best time of my life."[5]

Akhmatova felt very differently about war. In September 1914 she wrote one of her saddest lyrics, "Consolation," imagining the inner world of a widow and basing her consolation sternly on a Christian faith in the survival of the soul:

> *You will have no more news of him,*
> *Nor hear about him again.*
> *And you will not find his grave*
> *In the fires of wretched Poland.*
>
> *Your soul must be quiet and tranquil.*
> *He is no more a lost soul,*
> *but a new soldier in God's army.*
> *So do not mourn any longer.*
>
> *Your grief and tears are a sin.*
> *Don't weep when you are home.*
> *Think, rather, that now you can pray*
> *to an intercessor of your own.*[6]

She did not approve the Nietzschean idea of an elect beyond Good and Evil. For her, poetry was a mysterious gift which also had obligations and involved an imagination of human suffering. It was some time in the middle of December 1914 that Blok uttered his famous aphorism about Akhmatova's poetry, which has sometimes been used to contrast her with Marina Tsvetaeva: "She writes verse as if she is standing in front of a man and one should write as if one stands before God." It remains an interesting comment on Akhmatova's first two books of poems, but it was made at the very time her subject matter was beginning to widen and include the suffering of her country, as well as the pain in relations between men and women. This elegant woman, seemingly so concerned with appearance, was already making herself into the voice of a whole people.

The loss of young life in this savage war was unprecedented throughout Europe. A whole generation was being destroyed. The

Russian army was not as ill-prepared as historians have often claimed.[7] In manpower and weaponry it was indeed the equal of the German army, but the chain of command in military affairs, as in all fields of action, was hopelessly inadequate. Soldiers were badly equipped to fight in wintry conditions, and many were altogether untrained. Some could not load rifles. Some were not even provided with boots. Unsurprisingly, the army was soon disease-ridden.

The Russians suffered other disadvantages. The Russian railway network was unable to cope with the need to transport men and weapons, and their trains could not travel more than 200 miles a day. These military trains were, in any case, often filled with horses and fodder, which reflected an obsession with cavalry soon to be out of date in trench warfare.

By the autumn of 1914, when both Germans and Russians found the first bloody battles had ended in stalemate, the failure of Russian military strategy was already plain. At the end of a battle on 31 August, the Germans had killed and wounded 70,000 men and taken 100,000 prisoners at a cost to themselves of only 15,000 men. The reaction of the Russian high command to this disaster was casual to the point of callousness. Russia had not planned for a war longer than six months and had not imagined exchanges of heavy artillery fire which necessitated the building of trenches. Russian trenches were shallow and little was done to make them habitable. In winter they often filled with snow.

Village boys, who had hoped the army would offer them an escape from poverty, could not fail to observe the cowardly behaviour of some of their own officers, who continued to live far better than their men. Unsurprisingly, there was a rising percentage of deserters, who reported on conditions at the front. In less than a year, wives and mothers who were short of food themselves had come to believe that the war could not be won and thought their sons were being slaughtered without the least hope of victory.

Only when the war became a matter of entrenchment, with machine-guns and heavy artillery murdering impersonally, did Gumilyov face up to the brutal fact that his conception of the nobility of war was an anachronism. Even so, Gumilyov was decorated three times, twice with the St. George Cross.

Mayakovsky was another early enthusiast, though the army

refused to take him because of his politically suspect background. He soon changed his mind about the wisdom of fighting to defend the bourgeoisie. On 11 February 1915 at the Stray Dog, Maya-kovsky read his poem "To You" with Akhmatova in the audience.

> You, wallowing in orgy after orgy,
> owning a bathroom and a warm loo,
> how do you feel learning about the awards of St. Georgy
> from the papers in your morning room?

> Do you know, insentient nonentities,
> thinking only of how to fill your maw,
> that this moment, the legs of Petrov the lieutenant
> were ripped off by a bomb?

> And what if he, brought for slaughter,
> suddenly saw, unrepining,
> how you, with your mouths oily,
> lasciviously hum Severyanin?*

> To give my life for the sake of you—
> lips drivelling with lust?
> I'd sooner serve pineapple booze
> to the whores in Moscow bars.[8]

Akhmatova remembered "Mayakovsky standing absolutely calm on the platform, looking very handsome and smoking a cigar, while the audience howled abuse."[9] Although Akhmatova did not share Gumi-lyov's enthusiasm for the war, her patriotism was intense and her Cassandra-like intuition that a whole world was ending in the cata-strophe of war was soon to prove true. Russia lost more men at the front than any other country.[10]

Akhmatova's marriage to Gumilyov was essentially over, though they continued to meet, and she continued to respect his poetry. In January 1915 Gumilyov was sent on a mission to Petrograd, and the Stray Dog arranged a special evening of poetry readings in his hon-our. A snowstorm raged outside. The cellar was filled with cigar

---

* A fashionable poet from the rival Ego-Futurist camp.

smoke and the clinking of glasses. Gumilyov then returned to the front, until a severe illness necessitated a stay in a Petrograd clinic. Akhmatova visited Gumilyov in hospital only once in 1915.

Akhmatova took part in a series of fundraising events for the wounded. On 26 January 1915, she gave a reading of Gumilyov's poems at the Alexander Hall of the Petrograd Municipality since the Stray Dog had just been closed by the police as wartime censors found the tone subversive. Akhmatova appeared with Blok, Kuzmin and Mandelstam and had much flattering attention paid to her. At the end of January, Akhmatova read *At the Edge of the Sea* at the flat of her friend, the poet and translator Mikhail Lozinsky. Among those present were Nikolay Nedobrovo and Vladimir Shileiko, the specialist in ancient languages who was to become Akhmatova's second husband.

In April 1915, her book *Rosary* went into a second edition. It was hugely popular. Most of the poems in it had been written in 1912 or 1913 and in many ways it was a continuation of the lyrical diary of her first book, *Evening*. There are religious themes in the book, as the title suggests, but many deal with love and loss with colloquial vigour:

> *Don't you love me or want to look at me?*
> *O, you are so handsome, damn you.*[11]

In 1915, Akhmatova began to be very concerned about her mother-in-law, who had fallen ill with bronchitis and suspected tuberculosis. She was living in a flat that was cold, uncomfortable and ugly and Akhmatova's son Lev, now three years old, no longer had a nanny to help his grandmother look after him. Akhmatova accordingly spent several months in 1915 with her mother-in-law. Her emotional life still centred on Petrograd. It was in Slepnyovo, however, that she wrote most of *White Flock*, and she did so with her son close at hand. This is a book which opens with one of her saddest and most prophetic verses, written in 1915:

> *We thought we were beggars without property*
> *until we began to lose one thing after another.*
> *Then every day became a day of memory*
> *and we began to compose new songs*

about the wealth we once had
and God's generosity in the past.[12]

In fact, Russian losses had only just begun to make themselves felt.

Akhmatova received little news from Gumilyov, who had left for the front line again. As she wrote to the wife of the poet Fyodor Sologub: "I am having a very hard summer. Newspapers do not arrive every day, and news about the war is much delayed . . . Nikolay Stepanovich was transferred somewhere to the south and . . . writes even more rarely. I am getting well very slowly [from tuberculosis] but I am working a lot." It is with this letter she sends her harsh poem "Prayer" for publication in the yearly *Almanakh Muz*.[13] Written on 11 May 1915, "Prayer" declares she would be willing to sacrifice not only her lover but even her own son if the miserable slaughter of the Russian people could be brought to an end. It was a poem Lev must have read in later years and cannot have found easy to bear.

> *Give me bitter years of illness*
> *A fight for breath in sleepless fever*
> *Take my child and take my lover*
> *And my mysterious gift of song—*
> *Thus I shall pray at your liturgy*
> *After so many pain-filled days:*
> *Let the dark storm over Russia*
> *Become a cloud of glorious rays.*[14]

Luknitsky recalls that in the middle of August 1915 Akhmatova received a telegram saying that her father was very ill. In spite of her earlier antagonism towards him, she went to be with him on Krestovsky Island in Petrograd and nursed him for twelve days, alongside Yelena Strannolyubskaya, the woman he had been living with for many years. When her father woke at night and asked Akhmatova to find out when his son Viktor, then in the navy, would be back from manoeuvres, she pretended to know that Viktor would be arriving soon. But her father died two days later without seeing his son. He was buried in Volkov Cemetery in Petrograd on 27 August. Akhmatova's tuberculosis flared up again after her father's death and she was advised to stay in bed all through the winter of

1915–16. Luknitsky records Akhmatova's own words: "Every morning I got up, put on a silk peignoir and went to bed again."[15] In November, however, she was sent to a sanatorium. There she found it impossible to sleep, and begged to return to Petrograd. Allowed to do so, she began to recover.

In December of the same year, she sent a copy of her poem *At the Edge of the Sea,* cut from the current *Apollon* magazine, to Sergey Yesenin, and inscribed it for him. Yesenin was already a celebrity. He very much wanted to meet her but reported afterwards that she was completely different from her poetry. Akhmatova received him with kindness and hospitality, and Yesenin was unable to explain exactly what he had disliked in her. But they were never to be close friends.

In January 1916 Marina Tsvetaeva went to Petrograd in the hope of meeting Akhmatova. Akhmatova was not in the city at the time, and so we cannot know how these two extraordinary women would have related to one another in their youth. It seems likely that, as so often in Tsvetaeva's life, she would have been the lover rather than the beloved. Bisexual, she had only recently suffered the painful end of her love affair with the poet Sophia Parnok. On 19 June 1916, Tsvetaeva wrote the first lyric from a cycle of poems dedicated to Akhmatova:

> *Muse of lament, you are the most beautiful of*
> *all muses, a crazy emanation of white night:*
> *and you have sent a black snow storm all over Russia.*
> *We are pierced with the arrows of your cries*
>
> *so that we shy like horses at the muffled*
> *many times uttered pledge—Ah!—Anna*
> *Akhmatova—the name is a vast sigh*
> *and it falls into depths without name*
>
> *and we wear crowns only through stamping*
> *the same earth as you, with the same sky over us.*
> *Whoever shares the pain of your deathly power will*
> *lie down immortal upon his death bed.*
>
> *In my melodious town the domes are burning*
> *and the blind wanderer praises our shining Lord.*

I give you my town of many bells,
Akhmatova, and with the gift: my heart.[16]

Tsvetaeva's description of her Petrograd reading can be found in her memoir *An Other Worldly Evening.* Here she repeats the story Mandelstam used to recount about Akhmatova carrying the poems Tsvetaeva had written for her in a purse until they became shreds. When Lydia Chukovskaya read the piece to Akhmatova in 1958, Akhmatova replied that none of it had happened: "Neither the purse nor the shreds."

Gumilyov continued to have affairs with several other women, though often they were little more than a passing attraction: for instance, to Margarita Tumpovskaya, who was a believer in the occult and a convinced anthroposophist. In autumn 1916, however, he was to become seriously involved with Larisa Reisner, soon to be a prominent Bolshevik. Larisa was then very young and a student at the Institute of Psychoneurosis. Her father had been a landowner in Lithuania when Larisa was born, but had moved to St. Petersburg to study and practise law. She had begun to write fiction and poetry in 1915 and edited a magazine that made satirical attacks on Tsarist oppression. She and Gumilyov met at "The Comedian's Hat," which had taken on some of the qualities of the Stray Dog in the cellar of D. I. Rubenstein on the Field of Mars in central Petrograd. She liked Gumilyov's poems and they wrote one another tender letters when separated by the war.

Akhmatova also met Larisa once at the Comedian's Hat, where she had gone to see the rehearsal of a puppet show. While someone else was helping Akhmatova on with her coat, she gave Reisner her hand. To her surprise, since she had not heard of Gumilyov's involvement with Reisner, she saw Larisa had guilty tears on her cheeks. "Thank you. You're absolutely marvellous. I'll never forget that you were the first to give me your hand."[17] Afterwards, Akhmatova reflected, "And even if I had known, why wouldn't I have given her my hand?"[18] She did not deny that Larisa was a beautiful young woman. Reisner told Akhmatova later that Gumilyov had proposed to her but that she had found it impossible to hurt a poet like Akhmatova, whom she so much admired.

By now Akhmatova no longer cared about her husband's infidelity. She was pursued by many men. She had already met Nikolay

Nedobrovo in 1913, and told friends how much he had to teach her. He was an admirably cultured man, always elegantly dressed and noted for his handsome looks, slender figure and narrow, expressive hands. A close friend of his, Yulia Sazonova-Slominskaya, pointed out that his restrained manner concealed a bitter loneliness. "Nedobrovo appeared haughty and cold, but . . . he was a person who craved tenderness, loyalty and understanding."[19] A deeply religious man, Nedobrovo saw Russia not only as his homeland but also as a source of spiritual nourishment.

Nedobrovo was born in 1884 into an old noble family and grew up on his parents' estate in Kharkov. He was married to Lyubov Olkhina, herself a beautiful and sensitive woman who loved her husband and deeply minded his relationship with Akhmatova. When she had accepted him as a lover, however, Akhmatova was seemingly indifferent to Lyubov's pain and once remarked that she could not understand the basis of the Nedobrovo marriage, since his wife had so little understanding of poetry.[20] In a woman whose warmth and tenderness to her friends is so widely attested, this seeming callousness is surprising, but, as we shall see, Akhmatova was usually unkind about women who had claims on men she regarded as her own.

Gumilyov and Akhmatova continued to meet, even though their marriage had altogether collapsed. Gumilyov, who had grown obsessed with his Russian Orthodox faith, spent the winter reading religious books until in March 1916 he became a member of the Alexandrinsky Hussars. In the spring of that year, Akhmatova moved to Petrograd from Tsarskoye Selo and lived for a time in a dark, grey room, as she remembered it, where she became very ill again with bronchitis and tuberculosis. She would hardly have been able to look after a small child at this time, yet Akhmatova began to think of her son with a guilty sadness:

> *I know you won't be able to*
> *Remember much about me, little one:*
> *I didn't hold you, or even scold you,*
> *Or take you to Communion.*[21]

Akhmatova had four new poems in the *Almanakh Muz* in September 1916, and Mandelstam observed in them a new religious simplicity and claimed that her poetry had become one of the glories of Russia. The following month, she entered a sanatorium in Finland. She was attracting much glowing criticism, notably from Viktor Zhirmunsky, who comments on her "uniqueness of soul" and places her as "the most important of those poets who have overtaken Symbolism. Her poetic gift makes her the most significant poet of the younger generation."[22]

Nedobrovo had already written an article about Akhmatova's poetry which she regarded as perceptive. This had appeared in 1915 in *Russkaya mysl* and had a key paragraph:

> These torments and such complete humility—is not that a weakness of spirit, isn't that simple sentimentality? Of course not. Akhmatova's voice pattern itself, firm and rather self-confident in accepting pain and weakness, finally, the very abundance of the poetically transformed torments—all this testifies not to fearfulness in the face of life's trifles, but reveals a lyrical soul, firm rather than too soft, cruel rather than tearful, and clearly dominant rather than submissive.[23]

As another critic observed, Nedobrovo was able to discern the steel backbone within the elegantly languid poetess. Akhmatova herself commented, "How could he guess the severity and steadfastness to come? . . . Nedobrovo understood my path, my future, he divined and predicted it because he knew me well."[24]

For all her appreciation of his gentleness and intelligence, it was not to Nedobrovo, but to his friend Boris Anrep, that Akhmatova was to give her most passionate love. Akhmatova writes in her own notebook: "I made the acquaintance of Anrep during Lent 1915 in Tsarskoye Selo." Once they became lovers, Akhmatova guiltily wrote a tender poem to Nedobrovo confessing that the friendship between them could never become passionate love because her heart did not beat faster under his hand. Nedobrovo found this change in her affections hard to bear, all the more since in 1915 he learned that he had contracted tuberculosis, and for that reason spent his last years in the Crimea. Akhmatova saw him for the last time in 1916 in Bachchisarai. He died in Yalta in 1919.

Anrep had been both impressed and inspired by Nedobrovo since their days at a gymnasium in Kharkov. Their friendship, however, did not stop Anrep forming a relationship with Akhmatova. He was a romantic figure, a very charming man whose family tree included medieval knights, a General in the service of the Swedish King Charles XII and an illegitimate daughter of Catherine the Great. In 1908 he had married Yunia Khitrovo, before going first to Paris to study art, then to England, where he made friends with members of the Bloomsbury Group. Lady Ottoline Morrell invited him to her famous gatherings and particularly remarked on his youthful vitality and gaiety. It is not clear how much Akhmatova knew about his life in England; he had for some years been the lover of Helen Maitland, an American who had come to Europe in 1909. In Paris, Maitland had first been the mistress of Augustus John's friend Henry Lamb, then lived in Paris with Anrep from 1910 in a *ménage à trois* with his wife Yunia. When, in 1914, Maitland's first child by Anrep was born, Yunia went with her to England and helped to look after the child.

Helen Maitland was a close friend of Vanessa Bell. Duncan Grant first met her in Florence when he was twenty and she was leading a gypsy life with her mother, singing to the guitar. He describes her as bohemian, wearing long flowered dresses pinned at her bosom with a brooch and a shawl dripping from one shoulder, just as if she had stepped out of a picture by Goya or Manet. She seemed to him to belong naturally to studio life, and he remarks with amusement that whenever she sat in a chair artists immediately wanted to paint her.[25]

Anrep met Akhmatova after his return to Russia at the outbreak of war in 1914 to take up a commission in the Russian army. Yunia went first to Poland and then to southern Russia. Anrep's attachment to Maitland survived his relationship with Akhmatova. However, during 1915 Anrep frequently dined out with Akhmatova and went sleighing with her in the winter. It did not prevent him from planning his return to England.

In a poem written in spring 1915 in Tsarskoye Selo, Akhmatova speaks of Anrep as if she had waited all her life for him:

> *The evening light is yellow and wide,*
> *April is tender and cool.*
> *You have come many years too late*
> *but still I am glad you are here.*
>
> *Sit down very closely next to me,*
> *and look at me with amusement.*

> *I have filled this dark blue*
> *notebook with my childish poems.*
>
> *Forgive me, for writing of misery*
> *and not taking joy in the sunshine.*
> *Forgive me, for so often mistaking*
> *other people for you.*[26]

Her poems of spring 1915 circle around this love for Boris Anrep, whom she claimed as her own true love even though she knew he had other commitments apart from his legal wife. She talked of him to the end of her life. Neither Yevgeny Rein nor Anatoly Nayman could explain why she formed such a deep attachment to him, apart from describing his aristocratic style and good looks.

Anrep was a considerable artist in mosaic, but as a man light-hearted, irreligious, even frivolous. He had great physical confidence and was athletic enough to compete in the Men's Doubles at Wimbledon in 1920; much later in life he took an active part in the French Resistance during the Second World War. New research shows him to have exactly the cool dedication to his own pleasure which characterised so many of the men Akhmatova fell in love with. He was a free-living bohemian, already part of an international artistic world.[27]

Anrep met Akhmatova again when he returned from the front to visit his friend Nedobrovo on 13 February 1916. There he listened to a reading of Nedobrovo's tragedy, *Judith*, though he found it difficult to pay attention once he noticed Akhmatova was there. He sat down beside her. While Nedobrovo read from behind an Italian Renaissance desk—he loved beautiful furniture—Anrep could not take his eyes from Akhmatova's profile. The attraction was mutual. She pressed into his hand the black ring which her Tatar grandmother believed would protect her.

The heroine of her poem "The Tale of the Black Ring" speaks of giving it to her true love. Yevgeny Rein confirmed that Akhmatova thought of Anrep throughout her life as a love of great intensity and wrote many poems for him. There seems no doubt that Anrep was deeply affected by Akhmatova's beauty and presence, though he accepted a posting back to London as Military Secretary to the Russian Government Committee nonetheless in the middle of February 1916. He intended to return, or so he said, in six weeks, but he found England much to his liking and came back to Russia only for a brief period at the end of that year. The day before he left, Akhmatova sent him a copy of her book *Evening*, inscribed:

> To Boris Anrep
> One hope fewer now beguiles me
> But one more song I have for singing
> Feb 13 1916[28]

In exchange, Anrep gave her a copy of a poem of his own which she had sewn into a silken purse, and a carved wooden cross taken from an abandoned church in the Carpathian Mountains of Galicia, which found a place in several of her poems. His poem speaks of giving her a crucifix and failing to give her a pledge. When Akhmatova copied that poem into her album, she added a phrase which makes him recall that failure as evidence of his own stupidity.

She wanted to believe that was how he felt. Akhmatova saw his departure as treachery to herself, to the Orthodox Church and to Russia. She particularly objected to his casual mockery of the Russian Orthodox Church:

> By arrogance your spirit's dulled and swayed.
> You'll never know the light because of this.
> Our faith is nothing but a dream, you say,
> and but a mirage this metropolis.[29]

While waiting for letters from Anrep, Akhmatova wrote a sad poem in which a husband enters a house and confronts a wife stricken with conscience at her own behaviour: "Ah, it is you again. No longer a boy in love."

Akhmatova wrote a lyric—"I haven't drawn the curtains at my window"—and an acrostic dedicated to Anrep on 8 March 1916. On 11 July she dedicated "I know you are my reward" to him. It was as if his absence had increased the power he had over her imagination. It is reminiscent of her early passion for the chilly photograph of Kutuzov, her first lover.

In August 1916, Gumilyov left his regiment and travelled to Petrograd to take an exam for the rank of cornet (a minor lieutenant).

He visited his family, but rented a room on Liteiny Prospekt, where he lived until October, since his love affair with Larisa Reisner continued. On 25 October 1916, after failing his examination to become an officer, Gumilyov returned once again to the front.

In December 1916, Akhmatova was introduced to Yunia, Boris Anrep's wife, and was her guest at Belbek near Sebastopol. Yunia was by now separated from her husband and acting as a nurse, on leave from the war.[30] Akhmatova liked her and wrote a poem for her, even though she continued to wait anxiously for a letter from Anrep.

FIVE

Revolution

*The beginning of January 1916 was the
beginning of the last year of the old world.*[1]

—MARINA TSVETAEVA

emembering the reading she had given in Petrograd in
January 1916, Tsvetaeva compared the mood of the city
then to that of Pushkin's little tragedy *The Feast During the
Plague*, in which revellers offer blasphemous praise to the omnipres-
ence of death. The rich and the high-born lost themselves in love
affairs, drank champagne or spent their money on black market
caviar. Fortunes were gambled away in casinos.[2] There were reports,
almost certainly unfounded, about the Tsarina's sexual corruption,
both as mistress to the monk Rasputin and the lesbian lover of her
lady-in-waiting, Anna Vyrubova. These rumours signalled mainly
the huge popular dislike of the Romanov dynasty. The war was
going badly and the Tsar, who had taken over direct command of his
forces at his wife's insistence, was responsible for many poor decisions. All through 1916 the relentless slaughter of young men in the
trenches combined with strikes, crime and disorder at home to
induce mounting resentment.

There were many conspiracies hostile to the regime, but the only plot to succeed was the murder of Rasputin by Prince Youssupov, carried out on 16 December 1916 and greeted with joy in aristocratic circles, though evidently women in the court gathered to collect "holy water" from the river into which his chained and poisoned body had been thrown. The main result of this assassination was to make the Tsar more determined than ever to resist any attempt at reform and, as the hardship of the war continued, angry crowds began to gather in the streets.

Soon after her stay with Yunia Anrep in December 1916, Anna was declared healthy enough to travel and went first to Petrograd and then to Slepnyovo for Christmas and New Year with Gumilyov and Lev. There she enjoyed a sense of living in Pushkin's time, with sleighs, felt boots, snowdrifts and bearskin rugs. She remained in Slepnyovo until the middle of January 1917, meanwhile choosing poems to go into her next collection, *White Flock*. She found the choice difficult, as she wrote to Mikhail Lozinsky, asking his opinion on which should be kept and which removed, and begging for his corrections. As so many of the poems in *White Flock* relate to Anrep, it is not surprising that she spent much of her time in Slepnyovo musing about Anrep's betrayal, his admiration for red-haired women and the state of his soul.

Hers was an uneasy situation. She had no money of her own, her father was dead and her mother was living on a modest pension in the Crimea. Unless she wished to live in Gumilyov's house in Tsarskoye Selo, she was homeless. On returning to Petrograd early in 1917, she went to stay with her friend Valeria Sreznevskaya in her father's home at 9 Botinskaya Street. Dr. Sreznevsky's house and his psychiatric clinic were both in the Vyborg district of Petrograd.

A sense of disquiet filled the city. The usual buns, pies, cakes and biscuits were not on sale in restaurants even for visitors. There were few goods in the shops, and workers could not buy food for their families. Soon long queues began to form at bakeries and women were setting up beds outside any shops which were said to have stocks of bread and sugar. By early 1917, the average woman was spending around forty hours a week in line for necessities.[3]

In those queues the February Revolution of 1917 which deposed the Tsar was born. It started on the Vyborg side of Petrograd, where Akhmatova was living, when a group of women went off to rally their men from a neighbouring metal factory for a protest march to the centre of the city.

The first confrontation with authority came on Nevsky Prospekt on 25 February, when a crowd of protestors were brought to a halt by a squadron of Cossacks near Kazan Cathedral. Soldiers could be seen as workers and peasants themselves, and as such possibly sympathetic. On this occasion, a young girl offered the commanding officer a bunch of roses. To everyone's relief, he accepted the flowers as a gift and was wildly cheered by the mob.

Bloodshed, however, was inevitable. By 26 February a number of marchers had been shot and the centre of Petrograd looked like an armed camp. A demonstration on Znamenskaya Square was a turning-point: the deaths of several marchers emboldened others and soon it was far too late for repressive measures to work. A mutiny in the Petrograd garrison then turned the disorders of the previous four days into a revolution. Jubilant crowds opened all the prisons as a sign that the days of liberty had arrived, rather as the French Revolutionaries had opened the Bastille.

Akhmatova spent the morning the Revolution began at the dressmaker's, and only discovered what was happening in the city when the driver of her horse-drawn cab refused to cross to the Vyborg side of the river. She made her way home alone, through shouts, gunfire and confused rushes of people.

Since three of the most important revolutionary leaders of the Bolshevik Party—Trotsky, Bukharin and Lenin—were all abroad, the February uprising was an opportunity for Kerensky, a fiery speaker in the Duma, to take control. He was duly installed in the Winter Palace. Unfortunately, there had never been much of a tradition of democratic responsibility in Russia. The Constituent Assembly had little experience of power and, though they enacted a number of idealistic reforms, made no attempt to take Russia out of the war.

Many intellectuals greeted the February Revolution with wild euphoria. Alexander Blok wrote to his mother on 23 March 1917: "A miracle has happened, and we may expect more miracles . . . it is an extraordinary feeling . . . that nothing is forbidden."[4] Marina Tsvetaeva, in hospital in Moscow awaiting the birth of her second child, saw Kerensky as a second Bonaparte. The collapse of the monarchy had been so unexpected that people compared the experience to living through a dream or a fairytale. Power devolved to the Provisional Government and the Tsar was forced to abdicate. There was rejoicing throughout Russia. Red flags were hoisted in Petrograd, people sang the "Marseillaise" in the cities. In the countryside, however, peasants crowded uneasily into churches, afraid of the great change that had removed a Tsar they still thought of as protecting them. The new rulers believed in the innate goodness of the Russian people and hoped the transition to Western democracy would be unproblematic. They initiated a dazzling series of reforms, including freedom of the press and assembly, declared a general amnesty and removed all legal restrictions based on religion, class and race.

In spite of initial enthusiasm for these reforms, the Provisional Government failed to contain the mounting civil disorder. Over half a million workers came out on strike between April and July 1917, demanding higher wages, more food supplies and an eight-hour day. With mass parades, meetings on every street corner, and placards in Russian, Polish, Lithuanian and Yiddish, the Nevsky Prospekt became a kind of Latin Quarter with people hawking books and pamphlets on the pavement.[5] Most serious of all, the soldiers at the front wanted only one thing: peace, and this the Provisional Government failed to deliver. Almost a million soldiers began to desert between March and October and added to the general confusion.

An uneasy coalition of liberals, Mensheviks and Bolsheviks held together for a time in fear of civil war. Russian liberals spoke of ruling with the people instead of over them, and compared themselves to the French heroes of 1789. Well-meaning gentlemen they may have been, but they failed to consider the people's hatred for the propertied classes, which would soon immerse the country in blood.

Not everyone was so sanguine about the likely survival of organised government. Gorky, whose moving novels had described the cruellest inequities in Russian society, was appalled by the mob violence. He feared the mass of the people in their ignorance would be encouraged to give way to their basest instincts. On 14 June 1917, Gorky wrote to his wife in Moscow of his horror at what was happening in Petrograd in the wake of the February Revolution: "This is no longer a capital, it is a cesspit. No one works, the streets are filthy, there are piles of stinking rubbish in the courtyards . . . and all those base and criminal instincts which I have fought all my life . . . it seems they are now destroying Russia."[6]

Isaiah Berlin was seven and a half when he first saw the plywood banners bearing the slogans "Power to the Duma," "Down with the Tsar" and "Down with the War." Later, he witnessed a young policeman dragged off by a mob, presumably to his death: an image which remained with him all his life.

During the summer of 1917, Akhmatova returned for several months to Slepnyovo, not to a peaceful situation as she had hoped but to one in which neighbouring peasants were muttering with menace about the grand houses built on their bones. Deserters from the army planned to destroy Slepnyovo "just because there was a local holiday," as she wrote ironically to Mikhail Lozinsky.

Many of the liberal intelligentsia began to go into exile even before the Bolshevik Revolution began in October. Akhmatova saw the dangers of remaining but nevertheless refused to go into exile herself, although Anrep, of course, was already in London; and it may be his voice she imagines suggesting she do so in a poem written in 1917:

> *Come to me here and leave*
> *Your remote and sinful country.*
> *Leave Russia behind for ever . . .*
>
> *Peacefully, with indifference,*
> *I covered my ears with my hands*
> *So that such unworthy words*
> *Would not sully my sad spirit.*[7]

If she was tempted to follow him abroad, his silence in the following months convinced her she was forgotten. In summer 1917, she writes:

> *It is quite simple, it is quite clear*
> *And understood by everyone.*
> *You don't love me now,*
> *And I think you never have done.*
> *Why is it I am always drawn*
> *To someone else's man?*[8]

After that stark, bitter opening, she nevertheless envisages leaving Petrograd and Russia behind:

> *Am I wandering like a wretched*
> *beggar in some foreign capital?*
> *I am happy to think so. Well,*
> *then I may catch a glimpse of you.*[9]

She is now ironic about the reality of love itself and reflects lightly, in another poem dated 1917, that love is no more than fiction, even though people go on longing for one another and fearing to part.

Akhmatova continued to think of Anrep as a traitor. In the summer of 1917, she wrote a poem which begins by accusing him of apostasy:

> *You are a traitor, and for a green island,*
> *have betrayed, yes, betrayed your native land,*
> *abandoned all our songs and sacred icons,*
> *and the pine tree over a quiet lake.*[10]

She could not forgive his allegiance "to the calm English civilisation of reason, and not religious and political ravings."[11] He did not stay in touch with Akhmatova by letter, and as her own situation and that of Petrograd deteriorated, she felt altogether forsaken by him. In another poem of 1917 she imagines him hearing the news of her death:

> *And then he'll remember the winter skyline,*
> *and a snow storm whirling along the Neva.*
> *And perhaps he'll remember how once he swore*
> *to take care of his Eastern friend for ever.*[12]

Yet she continued to be obsessed with Anrep and to speak of him as a true "long-awaited lover, a bridegroom from whom parting cannot ever mean separation," as Amanda Haight puts it elegantly.[13] It is worth pausing for a moment to wonder again what it was about Anrep that Akhmatova found impossible to forget. It may well be his insistence on going his own way. As Nayman observed shrewdly, Anrep became like an *"amor de longh,* the distant love of a troubador, always desired and never attained."[14] He confirms Rein's comment that Akhmatova wrote more poems for Anrep than for anyone else. She cannot have admired his poetry other than sentimentally, but she may well have valued his dedication to art.

On the first landing of the main entrance of London's National Gallery you can still see Anrep's "The Awakening of the Muses," a marble mosaic set there between 1928 and 1933 which displays portraits of celebrated people. Greta Garbo stars as Melpomene, Muse of Tragedy, and other characters are played by his Bloomsbury friends, among them Virginia Woolf wielding an elegant pen as Clio, Muse of History, and the art critic Clive Bell as (a rather sober) Bacchus.

In 1945, Anrep was commissioned to make a fourth mosaic for the Gallery, entitled "The Modern Virtues," which included many other figures from English life, such as Bertrand Russell and Edith Sitwell. In this sequence he included a portrait of Anna Akhmatova as the figure of Compassion. He described it during a 1950s broadcast on Russian radio as follows: "A young woman is being saved from the horrors of war by an angel. The bones of martyrs are thrown into a mass grave as recorded in the documents of German concentration camps. It is not a portrait, but a memory of Anna Akhmatova in her youth, and the siege of Leningrad."[15] Perhaps the victims he had in mind were those of the Russian Revolution, but this could not be said in the Soviet Union.

Akhmatova's third book of poems, *White Flock*, was published in September 1917. Although there are poems for her lost lover, in many lyrics she has begun to speak for all the Russian people caught up in the suffering war had produced. Akhmatova was well aware of the horrors of the soldiers in the trenches and from this time onward this knowledge enters her poetry. She identifies with widows lamenting for their lost husbands, and the whole of Russia becomes the body of Christ:

> *They are wounding your holy body*
> *They are casting lots for your clothes.*[16]

Akhmatova felt she had been appointed by God to sing of this suffering and she continued to reject a world of warm, ordinary joys. Petrograd becomes a symbol for that dedication:

Not for anything would we exchange
This granite city of fame and calamity
The wide rivers of glistening ice
The sunless gloomy gardens
And, barely audible, the Muse's voice.[17]

The publication of *White Flock* came as Petrograd was falling into chaos. The book could not be transported to Moscow and there was consequently little distribution. The journals were closing down, as well as the newspapers. She could no longer count on readers of her poetry to bolster her self-esteem.

The situation in Petrograd worsened through 1917, and by 10 October 75,000 workers had downed tools in their dissatisfaction. On 17 October the new Lessner and Russian Renault factory workers left their work and came out on the streets singing revolutionary songs. By then, Lenin had returned incognito from Finland and with the help of Trotsky staged the Bolshevik Revolution.

Red Guards stormed the Winter Palace, from which Kerensky himself had managed to escape some hours earlier, and arrested the Provisional Government. The day the Winter Palace was taken, the bridge to the Vyborg district was raised to let Bolshevik torpedo boats through: an incident memorably recreated in Eisenstein's film *October*, which is otherwise notably inaccurate. Akhmatova was back from Slepnyovo and in Petrograd when the October Revolution ousted Kerensky and was standing at the edge of Liteiny Bridge as it opened. She watched trucks, trams and people hanging over the suddenly gaping bridge.

Anrep returned to Russia once more in the chaos of January 1918 hoping to meet Akhmatova. In his desperation to find her, he crossed the ice of the Neva on foot in order to reach the Vyborg district where Akhmatova was living with the Sreznevskys. She was visibly touched by his reckless concern, but pointed out calmly what a risk he had run and warned him that Red Guards were "grabbing officers on the streets." He showed her that he was wearing her ring on a chain round his neck to protect him. More practically, he had removed the epaulettes which showed he was an officer.

Anrep wrote a sentimental account of their meeting, which suggests an intensity of feeling his other behaviour does not: " 'Wear it always,' she said. 'Always,' I whispered, and then added, 'It is sacred.'

Her eyes clouded with emotion and she stretched out her hands to me. I burned with spiritual ecstasy, kissed her hands and stood up to part. Anna smiled gently, 'It's better this way.' "[18] That last remark strikes a false note, since so many of Akhmatova's poems are marked by the disappointment she felt at his leaving, and all the more since she and Anrep went out together that evening to watch the dress rehearsal of Meyerhold's production of Lermontov's *Masquerade,* a splendidly luxurious piece which would become famous and was playing to a packed house even though shooting continued in the streets outside. On stage, a spectacle prophesied disaster and the end of the world, while the excitement in the streets, with no trams and few cabs, resembled a carnival, albeit a celebration with blood flowing on the snow and stones.

Anrep, though cool and brave in a crisis, thought no good would come from a Soviet government and soon after this meeting took the earliest possible train for England. It is not clear whether he told Akhmatova of his long-standing relationship with Helen Maitland.[19] His absence continued to haunt many of Akhmatova's poems:

> *Everything is for you: my daily prayer*
> *The thrilling fever of insomnia,*
> *The blue fire burning in my eyes—*
> *And my poems, that white flock.*[20]

Anrep made an interesting life for himself in England, and his charm continued to create a favourable impression even in old age. Anne Wollheim, the first wife of Richard Wollheim, the philosopher, knew him many years later when he was living with Maud Russell, one of the patrons of the National Gallery mosaics, who asked the Gallery to keep her gift anonymous. Anne Wollheim remembers Anrep as "a delightful man, who liked playing chess and was probably quite selfish."[21]

After October 1917, most intellectuals were anxious about their likely place in the new Marxist state. Tbilisi in Georgia was an intermediate point of exile for the undecided, but many who had seen the violence in the streets went, as Anrep had, into exile in western Europe. All the old certainties had gone, and soon any semblance of an ordered life too. Money in the bank had lost all value, with food and fuel in short supply for everyone.

Mandelstam had never been drafted into the army and went to the Crimea in 1916. As he saw the new situation by 1918, his city, his family, all he loved had been given over to the power of death:

> *We shall die in transparent Petropolis*
> *Where Proserpine rules over us.*[22]

Mandelstam spoke of the city's degeneration even as he looked up at the night sky. A memorable refrain runs through one lyric:

> *If you are a star*
> *Your brother Petropolis is dying.*[23]

As the horrors of the war increased, Akhmatova continued to believe in a merciful God, but the suffering of so many people made her wonder whether this was God's retribution for the frivolity and callousness of the upper classes.

By now, in the south, an army of opponents to the Revolution had begun to form. On 5 September 1918 the Soviet of the People's Commissars made a resolution to shoot all people connected with White Army organisations, plots and uprisings. Nevertheless, those who opposed the Bolsheviks—including Tsvetaeva's frail husband, Sergey Efron—took up arms with the White Army, and a confused, cruel and desperate civil war began, of which the brilliant playwright Bulgakov gives a terrifying portrait, first as a novel in *The White Guard* (1924) and then as a play, *The Days of the Turbins* (1926).

In a war that lasted for three years both armies looted and murdered; there were peasant uprisings, retributory executions and other brutalities. Ordinary trade between the countryside and the towns ground to a halt. Over the following years, the population of Petrograd, once two million, dwindled to about 500,000 frost-bitten and emaciated people.

One evening, Akhmatova went to hear a boys' choir perform Mozart's *Requiem,* and on the way home encountered a procession led by an old priest. Akhmatova is said to have remarked, "Let's stop worrying about art. No one needs art. Let's open a tobacco shop."[24]

The situation in Moscow, where Tsvetaeva was living as a single parent with a newly born second child, was equally grim. Visitors were appalled by the conditions in which she lived. Yet, utterly impractical as she was, she buckled down to confront privation with one huge advantage: unlike Akhmatova, she had robust health. She was able to saw wood, light fires, wash potatoes in icy water and look after her precocious six-year-old daughter Alya, though she was forced to put her younger daughter into an orphanage, where the child died.

Tsvetaeva had noted in 1917 that Voloshin had prophesied the way the Russian Revolution would develop in the five years ahead: "the terror, the civil war, the executions, the *Vendée*, men turned to beasts and blood, blood, blood."[25] Not everyone shared this pessimism. As late as January 1918, when Blok wrote "The Twelve," it was possible for idealists to hope that the destruction of the old world would lead to a new fraternal brotherhood. Blok even portrayed Christ at the head of a group of marauding Red Guards. This remarkable poem opens in snow and wind, with an old woman bewildered at the waste of cloth in the many banners that bear the slogan "All Power to the Constituent Assembly." Twelve men with rifles, and cigarettes drooping from their mouths, take to the streets. In the bitter cold the sound of gunfire is heard. A prostitute tucks her gains into her stocking top. The Twelve go their way, under the Red Flag, murdering and abusing God's name through frost and blizzard. The poem follows them and comments in street language:

> *Open your cellars: quick, run down . . .*
> *The scum of the earth are hitting the town.*[26]

But in the closing lines, another figure joins them and we remember the number of Christ's disciples was also twelve:

> *soft-footed where the blizzard swirls*
> *invulnerable where bullets crossed—*
> *crowned with a crown of snowflake pearls,*
> *a flowery diadem of frost,*
> *ahead of them goes Jesus Christ.*[27]

Akhmatova, along with many others who did not think the violence of the Revolutionary Guards could ever be justified, was indignant at the blasphemy.

Mandelstam often came to visit Akhmatova in the days after the

Revolution, and they drove together in horse-drawn cabs over the ruts in the roads and between the bonfires, with the rumble of guns in the background. In 1917–18 Akhmatova saw a good deal of him while she was living at the Sreznevskys' and many of his poems dedicated to Akhmatova date from this period. Together, they visited poetry recitals at the Academy of Arts and there was some speculation about the nature of their relationship; Akhmatova, however, always insisted it was a deep and lasting friendship rather than a love affair.

Gumilyov had not been in Petrograd during the February Revolution, and when he returned he lived with Mikhail Lozinsky in the vacant flat of Sergey Makovsky. He then set off for Paris, hoping to become a foreign correspondent on *Russkaya volya* through his contacts with the émigré Mikhail Struve. In June 1917 he went to London, though, unlike Anrep, he had no intention of abandoning Russia. On his way to London, he sent a postcard to Larisa Reisner, advising her not to get mixed up in politics.

Anrep wrote no letters to Akhmatova after the October Revolution, perhaps because he had been warned it would damage her to receive letters from abroad. However, he continued to wear her ring around his neck and did attempt to send her a length of silk for a dress and a coin stamped with the profile of Alexander the Great when he met Gumilyov on his visit to London. Gumilyov responded like a proud husband and it is not clear whether Akhmatova ever received these presents.

While in England, Gumilyov met Aldous Huxley and many of the writers connected to the *New Age* magazine, such as Katherine Mansfield. He was entertained by Lady Ottoline Morrell and treated as a distinguished Russian poet. On his way home he travelled through Paris. There, he fell in love with Yelena Dubboucher, half-Russian and half-French, the daughter of a famous surgeon, to whom he gave the name "Blue Star." She inspired his next collection of poems and he remained in Paris as a result until his return to Russia in April 1918.

All Gumilyov's utterances suggest a lack of sympathy with the Revolution but, as much as Akhmatova, he felt himself bound up with the fate of his country. And he wanted to see Akhmatova and his son. Talking to Boris Anrep, he spoke of Akhmatova's "beautiful soul." Anrep, however, wondered whether he truly understood her spirit.

As soon as Gumilyov arrived in Petrograd, he telephoned Akhmatova at the Sreznevskys and discovered that she was visiting Vladimir Shileiko, the Babylonian scholar who had once frequented the Stray Dog. The following day, Akhmatova came to Gumilyov's lodging and stayed until morning, but on his next visit, once again at the Sreznevskys, she asked him for a divorce.

The news came as a thunderclap. When asked whether she was in love with someone else, she told him that she did indeed plan to marry Shileiko. Gumilyov was frankly incredulous, and not without reason. Shileiko, for all his being part of the crowd who frequented the Stray Dog and having published several poems, was a man obsessed with his own work: clay tablets, cuneiform script and yellowing ancient documents. His conversation was all about Egypt, Babylon and Assyria. Gumilyov found it impossible to believe Akhmatova was in love with Shileiko: he had a thin face, a wry grin and a caustic tongue.

Akhmatova herself described her choice of Shileiko as a form of almost religious submission, as if to the rules of a monastic order: "I felt so filthy, I thought it would be like a cleansing, like going to a convent, knowing you are going to lose your freedom."[28] Soon after Akhmatova had asked Gumilyov for a divorce, they went to Slepnyovo together to see Lev, and Gumilyov repeated his bewilderment at her request and entreated her to see there was no need for a divorce, whatever her relationship to Shileiko might be. Courteously, however, he thereafter made no difficulties for Akhmatova.

Shileiko was born in Peterhof, one of the Tsar's summer residences, and had attended Petersburg University. From 1913, he worked in the research section of the Hermitage until he was drafted into the army in January 1917. After the Revolution, Shileiko became an adviser in the translation section of Gorky's publishing house, World Literature, set up to make world classics available in Russia, and also worked as a professor at the Petrograd Archaeological Institute. He had been a tutor for the Sheremetev family before the Revolution and, because of his position in the Russian academy, was given a room in their palace on the Fontanka. This is a superb eighteenth-century building, but Shileiko was living there in some discomfort in an oblong room, with only a couch as a bed. An oil lamp left shadows in every corner. It was bitterly cold and he had to use his old army greatcoat as an additional blanket.

Despite the deprivations, the theatrical and artistic life of Petrograd prospered. The House of Arts opened in autumn 1918 in an apartment on the Moika River which had once belonged to a prominent businessman. Akhmatova was on the board, alongside Gumilyov, Korney Chukovsky, the critic Boris Eikhenbaum and the satirical writer Mikhail Zoshchenko. The board sponsored lectures and concerts, and sometimes provided rooms for poets. The entirely separate House of Scholars, which opened in December 1919 under the protection of Maxim Gorky, distributed rations, clothing, firewood and medical aid.

Gumilyov gave workshops at the House of Arts, and these attracted many students. He made a great impression walking about the streets in a Laplander fur coat and a hat with earflaps, and kept his coat on as he lectured, usually on modern poetry or the art of translation. He continued to believe that poetry could help answer the question: "Why am I alive?"

Akhmatova's divorce came through in August 1918, and she married Shileiko in December of the same year. She determined on a loyal, monogamous life, but Shileiko was to prove a difficult husband.

SIX

In a Time of Famine

We thought we were beggars without property.[1]

—AKHMATOVA

ot only Gumilyov found Akhmatova's choice of a husband surprising. Princess Salomea Andronikova, Akhmatova's friend from the days of the Stray Dog, was equally astonished, even disappointed. It is not clear whether Shileiko's friends also worried for him. Much later in her life Akhmatova remarked to Anatoly Nayman that the marriage had been a "sad misunderstanding" for both of them.[2] To Amanda Haight, Akhmatova spoke of Shileiko as the main reason she wrote so few poems between 1917 and 1921.

Some of the difficulties of their marriage arose from the hardships of the years of revolution and civil war. The urban life of northern Russia was returning to a prehistoric age. Everyone was short of food and desperate for fuel to keep their stoves alight. Lenin's decision to evacuate his capital to Moscow when the Germans began bombing the city on 2 March 1918 left the whole infrastructure of Petrograd to decay. Electricity, sewage disposal and water supplies no longer functioned, as Gorky had written to his wife in 1917.[3]

In the south, the Civil War raged with savage cruelty, bringing typhus, famine and even cannibalism to a desperate population. Both Reds and Whites committed appalling atrocities. Looting was commonplace: search parties of Red soldiers felt entitled to enter the houses of those thought to be rich, looking for valuables.

For Shileiko and Akhmatova it would prove a hard time to be setting up house. Their room was large, but damp and cold; the bed was behind a screen. The one bookcase could not accommodate all their books, which had to lie about the floor. Akhmatova had left Gumilyov's house without so much as a spoon or a cooking utensil and they had to borrow pans from their neighbours, although there was little to eat and not enough wood for the stove. Shileiko turned out to be as impractical as Akhmatova. It was Akhmatova who learned to light the oven, which was something of a triumph. She, not Shileiko, stood in line for rations, though it has to be said that only through Shileiko's position were there any rations to collect from the House of Scholars.

Valeria Sreznevskaya visited them in 1918, just before their marriage, and observed that Shileiko was a remarkable man who knew Babylonian poems by heart and dominated any conversation by telling stories of Assyrian legends. She also saw his egotism, however, and was concerned that Akhmatova looked so tired and pale. Both of them were suffering from tuberculosis. It is perhaps hardly surprising that, at the age of thirty, Akhmatova wrote of herself as an old woman who could only look to God for help. When Akhmatova's divorce came through on 8 August 1918, the legal paper was of little interest to her: "I didn't even bother to go anywhere, or talk to anyone about it . . . I just received the papers saying I was divorced. We were surrounded by hunger, by terror. Everybody was leaving, some of them leaving for ever."[4]

Nedobrovo had counselled Akhmatova—in the *Russkaya mysl* article she so much valued—to follow the advice of Pushkin and to go where her secret dreams led her. What secret dream led her to Shileiko? Primarily, it seems, Akhmatova wanted to be *of use* to a man of intelligence, and to be *needed* by him as neither Gumilyov in the upshot seemed to need her nor Anrep, who had chosen not to remain in Russia. Shileiko not only needed her, he demanded her undivided attention, and was so possessive of her that in one well-known poem she wrote of herself as a prisoner in his house.[5] She admitted that something in her welcomed this necessity for self-sacrifice. He was jealous, not only of other friends but also of the time and attention she gave to her poetry. For all the energy and articulacy of his speech and his earlier forays into writing poems, he knew Akhmatova's muse would never visit him.

For a time, she and Shileiko lived in Moscow, since Shileiko had found some work there, but they soon moved back to the Sheremetev Palace. Shileiko was ill, and often found it impossible to sleep. When he worked through the night, it was Akhmatova who got up and made tea for him. Most days she willingly took dictation of his translations, then went for a walk with him before he returned to work—sometimes until four in the morning. Shileiko could not do without tea and cigarettes and, according to Yevgeny Rein, spent money on both even when Akhmatova was in danger of starvation.[6] Shileiko also had generous impulses, however, once coming back in triumph with apples and matches for her.

She wrote little. While many poets remained optimistic about the new regime, Akhmatova was filled with anxiety about the Revolution from the beginning. Poems she had already written suggest that her silence was due to Shileiko's dislike of her writing life.

Shileiko, if we are to believe Akhmatova's version of events, was genuinely oppressive. Even in 1917 she wrote of him as a "strict friend" and characterised her love for him as "a testing by fire and steel." Apart from the situations she describes in her poems, Akhmatova spoke to several friends of the way Shileiko tormented her. According to Amanda Haight, this was because Shileiko wanted a wife not a poet, and "burnt her poems in a samovar."[7]

Akhmatova's willingness to accept Shileiko's domestic tyranny has to be pondered. In the first year of her marriage, she writes a poem which recommends him to tear at her consumptive breast with claws until blood from her throat stains the bed. This reads like an indefensible hyperbole. Akhmatova's poems about her relationship with Shileiko suggest he was a monstrous bully on whom she remained utterly dependent emotionally even as she expressed her bewilderment at his oppression:

> *You forbid me to sing and smile.*
> *Long ago you forbade me to pray.*

Yet if you will keep me by your side.
I don't care about anything else.[8]

There is also a hint in another poem that it was by Shileiko's choice that she had no more children. In 1918, she writes:

Ice floats by in chunks,
The skies are hopelessly pale.
Why are you punishing me?
I don't know what I've done wrong.

If you need to—then kill me
But don't be so harsh and stern.
You don't want children from me
And you don't like my poetry.

Let everything be as you wish.
I have been faithful to my promise.
I gave my whole life to you—
My sadness I'll take to the grave.[9]

However, there are other reports which emphasise the affection they obviously felt for one another. Tamara Shileiko, his daughter-in-law, who describes Shileiko as tender and affectionate, may not seem like an altogether independent witness, but Korney Chukovsky, too, observed on 19 January 1920 that, "She sometimes approaches Shileiko very gently, and strokes his hair. He calls her Anushka, and she calls him Volodia."[10] Among the pet names Shileiko used for Akhmatova was "Akuma" and he continued to use that name in letters to her, even after they separated. Both of them felt great affection for a St. Bernard dog, Tapa, a stray that Shileiko had taken in. Nayman remembers that Akhmatova spoke of Shileiko without any sign of resentment or reproach.[11] After she had broken with Shileiko, both of them tried to take care of one another.

In February 1922 she was still writing of Shileiko's "black jealousy":

He whispers: I'm not sorry
For loving you so intensely—

you have to belong only
to me, or else I shall kill you.[12]

Unlike so many earlier lyrics, when the recipient is far from clear, when she writes "my husband is an executioner and his home a prison," Shileiko seems unambiguously intended. However, it has to be said that Shileiko's jealousy was not without foundation. While still married to Shileiko, Akhmatova began a relationship with Artur Lurye, and also with the theatre director Mikhail Zimmerman.

Gumilyov had found a job as a member of Gorky's new publishing house. Bitterly hurt he may have been by his divorce from Akhmatova but, perhaps just because of that, he soon married again: another Anna, Anna Engelhardt, whom he had met while in a clinic for diseases of the lung in Finland. She was much younger than he was and he hoped she would be more malleable than his first wife. Akhmatova described this situation wryly: "He imagined Anna Engelhardt was wax, and she turned out to be—a tank."[13]

Gumilyov gave poetry readings and ran workshops wherever he was invited because he believed poetry and art kept people from becoming callous and from losing their dignity. Some of his teaching came from his need to support a new family, but he genuinely believed in the saving power of poetry. For her part, Akhmatova tried to avoid literary gatherings where they might meet. She wrote little: only two poems in 1919, and none in 1920.

Akhmatova saw Gumilyov was in pain, but thought it was mainly his pride that had been hurt by their separation. It did not soften her attitude but she was able to remain calm and friendly towards him. There was a coolness in her which went back to her childhood. She could never have written, as Tsvetaeva wrote of her husband, "Sergey Efron is my kin," or claimed, "I could never love anyone else."[14]

With the opening of the House of Arts and the House of Scholars, whatever fears the liberal intelligentsia might have, it looked as if culture was going to be encouraged and even supported by the State under the Bolsheviks. Akhmatova's opposition to the Bolsheviks remained deep-rooted, however, and on 11 May 1920 she refused to take part in a literary evening in the knowledge that Alexander Blok would be reading his poem "The Twelve," where, as we have seen, the figure of Christ is portrayed at the head of a group of Red Guards.

Gumilyov was writing some of his most startlingly original poems at this period, notably "The Lost Streetcar" (1919) in which he imagines himself walking down an unfamiliar street as if in a dream. An approaching streetcar bears down on him. Once aboard, he is possessed by scenes from his past: from his exploration of Africa to his honeymoon in Paris. As the streetcar swoops past a greengrocer, he sees a heap of decapitated heads on sale instead of vegetables. As he passes the home where he had once lived with Akhmatova, he pictures himself enjoying an altogether peaceful life with a dead cousin. The poem resolves inside the Cathedral of St. Isaac, where he imagines holy rites being said for that dead cousin as if such prayers offered the only answer to the terror of the world around him. The poem has the clarity of nightmare.

Akhmatova and Shileiko moved briefly to the Marble Palace, which had been built by Catherine the Great. There they had two rooms and a small kitchen, and their windows looked out over the Field of Mars, a one-time parade ground for Tsarist Guards. However, they soon returned to the Sheremetev Palace, as hungry as ever. They were on the edge of starvation when a friend of Larisa Reisner arrived with a bag of rice. Akhmatova gave the largest share of the rice to her neighbours and only kept two pans of the rice for herself. Soon after this, Reisner herself came to visit.

Larisa, now a well-placed Bolshevik figure, looked well-dressed and well-fed, and was wearing silk stockings and a beautiful hat. She had come to speak to Akhmatova about the ending of her own relationship with Gumilyov, but was shocked to see that Akhmatova and Shileiko looked so ill. She suggested that Shileiko should go into hospital immediately. That very night, at about half past eleven, she came back with a big basket of different kinds of food. The next day Shileiko was taken by car into hospital. Reisner invited Akhmatova to stay with her, and later that month she spent three days with Reisner at Tsarskoye Selo. On her return, however, the danger of starvation remained.

Chukovsky notes on 30 March 1920 that he met Akhmatova while walking with Alexander Blok. "It was the first time I had seen Blok and Akhmatova together. Blok's face remained absolutely impassive, and Akhmatova's also. Their eyes did not meet, nor did they smile at each other, but a great deal was said all the same."[15]

While Shileiko was in hospital, Akhmatova took a few tentative steps towards independence. She began to work at the Library of the Institute of Agronomy in May or June 1920, and when the government offered her a flat, she moved there. She now had a small salary and, in addition, the Agronomy Institute provided her with a ration card and a supply of firewood. When Shileiko came out of hospital, as Luknitsky notes,[16] he wrote to Akhmatova miserably to ask if she was abandoning him now that he was poor and sick. She replied at once: "No, dear Volodia, I am not leaving you . . . Move to my place."

This he did, though not without protest. The centre of power shifted as a result. Akhmatova was now the main breadwinner and the flat they were living in was hers rather than his. In August 1920, Shileiko's salary was only sufficient to buy food for one or two days a week. They were both enfeebled by illness and she had begun to feel emotionally stifled by the relationship. Indeed, no poems of Akhmatova's are dated 1920, the year when she began to work and live at the Institute. Work there required considerable stamina. The cold was so unbearable that everyone sat in coats, sometimes drinking cocoa heated up in the fireplace. Akhmatova's hot drink was usually prepared by someone else. She was still ill, but she was never depressing to visit.

Petrograd was no longer the brilliant capital of an empire in 1920, but a city altogether neglected, as Akhmatova wrote of it:

> The old Petersburg signboards were still all in place, but dusk, darkness and yawning emptiness lay behind them . . . You could pick a large bouquet of wild flowers in Gostiny Dvor.* The famous Petersburg wooden pavement was rotting. There was still a smell of chocolate wafting from the basement windows of Kraft. . . . All the fences of Tsarskoye Selo had been burned . . .[17]

In 1920, Korney Chukovsky visited Akhmatova and Shileiko and observed the dank room in which they lived. It was so cold there he had to put on two vests and an extra jacket before calling on them. Shileiko's tuberculosis was now complicated by pleurisy. Chukovsky marvelled that, although Akhmatova spoke quite brusquely to him, she was tender with Shileiko, sometimes "brushing away the hair

---

* A department store.

from his face."[18] Luknitsky recalled it was Artur Lurye who decided, some time in May or June 1920, that Akhmatova had to be rescued from Shileiko, and arranged for nurses to take the sick Shileiko to hospital again.[19] She did not leave immediately, however. It was a true *folie à deux*.

Both Akhmatova and Shileiko continued to be unwell, and on 12 August 1920 Akhmatova, seen at Sudeikina's flat, was described as "a horrible skeleton, dressed in rags."[20] All over Russia, those who lived in cities bartered for food, if they had the strength to go out into the countryside. Tsvetaeva describes in her journals *Earthly Signs* how she travelled into the countryside to exchange trinkets for flour. Akhmatova's health did not permit such forays.

Even Gumilyov, by then chairman of the Petrograd Union of Poets, could not find enough wood to keep warm in those terrible days, until he moved into the House of Arts, which was centrally heated. He continued to have young and beautiful mistresses. In 1920 the poet Vladislav Khodasevich remembers seeing Gumilyov arrive at a house which was feebly lit and choking with smoke from a smouldering fire, with Irina Odoevtseva on his arm in a low-cut black dress. He was shivering with the cold but he carried himself proudly: "He was playing that it was a ball. His whole appearance said, 'Nothing has happened. A revolution? I didn't hear anything about it.'"[21] There was no milk in the city for his younger child Lena and so he sent his wife and children to the country to be with his mother. However, his wife protested and insisted on being brought back to St. Petersburg. The child was put in a orphanage and there—like Tsvetaeva's younger child—she died of starvation.

By 3 February 1921, Akhmatova had moved from the Institute of Agronomy to the publishing house World Literature, where Gumilyov also worked. Her health improved. She was cheerful, looked much younger and began to put on a little weight. She said to Chukovsky, who met her there: "Why don't you come and see me later today? I will give you a bottle of milk for your daughter." Chukovsky reflected that, "No one else would give away a whole bottle of milk in February 1921."[22]

On 14 March Akhmatova met her ex-husband when she went to collect the card which gave her membership of the Union of Poets.[23] Gumilyov entered while she was waiting to see him, but busied himself with other matters. After a while the door of his room opened and she saw him talking to Alexander Blok. When Gumilyov eventually greeted her, he asked her to forgive him for making her wait. Akhmatova responded with a cool composure: "It's nothing. I am used to waiting." Gumilyov asked, "For me?" To which Akhmatova replied, "No, in queues." He signed her card, but gave her only a very cold kiss on the hand when they parted.

For all the depletion of illness, and her struggles within herself, Akhmatova's manner was often perceived as arrogant. In 1921 in the Writers' House, for instance, an acquaintance described her as reciting her poetry "standing very erect, haughty and with a fur of some kind on her shoulders." What was seen as arrogance was closer to the inward-drawn remoteness of misery, and this she described in May 1921 in a rare letter to Tsvetaeva: "I have not been so unhappy as I am today for a long time, and I wanted so much to talk about it. I don't write letters to anyone, and never have, but your kindness means a great deal to me. Thank you for that, and for dedicating your poems to me. I shall be in St. Petersburg before 1 July and want to read your new poems."[24]

All through the first half of 1921 Akhmatova was writing poems in which she rejected the thought of a violent end to her unhappiness: throwing herself under the feet of a bay horse, for instance, or sending her absent lover a poisoned handkerchief. Akhmatova's poems were now marked by a frank sensuality, as in August 1921 when she wrote:

> *I may kiss those shoulders*
> *in moist languor.*[25]

On 9 July 1921, Akhmatova was sitting in front of her window when she heard a voice from the street calling, "Anna." She was surprised, because Shileiko was in Tsarskoye Selo and she could not think of anyone else who would call her with such familiarity. It was Gumilyov, bearing sad news from her family in the south, from whom she had been cut off by the Civil War. He had been visiting her mother, Inna, and her only surviving sister, Iya (who was to succumb to tuberculosis in 1922). While there they had received news of her brother Andrey's suicide.

The story is a poignant one, as Akhmatova told it to Chukovskaya in March 1940. Andrey had poisoned himself when his child died of malaria.

> He left us a letter—a marvellous one. It ended like this. "I kiss Mama's hands, which I remember as so beautiful and delicate and which are now so wrinkled." His wife had taken poison together with him, but when they broke down the door and came into the room she was still breathing. She was saved. She turned out to be pregnant and gave birth to a totally healthy child.[26]

Even as Gumilyov delivered the appalling news of her brother's death, he suggested she might like to give a reading of her poems at an event that very evening. She was far too upset to accept but he, perhaps because he was cold and tired, rebuked her for not wanting to read in public any more.

That spring, Akhmatova received a moving letter from Alya, Tsvetaeva's eight-year-old daughter, who had read in her mother's poetry that Akhmatova had a son, and was curious about him. What Akhmatova felt about her son at this juncture is unclear. In 1918 she had been able to travel to see him, but this was now impossible. She thanked Alya now for her "kind thoughts" and Tsvetaeva for an icon she had sent, but of Lev she only writes: "In these last years I have lost touch with all my relatives and Levushka, after the divorce, stayed in the family of his father." This conveys the impression that custody of her son had been taken away from her, which was not the case. Perhaps she was ashamed of not taking more responsibility for his upbringing. Certainly her poverty, and her miserable living conditions, would have made that difficult. By 1921, however, Akhmatova confesses a sense of guilt at the separation in several poems:

> *The lot of a mother is a bright torture.*
> *I was not worthy of it.*[27]

and

> *Sleep, my quiet one, sleep,*
> *my boy. I am a bad mother.*[28]

—a line for which Tsvetaeva once said she would give up everything she had written.

Lev and his grandmother were no longer living comfortably in Slepnyovo. His grandmother had been forced to leave her estate when peasants threatened to burn it just before the Revolution. In 1918 she had moved to Bezhetsk permanently, renting a flat of three rooms there in which she lived for the rest of her life. It proved very difficult to keep the flat warm and pleasant. And indeed her only source of income—apart from money Akhmatova sent her when she could—were the earnings of her stepdaughter, who was a teacher in a primary school. Gumilyova and Lev were not starving, as so many people were in the cities, however. Bread, for instance, was not a problem, though potatoes with flax oil were a luxury.[29]

A further exchange of letters between Akhmatova and Tsvetaeva survives. Tsvetaeva had dedicated her poem "The Red Horse" to Akhmatova, and poured out her admiration in it. Since there are so many accounts—in the memoirs of Chukovskaya, for instance—of Akhmatova's impatience with Tsvetaeva's tale of her carrying the poems dedicated to her everywhere, it is something of a relief to read the warmth of her response.

In June 1921, Akhmatova wrote a poem for her friend Natalya Rykova which expresses her disgust at what was happening all round her, but finding consolation nevertheless in the unchanging beauty of the world. Called "MCMXXI," it gives the title to a whole volume:

> *Everything has been plundered, betrayed or sold;*
> *the black wings of death flicker over us.*
> *The pain of starvation gobbles everything.*
> *So why is it now so bright?*
>
> *By day the scents of cherry blossoms*
> *reach us from the woods nearby*
> *and at night there are new constellations*
> *in the translucent depths of the sky.*
>
> *And a sense of the numinous reaches*
> *these dirty, rundown shacks . . .*
> *No one, no one knows what it is,*
> *but we've longed for it for centuries.*[30]

In the summer of 1921, Akhmatova found it possible to leave Shileiko's rooms at the invitation of Artur Lurye, who had for some time been pressing her to join him in the flat he shared with Olga Sudeikina on the Fontanka. (Lurye employed a maid who lived in and looked after domestic chores: a privilege still not unheard of in the early days of the Revolution.) Leaving Shileiko was not an easy matter for her. "Somehow we managed to separate," she wrote:

> To put out the hateful fire.
> My old enemy, it's time to learn
> How to love someone else properly.
>
> Now I am free, everything is fun.
> At night the Muse herself will comfort me
> And in daylight Fame will drag herself here
> To sound her rattle in my ear.[31]

Once she had left him, she was determined to remain free from loving him. As she wrote:

> I swear by the garden of the angels
> I swear by the miraculous icon
> By our nights of burning delirium
> That I will never return to you.[32]

Her sexual involvement with Lurye is not in doubt; indeed Akhmatova refers to him as one of her "husbands."[33] The exact nature of this *ménage à trois* in Lurye's flat on the Fontanka has been disputed. Perhaps, as Anatoly Nayman thought,[34] Lurye was simply the fortunate possessor of an unequalled harem. If so, sharing a lover with Olga Sudeikina would give an important new meaning to Akhmatova recognising Olga as her double. However, there have been others, including Yevgeny Rein, who have suggested an additional erotic element in the relationship between Akhmatova and Sudeikina. Emma Gerstein—who only came to know Akhmatova well many years after this period—was emphatic nonetheless in her declaration that Akhmatova would have had no idea how to conduct herself in a sexual situation of the kind Rein suggests.

Whatever the nature of this experiment, Akhmatova was once

again able to write poems, after a year of nearly total silence, and remarked later: "If I had lived any longer with him [Shileiko], I should have forgotten how to write poetry."[35]

Artur Lurye was born in 1892 to a Jewish family in the Mogilev province, and came to St. Petersburg to study at the Conservatory in 1910. There he was influenced by the rising stars of the musical avant-garde and began to experiment with twelve-tone music. A former denizen of the Stray Dog, he played a Gluck gavotte in a modern arrangement to welcome Richard Strauss, who subsequently sat down with him at the piano. He thought of himself as a Futurist and, when Marinetti visited the Stray Dog, he delivered a lecture on the "Art of Noise" to welcome him. He had converted to Catholicism in 1913. A fastidious, well-dressed man, he wore a lorgnette on a gold chain.

Like many other avant-garde artists, he at first saw the Bolshevik Revolution as an opportunity rather than a disaster. He was intelligently active as Commissar of Music from 1918 to 1920, setting up a network of music schools and creating the orchestra that was to become the Leningrad Philharmonic. He also made sure that important new music was published, including that of Sergey Prokofiev. His dream was to transform the masses by bringing music of both the present and the past to them. However, in 1921 he was relieved of his position as Commissar. When he emigrated, he found his two years as a servant of the Soviet State counted against him in his efforts to find a foothold in the musical world.

It has been suggested that the last lyric of *Dark Dreams* refers to Lurye. This would imply that Akhmatova was unwilling to accept a docile role when she came to live with him and had no desire for an intense relationship:

> *Surrender to you? You are out of your mind*
> *I submit only to the will of the Lord.*
> *I don't want any more excitement or pain.*
> *My husband—is an executioner—his home a prison.*
>
> *Look, I came here of my own accord . . .*
> *It was December, there was a high wind.*
> *And if it was bright in your bondage,*
> *Outside the window, darkness stood guard.*[36]

A group of Akhmatova's new poems were published in *Plantain* in 1921, the year when the Civil War ended with the victory of the Bolsheviks. *Plantain* was a small book, only six inches by three, of the few poems written between 1917 and 1919. These poems were later incorporated in *Anno Domini MCMXXI*, published in early 1922. Certainly there are poems in *Anno Domini* about her unhappy failure to form successful relationships with men, yet the most important poems are about the horrors of war. There is a particularly poignant recognition of a mother's suffering which is not her own, since she had no son of military age:

> *Why then did I carry you*
> *long ago in my arms?*
> *Why then did strength flow*
> *into your blue eyes . . . ?*
>
> . . . . . .
>
> *At Malakhov Kurgan they shot an officer*
> *who had looked at God's world*
> *one week less than twenty years.*[37]

In one poem from *Plantain*, but written in 1916, the poet wants to give the Muse a white bird but finds the bird has already flown away after her beautiful "guest." Many lyrics speak of her desire to sacrifice everything for her country, even her gift of song.

In fact, these two years of Akhmatova's life were at once frivolous and amoral, and she may have enjoyed having no one particular man to whom she was devoted. Korney Chukovsky remembers forming the impression that the fame of her poetry was once again the most sustaining prop of her self-esteem. When she showed him notebooks with her new poems, he felt a great surge of pity for her, guessing that the pride she now took in her ability to earn money through her work disguised an inner bleakness. He remembered her saying with excitement, "I received 150 million roubles* for *White Flock* . . . I was able to buy a dress for myself, and sent some money to Lyovushka. And I want to send some to my mother."

---

* This was a substantial sum, though as the exchange rate changed twice a day it is difficult to give an accurate sense of what 150 million roubles was worth. However, in December 1921 a packet of matches cost 100 roubles, and teachers' salaries were about 500,000 per month. By March 1922, the same salary was 5 million roubles.[38]

There were two more unexpected deaths, both in August 1921, however, the first being that of Alexander Blok, who died at the age of forty-one. Blok, the greatest Russian poet of the Silver Age, had been in a serious depression for some time, disillusioned by the Revolution he had once hailed and speaking of himself as already dead. He suffered a heart attack in May 1921 after a trip to Moscow and, when it became clear he badly needed medical attention, Gorky and Anatoly Lunacharsky, Commissar for Education and Enlightenment, tried to arrange permission for him to go to Finland for treatment. Lenin refused, afraid Blok would speak out against the Soviet regime and knowing how important the change of mind of a poet like Blok could seem. Rheumatic fever followed the heart attack and Blok died on 7 August. His death came as a terrible shock for Akhmatova, who had continued to revere his poetry, though she disapproved of his political stance. At his funeral she wore a simple grey dress and when she came up to the coffin she bowed over him and crossed herself. She was crying freely and, though her face was hidden by a veil, many of the mourners recognised her. She would write many poems in Blok's memory, several of which Artur Lurye set to music.

Worse news soon followed. It was at Blok's funeral on 10 August that Akhmatova first heard that Gumilyov had been arrested on 3 August. Khodasevich had been with Gumilyov the evening before his arrest and describes him as being relaxed and cheerful and "intent on living to be ninety."[39] No news came from prison, and friends who inquired at the headquarters of the Cheka* about the charges against him were told to wait and come back in a week. However, the very man who received the delegation, the chairman of the Cheka, was involved in the secret meeting which concocted the so-called Tagantsev conspiracy. One of the conspirators was said to be Gumilyov.

In a letter from Shileiko, Akhmatova heard a rumour that Gumilyov had been transferred to Moscow, which could be taken as a sign that he might be released. Nevertheless, on a train from Detskoye Selo (the new name for Tsarskoye Selo), Akhmatova wrote a poem about her premonitions of his death by shooting. It is dated earlier than his execution, but whether that date is correct, or falsified to throw spies off the scent, is not clear.

---

* The Cheka, which became the OGPU, NKVD and later the KGB, was a Department of State set up to combat speculation and counter-revolutionary activity.

The truth about Nikolay Gumilyov's last days was uncovered by Vera and Sergey Luknitsky, the children of Pavel Luknitsky, in 1990 when the KGB offices in St. Petersburg were temporarily open after the collapse of Communism. Vladimir Tagantsev, a young professor of geography at Petrograd University, had claimed that in 1920 Gumilyov declared that if there were an uprising in the streets against the Soviet government, he would join it. Sailors at the Kronstadt naval base near Petrograd, who had initially supported the Bolshevik takeover of power in 1917, rose against the government in 1921. After the brutal suppression of this revolt in March 1921, Gumilyov realised the futility of such action and became politically inactive.

Once the Cheka had him in prison, however, he was interrogated four times. In his final interrogation, his inquisitor used all the means at his disposal to extract from him the names of other conspirators. Gumilyov remained defiant and no names were elicited. Nevertheless, Gumilyov was declared to be an enemy of the people and was sentenced to execution by shooting.[40] Gorky tried to intervene on Gumilyov's behalf but the poet had already been shot when Gorky arrived in Petrograd with an order for his release.

A few days after Blok's funeral Akhmatova had to go into a sanatorium in Detskoye Selo. Her friends the Rykovs were living on a farm nearby and she was visited by Manya Rykova when her father Viktor Rykov brought the terrible news that Gumilyov had been executed by a firing squad on 25 August with sixty-one others. He was only thirty-five. Akhmatova remembered returning to Petrograd and walking to the Marble Palace on foot to see Shileiko and share her grief with him. A Requiem Mass for Gumilyov was allowed, though his place of burial was kept a secret for nine years. Although she had not been close to Gumilyov for some time, Akhmatova felt his death with pain and fear. Perhaps she had never realised up until that moment how much Gumilyov had meant to her. At his funeral, it was she who was treated as his widow, although his second wife was present. On 27 or 28 August 1921, she wrote nakedly about Gumilyov's execution and the fear it had induced in her:

> *Terror fingers all things in the dark*
> *Leads moonlight to the axe.*

There's an ominous knock behind the wall:
A ghost, a thief or a rat . . .[41]

The last time Lev saw his father was in May 1921, three months before his execution. Gumilyov had come to collect his second wife and their daughter, and was in Bezhetsk for one day only. After Gumilyov's execution, Lev remembered that, although no one told him, he guessed it was the worst that could be imagined from his grandmother's grief. He never forgot the desolation he felt when he pieced together what had happened.

In the winter of 1921, three months after Gumilyov's execution, Akhmatova visited Bezhetsk in order to decide whether to take Lev back with her to Petrograd or to leave him with his grandmother. She decided the nine-year-old boy would be altogether better off with his grandmother because Petrograd had so little food or fuel. Her own situation was precarious after her divorce from Shileiko and she seems to have feared her son would disapprove of the way she was living. For this reason, she gave the boy a very full account of the reasons she was separating from her second husband. Lev remembered this visit vividly and was able to record her telling him that Shileiko had not allowed her to go out and insisted that, rather than doing her own work, she write out the contents of his books and articles at his dictation. Akhmatova told him that Shileiko always tried to debase her in her own esteem, show her that she was not talented, diminish her in every possible way.[42]

A precocious boy, Lev was similar to his father in appearance, gestures and independence of character, but he did not question his mother's version of those events. He saw too that his mother and grandmother could not find a common language. If Akhmatova was grateful to her mother-in-law for looking after her son for so long, she did not make that clear to anyone. An observant child, Lev could also see that his mother actively disliked his half-sister, Anna Ivanovna Sverchkova. The boy was a little homesick for Tsarskoye Selo, which he thought of as his "motherland," but he regarded Slepnyovo, the estate still owned by Gumilyov's mother, as his "fatherland" and was nostalgic for it all his life.

Strangely, Akhmatova had returned to the house she once shared with Gumilyov in Detskoye Selo only a few weeks before his death and taken from the attic all she could find of her correspondence. She did not take any papers that belonged to Gumilyov. Now she regretted that. After Gumilyov's death, Akhmatova was surprised by the number of letters that came to her from all over Russia. She was much saddened to think that Gumilyov had never realised how much and how widely his poetry was loved.

The dangers of writing about her misery after Gumilyov's execution were already obvious. In doing so, guardedly, she seems to be speaking with prophetic accuracy of what was to happen to her later under the Soviet Terror:

> *I brought destruction on those I loved*
> *and one after another they all died.*
> *This is my sorrow. I foretold*
> *their graves in my own words.*
> *It was as if my wild love songs*
> *were ravens, circling and smelling out*
> *the hot, fresh blood they desired.*
>
> *Now it is warm and sweet to be with you.*
> *You are as close as my own heart,*
> *but give me your hands, listen carefully.*
> *I warn you: go far away from me.*
>
> *And don't let me know where you are.*[43]

On 24 December 1921 Korney Chukovsky notes that when Akhmatova was living on the Fontanka, he found her lying on the bed in her coat while he was there. The woman who came to light a fire complained of a lack of wood and Akhmatova offered to help her saw more the following day. When she brought out a manuscript of a libretto for a ballet based on Blok's *Snow Mask*, Akhmatova apologised, saying she was not used to writing prose, and afterwards read her poems for Blok, which were so beautiful that Chukovsky wept.

Chukovsky pitied her harsh life and thought Akhmatova was sustained only by her fame and a belief in the importance of her poetry. She showed Chukovsky a new manuscript of her poems, but seemed worried that critics would say that she was only repeating herself in it.

In the wake of Gumilyov's death, the comforting support she had been able to take in the popularity of her poetry was soon to be snatched away from her. In January 1922, at an evening ominously entitled "The Purge of Contemporary Poetry," Mayakovsky gave a speech in Moscow declaring that her intimate domestic poetry no longer held any interest for him. In the aftermath of the Bolshevik victory, this assertion was a portent, though Akhmatova may not yet have understood as much.

When Lurye decided to leave Russia, and told Akhmatova so, she took the news with the outward calm that had become both her characteristic manner and her defence against emotional break-down. She told Luknitsky, "It was my calmness that finished him . . . When he left . . . it became easy."[44] Critics differ about which poems were written to Lurye, but losing him was clearly not the lifelong sorrow that she felt for Boris Anrep. Olga did not follow Lurye abroad until 1924.

Though once again abandoned, Akhmatova was not alone. The great poet Boris Pasternak met her in January 1922 and, in speaking of her kindness, remarked that she reminded him of a sis-ter. They were to be the purest of friends throughout their lives. In the middle of August 1922, he and his wife came to see Akhmatova to say goodbye before they left for Germany on a visit to see his father.

Akhmatova refused to consider the possibility of going abroad herself. She seemed to draw strength from her loneliness. She was separated from Nedobrovo by death, and from Anrep and Lurye by emigration. In a poem of 1922, she describes how her looks have suffered as a result of famine and illness:

> *My cheeks are sunken, and my lips without blood.*
> *He won't recognise my face;*
> *I am no longer beautiful, nor am I*
> *The one whose songs once troubled you.*[45]

A new defiance enters the tone of her poems: the steely defiance of which Nedobrovo had spoken.

> *I am not among those who left the land*
> *To be torn open by our enemies.*

And crude flattery does not influence me,
I will not give them my songs.

Still I feel some pity for an exile
Like somebody sick, or a prisoner.
A refugee has to walk a dark road,
And foreign bread has a bitter flavour.

Here in the smoke of blinding fires
What's left of our youth will be destroyed
And we won't be able to ward off
A single blow from ourselves.

Yet in the final totting up—and
We know each hour will be counted—
There is no people on earth more tearless,
More simple and more proud.[46]

However, Ida Nappelbaum, who remembers Akhmatova coming to her literary evenings in 1922 with Artur Lurye as her usual companion, observed that sometimes Nikolay Punin began to accompany her, even before Lurye left for western Europe. Punin was soon to be the most important figure in Akhmatova's emotional landscape.

The Civil War which had raged over southern Russia since 1918 ended in a Bolshevik victory in 1921. For many in the West as well as in Russia, that seemed cause for celebration. It is no longer possible even for a committed Marxist now to see that outcome as the victory of a long-oppressed people against more privileged classes, or to believe that Lenin was an idealist whose own good intentions were subverted once Stalin came to power. Rule by Terror was established under Lenin himself.[47] He set up the vast infrastructure of a police state, which employed more than a quarter of a million people. In prisons, the Cheka used tortures which were cruel beyond any that the Tsar's police had devised.[48] Nor was Trotsky any more humane. Indeed, he recommended that any Christian babble about the sanctity of human life should be put aside. Only Maxim Gorky spoke out against the Terror, writing directly to Lenin.

By now, the whole population was cooking in broken utensils, living in patched-up clothes and drinking from broken crockery; the economy was in ruins. There were seven million children living rough in derelict houses and on building sites, only able to survive by means of theft or casual prostitution. Roosters and goats roamed the streets. When Lenin introduced the New Economic Policy—which allowed a measure of market trading—peasants were quick to take advantage of it. Shops sprang up overnight stocked with butter, cheese, meat, pastry and fruit, which the peasantry had been unwilling to exchange for paper money. The hungry and the poor among the urban population, however, could only stare through the windows helplessly.

SEVEN

Infidelities

> *Our closeness is fragile.*
>
> —NIKOLAY PUNIN

midst Russia's turmoil, Akhmatova was about to enter the longest and most intense relationship of her life. Nikolay Nikolaevich Punin, an austerely handsome man of great intellectual authority, was an art historian. Punin's recently published diaries and letters suggest an extraordinary mind, a cold egoism and a man easily overwhelmed by sexual desire. These diaries, published for the first time in English after the acquisition of his papers by the University of Texas, Austin in 1996, and also L. Zykov's significantly different edition in Russian,[1] give a detailed account of his long, battling relationship with Akhmatova and a remarkable image of Akhmatova in her early thirties. Only Lydia Chukovskaya, recording her impressions of a much older woman, leaves us with an equally complex portrait.

It is not a simple story. Both Punin and Akhmatova were involved with other people when they became lovers. Akhmatova was living with Artur Lurye until he went abroad in 1922, and had taken up with Mikhail Zimmerman. Punin was married to Anna Ahrens, a hard-working doctor. He had also had several extramarital affairs before meeting Akhmatova, some of them at the same time. Akhmatova was not responsible for a breakdown in the Punins' marriage.

Punin felt some guilt towards his wife, whom he usually calls Galya in his diaries; nevertheless he managed to persuade himself that he loved her all the more tenderly because of that guilt. Anna Ahrens remained loyal to him throughout his infatuation with a beautiful young student he calls "N." His first erotic encounter with the seventeen-year-old N—brilliantly described in his journal—left him confused and guilty, yet quick to excuse himself by confessing his impatience with monogamous life: "I am here, in the study, Galya is in the dining room. Did I betray her? Yes. It offends her—from her point of view, yes; from mine, no . . . Again this childishness, why did I get married?"[2]

He was also involved with the notorious Lilya Brik, who lived in a *ménage à trois* with her husband, Osip Brik, and Vladimir Mayakovsky. Lilya was beautiful, with painted lips and darkened eyelids and "something impudent in her face," as Punin described her: a woman "who knows a lot about love . . . strong and controlled, spoiled, proud and reserved."[3] It says something for Punin's sexual arrogance that he was able nevertheless to tell her in 1920 that he "only found her interesting physically, and could only continue to see her if she would accept that as the basis of their relationship."[4] She seems to have agreed, and Punin wrote of her with some relish on 20 May 1920: "I cannot imagine a woman I could possess more completely,"[5] even though he cannot bear to hear her talk about art.

The tolerance accorded to sexual promiscuity all through this period never precluded violent jealousy. At the outset of his relationship with Akhmatova, Punin was particularly jealous of her association with Zimmerman but, in spite of his recurring doubts and suspicions, it seems likely that Akhmatova was soon more deeply in love with Punin than she allowed him to guess. This reluctance was not exactly a matter of feminine wiles. Her experience of emotional commitment had not been happy. Shileiko had tried to control her whole being while they were together and Anrep had abandoned her to go into exile. Perhaps she was not altogether willing to be bound to one man again. In the event, she and Punin were to be damagingly close for more than thirteen years.

Punin's father, a stern, traditionally religious man, was a doctor who had served in a military hospital in Helsinki. Indeed, both

Nikolay's mother and his stepmother were also traditional Christians but he lost his own Christian faith in adolescence. Punin's desire for an answer to his metaphysical uncertainties was probably the strongest emotion of his adolescent years. One of his earliest diary entries describes his failure to react to his mother's death, which his siblings found unfeeling. She had been a tender, loving mother and it is tempting to attribute to this early loss Punin's need for a woman who would make him entirely central to her life. At the same time, he found that no single woman was ever quite enough for him.

A precocious reader, he scoffed at superstition and determined to avoid sentimentality. Yet as the deaths of the First World War piled up, Punin could not bring himself to accept that there was no life beyond the one on this earth. As late as October 1916, Punin was still attracted to those who found strength in religious faith, while confessing: "I don't believe it. I don't protest all those vital sensations that are born of the religious state, but I do think it's insanity to project them on to something that stands outside of life. *Life* is God, and God is blind."[6] On 14 January 1917 he was writing: "There is nothing but death to talk about. Do we perish forever, or not?"[7]

He had no strong political convictions. Though he was drawn for a time to Socialism, he could not accept the materialism of the ideology. Early diary entries suggest how prone he was to depression, especially in spring. Like many of the men in Akhmatova's life, his own childhood, too, had centred on Tsarskoye Selo. They might have passed each other in their prams in Pavlovsk Park.

Punin had for some years made himself an articulate exponent of the Futurist movement, and while still in his twenties was a recognised arbiter of taste in the Russian art world. At the high point of his career, he wrote articles praising the art of Vladimir Tatlin and Kazimir Malevich but he was equally authoritative on icon-painting, Japanese art and Picasso. Punin was a gifted writer of prose. At the time of the Revolution he observes soldiers in yellow boots, merchants setting up shop on the pavements, prostitutes and milling crowds. In September 1917, he writes: "Here it is, the Revolutionary City in its time of troubles; hungry, depraved, frightened, abused, emergent, powerful and drunk."[8]

During the first years of Civil War Communism, Punin worked at the Russian Museum as deputy head of Fine Arts, and subsequently on the editorial board of the newspaper *Isskustvo kommuny*. In 1919 he was appointed head of the Petrograd Regional Visual Arts. For all his impeccable credentials as an expert in fine arts, however, he had an early brush with the Soviet authorities. On 3 August 1921, at about 2 a.m., he was arrested and taken to police headquarters. He was not questioned then but transferred without being charged to Cell 32 of the Depzit prison, where he was held until 6 September. During his time there he met Gumilyov briefly and observed he had a copy of the *Iliad* in his hands, which was taken away from him.

Conditions in general were difficult. While in prison, Punin wrote several cards to his father-in-law, Yevgeny Ahrens, giving a list of his most immediate necessities. Punin's wife replied with a touching letter on 13 August 1921: "My dear friend, how are you? Ask for whatever you need, we are sending all but the shoes . . . Can I send you books? I already sent one, did you get to keep it? All send kisses, greetings. I squeeze your hand. Your Galya."[9] There were some comic aspects to his imprisonment; his suspenders were given back to another inmate by mistake, for instance. But in the same month that saw Gumilyov's execution, the imprisonment was an alarming experience. Punin was only released through the intercession of Lunacharsky.

On 8 November 1921, Anna Ahrens gave birth to his daughter, Irina, by forceps delivery. By 20 November, Punin is reflecting once again that "the way to God is woman . . . the female face, mouth and the oval of the chin."[10] He is describing the appearance of his ideal face, which resembles that of his own mother, and indeed the face of Akhmatova.

His interest in Akhmatova went back to the days of the Stray Dog, though they were not then more than acquaintances. Punin first mentions Akhmatova in a diary entry of 1914, when she was already a celebrated poet. He travelled on the same train, and noted that she was "strange, pretty, pale, immortal and mystical." The next reference to her is 18 July 1920, when he saw her walking with Shileiko in the park of the Museum. He noted how well she carried herself but he was too shy to speak to her, partly because she was already so famous. He knew her history and disapproved of her earlier bohemian life, even suggesting he was "grateful that . . . she is not giving readings or publishing poetry now."

By September 1922, Akhmatova and Punin were passionately involved. The initiative may have been taken by Akhmatova. There are three notes from her to Punin which are undated, but thought to be written in September 1922: "I have a meeting at one of the commissions for the resolution of conflicts. Maybe you won't catch me. Then come on Thurs. in the morning, and until then, work and don't be sad. See, I can give good advice to my friends. And I am a bit sad that I will not see you. Kisses, Your An."[11] and "Nikolay Nikolaevich, today I will be at the 'Sounding Shell.' Come. A. Akhmatova."[12] Punin was overwhelmed by emotion when he read this note, and the following: "Dear Nikolay Nikolaevich, If you are free this evening, then it would be endlessly sweet of you to come and visit us. Until we meet, Akhmatova."[13]

By November of the same year Punin's diaries show him deeply in love with her, though he was well aware of her relationship with Zimmerman and knew Akhmatova continued to visit Shileiko, and to live in Shileiko's flat while he was in Moscow. This suited Punin well enough, since he wanted to remain married, and to keep his wife and daughter together with him. In January 1923, Punin recorded Akhmatova saying "she absolutely had to leave Artur's home. I asked her whether she would come live with me if I were alone. She answered: 'Then I would come.' "[14]

In his journal Punin often accuses himself of superficiality and the failure to be as creative as he would like to be. His own passion was to excel, and he berates himself for the triviality of his life and the limited use he had made of his talents. The wish not to be distracted from the main purpose of his life, as much as the torments of jealousy, led him to make several attempts to break away from Akhmatova, through 1922 and 1923. Akhmatova knew he was struggling to be free and tried to keep her own options open. At the same time, he gives us a sharp and insightful portrait of Akhmatova in her early thirties. In one of his diary entries, written in December 1922 when he thought a break was inevitable, he noted:

> Our love was difficult. Because of this it perished before its time. Neither she nor I could display it, talk about it, free up our lives for it . . . I still knew how to amuse her, but she never could comfort me. I often felt bitter and stifled with her, as if death were embracing and kissing me. Yet to this very moment, I love her lithe and sharp movements, the lines of her body, and I especially love her face, her mouth, and the sorrowful curve of her smile, her teeth with their lit-

tle gaps, the oval of her strong chin, her large forehead . . . It seemed to me that my mother had just such a face . . . A sweet face.[15]

At the end of December, Punin was prepared to cut free from his entanglement with Akhmatova altogether. Yet when he went to see her and found she was sitting by a cold, broken stove, and had some trouble with her heart, he at once melted with concern and the pleasure of her company: "I fixed the stove, then we walked in the Summer Garden. She cheered up, began to smile her sweet, womanly smile. We stopped by a bakery. She fed me pastries. We bought a Christmas tree."[16]

A note from Akhmatova to Punin—undated, but thought by Leonid Zykov to be written in December 1922—shows how very much Akhmatova admired him: "Thank you for the letter. You, it turns out, can write like the tenderest of angels. How glad I am that you exist. Until tomorrow, Anna."[17] Akhmatova was then at the height of her reputation and, though often sick, thin and dressing modestly, continued to hold herself like a queen. Punin guessed at an inner life as black as his own, however, and describes it more acutely than any of her lovers. As he wrote on 30 December 1922: "So empty—not her outer life—they don't bow to anyone as they do to her—but inside her, her life itself is empty, so much so that at times it even frightens me."[18] He thought she deserved an uncomplicated, light-hearted, simple love, and marvels at the pleasure she takes in the world around her: "She is often amazed at things to which we are already accustomed. How I love her joyful wonder at a cup, the snow, the sky."[19]

Punin was often furious to find Akhmatova enjoying a friendly life without him. One such occasion is recorded in "New Year's Ballad," which Punin mentions directly in his diary entry of 30 December 1922, while describing one of these angry departures: "It's finished. I left as easily as usual . . . But my heart was weary, as if I had swallowed poison. Life, why are you this way? So you didn't let me dine with you. I am the sixth guest at the banquet of death [here a poem of A. is written and crossed out] and all five drank to me, the absent one, but I have the feeling that I will never die."[20]

The poem "New Year's Ballad," dated 1923, opens on a table of friends collected together to celebrate the New Year. Ominous notes sound at once:

Why are my fingers covered in blood?
This wine burns like poison.[21]

A series of toasts follow. First the host raises his glass to the Russian soil, where they will all lie when they are dead. Another friend toasts Akhmatova's poems, "in which we shall all live," but a third guest,

unaware of when
he had abandoned this world, as if
in response to my own thoughts
muttered: "We ought to drink
to the one not yet here with us."[22]

The relationship with Punin continued to develop passionately but far from steadily. Changes of Punin's mood are recorded in his journal. One moment Akhmatova's treatment of him leads him to feel that their relationship is at an end; then, as it becomes clear nothing has ended, he notes soberly: "I cannot imagine a worse torment than that life might separate us."[23] Nevertheless, even at the height of his tumultuous passion for Akhmatova, Punin still needed Galya and felt guilty for what he was doing. When he went with his wife for a few days to Pavlovsk, he reflected in his journal: "Out of all this, the most tormenting thing is deceiving her, and the most horrible is tormenting her, and I am doing both."[24]

If Akhmatova felt guilty about Punin's wife, she kept it to herself. She had her own reasons to feel guilt about other matters. On 10 January 1923 she seemed particularly restless. This Punin attributed to the loneliness he often felt himself on public holidays. But at length Akhmatova brought herself to confess to him that she had recently betrayed him with her former husband Shileiko. "Then she cried, would I forgive her?" Punin responded with tenderness, perhaps reflecting he was hardly in a position to judge her, but nonetheless concerned about what her infidelity meant to him: "Knowing that you betrayed me, I know you will betray me, but I don't love you with the kind of love that can be betrayed."[25]

Punin was right to guess at Akhmatova's probable future infidelity. Only a few days later, on 17 January 1923, they arranged to go and see Zimmerman's production of *Khovanshchina*, but Akhmatova changed her mind about the outing. Punin observed she seemed

Anna Andreevna Akhmatova, 1922

ABOVE LEFT: *Andrey Antonovich Gorenko, Akhmatova's father, St. Petersburg, 1882*

ABOVE RIGHT: *Inna Erazmova Stogova, Akhmatova's mother, circa 1870*

BELOW: *Anna with her brother, Andrey, circa 1905*

Akhmatova as a young girl, Sebastopol, Ukraine, 1899

Paris   1911

ABOVE: Nude *(Anna Akhmatova), by Amedeo Modigliani,*
pencil on paper, circa 1911

BELOW: Portrait of Akhmatova, *by Nathan Altman,*
oil on canvas, 1914

Nikolay Stepanovich Gumilyov

ABOVE LEFT: *Nikolay Vladimirovich Nedobrovo, St. Petersburg, 1914*

ABOVE CENTER: *Osip Mandelstam, circa 1938*

ABOVE RIGHT: *Nadezhda Mandelstam at her dacha near Moscow, 1979*

BELOW: *Nikolay Gumilyov (extreme left) with Alexander Blok (third from the left), 1924*

Boris Anrep in his workshop in Paris, 1908

Olga Sudeikina with a doll in her hand, 1920

Nikolay Nikolaevich Punin, in the Gulag, 1950

ABOVE LEFT: *Artur Sergeevich Lurye, Paris, 1931*

ABOVE RIGHT: *Punin*

LEFT: *Anna Andreevna Akhmatova, Leningrad, 1924*

OPPOSITE: *Punin in his student days, 1919*

ABOVE LEFT: *Lydia Korneevna Chukovskaya, 1928*

ABOVE RIGHT: *Faina Grigorievna Ranevskaya, 1940*

BELOW LEFT: *Vladimir Georgevich Garshin, Moscow, 1948*

BELOW RIGHT: *Isaiah Berlin, 1940s*

Left to right, top to bottom: Lev in 1932, 1934, 1949, 1953 and 1956

ABOVE LEFT: *Boris Pasternak, 1930*

ABOVE RIGHT: *Joseph Brodsky, 1988*

BELOW: *Akhmatova receives her honorary Oxford degree, 1965.*
Back row (left to right), Gianfranco Conti, Geoffrey Keynes and Seigfried Sassoon.
Front row (left to right), Anna Kaminskaya, Akhmatova and Kenneth Wheare

ABOVE: *Anna Kaminskaya, St. Petersburg, 2003*

RIGHT: *Anatoly Nayman, Frankfurt, 2003*

BELOW: *Yevgeny Rein, Moscow, 2003*

Akhmatova, Leningrad, 1959

evasive about her new plans and became suspicious. He went to the theatre, found a ticket for himself, and soon noticed Akhmatova sitting in the eighth row. That evening, when he took her home, he listened to Akhmatova attributing her behaviour to her own humiliation. She had discovered new evidence of Artur Lurye's infidelity while he was living with her. Though this may seem a poor excuse, it may well be the case that her promiscuity sprang from the same insecurity that kept her dependent on men who abused her.

When she left Punin the next morning, he knew she was going to see Zimmerman, and sensed an imminent break-up. Perhaps there was something manipulative in her behaviour. Punin noted: "She said rightly that if she truly loved me, nothing in life could have intervened to destroy it. She doesn't love me."[26] Then he reflected with surprising justice: "But it seems she has the same right to think that I love her very little. I am preserving my home, what love is there in that?"[27]

When Punin walked her to the theatre on another occasion, supposedly to see Wagner's *Siegfried,* his suspicions were aroused again when she said she still wanted to go in even though they discovered upon arrival the opera was in fact *Onegin,* which she disliked. He correctly guessed that her obvious agitation meant that she had arranged to see Zimmerman that evening. He could not cope with the extremity of his jealousy over Zimmerman: "And what will I win, if I part with her out of pain? Only losing her before it was time . . . Is all that's left for me to do is watch this new love grow and not even lift a finger? . . . I saw there was no solution . . . then I felt how painful it was for Galya."[28]

A diary entry of 10 January 1923 shows him equally troubled by the occasional nights she still spent with Shileiko: "I don't know anyone in whom there has lived such a large and pure angel, in such a dark and sinful body."[29]

Punin had not altogether given up other sexual adventures of his own, although when he stayed with the Briks in Moscow on 20 March 1923 and Lilya made it abundantly clear that she was still sexually drawn to him, he says, "I remembered Anna and did not kiss her." When he returned from Moscow, he told Akhmatova he had made a resolution to see her only once a week and this made her very angry. She said it was the first time he had given her pain. Whatever his resolutions, he did not hold to them.

Punin's journal suggests a man in conflict with himself, but Akhmatova's poems of this period are coloured more strongly by her stubborn refusal to leave Russia and a desire to rejoin Anrep. She writes as if impatient with all those who fall at her feet weeping. In autumn 1922, for instance:

> *Here is the shore of a northern sea,*
> *the edge of our fame and misfortune.*
> *Do I care if you fall at my feet?*
> *I've had enough of condemned*
> *prisoners, hostages or slaves.*
> *I will only share bed and board*
> *with someone unyielding and hard.*[30]

Punin wrote her a long letter on 21 March 1923, wishing them at least "to endure the ending of their love together." Between April and May Punin's mood swings from lamenting the enormity of her need—"An. has become dependent on me, the affair has overflowed the bounds of love, has become my human affair"[31]—to once again losing any faith in their ever being truly together. He felt that the only hold he had over Akhmatova was sexual, that he had a "pathetic power to incite her unsatiated womanly blood, to arouse her animal passion,"[32] and spends all of June longing for her.

With such a volatile lover, it is hardly surprising that Akhmatova kept up contact with Zimmerman. On 8 July, Punin overheard her talking on the telephone to Zimmerman and, making out the word "tomorrow," laid a trap for her. He suggested he might visit her the next day. His suspicions were confirmed when she put him off. Punin wondered how he could go on loving her, faced with such duplicity, but he remains utterly ensnared. In his diary, he reflects angrily, "She doesn't love me and never loved me. What's more, she cannot love, she isn't able to."[33]

A few days later, they are happily visiting the islands just off the coast of Petrograd together, on a hot sunny day with a strong wind. Punin notes in his diary both Akhmatova's animation and her child-like quality, which he finds surprising in a woman "who already knows so much and is weary."[34] It may well be that her unpredictable behaviour engendered exactly the uncertainty which kept him so passionately in love.

By 2 August 1923, Punin was so overpowered by jealousy he could "do nothing the whole day because of the pain . . . An. asserts that she has sacrificed M. [Zimmerman] for me, yet her meetings with him are more frequent and last longer."[35] By 8 September Punin is seeing her daily. His emotions have an intensity he is not used to experiencing; indeed, his diary records a self-knowledge which includes the revelation, "Yes. I am a bit cold." More surprisingly, he discovers she is capable of causing him real pain. After a quarrel during which Akhmatova teased him, he records how he cried into his pillow in the coach that left to take him to Vitebsk. Even as he comes to acknowledge the depth of his feelings for her, he recognises the damage their relationship is doing to his wife: "Galya is undermined for ever."

All through November 1923 Punin's journal is full of his love for Akhmatova, although he records on 4 November "our closeness is fragile." Now Punin's journal includes notes from Akhmatova— sometimes with jottings in Punin's handwriting interrupting her, which gives an uncanny sense of overhearing the two lovers talking with one another: "Don't look at me like that. My head swims," Akhmatova writes. "We will be together, if only together" (this last in Punin's hand). "Now, now, Koty,* you'll quickly fall out of love with me."[36]

⌇

As the love affair with Punin developed, Akhmatova looked to be at the height of her literary success. She had already received a large sum of money for *White Flock* in 1917. From this she had given money to her mother and to her son. To preserve her mother's dignity, she pretended this money came from the pension her mother was entitled to as her father's widow, although this had in fact ceased long before. Sadly, this ruse led to her mother complaining that Anna was not sending her payments regularly, and sometimes even upbraiding her for not loving her enough. Akhmatova never explained the true situation, and simply endured the unjust reproach. This is the "steel" of which Nedobrovo had spoken. Akhmatova remained exceptionally fond of her mother, visited her frequently

---

* Punin's pet name, meaning "cat"; Akhmatova's was Olen, meaning "deer."

and, through the next few years, took care of her financially as well as she could.

For all the successful publication of *White Flock,* there were many signs that the new regime would not continue to look kindly on her poems. Her next volume of poems, *Anno Domini MCMXXI* (1922), contained many poems relating to her life in 1921; indeed, most of the new poems in the books were written in 1921, which had been a productive year for Akhmatova. In 1922 the critic Boris Eikhenbaum, in a book about contemporary poetry, wrote with much praise of Akhmatova's poems and coined the phrase which was to be used in later Stalinist attacks: "Here already we can see the beginnings of the paradoxical, or more correctly contradictory double image of the heroine—half harlot burning with passion, half nun able to pray to God for forgiveness."[37]

There were soon more serious signs of Party disapproval. In 1923, Mikhail Kuzmin, who had once written an introduction to Akhmatova's poems and been a friend and companion in the days of the Stray Dog, wrote that she was only significant now as a relic. Others, notably G. Levich, talked of her in Marxist terms, stressing her aristocratic origins. Two chapters of Leon Trotsky's *Literature and Revolution* appeared in September and October 1922 in *Pravda,* grouping her with Tsvetaeva and other women poets with an inauspicious disapproval: "The lyric circle of Akhmatova, Tsvetaeva, Radlova is very small. He [God] is a very convenient and portable third person . . . How this individual, no longer young, burdened with the personal and too often bothersome errands, can manage in his spare time to direct the destinies of the Universe, is simply incomprehensible."[38]

Punin, as a respected critic, was able to publish a reply to Trotsky claiming Anna Akhmatova as "the most original poet of the preceding generation."[39] He was well aware of the distress caused by the fallout from Eikhenbaum's book, which he found "shameless and insolent." The campaign against Akhmatova's poetry, however, had begun and was leading inexorably to a ban on her poetry by an unofficial Communist Party resolution that was not at first made public.[40] Akhmatova did not learn of it until 1927.

Although other voices were ready enough to mount accusations similar to Trotsky's, Akhmatova still enjoyed a wide readership and found an unexpected supporter in the celebrated Bolshevik Alexandra Kollontai, who declared Akhmatova's poems "reflect the soul of a woman of a transitional epoch, an epoch marked by a break in human psychology, the mortal struggle of two cultures."[41]

Punin's diaries record the difficult situations Akhmatova often faced socially. He had embarrassments of his own. When invited by Tatlin, a swashbuckling artist Punin had promoted, both he and Akhmatova accepted before discovering that Tatlin had also invited Punin's wife. Although this did not lead to a public scene, Anna Ahrens afterwards reproached Punin with hiding the nature of his meetings with Akhmatova. Punin describes Ahrens' tears and weeping and the way she berated him for his baseness: "And that I don't preserve any kind of even human relationship with her [Galya]. How could she say that, when all my relations with An. are destroyed by desire to keep G. at home and protect her self esteem."[42] Over a series of entries, in which Punin blames everyone but himself, he finds himself suddenly tempted by the thought that his wife might actually leave him.

Punin is not only shrewd, he writes brilliantly. When Akhmatova asks him whether he is glad she has come to see him, he answers tritely "of course." In his notebooks he muses:

> I was not glad but *happy*, with a full white happiness, so that everything became quiet and pure, like the snow . . . In my apartment the trees of the garden are right at the window. You can see their branches in the snow through the window. When An. came in, she filled the room so that it was as if winter herself had come to visit me, only it was warm. We drank coffee, and for some reason said very little.[43]

From 1921 to 1923 Akhmatova thought of herself as homeless and wandered from friend to friend as she would do in later life. In 1923, she found a base at 3 Kazanskaya Street and then in the following year moved to a new flat, once again on the Fontanka, that had been made from the former laundry room of the Sheremetev Palace.

Now, within the conversation book, they both record their thoughts; Akhmatova's usually much simpler. For instance, on 26 May 1924 she writes: "We were in Pavlosk in 1924," while Punin exclaims, "And I felt as if you were the end of the earth and there was nothing else." But her love is no less intense, as her rejoinder shows: "And I was amazed, that everything around was so green and fragrant. My Koty!"[44] It is rare to overhear such intimate confessions of love. Not all the exchanges are amicable, however. On 15 September, Akhmatova records: "Koty said that he has become so rooted in the Sherem[etev] House that he wouldn't exchange it for anything (i.e., for me).—Olen," and Punin rejoins: "I didn't say this—K[oty Malchik]."

Punin's notebook which runs from 1924 to 1925 collects a number of letters from Akhmatova, all undated but probably written in the summer of 1924 while Punin was travelling with Ahrens and Irina. If she misses him, these letters show more pride than love: "Very often you tell me that if I fall out of love with you and leave you it won't be hard for you to stay away from me. I remind you of this, and I remind you also of our last evening when you yourself asked so much for us to end 'this evil game' . . . It would be good if you could live in the country a bit longer, so I could leave the city before your return."[45]

The lovers in her poems seem once again to have become a composite figure of those she has lost. When she writes in 1924, in a poem titled "To the Artist," of being haunted by the "gold of lindens and the blue of water," Anrep comes to mind; but when she swears "by the passion of our night together, I will never return to you," she seems to be thinking of Shileiko.

Though she does not write poems about him, Akhmatova was far more deeply in love with Punin than he thought. She was, however, even more dedicated to poetry. She makes this explicit in 1924, when she wrote "The Muse," and Punin could well have taken a warning from that, but by then he was too much in love to draw away:

> At night, as I wait for her coming, my life
> Seems to hang by a thread. What are
> Youth, honours, freedom to me
> Compared with the flute in her hand.
>
> Look, here she is. She throws back her veil
> And fixes her eyes upon me with serenity.
> I ask, "Are you the one whom Dante
> Heard dictate the Inferno?" She answers "Yes."[46]

This is a daring poem, shivering with erotic excitement in the joy of creation, arrogant in imagining such a personal visit, and a direct connection to the great poet Dante.

Punin saw no threat as yet in Akhmatova's dedication to literature, but he is easily angered when he calls for her and finds that she has left to visit Shileiko. It is clear that Akhmatova was a long way from breaking with Shileiko altogether. Letters exchanged between Akhmatova and Shileiko show them continuing to use the same pet names for one another. Akhmatova was still looking after Tapa, the stray dog Shileiko had taken in when they were living together, and which had fallen ill. On 17 January 1925 she was to write: "I am still taking care of him and have put a muzzle on him." Shileiko's reply sounds genuinely concerned for her welfare: "You write you are ill and I am distressed about that. Don't go to the hospital and don't take my dog to hospital either. Both of you should come here in February to Moscow."[47]

Punin was maddened by so much uncertainty. On 24 March, when Akhmatova was entertaining friends, Punin suddenly came into the room wearing a fur coat. When she invited him to come in and sit, he said, very sharply and rudely, "You have enough people to entertain you," and left abruptly.[48]

About half the love poems in *Plantain* are to Shileiko, and many portray him as a jealous dragon. But she also wrote some of her strangest and most pitiless poems in 1924 and these do not concern her relationships with men:

> *Your heart must have no earthly consolation.*
> *You must not cling to either wife or home.*
> *Take the bread out of your own child's mouth*
> *and give it to a man you do not know.*
> *You must be the most humble servant*
> *of the man who was your desperate enemy*
> *and call the forest beast your brother.*
> *Above all, never ask God for anything.*[49]

Chukovsky's article in *Dom isskustv* about Akhmatova concentrated less on her subject matter than her marvellous simplicity and contrasted her with Mayakovsky, whom he found too much of a rhetorician.[50] The critic Vladimir Weidle, who saw Akhmatova often until 1924, thought that she had learned to endure everything—the corpses, the crowds, the hunger, the paupers, even Gumilyov's fate. She remained incapable, however, of looking after herself. On 6 May 1924, Chukovsky found her sitting in front of the fireplace, with a candle which she had to keep alight because she had no matches. He went out and bought some from painters working nearby.

On 8 August, Punin recorded in his journal a conversation between Akhmatova and himself in bed in which he asks her why she was still attached to Mikhail Zimmerman. Akhmatova denied that she was. Punin remained jealous all through August of that year, and threatened that if Akhmatova continued meeting Zimmerman at Fedorov's restaurant, as she intended, he would turn up there with Ahrens. Akhmatova adds her own ironic note to this diary entry: "Hail, Koty!" He was in an absurd position, as a married man and a womaniser, to make such threats.

One can see why Akhmatova loved Punin in these early years and she does not, it must be said, sound like a victim. Much easier to be sorry for his wife. In 1924, Ahrens had written a letter to her father telling him that she and Punin were separating, but did not send it because she was afraid it would affect his weak heart. Infatuated as he continued to be, Punin did not divorce Anna Ahrens and he and Akhmatova were never formally married, though she referred to him as her husband on several occasions.

Akhmatova remained, for all her impracticality, a loyal friend, and when Olga Sudeikina was ill with peritonitis through the summer of 1924, she nursed her with dedication, going every day to look after her. Sudeikina was a difficult patient, who often threatened to take her own life. It was only after her recovery that Sudeikina set off for Paris to join Artur Lurye. She left some of her dolls and trinkets with Akhmatova, who treasured them.[51]

On 23 September, Punin's journal gives an eyewitness account of the terrifying Petrograd flood. He was only able to reach Akhmatova at 10 p.m. in the evening and found her very agitated. Akhmatova is so often calm in the memories of friends that it is very revealing to have Punin record her anxiety so often and even to remark on 5 November: "What a worried woman! How can such a person live?"

Punin wanted her to accompany him to the Commissariat and register her change of address, but she remained uneasy about making such a commitment. Punin went to see Akhmatova at the Marble Palace on 8 November, and reports her in a terrible state, though "out of perniciousness she doesn't want to move in with me for five days." Akhmatova then writes: "Koty, I love you, things are bad for me. Now go home, tomorrow I will come and see you, my dear."[52]

In 1924, Pavel Luknitsky, a young man writing a thesis on the poetry of Nikolay Gumilyov, became acquainted with her. He gives many insights into her life over the years of their friendship. It is a little disturbing to have Roberta Reeder suggest that he was submitting reports on her to the Cheka,[53] but he certainly brought food and medicine when Akhmatova was seriously ill even if so.

When Luknitsky first met Akhmatova, she was living on part of Shileiko's pension. Although no longer with him, she collected his pension for him and sent it on to Moscow, where he was living in 1924. Her situation had improved in so far as she now had a maid to look after her, probably paid for by Shileiko.

In March 1925, Akhmatova's tuberculosis led her doctors to insist that she again spend some time in a sanatorium in Detskoye Selo. Her friends the Rybakovs found the money for her to stay there and passed on news of Olga Sudeikina. In a letter, Olga complained that Paris was repulsive and that she was longing to return to Russia, where she hoped—in total unawareness of the conditions there—to become a fashion designer. Although touched to hear that Sudeikina missed her very badly, Akhmatova knew her old friend would never be able to cope with earning a living in the Soviet Union. She herself was barely able to cope financially, and had no place she could think of as entirely her own. Akhmatova always claimed that the only reason she did not die, as her sisters had died, of tuberculosis, was because she suffered from Graves' disease, which she believed held tuberculosis in check. Perhaps this was a superstition current at the time. In the twenty-first century, medical opinion regards this as highly unlikely.*

---

* Professor Mark Pepys FRS, Professor of Medicine at the Royal Free & University College Medical School, London, pointed out that Graves' disease is an auto-immune disease and unlikely to boost resistance to TB. He speculated that Akhmatova's apparent thyroid over-activity, thyrotoxicosis, may not have been caused by Graves' disease but rather by TB of the thyroid, which can present as thyrotoxicosis. A spontaneous remission of her TB disease activity might account for Akhmatova's sudden "catastrophic" fatness after Tashkent. It is extremely unlikely that she would have undergone thyroid surgery at that time, and anti-thyroid drugs only became available in the 1950s at about the same time as anti-TB chemotherapy was first introduced.

In April 1925, she lived for a time in a *pension* in Detskoye Selo which Punin had found for her, and it was there she met and grew close to Osip Mandelstam's wife Nadezhda, who was also suffering from tuberculosis and was being treated by the same sanatorium. Akhmatova wrote in her autobiographical essay *My Half Century* that she was astonished by how attentive Mandelstam was to Nadezhda, noting that he would not allow her even a step away from him, "wouldn't let her out of his sight, didn't let her work, was insanely jealous and asked her advice on every word of his poems." Punin, too, visited every day and Akhmatova remarked ironically to Nadezhda that men were always charming and considerate when they came courting.

To Pavel Luknitsky, Akhmatova spoke of the way her relationship with Nikolay Nikolaevich Punin had developed. Even in 1925, probably their happiest year together, there were many angry quarrels. In July 1925, Punin wrote to her while she was away, referring to one such quarrel:

> Anna my dearest,
>
> You never gave me more pain than when you left today. Because I can't bring you back, I can't reach you and I can't tell you that you were wrong in what you said to me. Now I can only think about you, so lonely and proud, and feel the most horrible pain. Anna, please forgive me . . . everything you said in the morning was incorrect.[54]

Punin thought that Akhmatova had a cruel heart, although she could be tender. She, too, writes in their conversation book that K.M. (Koty Malchik) had a cruel heart and a wild temper. The force of their need for one another was inexorable, nevertheless. By April 1925 the lovers were spending almost every day together walking in the gardens of Pavlovsk Park and enjoying the spring weather. Their conversation book is now filled with an exchange of loving thoughts. This continues through May and June. On her birthday, 23 June, she promised to go abroad with him in the summer of the following year "if. . . ." The sentence is left uncompleted and suggests she was doubtful about her health. Punin's next comment in their conversation book confirms his own anxiety: "But only $\frac{1}{10}$ of Olen is left. She is tired after only 10 min.—still a queen. Her dear little elbows are the same."[55]

All through the summer they remained close, though from 21 to 26 July Akhmatova was in Bezhetsk visiting her son. Lev cannot have found that a very long visit, but would have seen that his mother was ill. Punin's conversation book that summer reads like an idyll: it was a high point of their relationship as lovers. In one undated remark, Akhmatova writes: "V[asilievsky] O[strov] is wondrous, coastal, quiet. Full moon. Sailing boats. Creaking. Very sad. One can never leave here."[56]

It was not until November 1925 that Akhmatova finally moved into Punin's flat in the Sheremetev Palace, where his wife and daughter continued to live. She had often spent nights there but this was a move which involved trust and commitment and was without mercenary motive. On the contrary, she had to pay Punin a steep rent for a room in his flat as well as sending money to her mother, Gumilyov's second wife, Anna Engelhardt, and even occasionally, in a *volte face*, to Shileiko—although more commonly he had been in a position to send money to her—as Luknitsky noted. This reckless generosity left her so pressed for money that sometimes she did not even have the 7 kopeks for a tram. In December 1925, she sent 50 roubles to Lev, and heard a sledge had been bought for him with the money. The letter acknowledging receipt of the money casually mentioned that Lev was suffering from an unknown fever and, as Luknitsky observed, Akhmatova became very worried.[57]

She received the note from Bezhetsk on the day of Sergey Yesenin's suicide. On 27 December 1925, the poet hanged himself in the Hotel Angleterre in Leningrad. Akhmatova had not much liked him when he was alive, and had little sympathy with either his peasant shyness or his swagger, but his profound disillusion with the Revolution he had thought would bring Russia Utopia was a grim hint at the times into which they were moving.

At this time, Luknitsky formed a friendship with Akhmatova's son Lev, who sometimes visited Leningrad, where he usually stayed at the Kuzmin-Karavaevs', relatives of Gumilyov's mother. Luknitsky visited him there, observing that Akhmatova had so little to eat herself, there was no way she could have looked after her son.

Akhmatova continued to feel responsible for Shileiko, and tried to keep things in order in Shileiko's apartment in the Marble Palace. She sometimes sent him frantic notes, for example when she discovered his electricity would be turned off if he did not pay the bill.

Although when they were living together he had felt jealous of her writing, she now valued his literary opinion and even sent him her poems for comment.

Akhmatova's conscience was not much disturbed by thoughts of Punin's wife and child and at first Punin took care she should not be troubled, as he commented: "I have never been so patient with anyone as I have been with her. She is amazingly and softly kind."[58] "Kind" is a word often used justly of Akhmatova but her compassion did not extend to the wife of the man she wanted. It is hard to believe she was unaware of the pain her move into the House on the Fontanka caused Punin's wife, but she only mentions to Chukovskaya that she always wanted to be friends with Anna Ahrens, and seems to reproach her for her lack of reciprocity.

Ahrens, who had weathered Punin's earlier affairs bravely, saw in Akhmatova an implacable and selfish determination to have Punin whatever the cost. And the cost was great. Anna Kaminskaya, Punin's granddaughter, of whom Akhmatova was very fond towards the end of her life, repeated her mother's description of Ahrens' misery,[59] which was so intense after Akhmatova moved into the Punins' flat that Ahrens was obliged to rearrange her work schedule at the clinic so that she would not be home at night.

When Lydia Chukovskaya asked Akhmatova which of her men she had loved most, she thought for a while and then replied she had stayed on living with Punin for two years after she knew she ought to have left him. Theirs was never an easy relationship.

EIGHT

The House on the Fontanka

An inhuman closeness.

—NIKOLAY PUNIN

he flat on the Fontanka now houses the Akhmatova Museum, and the wooden floors are buffed and shining, which gives the high-ceilinged rooms a sense of space and light. Although run-down when Akhmatova moved there, the flat was the kind people of the upper classes had lived in before the Revolution. Much of the furniture remains, including a desk and armchair that belonged to Akhmatova. Across this chair lies one of her shawls. When she moved in, she occupied the study with Punin, while Ahrens and Irina took the room beyond the living room.

The kitchen looks like a sensible farmhouse kitchen, with a stove resembling an Aga. In an adjoining room lived the Smirnov family. Tatyana Smirnova was the housekeeper for the Punin family and had two sons of whom Anna became particularly fond. Next to the kitchen was Punin's darkroom. An enthusiastic photographer, he produced sharply detailed portraits of Akhmatova, his family and the trees in the garden of the Sheremetev Palace. Irina recalls:

He would gather everything he needed on the large table in the kitchen: small baths, various powders, small boxes, special paper packed in black envelopes, and a lantern with red glass that was on during the major part of the work. During this time the light in the adjoining room would be off and light bulbs unscrewed just to be sure.

We would sit down in front of the camera while he covered himself in black while checking the focus. . . . He calculated the exposure with a light meter and at his signal we would stay still for what seemed to us an eternity. Papa would put some magnesium powder on a metal tray to be set on fire by the assistant, and would run to take his seat if he was to be among the people being photographed.[1]

Whatever else Irina observed as she was growing up, she remembers Punin vividly as a kind father. She recalled with particular pleasure, "wonderful lanterns on the Christmas tree. They were made of Japanese paper, and Papa would glue them together with our help."[2]

Through January and February 1926 Akhmatova still sometimes retreated to Shileiko's flat in the Marble Palace. While Akhmatova enjoyed being with Punin in the Sheremetev Palace, her old rooms in the Marble Palace gave her privacy. Sometimes Shileiko joined her there when he was not in Moscow. Although she had little money herself, she still occasionally helped him financially. Luknitsky notes that she sent him 45 roubles by telegraph on 15 January 1926.[3] Her letters continue to be filled with affection for him: "Write to me. Don't be lazy, and don't be angry with me. Send me kisses . . . Akuma."[4]

She did not doubt, however, that if she had not left Shileiko, she would have forgotten how to write poetry. In the early 1920s at least, poems poured from her again. In them she is still haunted by the thought of those who had gone into emigration. In "Lot's Wife," for instance, dated February 1924, she imagines an inner voice which would tempt the wife to think of the city left behind:

> It's not too late to look down now on
> The red towers of your native Sodom,
> At the square where you sang, the yard where you spun
> And the empty windows of the tall house,
> Where you gave birth to children for your dear husband.[5]

When Lot's wife has been turned to "transparent salt" and is rooted to the spot, Akhmatova asks us to pity her:

> *Who will weep now for this woman?*
> *Does her death have any significance?*
> *At least in my heart she is not forgotten,*
> *Because she gave her life for a single glance.*[6]

Akhmatova's health remained fragile, but her relationship with Punin, however unconventional, was beginning to give her a measure of happiness. And she had one less burden of responsibility: her brother Viktor, who recognised he had no future in the Soviet navy after the Bolsheviks took over and had refused to work for the Cheka, instead joined a group of bandits making a good living out of the fur trade on the island of Sakhalin. Having made some money in this way, he was able to send for his mother in 1925 and looked after her there until her death in 1930. In September 1926, moreover, the poet Fyodor Sologub, a powerful figure in the Soviet literary establishment, arranged for Akhmatova to have a pension of 60 roubles a month for Merit in Russian Literature. She gave 40 of these to Punin as rent.

Out of her sight, however, political changes were afoot at the centre of Soviet power that would affect the whole way of life of the Russian intelligentsia. Lenin had escaped death at the hands of an assassin's bullet in 1918, but his health began to fail in 1921 and he suffered his first stroke in May 1922. This stroke deprived him of speech for a time and paralysed his right side. Correctly guessing his days were numbered, Lenin began to concern himself with the problem of who should succeed him. Trotsky and Stalin were the main contenders for the succession. Lenin knew that Trotsky, for all his brilliant gifts, was perceived by most Russians as a Jewish intellectual and was as such likely to be distrusted, whereas Stalin had the reputation of "hardworking mediocrity." Lenin made Stalin the Party's first General Secretary in April 1922, a position without great political clout, but which Stalin was able nevertheless to make use of to build a huge power base. Lenin became more suspicious of Stalin's ambitions in the last year of his life and dictated warnings against his taking over the Party. These, however, were never read out to Congress as he had intended. He died on 21 January 1924. The screws were about to tighten on a new age, as Mandelstam had forecast in 1923:

> *My age, my beast, will be able*
> *To look into the pupils of your eyes*
> *And with his blood glue together*
> *The spinal bones of two centuries.*[7]

None of this directly affected the lovers as yet. A charming entry in Punin's diary gives a thumbnail cameo, which evokes the physical reality of Akhmatova at this time. He had taken her to the Commissariat for Aid to Scholars, so that she could exchange her ration cards for food, and she returned with him to have breakfast in his flat. His wife was not at home, and he lit the fire while Akhmatova sat in an armchair by the fireplace:

> She has grown terribly thin these past months. Why is that so sweet? To sit on the floor and kiss her hands, where does this sweetness come from? . . . I looked at her for a long time. Desire flitted across her face, and she looked into the next room—the bedroom—and looked away. What was she thinking? Was she jealous of G [Galya] or was she thinking about us, or was it just by chance?[8]

Akhmatova's clothes had remained in Shileiko's room in the Marble Palace, but Punin now arranged to have them brought to the House on the Fontanka. Shileiko continued to write sad letters to her, addressed to "My kind Akuma," which ask her to come and see him. "In my loneliness, I am becoming too much like a dog."[9]

The unconventional nature of her relationship with Punin is pointed up in an entry in Punin's notebook for 13 July 1925. The two of them entered into a contract, which Akhmatova signed without any apparent cavilling: "With this I allow N. N. Punin to have one child with any woman."[10] She demands no such freedom for herself. On the same page, Akhmatova agreed "not to see Zimmerman from this day forward." Perhaps the agreements were essentially frivolous, but Akhmatova's other comments added to Punin's journal have to be given weight. On 25 August 1925, she notes they have spent a golden day, and adds, "We are close." Punin then writes beneath her words: "An inhuman closeness."

For all the stormy times between them—which Akhmatova may well have enjoyed, if we remember Gumilyov's remarks about her love for war in a relationship—the lovers were indeed very close. Punin wrote in his journal: "People think that life knows two extremes: suffering and happiness; they may not be right. . . . I would never assert that A. does not torment me. . . . But I can breathe when I'm with her, and this means more to me than happiness."[11]

Punin was often bossy and tyrannical even in these early days of their life together, but perhaps this is hardly surprising given Akhmatova's stubborn independence of spirit. On one occasion, she came away from a phone call inviting her to have dinner at the Zamyatins.[12] Punin said he didn't want her to go and was offended when she insisted. They quarrelled bitterly and Punin was hurt and infuriated by her obstinacy. Akhmatova, however, fell asleep in the study without bothering to go to the Zamyatins. Punin could not understand how she could fall asleep without making up their quarrel. When Akhmatova read his unhappy journal entry about this disagreement, she added a note in her own hand in the margin: "What kind of a man is it starts to complain when he himself is to blame?" Akhmatova told Luknitsky that many of her friends disapproved of her relationship with Punin and did not always invite him to occasions where she was invited, which he found hurtful.

Shileiko had asked Akhmatova for a divorce, to which she made no objection, and on 17 December 1925 he married Vera Andreevna Konstantinova, who was only nineteen. Akhmatova's kindness to Shileiko continued nonetheless, as Luknitsky witnessed. When she travelled to Moscow, she telephoned and on one occasion went round with cheese and bread for his supper. She even read him her poems, which he was at first reluctant to listen to. On 22 January 1926, after hearing her read, Shileiko made the strangely prophetic comment: "When you are given a doctorate at Oxford University, remember me in your prayers."[13] Luknitsky says that she then read a little from his diary and Shileiko invited her enthusiasm: "You see how interesting it is. If you kept a diary like that you could be sure it would be read in a hundred years."[14]

Akhmatova had the keys to Shileiko's Moscow flat and still sometimes stayed there when she was in that city. Shileiko remained concerned for her, and once when he was away wrote touchingly to his young wife, asking Vera to look after her "in a strange land": "I am very worried about her. Write me whether she is all right. She is very lazy about writing letters herself."[15]

For all their many arguments, Punin remains altogether infatuated with her:

> Today Ani stayed on, to spend the night. I put her up in the study and all night long I could sense her presence in the house, even in my sleep. In the morning I went in to see her. She was still asleep. I had no idea she was so pretty asleep. We drank tea together, then I washed her hair, and she spent almost all day translating a French book for me. It is so peaceful to be with her constantly.[16]

Their closeness continues through 1926, with Akhmatova continuing to append her own notes to his journal entries, confirming their shared happiness. That it was happiness at the expense of Ahrens, who had been unable to move away from the family home, does not seem to have troubled the lovers. In a pathetic little note to Akhmatova, Ahrens apologises for something she said: "I realised you were hurt when you refused to come to tea and then NN confirmed my supposition. . . ."[17] Punin evidently felt he was entitled to reproach his wife for any words spoken that might disturb Akhmatova.

Akhmatova had already fallen under the spell of Punin's expertise in architecture, much as she had earlier been fascinated by Shileiko's knowledge of ancient texts. From now on, anyone meeting Akhmatova was impressed by her vast knowledge of Leningrad's buildings. Like any autodidact, she worked hard and with enormous dedication to make up for the education she felt she had missed. Indeed, she had once again found a brilliant man to whom she could be both companion and helper and once again she made herself as useful as possible. She transcribed for him the words of Cézanne from the French, prepared material on the French artist David and translated passages from a book about Ingres, which he needed for his lecture the following day.

Nor was it her only intellectual commitment. All through 1925 Akhmatova had dedicated much of her energy to helping Gumilyov's second wife, Anna Engelhardt, put together a book of memoirs of him. Luknitsky, who was also working on Gumilyov at this time, had brought Engelhardt to visit Akhmatova on 1 January 1925. She was glad to give her advice. However, when she had gone, Akhmatova remarked to Luknitsky: "What a heavy feeling I have after talking to her. She is somehow a little bit dull."[18]

In 1926, Punin's journals continue to include many moving entries in Akhmatova's handwriting, as if they had begun to share a mind. For instance, on 2 July, returning from the islands off the coast of Leningrad, Akhmatova wrote, with a hint of anxiety: "We are returning from the islands. Peace and quiet—what will be?"[19] The following day her residual uncertainty seems to have been allayed. Again adding her voice to Punin's diary, she notes: "I swam behind the yacht club. Nikolay took a picture of me. All day together in windy weather."[20]

Punin's own notes confirm their closeness, but the mood was as precarious as she had feared and on 21 July, back at the Marble Palace, Akhmatova wrote a curt note setting out areas of disagreement: "Nikolay! You repeat to me every day that I keep you from working, and obviously you don't wait to hear my reply that you, too, keep me from working. This obviously is not worth your attention, and every time I am so ashamed for you that I cannot say these words."[21]

The conversation book of the same year also reinforces Nadezhda Mandelstam's observation of Punin's verbal spite towards Akhmatova in public:

> Twice today you said to me in front of others that I am a do-nothing and that I pretend to be sick when I should work. It is true, and since you both [presumably Punin and Galya] work it is unpleasant for you to see me. That's why I immediately forgave you this afternoon. But it pains me that you once again repeated it in front of Luknitsky who, as you know, makes a note of everything.[22]

That some of the quarrels at this time were caused by Punin's continuing jealousy is likely; but other factors made the situation more difficult. With nowhere else to go because of the housing shortage, Ahrens and Irina had dinner and supper with Punin and Akhmatova in the dining room. Akhmatova later analysed with some perspicacity how exactly that arrangement suited Punin. She said he was unconsciously reproducing the situation of his own childhood,[23] but that she refused to behave like a typical stepmother from a fairytale. When Punin's wife was away at her medical practice, Akhmatova took care of Irina and taught her French. Indeed, from the late twenties to the early thirties, Akhmatova took her domestic responsibilities seriously, trying to be a mother to Irina and, after 1928, her own son Lev.

Akhmatova was once again writing few poems, though her longest period of silence had been during her years with Shileiko. In 1926 she put together a two-volume edition of her early poems and with this approached Gessen, the publisher. The manuscript was accepted and the contract proceeded to the point where Akhmatova was asked to correct proofs, but in 1927 the censors decided that only 500 copies could be printed. As this was quite uneconomic, galleys of the collection were transferred to the cooperative Publishers and Writers in Leningrad. Akhmatova was asked to remove eighteen poems from the first volume, and the following month she was told that forty more had to go from the second. On 9 February 1929, Luknitsky noted that it was now clear Akhmatova's collection would not be published at all.

Meanwhile, the most important Bolsheviks continued to jostle for power in the aftermath of Lenin's death. On 14 November 1927 Trotsky and Zinoviev were expelled from the Party. Bukharin had been in favour of prolonging the New Economic Policy, and even wrote an article in *Pravda* addressed to peasants who had profited as a result of the NEP, suggesting they need have no fear their gains would be taken away from them. Stalin cleverly outplayed them all, setting Zinoviev and Kamenev against Trotsky, packing Kamenev off as an ambassador and frightening Lenin's widow, Krupskaya, into compliance.

Akhmatova had been shocked by the death of Yesenin. A death that surprised and saddened her far more was that of Larisa Reisner, Gumilyov's former mistress, who had been so generous to Akhmatova when she was close to starvation, and had always seemed so exuberantly full of life. "She wanted so much to live. She was cheerful, healthy and beautiful," Akhmatova reflected.[24] Reisner died in February 1926 of typhus.

Moving in with Punin had given Akhmatova a roof over her head and she now had a measure of security. However, at a price: Punin showed his authority more and more sternly and she saw fewer of her friends. Mikhail Lozinsky, the great translator of Dante, with whom Gumilyov had often stayed and who was a close friend of Akhmatova, now hardly ever visited. She continued to see Shileiko, however, who she realised was seriously ill, and by 1929 she was to recognise that he did not have long to live.

NINE

The Vegetarian Years

1928–1933

When others praise me, it is no more than ashes, but even abuse from you is high praise.

—AKHMATOVA

Akhmatova used the phrase "the vegetarian years" to describe the late twenties and early thirties before Stalin's Great Terror took hold. In these years her relationship with Punin began to deteriorate. Punin had a biting wit and had begun to speak to her with a sarcasm bordering on cruelty. He liked to flirt with other women in her presence. "You can't imagine how rude he was during his numerous flirtations. He had to show all the time it was very boring for him to be in my company."[1] Nadezhda Mandelstam noted particularly that the least allusion to Akhmatova's stature as a poet led Punin to demonstrate his authority. He would send her to the kitchen with some absurd demand such as, "Annichka, go and clean the herring."[2]

Lydia Ginzburg, who first met Akhmatova in 1926, remembered her in the twenties as still young, slender and incredibly beautiful, and remarked cogently: "Her poetry of the 1910s and 1920s did not at all reflect her interest in history or literature or sharp, sometimes merciless, wit."[3]

For all his own flirtatious behaviour with other women, Punin's jealousy was pervasive. He seems to have disliked anyone who came to visit her. Even in April 1925, when Akhmatova was so ill that she really ought to have been in bed, Luknitsky noted that Punin watched him with suspicion as he tried to do things for her, and Akhmatova was able to see his distrust.[4] They often quarrelled passionately, and both of them were hurt by the words then spoken.

On her own behalf, Anna was beginning to develop a stoicism which could not have been predicted from her early frivolous days and this was underpinned by her deepening intellectual concerns. She continued her scholarly investigation of the work of Pushkin, for which Fyodor Sologub had helped her to get a commission in September 1926. Lydia Ginzburg observed an eccentricity in her passion for this work: Akhmatova, though capable of writing the most scholarly analyses of Pushkin's life, had begun to speak as if she knew Pushkin personally and felt "a peculiar jealousy of Natalya Nikolaevna [Pushkin's wife] and of all the women in Pushkin's life." Nor was it only Pushkin's life that animated her passionate personal involvement. Shakespeare's women were also scrutinised, almost as acquaintances. Ginzburg remembers her saying: "You know, Desdemona is charming, but Ophelia is a hysteric with paper flowers. She reminds me of Natalya Nikolaevna."[5] Nevertheless, Akhmatova's essays on Pushkin deserve their canonical status. Many of her guesses have been confirmed by recent research.[6]

She rarely spoke about her own financial situation, but Luknitsky saw with some shame that she was wearing rags and strangers' clothes and at the same time regularly sending what little money she could to the wife of Gumilyov. Whenever any money came her way, Akhmatova continued to be recklessly generous, though her finances remained so precarious that in May 1926 Mayakovsky and Pasternak arranged to perform their poems in public with the intention of allowing all the proceeds to go to Akhmatova, though this was not announced on the posters advertising the event.

Shileiko and Akhmatova remained affectionate. Indeed, when he wrote to her, he continued to address his envelopes to "A. Shileiko."[7] Many of her letters to him survive only in copies taken by Luknitsky before sending them on. If he was indeed working for the Cheka (or

OGPU, as it then became), his motives can only have been to show her life as politically blameless. She writes to Shileiko to tell him about the health of Tapa, his dog, and to advise him to take care: "Don't be too lazy to make a fire, eat like a human being, and stay indoors as much as possible—it's brutally cold."[8]

Tapa, however, gradually became a source of friction in the Punin household. On 1 September 1927, she reported to the sick Shileiko that "Tushin [another name for the dog] has completely worn me out—I'm nursing him myself again. . . . Send me your power of attorney. I need to pay the Punins for his keep, and I don't have any money at all. . . . Did Luknitsky write you about the plumber?"[9] Akhmatova and Luknitsky had taken over the responsibility for repairs to Shileiko's flat and the plumber was necessary, as a later letter makes plain, because the tap in the hallway had been removed and there was no water in the apartment. By August 1928 she was writing:

> Things with Tapa are very bad. He has cancer. The operation is today. I've been fussing over him all summer—but he's just getting worse. He's been in hospital a week now, and they say they have to cut him open. The operation costs nothing, his keep is one rouble a day. I've already paid for the medicine. They've already taken out the faucet in the hallway; there's no water in the apartment.[10]

Her own health, too, was once again poor. On 12 July Akhmatova wrote, "I've been really sick for a month now. In the next few days I'll be going into the hospital for tests." A far more serious disturbance to the balance of the household, however, was the arrival of Akhmatova's son Lev.

In 1928, Lev, now sixteen, left his grandmother's home in Bezhetsk and came to live with his mother and the Punins in the House on the Fontanka. It would have changed the dynamics of any household, and this one was already tense. Lev needed to be in Leningrad to have any chance of a good education, since he already found himself regarded with intense suspicion by the authorities, who feared that children of their victims might harbour thoughts of revenge. With the help of Punin's brother Alexander, however, Lev obtained a place at the school where Punin's brother was headmaster. He intended to enter Leningrad University, where he wanted to study Central Asian history. His father would have been delighted with his range of interest.

Lev was already a boy with a troubled history. The last time he saw his father was in May 1921. Gumilyov became his hero and legend for the rest of his life. Gumilyov had only travelled to the province of Tver two or three times, but Lev remembered those visits vividly, particularly his encouragement to study history. Gumilyov gave Lev books about the conquest of Italy by the Goths, which his grandmother considered too difficult but which the child relished so much that "I didn't just understand them, but I remember everything in them even now."[11] It is interesting that he starts his account of his own life in Lavrov's *Sudba i idei* with this memory of his father's encouragement. It is the only mention of active interest taken by his father in his education—and he goes on to contrast this with Akhmatova's disapproval of his chosen career. Lev remembered Gumilyov drawing pictures of the labours of Hercules, and adding literary captions. The pictures do not survive, but Lev could recite all the poems his father taught him correctly.

His life in Punin's unconventional household cannot have been easy. The discomfort was not only psychological. There was simply no room in Punin's flat for an extra person—Lev had to sleep on a trunk in the corridor. And he guessed Punin was anxious that the son of an executed poet would bring danger to his family.

Lev was never going to like Punin, and it wasn't just because of his unconcealed dislike for himself. Sergey Lavrov, who only knew Lev in later life, claims, "I think that Lev Gumilyov knew Punin's article denouncing his father." Lavrov quotes the denunciation printed in *Isskustvo kommuny*.[12] This article, written three years before Gumilyov's execution, makes unpleasant reading as it has an ingratiating tone and particularly approves of the absence of Gumilyov from the literary world:

> With what effort, and only because of the powerful Communist movement, did we, a year ago, leave behind longstanding oppression by the dreary effeminate-licentious bourgeois aesthetic. I admit that I have personally felt cheerful and vivacious during this whole year in part because several "critics" and several "poets" [Gumilyov, for example] stopped writing, or at least stopped being printed or read.[13]

Punin and Nikolay Gumilyov had, as we have noted, met briefly in August 1921 in the yard of Depzit prison. Young Lev couldn't have known about this when he arrived in the Punins' flat. Whatever the reason, Lev's account of his treatment by Punin accords with that of Akhmatova and Emma Gerstein, though it should be remembered that he showed an equal bitterness against his mother, and often unjustly. It seems likely that Punin's possessiveness made it difficult for him to relate generously to Lev. Although he was a brilliant boy with a passion for study, he was too clearly a competitor for Akhmatova's attention, and Punin, however unfaithful he might be, wanted that attention for himself.

Akhmatova always recalled with pain[14] Punin's resentment at Lev's presence, but his daughter and granddaughter contest her description. Punin's character has been hotly debated. Irina Punina,[15] who was a child of seven when Lev entered the household, speaks very warmly of her father's kindness. She insists that Punin was always kind to Lev, too, and points out that helping him to find a place in his brother's school, when Lev's father had been executed as a criminal, was an act of some courage in itself. She goes further, in claiming that relations between Lev and Punin were very good and describes the cheerful lamp, shelves for books and other comforts Lev enjoyed in his corridor room. Her daughter, Anna Kaminskaya, also paints a picture of her grandfather very much at odds with Akhmatova's, though it has to be said that when she describes Punin's treatment of Lev in the thirties she is only reporting what she has been told by her mother.

Lev's own resentment—of his mother as well as his stepfather—perhaps amplified by later experiences, is vouched for by all of his friends: ". . . I must say, it was very hard for me to live in Punin's flat, because I had to sleep in the corridor on a trunk. The corridor was not heated and was cold. Mama spared me attention only as far as she taught me French. But thanks to her lack of skill as a teacher, I took it in with difficulty and learnt French properly only after entering University."[16]

Akhmatova was ill when her son arrived from Bezhetsk and Kaminskaya reports disapprovingly that when Lev appeared at the House on the Fontanka, Akhmatova immediately went off for twenty-four days to a sanatorium.[17] For all her devotion to Akhmatova at the end of her life, Kaminskaya is now highly critical of her treatment of Lev. She speaks of Akhmatova "abandoning" her son to the care of Gumilyov's mother, and attributes that decision to Akhmatova being a poet, who could not bear the chores of washing clothes or cooking for other people. She knew very well that Anna loved children, but thought it was "chiefly other people's children, for whom she did not have to take responsibility, like the Smirnovs. All her life she had not been able to concern herself with practical matters."[18]

This last accords with many other observations, but it is not clear why a dedicated doctor like Kaminskaya's grandmother Ahrens would not be as busy outside the house as a poet would within it. The idea of a poet as prevented by his or her very nature from taking practical action is peculiarly Russian, and perhaps particularly in the Soviet period.[19] Up till then in Punin's house, however, there had been no need for Akhmatova to concern herself with housework. Tatyana Smirnova washed floors and clothes and did all the house-keeping until 1930, when Punin ceased to employ her.

As in a very real sense a lodger herself, Akhmatova was unable to speak up for her son, and Lev observed as much with anger. When the passport system came in, which required all citizens to register their permanent address, Akhmatova was not in a position to give her son the necessary documentation, as Yevgeny Rein explained to me:

> Akhmatova herself was not the mistress of the flat where she lived, which technically belonged to the Punin family. . . . And they hated Lev and would not allow him to be a resident of this flat. Akhmatova could have gone to the courts to compel this . . . but she was a very special person and did not want to go to a Soviet court, where people would say horrible things to her.[20]

Rein's memory of what Akhmatova said about Punin is consistent with many of her own written comments. She could not even prevent Punin using hurtful sarcasm towards her son. Lev remembers:

> When I finished School, Punin wanted me to return to Bezhetsk, where there was nothing to do, nothing to study and nowhere to work. I had to move to an acquaintance's [in St. Petersburg] where I helped with housework—not quite as a home help, but so to say, to carry the shopping. From there I went off on an expedition which

was a work exchange organised by the Geokomitet. When I returned, Punin met me and said, opening the door, "Why did you come? There is nowhere even for you to spend the night." Friends had to give me shelter.[21]

Kaminskaya agrees that Lev left the House on the Fontanka to live for a time with Lev Ahrens, Anna Ahrens' brother, but denies this related in any way to arguments he might have been having with Punin. "There were some heated discussions," she concedes—presumably remembering the post-war period—"but they were on intellectual matters, which those who overheard them could not understand." When asked about the sentence in Punin's famous letter from Samarkand,[22] in which he repents about his treatment of Lev, Kaminskaya thought this must refer to the fact that he felt guilty about Lev's arrest in 1938, even though it was not his fault.[23]

Kaminskaya repeats her mother's claim that the niche in the corridor was altogether pleasanter than Lev remembers. Her evidence about the twenties and thirties is important chiefly as a sign of the way Punin was able to inspire affection. When Kaminskaya lived in the House on the Fontanka again after the Second World War, she found Punin a kind grandfather, who liked playing with her. He often made toy animals for her at a time when there was no money to buy them, and she particularly remembered his making hoops which they could throw over a hook, for instance, and waking on her birthday in May 1949 to find a whole table covered with handmade toys.

Akhmatova had other problems, since she was coming to realise that the Soviet regime was unwilling to see her poems published. Stalin had always understood that artists could be a central prop for the new State he envisaged. That was why he had tempted Prokofiev back to Russia with a carefully choreographed vision of Soviet privilege, and Gorky, who had left in 1922, was flattered into returning by a campaign of praise in the Soviet press. Both were bitterly to regret their choice.

The unpublished decision to ban Akhmatova's work had been made in 1925. Later recorded conversations suggest the policy originated with Stalin.[24] Akhmatova was not the only writer to suffer censorship. Osip Mandelstam continued to publish critical essays and prose but by 1928 could only earn his living by means of translations and journalism. For some years, Bukharin had been able to help him. But Bukharin's disagreement with Stalin over the collectivisation of agriculture meant that he was soon to be in danger himself.

In August 1929, there were public attacks on Boris Pilnyak and Yevgeny Zamyatin in the Soviet press. Zamyatin's *We*, which predicted the sterile world resulting from a planned society, had been published in Prague in 1927. Pilnyak's *Red Mahogany*, which explored the disintegration of the revolutionary ideals and the corruption of the NEP, was first published in Berlin in 1929. Quite apart from the subject matter, publication abroad was by this time regarded as a serious offence in itself, and the two writers were asked to resign from the Writers' Union. In a brave protest, Mikhail Bulgakov and Boris Pasternak also resigned. Akhmatova, too, wrote a letter of resignation, which she gave to Luknitsky to deliver on 13 October 1929. He did not do so, however, perhaps understanding the dangers of her situation far better than she did.

Akhmatova was as yet unafraid for herself and even continued to hope that her own poetry might still be published. She went to see the Bolshevik poet Demyan Bedny, a favourite of Stalin, who wrote propaganda jingles in the manner of popular songs, knowing he was influential. Demyan Bedny was in fact a pseudonym, taken to conceal his identity as the illegitimate son of a Grand Duke. He and Akhmatova dined together in the Moskovskaya Hotel but nothing came of the meeting. Zamyatin and his wife soon left Russia, and began to send Akhmatova food packages and money from the West, guessing that her situation would become even more dangerous. Pilnyak was less fortunate. Although Stalin's purges were not yet under way, a close eye was kept on writers who were suspected of disloyalty. And Akhmatova already guessed that her works were under an official ban.

Although Bukharin was no longer head of the Comintern and had been expelled from the Politburo, he still retained some power and had been able to arrange for Mandelstam and his wife to travel. Mandelstam's *Journey to Armenia*, published in 1933, was his last book to appear in Soviet Russia for thirty years. Other writers, including Bulgakov, fell into Stalin's cat's-paw. Bulgakov's play *The Days of the Turbins* had been one of the great successes of the Moscow Arts Theatre in the 1920s. Rather surprisingly, since few Bolshevik sympathies were expressed, Stalin enjoyed the play so much that, according to theatre records, he went to see it fifteen times. However, none of Bulgakov's later plays were performed in his lifetime. Nor was he allowed to leave Russia, though he made a brave, direct appeal to Stalin for permission to do so. His novel *The Master and Margarita* did not appear until a quarter of a century after his death in 1940.

By 1928, Stalin had consolidated his political position, and initiated his plan for collectivising the land. Any landed peasant was at the mercy of the decisions of the local OGPU, the department of State security. The prosperous, designated as kulaks, were loaded on to carts and taken to the far north, where most would perish. Many ordinary Party members lost their jobs that year. Often, the charge against them was no more than showing undue leniency to peasants during collectivisation, which in Stalin's hands had become a brutal affair. Some peasants, unwilling to give up their land, fought back by destroying their crops. But they were dealing with a ruthlessness they had not bargained for. Stalin's response to their defiance was to allow famine to develop, and soon hunger and disease were taking the lives of peasants all over the Ukraine. Peasants died, leaving scribbled notes pinned to their bodies which are still moving: "My son. We couldn't wait. God be with you."[25] Those peasants still alive were forcibly transported in scant and unsuitable clothes to Siberia, where the vast majority died.

Pasternak, who travelled round southern Russia in the early thirties, was so affected by what he saw that he was brought to the edge of madness. Yet it was in these years that Bernard Shaw, who travelled through Russia with Lady Astor—the wife of a wealthy newspaper proprietor—found it possible to write: "Stalin received us like old friends and let us say all we wanted before modestly venturing to speak himself." Shaw was far from the only idealist Western writer to see only what he wanted to see.

The early darlings of the Revolution had already begun to fare badly. Yesenin, the peasant poet, who had come to St. Petersburg in the 1910s dressed like an unsophisticated rustic, with a love of Rimbaud, had once sung about a Utopia of people close to nature. As we have seen, he had taken his own life in 1925. Mayakovsky, whose loathing of the bourgeoisie made him one of the resounding voices of the Revolution, had been unkind about Yesenin's suicide, even writing a poem to rebuke him for it:

> *To die*
> *is not such a hard matter.*
> *Creating life*
> *is far more difficult.*[26]

In fact his own life was to grow more and more difficult. His play *The Bedbug*, directed by Meyerhold in 1929, was savaged by the critics. His exhibition of twenty years of his literary work at the Press House in February 1930 was boycotted by many writers, already afraid to be associated with a failure that might be manipulated from the centres of power.

At a meeting of students on 9 April 1930, Mayakovsky was baited with demands to prove anyone would be reading his work in twenty years. A few days later, on 14 April, he shot himself. There were many elements in his unhappiness. He had been taunted by students, reviewed with hostility, and been rejected by a beautiful young Russian, Tatyana Yakovleva, whom he had met in Paris. But the political changes all around him were part of his dismay. He left a poem as a suicide note, asking his mother, sisters and friends to forgive him, and wishing happiness to those who remained alive:

> *. . . love's boat*
> *was smashed*
> *against existence . . .*[27]

Akhmatova had not altogether forgotten that Mayakovsky raised his voice against her own poetry, once reading out her lyric "The Grey-Eyed King" to the melody of a popular tune, and on another occasion calling her a relic of the past. But, as she told Anatoly Nayman,[28] she genuinely liked Mayakovsky's poetry early in the century, even though it was the polar opposite of her own. Tsvetaeva always admired Mayakovsky's virtuosity and energy and defended him against émigré critics when he visited Paris. Akhmatova was dismayed by the news of his death, as indeed was Pasternak, who went to see his body and was moved by the solemn austerity of Mayakovsky's dead face.

Screws were tightening on Akhmatova, too. Punin began to be grudging about the expense of Lev's keep, and on one occasion insisted that the butter on the table must go only to his daughter Irina. Akhmatova remembered particularly the embarrassment on Lev's face and her own inability to stand up for her son. Much later, in 1940, talking to Chukovskaya, she reflected that this period of her life had altogether crushed her spirit. She had no regrets about trying to find domestic happiness, but was now further away from it than ever. Nevertheless, to Vsevolod Petrov, a young man working with Punin, he and Akhmatova seemed the living embodiments of a Russia that had disappeared. He described Punin's eloquence and the excitement he generated whenever he spoke, declaring that his response to paintings was analogous to those who have absolute musical pitch.

At forty-three, Akhmatova was still elegant whatever she wore, and very thin. Whether or not suffering from Graves' disease,[29] an overactive thyroid gland accounted for her skinny appearance. Photographs of her at this period show fatigue around her eyes and mouth. For all her poverty, however, she was instantly recognisable as a member of the old aristocracy. This was made manifest on a car ride with Pilnyak in 1930 when a slight accident caused them to stop the car. Workers on a collective farm came running up to help but one woman turned on Akhmatova, saying: "She's a noblewoman. Can't you see she is?"[30]

Yury Olesha, who met her in the early thirties when he was rather full of his own importance, was reduced to feeling like a schoolboy when Akhmatova talked about Shakespeare. She had begun to translate *Macbeth* and, in a poem written in 1933, before Stalin's Terror came close to her own family and friends, she evokes the parallel between Scotland under Macbeth and Russia under the Bolsheviks. The poem begins innocently enough:

> *Wild honey smells like freedom,*
> *And dust like a ray of sunshine,*
> *A young girl's mouth, like violets*
> *While gold smells of nothing at all.*[31]

But the first verse closes ominously:

> *But we have learnt one fact for ever:*
> *Blood only smells like blood.*[32]

The last verse brings together Pontius Pilate's attempt to cleanse his hands with Lady Macbeth trying in vain to wash her own hands clean. The contemporary Soviet echoes are hard to overlook.

Akhmatova made an attempt to leave Punin in 1930 when a friend offered to find her a room elsewhere. But Punin told the friend that it was a matter of life and death to him whether she stayed, and her resolution weakened. She continued to live with him at the House on the Fontanka without the strength to leave, except for two occasions in the summer of 1931 when she looked after people who were ill: first Valentina Shchegoleva, the wife of a noted Pushkin scholar, and then her young "stepdaughter," Irina Punina.

At this point another witness enters the story: Emma Gerstein, who became Lev Gumilyov's most devoted friend and lover. She was the daughter of a distinguished surgeon and a close friend of the Mandelstams, whom she had met in a sanatorium. She sometimes offered them a place to stay in her own Moscow flat. In autumn 1933, they were installed in a Writers' Union flat in Nashchokin Lane, and Osip and Nadezhda's first invitation was to Akhmatova. It was through the Mandelstams that Gerstein first met Akhmatova, for whom she had felt admiration all through her life.

Lev introduced himself to Emma Gerstein in October 1933 at the Central Bureau of the Department of Research Workers, where she was employed, and asked for help to realise his academic ambitions. She took up his case with great zeal. At this period "he took little interest in girls and adored his mother."[33]

Gerstein was in love with Lev Gumilyov from the day they first walked home together talking. In the years when they were lovers, she writes, "I looked at the slender neck above the fur collar, and the bowed head in the peaked cap, and I loved him."[34] Although her memoirs are filled with admiration for Akhmatova, some of her observations may be warped by the intensity of her involvement with Lev. She gives a vivid and detailed account of his passionate bitterness. When summoned to see the OGPU on one occasion, he asked Gerstein to see him off at the station, remarking characteristically: "No one has ever met me or seen me off in my whole life." They said tender farewells on the platform. Later, she learned that on this occasion the OGPU only wanted to return some documents to him, but a friend picked up at the same time had been sentenced to five years' imprisonment.

After spending an extra year at school in Leningrad studying history, Lev tried to enter the German language course at the Gertsen Institute in 1930, but was refused because of his parentage. Mikhail Ardov, the young son of the family of Akhmatova's great friends, and a close friend of Lev in later life, very well understood Lev's bitterness. Now a priest, he told me, when we met outside a church in St. Petersburg:

> He had many reasons to feel hurt by his mother. From his early childhood he didn't live with her but with his grandmother in Bezhetsk. And of course he couldn't have liked the kaleidoscope of Akhmatova's so-called husbands. He was also jealous of Akhmatova's "stepdaughter," Irina Punina. . . . But the most important pain in Lev's whole life was the thought that Akhmatova didn't care enough to get him out of the camp. It was not true . . . she cared only too much and I know this.[35]

What Gerstein shared with Lev was an incisive intelligence, which in her case she was able to devote to original archival research on Lermontov. Her literary criticism was acute and sensitive. Lev recognised as much and liked to read poems he had written to her. Gerstein saw the heavy debts to Akhmatova in his poems and decided he was more likely to develop into a scholar than a poet; sometimes her honesty impelled her to respond to them tactlessly. But she gave him warmth and unconditional affection and it is easy to understand how they became lovers, though Gerstein was not beautiful.

The Mandelstams did not approve of the relationship; indeed, Osip composed a spiteful epigram about the fact that Gerstein was nine years older than Lev. A poem Lev had written, which Emma regarded as one written for her, was declared by Nadezhda Mandelstam to be intended for the pretty poet Maria Petrovykh.

When Gerstein visited Akhmatova just after Lev heard he would be allowed to enter the History Faculty in Leningrad University in 1933, she found him in his raincoat and peaked cap, running around with a saucepan full of hot water and very excited—at the sight of her, she thought. Akhmatova saw Gerstein's happiness and told Lev quietly to put the saucepan down. Many people have spoken about Akhmatova's opposition to Gerstein as a daughter-in-law. She did not see Gerstein as a suitable wife for her son if only because of the age gap.

From time to time, Akhmatova appeared in Moscow and once, while staying with Gerstein, seemed preoccupied by her relationship to Lev. She scrutinised Gerstein closely, commented on her pasty skin and then, for no apparent reason, exclaimed: "Emma, I want a grandson." "She began to tell me how hard it was living with Punin, and that Lyova was her only hope."[36] When he left university she wanted them to live together and then confessed Lev had "a mad passionate longing to live in Mongolia." However, she need not have worried: Emma and Lev had made no plans for the future.

Emma's circle of friends also had doubts about the relationship. When Emma was staying on Vasilevksy Island at the apartment of Mandelstam's brother, Yevgeny, he warned her to keep clear of Lev because he was afraid he had "bad acquaintances." Her response was to move away from Yevgeny's apartment and stay with childhood friends instead.

When Gerstein next visited Akhmatova, she found her looking rather unwell, lying on a divan. Nikolay Punin had taken Irina and his wife to Sochi, and left Akhmatova and Lev their ration cards but no money to use them. She and Lev were weak and Lev had even gained a low mark in his exams because he was faint from hunger. This is striking independent evidence of Punin's seeming indifference to Akhmatova's welfare by this time.

Yet, for all the bickering that had poisoned their relationship, a strong emotional bond still held Akhmatova and Punin together. There is something peculiarly touching in Emma Gerstein's memory of watching Akhmatova say goodbye to Punin before leaving Leningrad on a trip to Moscow: "He was standing on the platform in front of the train car window. But the window was covered with frost, so he tapped against the glass. She answered him, and they continued to tap to each other until the train began to move."

TEN

The Terror

1933–1938

Who can refuse to live his own life?

—AKHMATOVA

khmatova's verdict on the last years of her relationship
with Punin is given in her poems, in conversations
recorded in Lydia Chukovskaya's diaries and twenty
years later in her memories shared with the young poets Yevgeny
Rein and Anatoly Nayman.[1] A consistent picture emerges of her as a
defeated woman. Observers bear out how Punin seemed to enjoy
putting her down in company. His daughter Irina's memory of this
period, however, is of an altogether more generous man. Her observation must be given due weight, but Akhmatova's depression is
incontestable and by 1933 there was no public acclaim to sustain
her.

If she hoped for affection from Lev, it was only intermittently
forthcoming. As Mikhail Ardov pointed out, Lev had every reason
to resent the way Akhmatova had abandoned him as a child with his
grandmother. Lev's sense of being given insufficient attention was
already present when as a young child he asked his mother how

many minutes a day she spent thinking about him. Quite soon, as Stalin tightened his grip on the Soviet Union, Lev was to find new reasons for bitterness.

In 1933 Stalin's wife Nadezhda Alliluyeva committed suicide, perhaps in horror at what her husband was doing, and Stalin wept at her funeral. At the graveside, he and his sons threw handfuls of earth on her coffin. For all the genuine grief and anger, Stalin did not mitigate the severity of his rule. A decree was passed depriving those who were accused of terrorism of any right to defence. Thousands were arrested, among them Lev Gumilyov.

Lev had been visiting a colleague, the Middle Eastern scholar Eberman, to consult him about a translation when there was a knock on the door and secret police rushed in and seized both of them.[2] On this occasion Lev only spent nine days in prison and was not handled roughly. Eberman, however, was never to appear again. It was a sign of the gathering threat which was soon to engulf the whole of Russia.

The first of Akhmatova's friends to attract the serious attention of the NKVD—formerly the OGPU—was the poet Osip Mandelstam. He and Akhmatova had grown very close. They had much in common, sharing an Acmeist past and an admiration for Gumilyov. As a poet no longer permitted to publish, Akhmatova's thoughts at this time were primarily dedicated to her intellectual discoveries. In 1933, both Mandelstam and Akhmatova had soaked themselves in Dante's poetry, which they were able to share together in Italian. On one occasion, when Akhmatova recited a part of the *Purgatory* to Mandelstam, he was so moved to hear Dante's words in her voice that he broke down and wept.

Both Akhmatova and Mandelstam spoke of their own poems beginning as a musical phrase ringing insistently in their ears. Mandelstam usually waited until it was clear enough as a poem to write it down, then he liked to offer the poem to a listener. Between 1933 and 1934, Lev was often his first listener, since he stayed with the Mandelstams in Moscow, where he was warmly received. "It so happens that all of Mandelstam's first listeners came to a tragic end," Mandelstam's wife Nadezhda recalls laconically.[3]

The friendship between Akhmatova and Mandelstam took on great intensity in the early thirties. Nadezhda reports Mandelstam saying that Akhmatova was a woman made "for comradeship, not for

love," and observed, "It would seem that love played a very important role in Anna's life but at the first crisis each of her affairs crum-
bled around her like a house of cards. Yet her intensely personal and
ardent relationship with Osip withstood every test."

Akhmatova, much heartened to be in the presence of her friends,
visited Moscow whenever she could gather the fare. Together they
generated an atmosphere of great excitement. Indeed, Gerstein
records that on one occasion when Akhmatova left, taken to the station by Lev, Mandelstam exclaimed: "How good that she's gone.
That's too much electricity for one house."[4]

It became easier for Akhmatova to stay with the Mandelstams
once they had been given their new flat in Nashchokin Lane. This
was not luxurious but had a bathroom and a large room with
unpainted boards stretching along a whole wall filled with Mandelstam's books. According to the laws of that time, a tenant could not
be evicted once his bed stood on the undisputed territory. Emma
Gerstein gives an amusing picture of Nadezhda taking up her post
the night before the flat became vacant so they could move their
mattress in ahead of any rivals. Mandelstam's father, Emil, normally
stayed with his son Yevgeny in Leningrad, but the new flat also made
it possible for him to stay with Osip from time to time. Later,
Nadezhda's mother Vera Yakovlevna shifted all her belongings from
Kiev to Moscow. Once she had moved in, she "valiantly endured the
astounding disorganisation of her children."[5]

Visitors who met Akhmatova at the Mandelstams could not mistake her poverty. She had been travelling for twenty years with the
same suitcase, which did not have a lock and had to be secured by a
strap. She had only one old cap and a light coat, which she wore no
matter what kind of weather, though later her friend Valentina
Shchegoleva bequeathed her a fur coat. Indoors, Akhmatova usually
wore scarlet pyjamas. She retained her famous fringe.

On the ground floor lived the satirical writer Viktor Ardov with
his young wife, Nina Olshevskaya, an actress at the Moscow Arts
Theatre, and her little son from her first marriage, Alexey Batalov.
Nina was one of the first graduates of the Stanislavsky school of acting and was very beautiful. As well as working in the theatre and
vaudeville, she was also an adept amateur caricaturist. Because there
was no room for both Akhmatova and Lev to stay in the Mandelstam
flat, Lev gave up his bed to his mother and went off to stay with the

Ardovs. Their whole ambience of artistic worldliness was glamorously different from anything else in his life. He was impressed by Nina's beauty. Above Nina's divan hung portraits of all the famous poets who had been in love with her. She flirted with Lev, too, and he once confessed to Emma Gerstein: "I cannot remain indifferent when she lies there with her bosom half uncovered and gazes at me with her brilliant black eyes."[6] Nina had admired Akhmatova since the first time she had seen her majestically ascending the stairs to the Mandelstams' flat. They became close friends.

Akhmatova had spent a month with the Mandelstams in Nashchokin Lane in early 1934. On 13 May, she returned on a second visit, bringing with her a statuette of herself (by Yelena Danko) which she intended to sell to pay for the return journey. Lev, who was staying with the Mandelstams at the time, had gone to the station to meet her and managed to miss her. This upset Akhmatova a great deal, though whether because of her son's absence or because she preferred to be met by Mandelstam is not entirely clear. Mandelstam usually had a stream of jokes to tell her, and she was not visiting Moscow primarily to meet her son but in response to Mandelstam's urgent telephone calls.

Akhmatova was used to sleeping in the Mandelstams' small kitchen. The gas had not yet been connected, so Nadezhda usually covered the cooker with an oilcloth and cooked on the kerosene stove. On this occasion, with nothing to cook, Mandelstam had to go round his neighbours looking for an egg for Akhmatova's supper.

At one o'clock in the morning there was a knock on the door and several agents of the Soviet secret police entered the flat and checked everyone's identity papers. They began to search everywhere, making a pile of papers on the floor and turning the whole apartment upside down looking for incriminating material. Then they presented Mandelstam with a warrant for his arrest, signed by Genrikh Yagoda, head of the secret police: "Suddenly Akhmatova said that Mandelstam should eat something before he left, and she held out the egg to him. Mandelstam took it, sat down, put some salt on it and ate it."[7] The NKVD continued to search the apartment all through the night, before taking Mandelstam away with them. Sitting together the following day in the ransacked apartment, Akhmatova suggested to Nadezhda that it would be wise not to clear up but leave the papers where they had been scattered.

At first light, Lev arrived to see his mother, knowing that the Mandelstams were early risers. But Nadezhda urged him to go away at once in case he, too, should be put in danger. Nadezhda gives a wonderful description of Lev, still a youth but so alive with ideas that wherever he appeared he always caused a stir, either because people sensed the strength in him or perhaps they guessed that he was doomed. "Now our house had been stricken by plague and become a death trap for anyone prone to infection. . . . 'Go away,' I said. 'Go away at once. Osip was arrested last night.' "[8]

Soon afterwards, the NKVD did return and collected more manuscripts. Akhmatova and Nadezhda were in no doubt what they were looking for: Mandelstam's "Wolf," a reckless poem lampooning Stalin's ugliness and his cruel treatment of peasants. For a man of no great physical stamina, it was an act of almost insane courage to write it and read it to chosen friends. Not for nothing did he tell Akhmatova in February 1934 that he was ready for death.

Akhmatova stayed on for a while to comfort Nadezhda, before leaving to beg help from Pasternak, who in turn went to Bukharin, then editor of *Izvestiya*. Akhmatova went to the Kremlin to see Stalin's old comrade Avel Yenukidze. It is not clear whether either intervention had any effect. At this time, Stalin made a completely unexpected phone call to Pasternak, asking him for his evaluation of Mandelstam's stature as a poet and, when Pasternak hesitated, perhaps wondering what answer would help Mandelstam most, Stalin said he would have known much better how to speak up for a friend. When Pasternak said he wanted to talk to Stalin about other matters—life and death—Stalin rang off and when Pasternak tried to ring him back, refused to take the call. There are many versions of this phone call, but though Pasternak agonised about it for many years he did say that Mandelstam was "a master."

The dangerous poem had never been written down on paper by Mandelstam. This proved no defence once he was inside the Lubyanka, however. Ways of undermining sanity in prison were quite systematic. In his cell, Mandelstam often heard a woman's voice which he thought belonged to Nadezhda and by the time she was allowed her first visit to him he was already confused and broken.

Akhmatova also asked for help from the writer Lydia Seifullina, who had friends in the secret police and who advised her, doubtless understanding Akhmatova's own vulnerability, not to get involved in the case. When Nadezhda was lucky enough to be given a meeting with her husband in the Lubyanka, Mandelstam managed to tell her that his interrogator had the text of his poem and that it was the first version which had "the murderers of peasants" in the fourth line.

In the record of Mandelstam's interrogation,[9] he recited the whole of his poem about Stalin to his inquisitors, saying, "Yes, I am the author of the following verse," and adding, with some pathos, "I gave no one copies but read it to my wife, my brother, the writer Anna Akhmatova and her son Lev Gumilyov." Pasternak, Akhmatova and Emma Gerstein ended up on the list extracted from him by the NKVD as people who had listened to the "Wolf" poem. Emma Gerstein knew of fourteen people who had heard the poem. One of them must have reported it to the NKVD. According to Nadezhda Mandelstam, the interrogator already had a version of the poem in Maria Petrovykh's handwriting, which suggests some involvement with the NKVD, but Akhmatova claimed that she had heard directly from Mandelstam how that came about, and her friendship with Maria Petrovykh through the next thirty years was undiminished.

In the event, Mandelstam's sentence was less severe than might have been feared. He was exiled for three years to Cherdyn, a small town on the River Kama in the Urals. Nadezhda was to be allowed to accompany him into exile. However, Akhmatova left for Leningrad without being able to see Mandelstam again, which meant that he could not rid himself of the fear that she lay dead in the ravines of Cherdyn. Mandelstam was still mentally ill and convinced that, in spite of his release, he would nevertheless be shot. He dreamt that Akhmatova had been arrested and was even then undergoing interrogation. While in hospital in Cherdyn, he broke his arm jumping out of a hospital window. With Bukharin's help, Mandelstam's place of exile was commuted so that he could choose any city to live in other than the twelve major cities. The Mandelstams settled on Voronezh.

Mandelstam's arrest filled Moscow's literary intelligentsia with dismay and foreboding. Bulgakov's wife burst into tears when she heard of his sentence. About this time, as Emma Gerstein reports, Lev appeared in an "awful jacket and trousers, with enormous patches on the knees." He had grown a thin Tatar moustache that drooped round his mouth, and he was on his way through Moscow for a day, returning from an expedition in the Don area. He told Gerstein that conversations in the Punin household, which had been overheard and misunderstood—which would fit with Anna Kaminskaya's account—had been reported to the authorities and that a friend had been interrogated and arrested that summer. After visiting a church, they came back to Emma's flat, where he announced, "When I get back to Leningrad, they'll arrest me." His apprehensions were mistaken on this occasion.

Exile and isolation were alarming, but the real Terror only began after the assassination of Sergey Kirov. On 29 November 1934, Bulgakov's wife, Stalin and Sergey Kirov, Stalin's close friend and his chief lieutenant in Leningrad, attended the Arts Theatre in Moscow. Nothing could have looked more amiable. Kirov was a cheerful, handsome man whom most women liked. He enjoyed a life of mountaineering and camping, though he listened to opera, watched ballet and liked singing operatic arias. To all appearances he was a favourite of Stalin, who inscribed a book to him, "My friend and beloved brother." Perhaps Kirov should have worried, however, when he gained a larger vote than Stalin at a Party Congress.

Two days later, Kirov was shot in the back of the neck in Leningrad by Leonid Nikolaev, a young man who then tried to shoot himself but was prevented by a bystander. Rumours that Stalin may have organised the assassination have been persistent. Among the leaders, Khrushchev hinted as much, though he had no firm evidence, and Mikoyan also came to believe that Stalin was involved in the murder.[10] Whether this is true or not, Kirov's murder gave Stalin the pretext he needed to establish a reign of terror.

Stalin's vengeance spread out more and more widely: he passed an emergency law that decreed the trial of terrorists must take place within ten days of their arrest and that there should be immediate execution after conviction. In the month of December 1934 alone 6,501 people were shot, a figure which included the innocent families of those arrested. By mid-January 1935, one tormented prisoner had been encouraged to implicate the old Bolsheviks Zinoviev and Kamenev. At first, Kamenev refused to confess, though a regime of threats and sleeplessness was used against him. Yezhov, then head of the secret police, threatened that Kamenev's son would be shot, which soon changed that. Kamenev behaved with some dignity at his trial, but both defendants had agreed to plead guilty, providing there were no shootings and their families were protected. They were sentenced to ten years and five years respectively. When they were interrogated further, the net of arrests spread wider. Stalin was soon purging his most intimate friends. His own bodyguard was killed in a dubious car crash. Soon the flood of arrests grew so huge that the camps were deluged by "Kirov's torrent."

Everyone was frightened. In the summer of 1935, Akhmatova saw Pasternak again on his way back from the International Congress of Writers in Paris. Both poets were finding it difficult to write, and Pasternak confided some of his mental problems to her. Akhmatova herself felt as if her muse had abandoned her altogether. To Nina Olshevskaya, she wondered gloomily if she had not already written all she would ever write, since poems no longer came into her head.

This is the context in which Lev was arrested again in autumn 1935. Punin was arrested at the same time, and the situation looked altogether more serious for both of them. Lev was taken in along with several students from the History Faculty who were doing well in their courses, and all were declared guilty of belonging to an anti-Soviet organisation. "We all found ourselves in the Big House—Leningrad's equivalent to the Lubyanka—a new building of the NKVD on Liteiny Prospekt."[11] Akhmatova and Punin's wife immediately set to work to burn every document that could in any way appear compromising to Punin.

Anna Kaminskaya gives a new insight into the reasons behind the arrest of Punin and Lev. At a family dinner in May 1935, Punin took a photograph using an unusual chemical flash. He then joked to his startled guests that with such a camera it might have been possible to kill Kirov, and even to murder Stalin. Presumably he meant the noise would conceal a shot. This remark was reported to the NKVD, Kaminskaya maintains, by a friend of Lev, whose name Kaminskaya remembered as Arkady.[12] Lev's friend was very often at the house, mending furniture and doing other household chores, and the family fed him. It is not clear what motivation he would have had in betraying them, but there could be many explanations for it: fear, greed or the wish to protect his own family. In those days it was commonly observed that in any gathering of ten people one would always be a spy. Punin's joke was certainly exceedingly reckless.

Some days after Lev and Punin had been arrested, Emma Gerstein found Akhmatova sitting outside her flat with her ancient, battered suitcase. She had been there for several hours. Emma brought her in and she stayed the night, sleeping in Emma's bed. Emma observed that her eyes were sunken and that triangular recesses had appeared round the bridge of her nose. They would never vanish thereafter. Emma compared her appearance after Lev's arrest to that of a shot bird. People who recognised her as she passed them in the street saw the change in her with horror and pity.

Among the friends who tried to help Akhmatova were the Bulgakovs and the writer Lydia Seifullina, who had contacts both with officials in the Communist Party and the NKVD. Akhmatova wanted to see Seifullina but had forgotten her address. After much prompting, Emma discovered Seifullina was living in a writers' house on Kamerger Street. Akhmatova could hardly cross the road to a taxi and seemed almost to have lost her mind, muttering incoherently to herself. Many years later, Akhmatova read a new poem to Emma which seemed oddly familiar. She was told by Akhmatova that the poem had been composed in her head as they drove along in that taxi.

Seifullina advised Akhmatova to write directly to Stalin, and assured her that Stalin's secretary, Alexander Poskryobyshev, would deliver her letter. The next day, Akhmatova was driven by her friend Boris Pilnyak to the Kremlin to hand over her letter, which is very moving. It is a proud letter, uncompromising, even assertive:

Much respected Iosif Vissarionovich,

Knowing your attentive attitude to the forces of culture in our society, and especially authors, I dare address myself to you with this letter. On 23rd October in Leningrad Nikolay Nikolaevich Punin (Professor of Arts) and my son Lev were arrested by the NKVD. Iosif Vissarionovich, I don't know what kind of accusations have been brought against them but I give you my word of honour that they are neither fascists, nor spies, nor members of counter-revolutionary societies. I have been living in the USSR since the beginning of the Revolution. I never wanted to leave a country to which I am connected by heart and mind, despite the fact that my poems are not being published any more, and critics' reviews give me many bitter moments. I have never allowed myself to become depressed; I continue working in very difficult moral and material conditions and I have already published one research paper about Pushkin. The second is in press. In Leningrad I live in solitude, and I am often ill for long periods of time. The arrest of the only two people who are close to me gives the kind of blow from which I shall not be able to recover. I ask you, Iosif Vissarionovich, to return my husband and my son to me. I am sure you would never be sorry after doing so.[13]

It was signed "Anna Akhmatova, 1st November 1935." Pasternak wrote on the same day, and very courageously:

Once you reproached me with indifference to my comrade.[14] Apart from the value Akhmatova's life has for us and for our culture, I am a witness to her honest, difficult and uncomplaining existence. I ask you, Iosif Vissarionovich, to help Akhmatova and free her husband and son. Her attitude towards them is a categorical guarantee for me of their honesty.

These appeals brought results.[15] The evidence of it is in a signed resolution written in Stalin's hand across Akhmatova's letter. It reads, "To Comrade Yagoda. To free from detention both Punin and Gumilyov and reply that this action has been carried out. Stalin."[16]

As Boris Pasternak told Akhmatova, he usually refused to write letters for anyone, and she understood he had taken a risk for her sake. She spent some time that day with the Pasternaks and was put to bed in their apartment. The next morning they were able to show her a telegram saying that both Punin and Lev had already been released. Punin had been so surprised by this release, that when they woke him in the night to tell him about it, he asked permission to stay until the morning when the trams would be running. Even though her relationship with Punin had disintegrated, Akhmatova's relief was intense.

Lev owed his release directly to his mother's intervention and her literary connections but he believed that both he and the students were freed "because the man charged with being the main organiser of the criminal group, that is Nikolay Nikolaevich Punin, had been freed." All of them were released in November 1935 but Lev reflects angrily on the much more comfortable situation Punin enjoyed after their release:

I suffered more than the others because they expelled me from the university and I lived in misery for the whole winter, even going hungry because Punin took all of Mama's ration cards and forbade her to even give me lunch, announcing that he "couldn't feed the whole city"; thus showing that I was for him a completely foreign and unpleasant person.[17]

As Sergey Lavrov comments, Lev continued to resent the priority he sensed in Akhmatova's emotions. Lev's feeling of neglect no doubt goes back to his childhood but some of his impressions are confirmed by Emma Gerstein, who remembers that when Akhmatova had telephoned her with the words, "Emma, he's at home," Gerstein asked her, "Which he?" " 'Nikolasha, of course,' she replied. 'And Lyova?' I asked timidly. 'Lyova as well.' "[18] The implication that Akhmatova cared far more for Punin than her son is unnerving in so scrupulous an observer. Lavrov quotes with horror Lev's laconic "Punin returned to his work and I was thrown out of the University. During the winter I was on the edge of starvation."

Lev's account of his situation is bleak. On his release, he moved out of the House on the Fontanka and lived with Axel, a like-minded student friend, while continuing to take his meals with his mother. He had no permanent job and was usually hungry. Other university friends recall stories about the humiliating treatment he had to endure. As Lev remembered it, when Akhmatova had guests, she used to tell them that he was going to leave soon and it was often Ahrens who found something for him to eat in the kitchen. It is hard to reconcile such mean behaviour with Akhmatova giving food away in time of a general famine in earlier years, but that is how Lev perceived the situation in this period of his life. It is possible that Lev's intense, brooding presence made ordinary conversation impossible. Emma Gerstein recalls Lev in a state bordering on the unhinged. Punin's manner, too, had changed: "Often he sat at the table for hours in a red dressing gown, playing patience. At other times he shut himself up in his study, coming out only to gulp down a cup of tea and comment under his breath, 'How well the work's going. I've already turned out a whole twenty five pages.' "[19]

When a dish of carved slices of meat was brought in, Punin had to urge all the young people not to put too much on their plates. Conversation over meals was stilted. Emma Gerstein reports that once, when she was eating at the same table as Punin, Anna Ahrens, Akhmatova and Lev, the subject of people "who don't like to work" came up. Punin's wife remarked, "I wonder who doesn't earn their own food here." Lev and Akhmatova "stretched their backs at once. For a few minutes I could not see anything but those proud and insulted figures who looked as if they were tied by invisible thread."[20]

After Lev left gaol, Gerstein asked Akhmatova to take a letter to him from her, but Akhmatova refused to do so. She was now afraid of letters and there was indeed a real risk they could be discovered if there was a search on the train. Gerstein gave Akhmatova verbally the good advice she had been going to give Lev: that he should use his time to study for a degree as an external student. Akhmatova was touched by that concern. As she was leaving, she gave Gerstein a rapid but tender kiss. Nevertheless, Gerstein let her later bitterness spill into this story when she came to write her memoirs. She found a means of sending a letter through the painter Alexander Osmy-orkin, and in due course Osmyorkin brought back a reply from Lev which detailed all the harassments he had suffered at university in Leningrad and ended, as she remembered: "The only solution is to move to Moscow. Only with your support can I lead a normal life and at least do a little work."

This suggests a dependence on Gerstein at this time which was stronger than his dependence on his mother. Unfortunately, in 1938 Gerstein was forced to burn the letter, fearing it would damage Lev, and we have no documentary evidence to support her memory. At the very end of January 1936, Akhmatova came through Moscow on her way to see the Mandelstams in Voronezh. Gerstein showed Akhmatova Lev's letter then, and when she read it through to the end Akhmatova replied "in a voice of iron," "Lyova can only live with me." According to Gerstein, after this Akhmatova would not let him visit Moscow.

Akhmatova had never shown herself to be a possessive woman in relation to her husbands, but her maternal role had come to be the most important relationship in her life. To this, she may have felt Gerstein's devotion was a threat. Gerstein certainly believed so. Some time in the spring, Akhmatova went to stay in Starki on the estate of Vasily Shervinsky, and on her return in July Gerstein reports that "she met me as a woman meets a vanquished rival. 'Lyova was so keen to see me that he came to Starki from Moscow on his way to join the expedition,' she declared."[21] As Gerstein had no idea that Lev had even passed through Moscow, she was badly hurt to hear that he had failed to contact her. Akhmatova would have known as much, always supposing that Gerstein is remembering the words correctly. The story occurs in Gerstein's memoirs as part of the section "Unwanted Love," which was only published in 1998, when it produced much indignation in Moscow. Anatoly Nayman remarked that it was impossible to understand how a woman as intelligent as Emma Gerstein could write as she did about Akhmatova.[22]

In 1936 many of those said to be followers of Trotsky were arrested. Many convicted of such offences were shot out of hand, but for the most eminent there were to be political show trials. Stalin had told the NKVD that confessions were essential. Maxim Gorky was now ill and depressed by the little he was allowed to know of what was going on. (The NKVD actually printed false issues of *Pravda* especially for Gorky, so that he would not read of the persecution of his friend Kamenev.)[23] In the event, Gorky died on 18 June. There were other deaths. In February, Alexandra Kanel, the dearest companion of Gerstein's father, had died in mysterious circumstances. She had been a doctor to many of the most important Communist leaders, including Molotov, and in 1932 had been called in at the time of the suicide of Stalin's wife, Nadezhda Alliluyeva. Along with two other doctors, she had refused to sign a certificate giving the cause of death as appendicitis, and in 1935 she had been dismissed from her post. Her sudden death in 1936, though four years after this episode, was felt by Gerstein to be suspicious and proved a frightening portent of what was to come.

In 1936, Akhmatova undertook an exhausting thirty-six-hour journey to visit the Mandelstams in Voronezh. Osip's brother, Yevgeny, who saw her on to the train, had not thought to order bedding for her, but when he apologised, she replied with queenly negligence, "No matter." She arrived looking old and distressed but she became animated as soon as she reached the Mandelstams and in her animation recovered her old beauty.

In 1936, Viktor Ardov, who knew that Lev was still not allowed to enter Leningrad University, arranged for him to start as a first-year student at Moscow University. Lev, already twenty-four, rejected this proposal angrily. Seeing his pain and humiliation, Emma Gerstein found the right words to help him. She assured him he would be a historian whether Leningrad admitted him or not. Partly because of this loyal encouragement, he told her that she was the only woman he loved. By the next morning, however, he was weeping and subdued and talking about his mother.

Ardov arranged for him to have a room in Moscow, and Gerstein believed he had resigned himself to taking up the place at Moscow University, even if it did mean going back to being a first-year undergraduate. She was overjoyed at the chance this would give for them to be together. He returned to Leningrad, intending, she thought, only to pick up his things. To her disappointment, silence followed. Through November and December 1936 Gerstein heard nothing from him. Akhmatova sent no news of any further arrest, so Gerstein concluded that Lev had indeed changed his mind and decided to abandon her.

Akhmatova herself had bad news, as she wrote to Gerstein on 31 December 1936: "They have taken away my pension. You can imagine how that complicates my existence. I should come to Moscow but I have not the strength."[24] Without her pension, her only income,* she was now entirely dependent on Punin's goodwill.

Several poems written in 1936 relate to her loneliness while her relationship with Punin disintegrated. He had taken a new mistress, Martha Golubeva, an art historian who collaborated with him on several articles. Martha lived in her father's house on the Fontanka and did not seek to become part of the Punin household, though she was Punin's closest friend for the rest of his life. With no entries in Punin's journal for 1935–6, we can only guess at his feelings. Akhmatova drew away proudly but unhappily:

> *I have hidden my heart so well from you*
> *I might have tossed it in the Neva . . .*
> *Now I live here in your home,*
> *Tamed and without wings.*
> *At night I listen to creaking . . .*
> *What's there in the strange gloom?*
> *The Sheremetev lindens,*
> *The spirits of the house*
> *And they come closer cautiously,*

---

* It was only enough to keep her in cigarettes.

> *Like the sound of quiet waters*
> *While the black whisper of ill-luck*
> *Is warm in my ear, murmuring,*
> *As if it were the night's business,*
> *"You wanted comfort, did you?*
> *Do you know where it is—your comfort?"*[25]

If there is a suggestion in these last lines that her only comfort would be found in death, Akhmatova nevertheless sturdily rejected suicide and continued to do so when she experienced even greater disasters. She went away more often to Moscow, however, where she usually stayed with the Ardovs.

Punin was far from free of her. On 30 July 1936 he wrote in his diary, "An. has won this fifteen-year war,"[26] and was deeply upset by Akhmatova's poem, "A Last Toast," which acknowledges the wasteland of their relationship:

> *I drink to my ruined house*
> *My life of viciousness*
> *The loneliness we shared.*
> *Just so, I drink to you—*
> *To the lie of treacherous lips,*
> *To the deathly cold of your eyes,*
> *To this cruel rough world,*
> *Where God does not save anyone.*[27]

He sent telegrams—and gifts of money—to Moscow after her, saying that he loved her. When she did not reply, he went himself on 1 August and was hugely relieved to discover that she had received neither telegrams nor money, and was glad to see him. They spent a few days together but there was no happy ending. In the same month, Akhmatova wrote a poem identifying with Dante in his exile from Florence, which she felt was comparable to her own sense of alienation from St. Petersburg.

There were a few illusory signs of hope. In January 1937, Lev was readmitted to Leningrad University at the urging of Punin and allowed to enter the third year of the course. He was not living at the Fontanka but with Axel, who had a portrait of Nikolay Gumilyov hanging on the wall. The bedding was unsavoury and Lev slept on the floor on a bearskin, perhaps with habits of Asian tribes in mind.

He went away for some time to live in a village with his half-brother Orest, of whose existence neither he nor Akhmatova had been aware until a short while before. He was the child of Olga Vysotskaya, the actress at the Meyerhold Theatre who had borne Gumilyov a son in 1913. Lev was overjoyed at the discovery of an extension to his family, and Akhmatova acknowledged Orest at once, saying, "He has Nikolay's hands."28

Lev also continued to visit Moscow as a protégé of the Ardovs. By 1936 Ardov and his family were living on the Ordynka—a place mentioned in almost all the memoirs written about this period of Akhmatova's life—in some style. Ardov was able to take Lev to the Metropole Hotel and ride round with him in taxis. Lev told Emma: "I've come to Moscow to see you, but I can't resist good living."

Mandelstam was allowed to return from exile in Voronezh in May 1937. Akhmatova described meeting him in the autumn that year when he and Nadezhda came to Leningrad for two days and had absolutely nowhere to stay. "Osip had great difficulty breathing and gasped at the air with his lips . . . Someone who arrived after me said that Mandelstam's father had no warm clothing. Osip took off the sweater he was wearing under his jacket so that it could be given to his father."29

Akhmatova's own isolation from the literary community was now complete. She did not even receive an invitation for the celebrations on the centenary of Pushkin's death and spent the evening alone and sad. In 1937, when she went briefly into the Obukhov hospital for a check-up, Lev clung tenderly to her but he was generally too nervous or drunk to offer much affection. Her loneliness was profound.

Lev's opinions were radically opposed to his mother's. Akhmatova was markedly philo-Semitic. Many of the men she loved (Modigliani, Lurye, and later Isaiah Berlin) were Jews, while Lev had reactionary views which were close to those of the extremely right-wing "Black Hundred" groups active under the Tsar. Many people mention his anti-Semitism. He had come to believe that only a Fascist Russia would bring about a happy state when, as he explained to Emma Gerstein, who was Jewish and very aware of being so, "a Jewish parent will not be allowed to do anything and, like mulattos and half-castes, they won't be accepted in society."[30] In 1937, although many Jews had suffered in the 1937 purges, anti-Semitism as such was not avowed State policy and was still frowned upon in ordinary domestic contexts. I have been given many explanations for Lev's dislike of Jews, some relating to his later ill-treatment in the camps by Jewish interrogators, but his convictions were formed long before his imprisonment.

Soviet citizens had been taught to believe that enemies, suborned by foreign powers, were at work in their society and had to be rooted out at every level. When their neighbours were investigated for complicity, they were not at first afraid for themselves. Under the cruel rule of Yezhov a period of show trials and executions began, especially among the intelligentsia. By 1937, the year Russians call the "Yezhovchina," millions of bewildered citizens, convinced that some mistake had been made, had been arrested. Torture was now routine and confessions were extracted, so those still untouched could delude themselves they were in no danger, but most recognised that extreme caution was advisable.

The first of the famous show trials had opened on 19 August 1936. *Pravda* and the popular poet Demyan Bedny called for the blood of the enemies of the Soviet Union. Almost anyone in the arts could be so defined and could be brought into line. Eisenstein, who had been working in Hollywood, was lured back to work on *Bezhin Meadow*, but he was ordered to cut his film *October* according to Stalin's wish so that there should be no mention of Trotsky.

By 2 July 1937 those arrested were no longer specified by name, and no precise charges had to be answered. Quotas in thousands were recommended to local Secretaries: Category One were to be shot out of hand; Category Two were to be deported. Stalin continued, however, to insist that his victims sign elaborate confessions of their crimes, elicited by torture or threats to their families, before they died.

Bukharin, now under arrest himself, wrote to Stalin when he was in prison that there was something "great and bold about the political idea of a general purge." He was soon to become a victim of the monster he had praised. Most people tried to believe that there was some reason in the arrests and executions, in the hope that their own innocence meant they were safe. Akhmatova was impatient with the question about the reasons for a particular arrest, and often declared that "people had to understand you could be arrested for *nothing*."

When Meyerhold was arrested, at the airport where he was supposedly boarding a plane for the West, Akhmatova pointed out to Emma Gerstein immediately how unlikely it was that he would be planning to leave Russia without his wife Zinaida Raikh. Then came a warrant for Gerstein's father. The NKVD searched the flat, looking for one particular document, which it seems they did not find.

Ironically, 1937 found Lev restored to the History Faculty of Leningrad University and once more allowed to take examinations. This miracle was attributed by Lev to the courage of the Dean of the University, Professor Mikhail Lasorkin. Unfortunately, in the same year Lasorkin was arrested, along with his wife, and subsequently shot in the course of interrogation. His body was thrown from a window so that it could be claimed he had committed suicide. In 1938, when Lev was in his fourth term at university, he was arrested for the third time, a disaster he may well have brought on himself, as he acknowledges.

He was listening to a history lecture, given by Professor Pudansky, on the subject of Russian literature of the twentieth century, when the lecturer began to mock the poetry and personality of his father, Nikolay Gumilyov. As Lev remembers, the lecturer claimed, "The poet was writing about Abyssinia, but he had never gone further than Algeria." "I couldn't bear it, and I shouted from my place so that the Professor could hear, 'No, no, he had *never* been to Algeria. He had been to *Abyssinia*.' The Professor dismissed my comments patronisingly: 'Who knows better, you or me?' I answered, 'Of course, I.'"[31] These were rash words in such a political climate, all the more from someone who was the son of an executed prisoner. At the end of the lecture, the Professor complained about Lev's impertinence to the new Dean of the University, who evidently took the matter further.

Lev was arrested on 10 March 1938. Orest was staying overnight on Sadovaya Street, and it was he who brought the news of it to Akhmatova. Lev was taken into the Kresty prison, which is part of Leningrad folklore. This time his interrogators were far rougher than they had been in 1935. As Lev described his treatment, his interrogator swore at him and assaulted him. "By this time torture had become commonplace. They tried to make people confess and sign

the verdict of guilty which the interrogator had prepared beforehand. Because I didn't want to confess to anything which I didn't do,
they continued beating me for eight nights."[32]

He was not the only student arrested. Three others were also
charged at the same time. All were accused of conspiring to over-
throw the regime by means of assassination. They were tried by a
military tribunal of three men, the so-called Troika, in a trial that
lasted only fifty minutes. All were found guilty. Lev was sentenced to
ten years in a prison camp, plus four years in which he would have
no ordinary citizen's rights. All his property was to be confiscated
but, since he had little, this was a minor matter. After sentence had
been passed in October, Akhmatova was allowed to see her son in
prison, and Emma Gerstein remembers being told that Lev tried to
look his best so as not to alarm her, wearing a scarf borrowed from
another prisoner to hide marks of ill-treatment. He told her he had
been given the same sentence as Radek, a repentant supporter of
Trotsky. Akhmatova remembered that Radek, who was sentenced to
ten years, died after two years in gaol. Rumour had it that the
Moscow prosecutors thought Lev's sentence too light and that he
would be shot.

Once, when Akhmatova had been staying with Moscow friends,
she fell ill there. In spite of this, she returned to Leningrad, determined to see Lev, or at least hand in a food parcel. She was told he
had already been sent away to work on the canal being built to con-
nect the Baltic to the White Sea. The guards took in the parcel any-
way, which included 200 roubles saved with great difficulty by
Gerstein.

Akhmatova continued to make regular trips to Moscow in the
hope of finding someone who would intercede for her son. Soon
afterwards she asked Gerstein to burn all Lev's letters, frightened
that some piece of paper might be used against him. Akhmatova herself put the letters in the stove. Gerstein, who was well aware that
sentimentality might be dangerous to Lev, describes the experience
as an *auto-da-fé*.

Talking about Punin in Moscow some time in the last months of
1937, Akhmatova told Gerstein he was "fed up with me,"[33] and drew
her hand across her throat. By the autumn of 1937, Akhmatova was
involved with another lover herself, the doctor Vladimir Garshin,
whom she met in Kuibyshev hospital where she was being treated

for her thyroid condition by the endocrinologist V. G. Baranov. Garshin visited Akhmatova a few times in hospital, though it was not their first meeting: they had been introduced for the first time at the house of the literary historian Mikhail Engelhardt. When she was able to return home to the House on the Fontanka, their friendship deepened, encouraging a good deal of gossip in the university about Garshin's meetings with Akhmatova.[34]

Garshin stood out among the university professors of his faculty, not only for his exceptional intelligence but also for a remarkable personal magnetism.[35] He had dark chestnut hair and was considered very handsome. His manner of speaking was also very attractive: penetrating, and without the least affectation, with an unusually resonant voice. Many women fell in love with him.[36]

He had not had an easy life. In the Civil War, he had been an officer in the White Army, and his brother had chosen to emigrate. His father committed suicide, and he himself was once sentenced to be shot.[37] His present home situation was also difficult. He and his family occupied three small rooms in a communal flat on the south side of the Fontanka. There he lived with his wife Tatyana Vladimirovna and his two sons, Yury and Alexey, his sister Yulia Grigorievna, and her daughter. His sister was mentally ill. In 1936, his elder son Yury married and brought his wife to live in the same flat. His younger son Alexey, whom Garshin loved tenderly, had a serious speech impediment. He made many drawings of ships or boats of which his father was very proud, but his friend I. D. Khlopina,[38] who lived nearby, remembered both his pride and the sadness she felt because the drawings were not very good.

Tatyana Vladimirovna did not work and, although Garshin had a professorial salary, they had very little money: partly, it must be said, because Garshin was a coin collector who spent more than he could afford on his hobby. Garshin's relationship with his son Yury was put under strain once Garshin began seeing Akhmatova and after a serious disagreement with his father Yury left home altogether.

Garshin usually visited the Khlopins without his wife, and only entertained them once in his own flat. He was uninterested in cards, and did not go very often to theatres or concerts. Lydia Chukovskaya describes his irritated and sometimes infantile tone, but she admired his unmistakable sensitivity and saw he was a very handsome man.

Nineteen thirty-eight was a long, terrible year. Akhmatova continued to visit the Mandelstams until they took the advice of Isaak Babel, soon to be in trouble himself, who suggested they might be better off in Kalinin, an industrial city on the River Tver, while waiting to hear whether there was any chance to secure a work permit. Given vouchers for a workers' rest home, they felt a measure of relief since they were well looked-after there. In May 1938, they listened to the May Day celebrations without going to join them. The next morning, Mandelstam was rearrested. Sick and with no one to protect him, he went off into the wilderness of the Gulag with little hope of survival.

Akhmatova did not separate from Punin until September 1938, when she approached Anna Ahrens and suggested that they simply exchange rooms. Ahrens, who evidently still loved her husband very deeply, agreed. Punin was present but, as Akhmatova describes it, both women began moving their things while he could do nothing but look on in silence and accept the new arrangement, though when he found himself alone with Akhmatova "he complained that she might have remained with him for another year."[39] She must have smiled ironically at that, remembering how many years she had gone on living with him unhappily, only realising after she separated from him that she had been too depressed to move earlier.

Anna Kaminskaya gave me a rather different account of the way Akhmatova's relationship with Punin came to an end. Kaminskaya says that the relationship only finally ended in 1938 when Irina discovered she was pregnant. It was then, according to Kaminskaya, that Punin asked Akhmatova to move from the room they had been sharing to the "Memorial Room."[40]

As Akhmatova told Chukovskaya, these years had crushed her spirit, adding: "That's what my life, my biography is like. Who can refuse to live his own life?"[41]

ELEVEN

The Lamb

That was the time when only the dead could smile,
happy to be at rest.

—AKHMATOVA

*I*n November 1938, Lydia Chukovskaya visited Akhmatova in the Punins' shabby flat. She became one of Akhmatova's most loyal friends through the terrible years ahead, and it is through her that we see Akhmatova as she coped with the uncertainties of Lev's fate. Chukovskaya has an unsentimental eye and a sharp literary intelligence. Akhmatova came to depend on her human warmth, emotional strength and the editorial skills she had gained from working in a publishing house.

Chukovskaya was still an attractive young woman of thirty-one as she walked through the kitchen of the Punins' flat, where the winter washing hung on clothes lines, along a corridor with wallpaper hanging in scraps on the walls, into the room Akhmatova had occupied since her separation from Punin. The general appearance of Akhmatova's new room was one of neglect and chaos. By the stove stood an armchair with springs protruding from the seat. It was only possible to sit safely on the chair, which lacked a leg, by propping it up on a small chest. The beautiful furniture that was still there, like her own carved chair or the mirror in a smooth bronze frame, only emphasised the squalor. Akhmatova remained as unworldly about "things" as could well be, often using lovely plates with drawings in the style of David on them which most people would have felt should be kept aside for special occasions. Her treasures included painted Easter eggs, of which her favourite was one given her by her son. The bottom drawer of a cupboard would not close because of the biscuits she was collecting to send to Lev. On the floor lay another bag of provisions, including tinned food which Emma Gerstein had brought to send to Lev. The floor was unswept. Akhmatova herself was wearing a black dressing gown, torn from under the arm to the knee, a fact which did not seem to bother her. She often sat huddled up in a big armchair with her feet tucked underneath her.

Chukovskaya could only guess at the complexities in the household. Punin, as we have seen, had moved into his wife's room when their daughter Irina became pregnant, and Irina gave birth to her daughter Anna in 1939. Nevertheless, his relationship with Martha Golubeva continued. His own feelings at this time for Golubeva and his wife are unclear since for six years, from 1935 to 1941, he did not keep a diary. From the tone of the first passages, written when his diary restarted in 1941, it looks as though he had given up doing so deliberately.

Akhmatova's new admirer, Garshin, an anatomical pathologist in the Military Academy of Medicine, brought her tea and flowers and did all manner of chores for her. Perhaps she loved him, though never as she had loved Punin. Garshin was devoted, although married, and in her loneliness she leaned on him as she leaned on Chukovskaya. Garshin was always solicitous for her welfare. In December 1939, when he heard she was returning from a visit to Moscow to plead for Lev, he went to her flat, lit her stove and tidied up, though he was unable to meet her train since he could not leave work that morning. Chukovskaya went to the station instead.

Chukovskaya did not find Punin in the least concerned about Akhmatova's welfare. On the contrary, she observed that when the Punins held parties they frequently played their gramophone to all hours and that it was often noisy in Akhmatova's small room. Sometimes Punin could be heard stamping in the corridor and talking ceaselessly. There were other irritations. Punin used all the space in their joint shed to store his wood, which left no space for Akhmatova to put wood of her own. Sometimes he or his wife borrowed her kettle and left it in their rooms when they went out so she could not even make herself a cup of tea. Punin seemed to take only a perfunctory interest in Akhmatova's health even though, in addition to heart problems and continuing tuberculosis in her lungs, she was now suffering from Meniere's disease, which made it difficult to keep her balance and left her dizzy and nauseous when she turned her head.

On her first visit, Chukovskaya had come to see Akhmatova on business. She had heard rumours that Akhmatova's letter had helped to procure the release of Lev and Punin in 1935 and, though she knew Lev was once again in custody, she wanted advice about what actions she herself could take. Her own husband, Matvey Bronstein, had been sentenced to ten years for nothing more than bearing Trotsky's real name. Chukovskaya, by recording Akhmatova's day-to-day words, became something like a Boswell. In doing so, she has transformed the silent, beautiful creature of paintings and photographs into a living woman, whose comments on the great figures of Russian literature are often acerbic and sometimes spiky.

On the occasions when Akhmatova visited Chukovskaya, "she sat on my divan, magnificent, her profile like on a medal, smoking."[1] Yet, for all her imperious presence, she was as helpless as a child. She always needed Chukovskaya to walk her home, to the very door of her flat. The deep stone stairs of the House on the Fontanka did not have a single light, though in 1938 Akhmatova could still climb those stairs without panting. She also needed help in crossing roads, which made her very fearful. She attracted several such devoted helpers. Gumilyov's former mistress, for instance, Olga Vysotskaya, also looked after her, and indeed Akhmatova confessed ruefully that, "I only eat now when Olga Nikolaevna feeds me. She somehow manages to make me."[2]

Akhmatova made several trips to Moscow, partly to see loyal friends like the Ardovs who could alleviate her loneliness, but mainly to see what else could be done to help Lev. At this period her son seemed convinced that he was held not because he was related to Akhmatova but because of his relationship to Gumilyov:

> The interrogator/investigator announced that I was arrested as the son of my father and said "we don't love you for it." It was completely

absurd because all of the people who had taken part in the Tagantsev business in 1921 [like his father] had been arrested and shot by 1936. But the interrogator, Captain Lotyshev took no account of this and after seven nights of beating I was offered a protocol to sign, which I did not write and didn't even manage to read, being very beaten up. I heard that Captain Lotyshev was himself shot in 1938 or 1939. The tribunal tried me and two students whom I scarcely knew (or I only recognised them by sight from the university; they were in a different faculty). We were accused of terrorist actions according to that false document, although none of us could shoot or wield swords, or even owned any type of weapons.[3]

In December 1938, Lev and the other students were given the usual winter work of prisoners—felling trees in woods. At this period he did not think that any letter written by his mother, even if it reached its addressee, would have effect. He writes of his mother as naïve, someone who thought verdicts of guilty were the result of judicial error: "My mother was a very naïve soul, as many other people who are innocent in their thoughts, so she thought that the verdict of guilty was a result of judicial error, chance or oversight . . ."[4] In this he was completely mistaken. Akhmatova, alongside her friend Nadezhda Mandelstam, had long realised the seemingly haphazard nature of Stalin's Terror was a matter of policy and that this was not a question of a particular court making a mistake. However, Lev was right to understand that she could do little to help him.

By 1938 the Revolution had almost completely devoured its own children. At the show trials of Zinoviev and Kamenev, which had opened on 19 August 1936 and led inexorably to their execution, Western observers were amazed by the docility of the accused. Bukharin was tried in March 1938, as was Yagoda, former head of the NKVD. Yezhov, who had presided over the Terror, was himself removed from his position in the NKVD. Soon he was to disappear for ever. As a result of his fall, the lawyers representing Lev and the students accused alongside him appealed to the Military College of the High Court of the Soviet Union for his case to be reviewed.

At the same time as this sudden hope at the beginning of 1939 came terrible news. Mandelstam had died in the camps. "I received a short letter from a friend in Moscow which read, 'Our friend Lena has had a child and our friend Nadya is widowed.'" Such was the coded way that the horrible news reached Akhmatova. The loss of such a close friend made her even more lonely, and her fear for Lev was naturally intensified.[5]

Lev's position was indeed perilous. When his sentence of ten years on the White Sea Canal was reviewed in 1939, the charge against him was upgraded to "Terrorist Activity." He was condemned to be shot and was accordingly brought back to the Kresty prison. However, paradoxically, being brought back to Leningrad at that point probably saved his life, as he explains:

This time I was saved, not by Stalin but, as sometimes happens, by a lucky coincidence of circumstances. By 1939 I was almost dead. [He uses the prison-camp term *dokhodyaga*, which means someone starved, ill and weak beyond recovery, rather like Primo Levi's *Mussulman*.] I was very thin, with stubble on my chin, and hadn't been able to wash myself for a long time. I could hardly move my feet when walking from the prison barracks to the forest to fell trees. It was an icy forest, where snow reached to your waist, and I worked there in torn boots without warm clothes, with the only nourishment *balanda* [prison soup] which was little more than water, and a meagre ration of bread. In front of one particular fir tree, which had almost been sawn through, my axe fell from my weakened hands. To my peril, I had sharpened it the evening before. The axe easily penetrated the thick leather of my boot and cut my foot almost to the bone. The wound infected and probably that would have been the end of me . . . but fate decided otherwise. I was summoned to Leningrad for a new investigation. It saved my life.[6]

While Lev was in prison waiting for his retrial, he began to think very deeply about the way clans or tribes became a nation, forming theories which were to be the basis of his future work.

With Lev in the Kresty prison, Akhmatova stood outside in the long queues in the hope of learning something about him, or to beg the guard to take in a food parcel for him. Lydia Chukovskaya often waited with her in the same queue, hoping to have news of her husband. Unknown to Chukovskaya, Bronstein's sentence of "ten years' exile without benefit of correspondence" was in reality a euphemism for execution and he had already been shot.

Akhmatova did not ask for help, but she attracted it from those who stood with her: "From time to time one of us managed to get Anna Andreevna out of the queue and to make her sit down—even if it was only on a block of stone . . . But she left the queue unwillingly . . . She stood in silence. . . ."[7] The next day her feet were so badly swollen she had to take off her shoes and walk across the yard in her stockinged feet. She was looked after by Chukovskaya who, even in her own distress, regarded it as a privilege—partly because Akhmatova was so visibly ill, partly because she felt such admiration for her poetry. As Chukovskaya saw: "The hot day waiting in the courtyard to hand in clothing seemed endless. Torture by standing."[8]

So it was that Akhmatova once again took her place with the mothers and wives in the queue at the wall of that prison. As she wrote "instead of a preface" to her great poem *Requiem*:

> In the terrible years of the Yezhov terror I spent seventeen months waiting in line outside the prison in Leningrad. One day somebody in the crowd identified me. Standing behind was a young woman, with lips blue from the cold, who had of course never heard me called by name before. Now she started out of the torpor common to us all and asked me in a whisper (everyone whispered there), "Can you describe this?" And I said, "I can." Then something like a smile passed fleetingly over what had once been her face.[9]

Akhmatova was too afraid of the likely danger to commit the poem to paper. She and Chukovskaya both learned the poems by heart, and that is how they were preserved. The transformation of the "gay little sinner from Tsarskoye Selo" into the voice of a whole people's suffering had begun.

Akhmatova reflected scornfully on the support her remaining fame gave her in those terrible days. With characteristic wryness, she pointed out to Chukovskaya that it was one thing to take pleasure in being recognised while travelling in a soft landau under a little umbrella, and quite another when standing in the snow queuing for herring.

In the new investigation, Lev was charged, among other falsities, with being incited by his mother to murder Andrey Zhdanov, the leader of the Party in Leningrad. On 17 July 1939 there had been a Resolution of a special committee of the NKVD about the imprisonment of Lev Gumilyov for "participation in anti-Soviet organisation and agitation."[10] On 29 July 1939, Akhmatova told Lydia with great excitement that Lev's friend, Nikolay Davidenkov, arrested at the same time as Lev, had been released; but Lev was transported to Norilsk prison camp in the far north on 17–18 August nevertheless.[11]

On 28 August Akhmatova received the news that Lev was going to be sent back to the north, and was in urgent need of warm clothes. Chukovskaya came to her aid, since Akhmatova seemed too wretched to be practical: "I managed quite quickly, by phone, to arrange for a hat, a scarf and a sweater. Everyone I called understood everything immediately, with no questions. 'A hat? No, I don't have a hat, but do you need some mittens?' . . . We went to fetch the boots together. . . ."[12]

Akhmatova was so distraught she was not even able to drink a cup of tea offered by one of her friends and could not remember the address of the friend to whom she had lent boots, or the correct trolleybus to take, but knew she had to look smart herself for an interview with the authorities the next day. When asked whether she could possibly do so, she said, "All my life I've been able to look however I wanted to; from a beauty to a hag."[13] When a wardrobe of warm clothes had been assembled, Chukovskaya helped Akhmatova bring them back to her room. When they parted, Akhmatova said, "I'm not going to say thank you. You don't say thank you for something like that."

The new trial had reduced Lev's sentence to five years, after which he could hope to be allowed to leave the far north. In Norilsk, he was allowed to study geology and by the end of his prison term had become an efficient lab technician, working on the copper, nickel and platinum to be found there. Attitudes to prisoners held in Siberia were, rather surprisingly, better than in European Russia and it was possible for prisoners to gain educational qualifications. Lev began by digging the earth, then became a copper miner and at length a geology technician. It was a very hard life, whatever he was able to learn. He spent one and a half years in the north and in his own words, "after that the front line looked like a resort." His bitterness against his mother now began to mount, as he confided in a letter to Emma Gerstein:

You ask how many friends I have and also about the women in my life. I have workmen who work for me, and as for women—during the whole year I saw three of them: a female deer caught in a snare and a female hare and a tree squirrel who was killed by a club. There are no books and nothing at all. *My mother doesn't write to me and doesn't send telegrams. She is probably in good health.*[14] [Author's italics.]

Not so, though it is hard to be sure just how ill she was at this stage. A reader of Chukovskaya's journal might be suspicious of the way Akhmatova pointed out on 26 February 1939 that a small, dark brown lesion on her forehead was probably cancer. (It wasn't.) There was nothing hypochondriac, however, about her heart problems, a thyroid disorder and recurring bouts of tuberculosis through 1938 and 1939.

When she returned from the queue, Akhmatova's feet had always been badly swollen and on 16 September 1939 Garshin was so alarmed by what had happened to her toes that he arranged for her to see another doctor. It was not gangrene, as he had feared, but traumatic neuritis. On 15 October Akhmatova went to a second doctor and to her indignation was pronounced physically healthy. It would not be surprising if there were a psychosomatic element in her symptoms, given the level of her anxiety for Lev. His sentence of five years was relatively light but she knew it was quite possible she would never see her son again.

Out of this mix of physical distress and misery rose one of the greatest lyrical sequences in the Russian language: *Requiem.* It can now be heard, in Akhmatova's own voice, downloaded from the Internet;[15] or through a tape recording made by Peter Norman in Akhmatova's hotel in London after her visit to Oxford in 1965.[16] She has a dark, low voice and reads with a strong, pounding rhythm. All the lyrics are carefully dated. One short poem, of 1935, must refer to Punin, since Akhmatova was in the flat when he was taken away, while she was not a witness to Lev's arrest in the same year:

> *At first light, they led you away, and like*
> *a mourner at a funeral, I followed.*
> *Children were crying in the front room.*
> *The candle was guttering under the icon*
> *and your lips were cold as painted lips,*
> *your forehead deathly wet.*

> *These moments I shall never forget:*
> *I shall howl like the wives of the Streltsy*
> *underneath the towers of the Kremlin.*[17]

By 1939, most lyrics are explicitly about her fear for Lev:

> *I cried out for seventeen months,*
> *to call you home again, and*
> *threw myself at the hangman's feet—*
> *you are my son and my terror.*[18]

In some poems, she seems to be looking down on her own suffering as if from above and at a stranger. The tone is deliberately flat, the lines short:

> *This woman is ill.*
> *She is all alone.*
>
> *Her husband is in the grave, her*
> *son in prison: pray for her.*[19]

Since Punin was not dead or imprisoned at this point, she must have been thinking either of Gumilyov or Shileiko.

In another short lyric, she reminds herself how she had once been a frivolous "mocker" of conventional morality and wished she had been shown:

> *What would happen in your life:*
> *And how you would stand with a parcel*
> *Three hundredth in line by the prison.*[20]

Unforgettably, she describes the sounds of summer rustling outside her window, and recalls how once she had a premonition of terrible events which would happen on "a brilliant day, in this deserted house."

On 19 August 1939, in a poem written in the House on the Fontanka, she speaks to Death using the familiar form of "you"—*ty*—as if speaking to a close friend:

> *You will come in any case—so why not now?*
> *I am waiting—I can't bear any more.*
> *I've put the light out and opened the door*
> *for you: so simple, so miraculous.*[21]

The manner of her death no longer matters to her:

> *You may take whatever shape you choose,*
> *Burst in upon me as a gas shell does*
> *Or creep in like a bandit with his cosh*
> *Or else infect me with a typhus vapour.*[22]

Lev was later to voice some objection to the title of the sequence, since a Requiem Mass is said for the dead. He particularly disliked lyrics such as "The Crucifixion," in which Akhmatova appears to identify with the Virgin Mary, notably one written in 1943 in Tashkent, which has the lines:

> *Mary Magdalene beat her breast and wept,*
> *The disciple He loved most was turned to stone,*
> *But no one dared to glance towards His mother*
> *Where she was standing silent and alone.*[23]

The finest poem from *Requiem* known by heart by many Russians is the "Second Epilogue," written in 1940. She speaks there of a hundred million people "screaming through her exhausted mouth." It is not only her own anguish she is recording. Hence, her bold demand that if her country ever decides to set up a monument to her, it should stand neither by the sea where she was born, nor in the garden of the Tsar:

> *But here, where I stood for three hundred hours*
> *outside those gates that never opened to me.*
>
> *In case in blissful death I might perhaps*
> *forget the rumbling of those black marias*
>
> *or how the hated door banged shut against*
> *an old woman howling like an animal.*

May the melting flakes of snow then flow
over bronze eyelids, as if they were tears,

and let a prison dove coo somewhere in the distance,
while the ships on the Neva sail quietly on.[24]

Akhmatova told Chukovskaya that Punin had asked her to move out from his flat altogether, but she had nowhere to go. She reflected that she had begun to think badly of men, who were very rarely to be found in the queues waiting outside the Kresty. (There were more inside, however.) Akhmatova was often witty about her disappointment over her treatment by men, in a way only a great beauty could allow herself: "I have always dreamt that my husband would hang my portrait over the table. But none of them did—not Kolya, not Volodya, nor Nikolay Nikolaevich. He's only hung it up now that we've separated."[25]

In 1939 other shocks followed. The Fascist powers, so often excoriated in the Soviet press, were suddenly transformed into allies. The Nazi-Soviet pact was signed on 23 August 1939, for reasons more fully discussed in Chapter Twelve.[26] Nine days later, Hitler invaded Poland and France and England declared war on Germany. Akhmatova, even in her own distress, was shaken by the news. The Soviet press was ordered to remain completely silent about what was happening to Jews and Socialists in Nazi-occupied Europe. Meanwhile, Russians like Akhmatova, whose natural sympathies were with France and Great Britain, were dismayed to watch the course of the war going entirely in Hitler's favour.

On 12 December 1939, Lydia Chukovskaya received the news that her own husband was dead. Nevertheless, when Akhmatova summoned her in her usual peremptory, needy way, Chukovskaya went round to see her. By now Akhmatova's room looked even stranger than usual, with newspaper stuck over the window panes and a twisted piece of shawl hanging from the ceiling. She found it impossible to keep up their usual conversation, however, and when Akhmatova noticed something was wrong, Chukovskaya confessed what had happened. Akhmatova was stricken with horror at her friend's pain, and her courage in concealing it: "My God. My God, and I didn't know. My God."[27]

Just as she had been a good "stepmother" to Irina, Akhmatova was now fond of the sons of her neighbours, the Smirnovs, Valya aged seven and Shakalik eighteen months. Akhmatova often acted as a babysitter for the younger child when the Smirnovs were at the cinema and was very unhappy to hear Tatyana Smirnova beating her son Valya. When she tried to talk to her about that, Smirnova rebuffed her. Akhmatova valued the children's affection and was hurt when, after a short trip to Moscow on Lev's behalf, Shakalik seemed to have already forgotten her on her return.

In 1939, there seemed unexpectedly to be a chance of publishing her poems. She was invited to prepare a selection of poems, to be called *From Six Books*. Her voice was ironic as she wondered whether asking her to put a new collection together meant someone believed she was at last writing about collective farms. In December 1939, when she was in Moscow trying to help Lev, she read "To Death" from *Requiem* to Pasternak.

By 1940, Akhmatova's position in the literary world seemed to be inexplicably changing for the better. On 5 January, she was accepted as a member of the Leningrad Writers' Union and was admitted with ceremony. She had been invited to join in 1934, but Mandelstam's arrest had shaken her and she had not filled in the form. In 1935, she had told a friend that she felt she had written all the poetry she could. Then in 1936, in her pain and anxiety, poetry unexpectedly began to flow. On 11 September 1939 Akhmatova had written to apply to the Union of Writers. "Please accept me as a member of the Union of Soviet Writers."[28]

Now, in 1940, Mikhail Lozinsky, the foremost translator of Shakespeare into Russian, welcomed her with a speech in which he said her poems "would last as long as the Russian language exists, and every last grain of them will be garnered like lines of Catullus." This she repeated to Chukovskaya with many self-deprecating comments about its absurdity, but clearly enormously pleased. Lozinsky, whom she had known for thirty years, was a man of integrity. Chukovskaya noted that, although she continued to complain of insomnia, she looked rather healthier.

Other efforts were being made on her behalf. Alexander Fadeev, a talented novelist and then Secretary of the Writers' Union of the USSR, wrote a letter to A. Vyshinsky, the Vice Chairman of the Soviet Narodnykh Komissarov:

In Leningrad, a famous poet Akhmatova lives in exceptionally difficult financial and housing circumstances . . . who, despite all the
incongruity of her talent with our time, remains the greatest poet of
pre-Revolutionary times . . . In my opinion, she should be given
some accommodation ahead of any queue . . . I ask you to interfere
in this matter.[29]

In fact, Akhmatova did not want to have a new flat found for her,
saying she was used to living on the Fontanka and hoped only for an
extra room when Lev returned from the camps. In early 1940 she
was pleased to receive a sum of 3,000 roubles from the Writers'
Union in Moscow and her pension was reinstated at about 700 roubles a month.

On 13 January 1940, when Chukovskaya returned from a rest
home where she had been writing her novel *Sofia Petrovna* (*The
Deserted House*) about the events of 1937, Akhmatova had insomnia
and numb feet, as she reported, but in fact looked rather better. Her
hair was done with a comb placed carefully in it. Some part of her
recovery must have come from the revival of her literary fortunes.
On 23 February she signed a contract with *Leningrad* for several of
her poems. This would mark her first publication in the Soviet press
for fifteen years. One of these was "To hide my heart from you,"
about her relationship with Punin. When the magazine appeared in
April, Akhmatova told Chukovskaya that Punin was very angry, with
a face like a thundercloud.

Yet the new atmosphere in some way unnerved her. She was worried because two publishing houses now wanted a book of her
poems, and had sent her contracts simultaneously. She did not know
how to handle the situation. When Chukovskaya arrived, it was
necessary to look everywhere for the contracts, which were discovered beneath the armchair under a heap of papers. The pressures of
putting a collection of poems together after so long a gap in her
publishing life seemed to be almost too much for her. By 23 January,
Akhmatova had gone completely to pieces and was refusing to eat
or drink. Garshin noted she was turning night into day and was
totally disorganised. She complained to him that the publishers
were sending someone for the manuscript of her poems and they
were not ready. It was Chukovskaya who found a typist. In February

Garshin arranged to have her room washed and cleaned by Smirnova.

The mood of the times had changed so emphatically that in July 1940 Pasternak asked Akhmatova innocently whether Lev had been released from prison yet as so many others had. Lev remained in the far north, however. Nevertheless, Fadeev, Pasternak and A. Tolstoy considered it was feasible to suggest the text of Akhmatova's *From Six Books* for the Stalin Prize, which would have been unthinkable at the height of the Terror.

And Akhmatova was writing poems again. Indeed, she was not sleeping and had taken to writing all night through. Between 1936 and 1940, she had widened the focus of her work decisively. There remained considerable friction with Punin. Rather bitterly, Akhmatova reflected that Punin had "discovered a new reason to take umbrage at me": "Why didn't I write when we lived together, when I write so much now? . . . Now at last I have understood: for Nikolay Nikolaevich, Anna Evgenevna was always the model wife: she works, earns 400 roubles a month and is an excellent housekeeper."[30]

Although Akhmatova continued to do all she could to secure Lev's release, his complaints about her intensified. Many of these concerned the style and frequency of her letters. Such letters as she wrote were indeed short. She worried that some phrase in them could be used against her son, choosing instead to write cards, which were treated much more cursorily by the censors. Telegrams were her preference to convey necessary information.

This was not, as he imagined, a sign of indifference. On the contrary, her well-being seemed to depend largely on news of Lev. When she had any cause to feel optimistic about him she looked radiant. On 2 May 1940, Chukovskaya reported, following a visit, that she was "dressed up and almost rosy,"[31] but only a few days later her air of youth and triumph had completely gone and she once again had a "sallow, pinched, old face."[32] By 14 May she was speaking unhappily of another failure in her attempts to help Lev. She gave Chukovskaya another poem from *Requiem* to read, and then they burnt it together over an ashtray.

Akhmatova's health in June 1940 was poor once again and she was registered as an invalid "of the second category." She remained hopelessly dependent on the streets: needing to be walked home and finding it particularly difficult to cross Nevsky Prospekt. In her old mackintosh, an absurd old hat and worn-down shoes, she remained stately, with a beautiful face and tangled grey fringe. She was beginning to complain again of her heart, though whether of angina or arrhythmia is not clear. Chukovskaya writes of "five heart attacks in five days." She cannot mean infarcts but she might mean either attacks of fibrillation or angina. Five infarcts in as many days would surely kill anyone. When Garshin said she must go into hospital, Akhmatova recovered immediately.

One of her major anxieties, as she explained to Chukovskaya on 8 June 1940, was that Tatyana Smirnova had been assigned to spy on her. We know now this is very likely, bearing in mind documents unearthed by Irma Kudrova about the level of spying by the NKVD around Tsvetaeva in her husband Sergey Efron's *dacha* in Bolshevo. Kudrova gives us details of the way people close to the Efron household—including Samuil Gurevich, the man whom her daughter, Alya, loved—routinely reported to the NKVD. By 13 August Akhmatova's suspicions of NKVD spying were confirmed. She set a trap for anyone who might be reporting on her by placing a hair in a notebook containing her poems when she went out. When she came back it was gone. This sent her almost insane with worry, because if she was being watched so intensively this might well affect the way Lev was treated.

On 18 June, Akhmatova was astonished to find herself talked about very favourably in the magazine *Leningrad,* but her pleasure was short-lived. On 26 June, a representative of the house publishing *From Six Books* came to visit and asked her to remove two poems: "Everything is ravaged, bartered, betrayed"[33] and "I am not one of those that left the land."[34] The worst of the Terror seemed to be passing but, although she continued, with Chukovskaya's help, to put her book of poems in order, Akhmatova suspected that once again something would prevent publication. The difficulties of ordering her manuscript seemed insurmountable to her. Chukovskaya came to her rescue once again, and in the outcome it was she who had to check the poems and read the proofs. By 26 August, as Akhmatova told Korney Chukovsky, the production of her book had been halted altogether. "They say there is no paper, but that is out of politeness."

Her visit to Fadeev in Peredelkino that summer concerned another matter. She had already spoken to him about some intervention he promised to make for Lev, and she wanted to know how it had gone. On 27 August she received a letter from Fadeev saying he had indeed managed to find the right man and that he would arrange for her to meet him. Thereafter, she had waited for news. Chukovskaya, with careless cruelty, responded to her pessimism about the likely result by reminding her that she could at least have *hope,* while Chukovskaya could not, since discovering her husband was dead.

So it was at the end of August 1940 that Akhmatova went to see the State Prosecutor of the USSR on Pushkinskaya Street. Chukovskaya accompanied her but Akhmatova spent only a short time in his room before being ushered out, by a rudely shouting man much smaller than she was. Akhmatova's desolation was complete. Later, while reporting as much to Chukovskaya, Garshin began to cry, aware that he wanted to throw in his lot completely with Akhmatova and could not do so "without committing a sin." Chukovskaya too was affected by her own helplessness.

However, a few days later Akhmatova had recovered enough to attend to combing her hair and read to Chukovskaya, who marvelled at the way she could turn the broken fragments life had thrown her way into gold. She recited three poems. "But I give you solemn warning," "No, it's not I. Someone else is suffering" and "Thus dark souls take flight." Chukovskaya made the tea. There was no food since Tatyana was ill and so had not been shopping.

Akhmatova's domestic situation remained unhappy. While Chukovskaya was there, Punin put his head round the door and asked to borrow 15 roubles. Tatyana Smirnova had taken one of Akhmatova's copies of her poems without permission and now wanted to sell it back to her for 100 roubles. But what Akhmatova found most unbearable was hearing Tatyana shouting at her son— "You beast, you bastard"—when she wanted Valya to do his homework.

On 3 September, she began the first of her beautiful *Northern Elegies,* a poem she later completed in Tashkent. It has an epigraph from Pushkin: "I no longer live there." And it is set in the Russia of Dostoevsky, to whose spirit it is essentially a tribute. The Leningrad she evokes is a lithograph of St. Petersburg in the nineteenth century, with *droshkies,* girls' dancing classes, ubiquitous dress shops with French names and money-changers. She remembers the kerosene lamps and plush armchairs of her own childhood, alongside Dosto-evsky's world of lands often mortgaged, and roulette in Baden-Baden. It is in this context that she also remembers her mother's beauty and kindness. Dostoevsky enters her poem as she imagines the emer-gence from non-being, which was the moment of her own birth, as a kind of loss,

> *The country shivers, while the convict from Omsk*
> *knew how the world goes, and gave up on all of it.*
> *Look, he has shuffled everything around;*
> *his spirit rises over primordial chaos.*
> *Midnight strikes. We can hear his pen squeaking:*
> *page after page stinks of Semyenov Square.*
> *And this was the moment we chose to be born.*
> *How perfectly we timed it, so as not to miss*
> *a single one of the spectacles to come*
> *as we decided to give up non-existence.*[35]

During the night of 1 October Akhmatova had a serious cardiac crisis. The following day she was "in disarray, unkempt and hag-gard." There had been some bad news about Lev, and 1 October was his birthday. On 13 October she received a letter from Lev which distressed her very much. Chukovskaya observed that her eyes had sunk into her face and that she was lying down, looking wretched: "I received a letter. Today. At eight o'clock in the morning. Not getting letters is horrible—not a single letter in three months—but getting them is even worse."[36]

Other troubles followed. Whatever frail prop her literary hopes had given her was taken away. Some copies of *From Six Books* had been printed, for all the talk of paper shortages, but on 29 October it was banned and all copies taken from the shops. On 7 November Akhmatova, who was suffering from bronchitis, had a further heart crisis in the night which took her into hospital. There, she was very moved when a cleaner asked her to write a little verse for her. "It turns out that whenever she writes home to her village, she ends with a poem and her correspondent does the same." Akhmatova is touched at the thought of such simple people in Russia loving poetry. "I don't know any country in which people love poetry more than ours."

While she had time to brood in hospital, she became convinced that her new troubles were of her own making. On 13 November Akhmatova told Chukovskaya:

> You know, these last few days I've understood that I myself am to blame for everything. For everything that happened with the book. The Central Committee is absolutely right. . . . The publishing house selected some poems and took them to Moscow. There they were approved. Then, out of the blue I took it upon myself to add new ones, and, as if that weren't enough, I put the saddest poem in pride of place. . . . *And if I had not done this, Lyova would be at home.*[37] [Author's italics.]

Chukovskaya could not shake this logic, although she reminded Akhmatova that it was the publishing house that had asked for new poems and no one had known what they wanted.

On 22 November, Akhmatova's childhood friend Valeria Sreznevskaya fell ill. Akhmatova visited her several times as she lay on her bed in a torn nightdress, delirious. Her madness and later her death distressed Akhmatova profoundly.

Early in 1941, Chukovskaya had to leave Leningrad because her novel, *Sofia Petrovna*, had come to the attention of the "Big House" and she was under constant surveillance, particularly by her maid, Ida. She did not tell Akhmatova of her misfortune. Akhmatova was already tormented enough by her fear for Lev. Chukovskaya went into the Uzkoe sanatorium in February 1941.

～

While in Moscow, Akhmatova usually stayed with the Ardovs and there in early 1941 she met Marina Tsvetaeva twice: the only times the two women had seen each other face to face, although Tsvetaeva had written ecstatic poems in praise of Akhmatova's beauty and poetry before leaving Russia for Prague and Paris in 1922, and there had been a few letters between them.

Marina Tsvetaeva is one of the greatest Russian poets of the twentieth century, recognised as an equal by Akhmatova, though she had reservations about the violence of her emotions, the ferocity of her expression and the wholeness of her self-exposure. She knew that

Tsvetaeva had remained dedicated to poetry through a life that was a history of loss and unremitting poverty after she and her surviving daughter followed her husband into exile in France. Tsvetaeva, too, had seen her early fame vanish and learned to accept loneliness and rejection.

Tsvetaeva's marriage to Sergey Efron went back to a childhood meeting on the shores of the Black Sea and, though she may have loved other men more passionately, theirs was as close a bond as that of siblings. Most biographers have been inclined to feel some impatience with Efron's inability to find work, his constant sickness, his changing political allegiances. Tsvetaeva's return to the Soviet Union from Paris in 1937 was precipitated by the unexpected exposure of Efron as an agent of the NKVD. He was forced to flee to Russia. Tsvetaeva always refused to believe in Efron's involvement in the murder of Ignace Reiss—an NKVD agent who had defected—which had led the French police to investigate him.

Her daughter Alya, a convinced Communist, had already returned to Russia; her adolescent son, Mur, longed to be in the homeland he had never seen; the émigré community in France was largely hostile. Her decision to follow Efron was therefore perhaps unsurprising, but it proved a tragic mistake. She found her country in the grip of Stalin's Terror, and her sister already in prison. Not long after her return, Alya and Efron were arrested.

In the crowded *dacha* in Bolshevo allocated to Efron by the NKVD, Tsvetaeva found that his belief in Communism remained unshaken even after the arrests of both her own sister Anastasia and D. S. Mirsky, the literary critic who had been their close friend. The Klepinins, whom Efron had recruited into the Soviet secret service, also lived there. Tsvetaeva found herself intensely lonely. Alya remained as convinced as her father about the aims of Soviet society. Nevertheless, Alya was arrested on Sunday, 27 August 1939, between the Nazi-Soviet pact and the invasion of Poland. Emilia Litauer, a French Communist of thirty-five and a frequent house guest, was arrested at the same time, and the prisoners were questioned about one another.

Alya began to "confess" within a month of her arrest. Irma Kudrova,[38] who had read the file of her interrogation, assesses Alya's confessions with caution and it was only after Khrushchev's Twentieth Party Congress in 1956 that Alya was able to write about the vicious treatment she received in prison: "I was beaten unmercifully with rubber truncheons, for twenty days and nights. I was deprived of sleep . . . kept in a cold incarceration cell, undressed, standing to attention; they staged a fake execution."[39] It is not surprising that she finally gave them what they wanted: a declaration that Efron had been a double agent. "Not wishing to conceal anything from the investigation, I must report that my father was an agent of French intelligence."[40]

Five days later, a warrant for Efron's arrest was drawn up and, after a delay which suggests that someone higher up the chain of command had to be consulted, Efron was brought in, on 9 October 1939. He was a sick, unhappy man, yet his NKVD file shows him behaving with exemplary courage. He was not evasive. He gave a detailed account of his years in emigration, his motives for organising the Democratic Union of Russian Students, and named all the leaders of the Eurasian cell in Paris, most of whom were safely in France. We can assume he was not treated gently. Yet it was only when he was told that his friend Emilia Litauer had unmasked his antisocial behaviour, and that his own daughter had confirmed as much, that he was overwhelmed. The files reveal that he then asked for a break in interrogation: "Right now I can't talk. I'm very tired."

Tsvetaeva, of course, knew none of this when she met Akhmatova in Moscow two years later. She had travelled there with her son in the hope of finding someone who could help her secure the release of her family. As an émigrée, with a family in prison, she found it difficult to meet old friends though she was in touch with Pasternak. And Akhmatova, for all her nervous anxiety, could always make herself do what she felt to be right.

Pasternak telephoned Viktor Ardov's wife, Nina Olshevskaya, who told him that she would ask Akhmatova to call back and arrange a meeting. Akhmatova did so and, after a very brief conversation, Tsvetaeva was invited to the Ardovs' flat on the Ordynka. It is worth mentioning that Akhmatova was willing to go out and meet her if it was more convenient, but Tsvetaeva, who had no base in Moscow, preferred to come to the Ardovs' flat.

Viktor Ardov recalls letting her in, and watching the two women press one another's hands before going off to the tiny room in which Akhmatova always stayed. They remained there alone for the best part of the day and Akhmatova never spoke of what had been discussed. She remarked only that Tsvetaeva seemed to be a completely normal person, deeply concerned for her family's fate. The following day they met again, this time at Nikolay Khardzhiev's apartment, and sat there talking and drinking wine. Khardzhiev found Tsvetaeva sparkling: "She was full of Paris and talked brilliantly." Akhmatova felt herself to be dull and cow-like in contrast. But Khardzhiev, who saw the quicksilver in Tsvetaeva, was more struck by what he describes as Akhmatova's "complete and utter genuineness."[41]

Ardov and Akhmatova had planned to go that evening to see Olshevskaya, who was acting in *A Midsummer Night's Dream.* Tsvetaeva insisted that plans should not be changed on her account. As they left Khardzhiev's house together, a figure stepped out of the shadow and began to follow them and Akhmatova wondered, "Her or me?"

Once back in Leningrad it is easy to see how Akhmatova came to depend on Garshin's tenderness. Though Akhmatova was surrounded by many loving friends, not all of them approved of this behaviour. Surprisingly critical was Nadezhda Mandelstam, to whom Akhmatova had always been so loyal. On 9 May 1941, a letter from Nadezhda written from Kalinin to the biologist B. S. Kuzin[42] speaks unkindly of Akhmatova being afraid to visit her, presumably afraid to damage her son by being discovered with the wife of an executed criminal. "But I fear that old woman has, not just a persecution complex but megalomania. Doesn't it look that way? Besides, she has been in love for three years now—and that's not healthy at her age."[43]

Akhmatova's anxiety about Lev was unremitting and in a mournful imitation of the Armenian poet Tumanian, she addressed a Padishah, who must be thought of as Stalin himself, in the voice of a ewe lamenting for her lost lamb:

> May God preserve your own child . . . How was the taste of my son?[44]

$\mathscr{W}ar$

Who now will rescue Leningrad?[1]

—AKHMATOVA

*I*n the years of the Great Terror, the Russian people were mainly afraid of Stalin's murderous whims. But there was another, European, danger, as the intelligentsia were well aware. Hitler had been in charge of Germany since 1933, building up his armed forces and menacing his neighbours. Europe was a "poker game," to use Stalin's words,[2] in which Adolf Hitler's Nazi Germany, the Western democracies and Stalin's Soviet state were all hoping to see the other players attack one another.

Stalin regarded the Western democracies as at least as much a threat to the Soviet Union as Germany, even after Hitler had ingested Austria and Czechoslovakia. Moreover, the Munich Agreement convinced Stalin that the West was not serious about stopping Hitler. When Britain and France guaranteed Polish borders on 31 March 1939, he suspected they would find some excuse to placate Hitler when the time came and that this would leave Russia alone and exposed. Rather than seeking an alliance with the Western democracies, therefore, Stalin opened negotiations for a peace deal with Hitler. The Nazi-Soviet non-aggression pact of 23 August

1939 allowed Stalin to annex the eastern part of Poland when hostilities broke out. On 1 September, Hitler invaded Poland. Many sections of the intelligentsia were dismayed, notably members of the Jewish Anti-Fascist Committee, who had been used by Stalin to drum up support for Russia in the United States. The novelist Ilya Ehrenburg, a resilient survivor, fell into a black depression at the news.

Akhmatova was in hospital with an inflamed jaw in the days leading up to the outbreak of war between Hitler and western Europe. Garshin and Chukovskaya visited her and, although she had to undergo painful surgery, she gave a characteristically ironic account of her operation, though there is a touch of pride, too, in the pleasure she took in the surgeon's praise: "Vladimir Georgievich [Garshin] told me later that the doctor was amazed how much I could bear. So when was I supposed to scream? Before—it didn't hurt; during the operation—I had the forceps in my mouth, I couldn't scream; afterwards, it was no longer worth it."[3]

To Chukovskaya, she reported more serious problems: she had cavities in both lungs, and continued to suffer from dizziness and nausea, which she attributed to Meniere's disease. By 16 September, she was once more in bed, at home, under doctor's orders. Towards the end of the month, Punin returned to his section of the flat and could be heard shouting at his family in a horribly bad temper. Akhmatova thought his anger was due to a shortage of money. By the middle of October, her face was grey and sickly, her insomnia seemingly incurable. She was finding it difficult to eat. She had decided to sell a painting to Boris Grigoriev,[4] in part to fund a trip to Moscow during which she made strenuous efforts on behalf of Lev.

For all her scepticism about the likelihood that her poems would be published, Akhmatova had already been sent a lump sum of 3,000 roubles from Moscow,[5] and her pension was raised to 700 roubles a month in January 1940. If it had not been for Lev's continuing imprisonment, Akhmatova might have begun to imagine that the authorities had changed their mind about her. That she was not thinking on such lines is suggested by her enigmatic *Poem Without a Hero*, deeply troubled by the theme of sin and atonement rather than celebration, which she began that autumn.

Meanwhile, Hitler turned his attention to the Low Countries and France. His blitzkrieg was swift and merciless, and France sued for peace on 17 June 1940. Stalin was astonished and appalled at the French lack of resistance. Akhmatova was altogether dispirited. She found the news of the Blitz on London particularly horrifying and she continued to follow the course of the war anxiously.

On 5 June 1940, Akhmatova visited Ilya Ehrenburg and read to him her poem about the fall of Paris, which speaks of burying a whole epoch of Russian love for that city and closes sadly on scenes of humiliation and grief, over which:

> *The moon moves like a pendulum.*
>
> *That's how it is, over ruined Paris,*
> *Just such a silence hangs overhead.*[6]

In 1940, she also wrote a poem, "To Londoners," about her unhappiness in reading about the Blitz. She called the destruction of London "the twenty-fourth tragedy of Shakespeare":

> *Only not this, not this, not this—*
> *we don't have the strength to read it.*[7]

Suspicion of internal enemies was far from over. Lydia Chukovskaya had already found herself under new and serious surveillance by the NKVD, interested in manuscripts relating to 1937 and her novel *Sofia Petrovna*. In May 1941, six weeks before Germany invaded Russia, partly to escape this surveillance and partly to protect Akhmatova from it, Chukovskaya went to Moscow to have surgery. Akhmatova, once again trying to drum up support for Lev's release, visited her in hospital there.

Most apologists for Stalin have maintained that the agreement with Hitler was entirely a device to buy time so that Soviet armies could be put on a war footing. However, Stalin seems to have genuinely hoped that war with Hitler was not inevitable and was suspicious of any intelligence reports that suggested otherwise, particularly those which originated from the West. He had no intention of being jerked into a war by Western reports which he felt were designed to produce exactly that outcome. He avoided all actions which might annoy Hitler, and initiated several anti-Semitic measures to placate him. Nor does he seem to have used the time bought with much prescience. When the first news came through that Hitler's Luftwaffe were attacking Russian cities on 22 June 1941, even as three million German soldiers began one of the most brutal invasions of all time, Stalin issued orders to avoid provoking his fellow dictator. German bombers strafed Kiev and Sebastopol, while Stalin continued to urge Soviet forces not to cross the agreed borders.

Punin remembered hearing that war had begun from Akhmatova, who ran in with dishevelled greying hair in her black silk Chinese robe to report Molotov's speech on the radio.[8] Crossed paper strips were pasted on to the windows to minimise slivers of glass in anticipation of bombing. Punin sat at his writing table while Martha Golubeva ironed in the kitchen, and thought how strange it was that, although a large number of people would obviously die, nobody thought it would be himself. He saw in this a similarity to the year of Yezhov's terror.

By 28 June, the full scale of the catastrophe was apparent. The Germans had penetrated 300 miles into Soviet territory and encircled 400,000 men. Minsk, the capital of Belorus, was in their hands. The road to Smolensk was open and the Germans were advancing on all fronts. Within three weeks of the start of the war, Russia had lost two million men and 3,500 tanks.

The brutality of the Germans as they advanced galvanised the natural patriotism of the Russian people as they witnessed the behaviour of German troops, who had been taught that Slavs, like Jews, were sub-human. They bundled villagers into churches and set the churches on fire; they butchered, murdered and raped. Russian bewilderment at what had been happening to them under Stalin was forgotten in a primitive rush of hatred for the German invaders.

Leningrad lay in the German path and air raid sirens and enemy aircraft could soon be heard every night. The city braced itself for a siege. Yet in spite of Leningrad's obvious peril, Akhmatova returned there from a visit to Moscow. The writers and artists in the city were staunchly involved in its defence. Once the terrible siege began on 8 September, three and a half million people began to die of cold and hunger. By autumn 1941 a single lifeline was open, across Lake Ladoga, north-east of the city, which freezes for two months in the north, and four months in the south every winter.

On 30 June, when a call went out for civil helpers, writers and artists clamoured to play their part. Dmitry Shostakovich volunteered, but his application was rejected. One evening, he happened to be playing themes from his Seventh Symphony to a group of friends. At the end of the first movement, he sent his wife and children to the air raid shelter but continued to play though the sound of aircraft guns could be heard in the background.

The poet Olga Berggolts broadcast to the people of Leningrad every day and Akhmatova, too, broadcast, though she was ill and had to be recorded from her bed. Luknitsky went to visit her before she spoke on the radio and noted, "She was lying down. Ill. She greeted me very hospitably. Her mood is good. She is a patriot and the knowledge that at this moment she and everyone else are thinking alike cheers her."[9] What she said in the broadcast was simple and stirring: "My whole life has been connected with Leningrad; in Leningrad I became a poet, and Leningrad inspired and coloured my poetry. I, like all of you at this moment, live only in the unshakeable belief that Leningrad will never fall to the Fascists."[10]

She did not only broadcast. When she was well enough, she went into the streets with a gas mask over her shoulder and took on her stint of fire-watching, and even sewed sacks for sandbags. Akhmatova felt a huge relief at finding herself united to her fellow countrymen in a common aim, but she still needed people to look after her.

In the first air raid on 8 September at 11 p.m., the Punins did not leave their apartment because "It still didn't seem terrifying. . . . We put out the lights and stood at the open window."[11] Gradually, as they listened to the whistle of bombs and the sound of blasts, they began to appreciate the danger.

The very next morning, Irina Punina reported that one of the bombs had fallen on 22 Fontanka, the house of Martha Golubeva's father. With endless air raid sirens that day, Punin only reached the house by the evening. He found the ceilings fallen in, the building likely to collapse and a huge crater in front of the entrance. Both floors had come off the foundations. "Since that day we have spent all our free hours dragging Tika's [Martha Golubeva's] remaining things to my apartment."[12]

The poet and writer Vera Inber gives the best crisply factual account of what it meant to be under siege, in a diary she kept from the beginning to the end of Leningrad's ordeal. She wrote on 16 September 1941: "It gave me a strange feeling when the phone rang and a fresh young voice said, 'The telephone is disconnected until the end of the war.' "[13] Reading Inber's diary, it is possible to understand how the radio voice of Stalin seemed a "great shining consolation"; how dismaying it was to hear on 22 September of the loss of Kiev, and make out the heroism of a city contending with bombs, fires and often forty degrees of frost.

By 16 September, Ahrens and Martha Golubeva were both on civil defence duty. At night the sound of anti-aircraft fire, bombs and terrifying blasts was inescapable. On 25 September, after a day of unremitting air raids from dawn till dusk, Punin wrote in his dairy about the numbers of victims: "The bodies are taken in carts to the graveyard. The ration of bread is 500 grams a day; there is nothing in the markets. Some people I hardly recognise, they have grown so thin . . . it will soon be a month since we were surrounded. *What are 'they' hoping for, why don't they surrender?*"[14] [Author's italics.] In his wish for an end to the siege, though seemingly rational, Punin was not in fact as wise as those to whom stubborn resistance was instinctive. No one could have known at the time, but surrender would have meant mass destruction for Leningrad. Hitler had given an order that when the population of Leningrad had been bombed and starved into submission, they were to be driven out into the snowy waste to die, while the city was to be erased from the face of the earth. "After the defeat of Russia there will not be the slightest reason for the existence of this large city."[15]

At the outbreak of war, Punin is said—by Zoya Tomashevskaya, among others—to have taken his family to the basements of the Hermitage Museum for safety and left Akhmatova alone in the flat on the Fontanka. On the evening of 25 September, Punin mentions that Akhmatova had "long ago" left the flat in the Fontanka and was now living with the family of the Pushkin scholar Boris Tomashevsky. Anna Kaminskaya, however, maintains that the Punin family continued to live on the Fontanka until February 1942 when they were evacuated to Samarkand.[16] While this may well be so, Punin's note on the evening of the first bombardment, 8 September, does not mention that Akhmatova was there. In his journal he records the buzz of the planes, the whistle of bombs and the shaking of the buildings, and admits, "Lately I have begun to go to the bomb shelter at the Hermitage. There it is almost inaudible."[17] As the bombing increased, Tomashevsky took Akhmatova into his home at the House of Writers on the Griboyedov Canal.

Akhmatova moved to the Tomashevsky flat because she was afraid.[18] For a time, she shared a fourth-floor apartment with them in a block with a broken lift, until the caretaker made them somewhere safer to stay in the basement. E. I. Schwartz confirms Akhmatova's presence in the shelter on the Griboyedov Canal on 28 September. It had already been suggested to her that she should be evacuated, but she did not want to go without a companion. She wanted Olga Berggolts to accompany her but Olga firmly refused to leave Leningrad[19] and stubbornly remained there throughout the blockade, working for the city's radio station and keeping her own daily record of events in prose and verse.

Meanwhile, Akhmatova slept in a wide basement corridor at the Tomashevskys where the heavy stone arches offered some protection from the shelling. Once, making her way home with Tomashevsky, they took shelter in a cellar below street level and found they had stumbled into the premises of the old Stray Dog cabaret, long shut but still recognisable. Akhmatova was amused. Coincidences abounded in her life. When Garshin visited her, he brought food. He had little to do with the Tomashevskys. His job as a doctor was exhausting and, as medical supplies became more scarce, he faced a dispiriting struggle against widespread disease and malnutrition.

On 25 September, Punin dropped in on Garshin and told him that Akhmatova was flying out of Leningrad the day after tomorrow. Garshin burst into tears and said, "Well, Nikolay Nikolaevich, so another period of our lives comes to an end." He gave Punin a note to give to Akhmatova. Punin's response was altogether cooler: "It's strange to me that Anya is so afraid: I am so used to hearing about death from her, about her desire for death. But now, when it is so easy and simple to die?"[20]

Before Akhmatova left Leningrad, an old friend, Nadezhda Chulkova, gave her an absurdly generous treat: an omelette followed by coffee and cream.[21] While relishing this amazing gesture, Akhmatova confided that while she had been sitting in the garden with a child in her arms (perhaps one of the Smirnov children) one day, listening to the bombardment, she had reflected on how immorally she had lived her life, and how unready she was to face divine judgement. This goes some way to explaining her new fear of death. These thoughts fed into her *Poem Without a Hero*.

Pavel Luknitsky records on 28 September 1941 that Akhmatova

came to tell him that she and Zoshchenko were being evacuated by air—she thought to Central Asia—on the instructions of Alexander Fadeev. She was ill and weak, but talked to Luknitsky about ancient myths which told the story of the earth surviving, myths which gave her hope even as the buildings around them were being destroyed. Akhmatova left Leningrad at the end of September and wrote on the aeroplane:

> *The birds of death are flying high.*
> *Who now will rescue Leningrad?*
>
> *Be quiet, the city is still breathing,*
> *it is alive and listens to everything,*
>
> *for instance, her sons who groan in their sleep*
> *at the bottom of the Baltic sea,*
>
> *or the cries for bread that rise from within*
> *and reach up to the skies.*
>
> *This hard earth is without pity.*
> *Death stares out from every window.*[22]

On 2 October, Akhmatova sent a postcard to Garshin to tell him she had arrived safely in Moscow and was staying at the flat of Samuel Marshak, the translator and children's author. "Where next? I don't know."[23]

During the first air raids, and after the outbreak of war, Chukovskaya was in a *dacha* at Peredelkino near Moscow and too feeble to go back to Leningrad. On 28 July 1941, she was sent with her daughter and four-year-old nephew by steamer to Chistopol. In October 1941 Akhmatova was told to join a group that the Writers' Union were planning to transport from Kazan to Chistopol. When Chukovskaya heard of this she reflected that it was as hard to imagine Akhmatova in the wilds of Chistopol as to imagine the Admiralty arch there. Chistopol was a wretched small town in the Tatar autonomous republic. In some places mud came up to the waist and for many evacuees, including Chukovskaya, there was unlikely to be any means of earning a living.

Meanwhile, by 26 November Punin found himself weak from hunger, though luckier than many; he was sometimes given a soup made from oats and stewed cabbage at the House of Scholars. The less fortunate stood in the freezing cold waiting for bread. The daily horrors of bombing continued and bombs often fell on people standing in line. "But mainly the starvation is even more terrible. Many are already falling in the streets and dying."[24]

In late November a bomb fell close to the House on the Fontanka and all the glass in the windows was blown out. Punin returned to the house to collect some valuables and there met Garshin with a toboggan collecting Akhmatova's papers and most valued possessions to store at his place. Garshin's loyalty and love for Akhmatova at this period is unmistakable. The Soviet authorities were trying to evacuate as many notable artists and important or useful people as they could while the Germans advanced. Garshin, who could have been evacuated himself, preferred to remain with his wife and children in Leningrad throughout the blockade.

Marina Tsvetaeva had been in Moscow hoping to find friends after her husband's and daughter's arrest. When bombing began there, she evacuated her adolescent son Mur and herself to Yelabuga, across the river from Chistopol, where the Writers' Union was housing its members. In August 1941 she went to Chistopol to beg the writer Nikolay Aseev for a residence permit to live there. This was arranged for her, despite some initial reluctance, but she could see she would have difficulty finding employment. She returned to Yelabuga and took her own life only a few days later.

Many factors led to her despair. She knew nothing of her husband's fate, or what was happening to her daughter. Her sister, Anastasia, believed she may have killed herself in the hope that her son Mur would have a better chance of acceptance without her. However, Anastasia was imprisoned herself at the time and has no evidence to support this. Maria Belkina, who knew Tsvetaeva in Moscow, attributes her death to the onset of mental illness.

When Mur wrote in his diary, "Few people will remember me with a good word," he was sadly prescient. He has been blamed in most memoirs for showing too little appreciation of his mother's poetry even before they left France, and for a selfish lack of concern for his mother's welfare in her last weeks. There is strong evidence of his quarrelling with Tsvetaeva on the last night of her life. Tsvetaeva's suicide note to fellow Muscovites nonetheless asked them particularly to take care of Mur.

Tsvetaeva's own journals show a loss of the will to live even before she left Moscow. She had already written that she was "looking for a hook." Yet Lydia Chukovskaya, a first-hand witness in Chistopol, denies that Tsvetaeva's state bordered on mental illness. She recognised that, in spite of Tsvetaeva's despair, an energy flowed from her whenever she spoke.

Tsvetaeva had written little for more than two years. Her daughter Alya, after she returned from the camps, counted Aseev responsible for her mother's death: "He's a murderer and this murder is worse than that of d'Anthès"[25]—the Frenchman who killed Pushkin in a duel. But whatever anxieties Aseev may have had about associating with Tsvetaeva, he did nevertheless fix her residence permit for Chistopol. Even when the Committee of the Writers' Union announced that good news, however, Tsvetaeva's inner state had remained bleak. Lydia Chukovskaya reported her saying: "I won't find anything. Even if I find a room, they won't give me any work. . . . Tell me, please, why do you think that it's still worth living?"[26] Chukovskaya, helping Tsvetaeva to cross a slippery bridge, expressed relief that at least Akhmatova was not there because she would not be able to bear it. Tsvetaeva, who was at the very end of her tether, was astonished, but to the end people always thought she was stronger than Akhmatova.

Tsvetaeva's last note to Mur is unbearably sad:

Forgive me. It would have been worse to go on . . . I'm *terribly* ill. I'm no longer myself. I love you madly. Tell Papa and Alya—if you see them—that I loved them until the last moment and explain *that I had come to a dead end.*[27]

When she heard the news of Tsvetaeva's death, Akhmatova was desolate. A year earlier she imagined the act of suicide as she wrote of Cleopatra's death, but she remained a believing Christian and always rejected it for herself.

Cleopatra

She has already kissed the dead lips of Antony
And on her knees poured out her tears for Caesar.

Her servants have betrayed her. In the darkness
Victorious Roman trumpets sound in the streets.

And then comes the last captive of her beauty.
A tall man bends to whisper in her ear:
"You will be led like a slave in the Triumph he plans."
The shape of her swan's neck does not alter.

Tomorrow they will fetter the children. Little remains
To be done on this earth except to joke with the fellow.
Then place the black snake with an indifferent hand
On her dark breast in compassionate farewell.[28]

Chukovskaya's belief that Akhmatova would avoid the Tatar wastes of Chistopol was mistaken: she was evacuated there. Among long queues of writers waiting to board the train from Moscow to Chistopol with Akhmatova were Boris Pasternak, Alexander Fadeev, Samuel Marshak and artists and actors from the Vakhtangov theatre. The train had no upholstery or any other comfort. The Jewish poet Margarita Aliger was also there, and kept notes of the occasion. Aliger, whose poems I have translated and whom I met several times both in Moscow and Cambridge, was a short, animated woman of immense seriousness. Her life had been a hard one: she had lost her first husband in the war and though she had a child with Fadeev, he took little interest in his daughter. Aliger was still attractive in her middle years, without being conventionally pretty.

Aliger had first met Akhmatova at the Ardovs in 1940, and was taken into the small room Akhmatova usually occupied there. "I saw only her. The room was full of her alone."[29] Now she observed Pasternak and Akhmatova entering the same compartment, talking quietly and calmly. Other people were understandably agitated but these two seemed almost oblivious of their uncomfortable surroundings.

When they arrived at Kazan, they were taken to the docks and put on a steamer which was going to take them all by river—first the Volga, then the Kama—to Chistopol. With Aliger, whose husband had just been killed, Akhmatova reflected on the enormity of the war that had broken out. She saw it as a war between good and evil and, as such, unlike the meaningless waste of life in the First World War. She was convinced that Russia would be bound to win it.

At Chistopol, a freezing, lonely place, Akhmatova soon learned she was going to be transferred south to Tashkent. Nor would she be alone. Her friends Lydia Chukovskaya and Yelena Bulgakova, the wife of the playwright, were also to be sent south, along with the amazing comic actress Faina Ranevskaya.

On the long train journey to Tashkent, Chukovskaya watched as Akhmatova stared out of the window, saying simply that she was glad to see so much of Russia. Akhmatova seemed to respond to huge changes in her circumstances with a strange impassivity. Joseph Brodsky, in an interview with Solomon Volkov, speaks of her temperament as "phlegmatic," using the word in the sense of the medieval humours.

She and Chukovskaya arrived in Tashkent on 8 November and found themselves in another world, amazing after the frozen wastes of Chistopol. Brown-skinned women offered oriental sweetmeats and flat white loaves of bread in an eastern marketplace. Akhmatova and Chukovskaya marvelled at camels in a majestic caravan, looked around at almond and apricot trees and an abundance of flowers. It was a city of one-storey houses, each with its own garden, where people often lived and worked outside in the shade of a mulberry tree.

Chukovskaya's father, Korney, met their train and took them to a hotel. After a few days, Chukovskaya went to stay with her father, and Akhmatova was given a small room under the eaves in the "House of Moscow Writers" at 17 Karl Marx Street. With an iron roof and only one window, the room was often airless in the heat. Akhmatova stayed there until May 1943. Nadezhda Mandelstam lived in the same house. As all the displaced northerners were penniless, they had to look at the grapes and peaches in the marketplace without any hope of buying the luscious fruit. Akhmatova used to gaze hard and longingly on bunches of purple grapes.

It is not clear how much she missed Garshin. He thought of her often, wrote many letters and sometimes sent her financial help. His wife died in the street from hunger in the first terrible winter and when Garshin told Akhmatova of her death, he stressed his loneliness and his great need for her.

Akhmatova completed the second of her *Northern Elegies* in Tashkent by March 1942.

> *So I have come to it, the very landscape of autumn*
> *Which has terrified me all my life.*[30]

The poem opens in Leningrad with the sky in flames, and she sees the familiar window of the House on the Fontanka squinting at her disapprovingly. She remembers the fifteen "granite" years she lived there with Punin, teaching herself to become another kind of granite. What frightens her most is hearing her own voice in the darkness, grieving for the happiness she had felt when she moved in to be with the man she has left behind. She concludes bitterly:

> *So this is your silver anniversary.*
> *Send for your guests, dress up, celebrate.*[31]

The literary world was perhaps more vital in Tashkent than it had been in Moscow or Leningrad. The city was packed with writers, including Zhirmunsky and Alexey Tolstoy, and there were many social occasions; poetry was often the main entertainment. Akhmatova read her poems at poetry readings, sometimes in hospitals. She was treated with respect and honour by most writers in Tashkent, but several women writers—whom Akhmatova called "the knitters"—were envious of her mixture of helplessness and authority. Chukovskaya continued to visit Akhmatova every day, bringing her food and coal and standing in line for rations. Nevertheless, during Akhmatova's time in Tashkent she and Chukovskaya had a quarrel which led to a break of several years. It now seems clear that this disagreement was connected to Akhmatova's new friendship with the actress Faina Ranevskaya.

As early as December 1941, Chukovskaya complained in her journal that Ranevskaya sometimes came to visit Akhmatova "completely drunk" and bringing a group of other people who disturbed their quiet conversations. She admits that on one occasion Ranevskaya succeeded in making the stove heat the room more effectively, intoxicated or not, and demonstrated a remarkable wit the while, which made Akhmatova laugh. However, Chukovskaya disliked Ranevskaya's manner and thought she encouraged Akhmatova to drink heavily.

By 17 April 1942, Chukovskaya observed that Ranevskaya and her friends came to see Akhmatova even when she was ill with a cough. Chukovskaya saw that Akhmatova was exhausted by the number of guests who wanted to visit her, so she put a note on her door, saying Akhmatova was working. Most people read the note and went away, but Ranevskaya did not, and this made Chukovskaya angry. She disliked the obscene language Ranevskaya chose, a disapproval which increased as Akhmatova received her visitor with great cordiality while losing her temper with Chukovskaya, who was washing the dishes.[32]

Whatever the coarseness of her language, Ranevskaya always showed Akhmatova great respect. Even when she had known her many years, she never addressed her as "*ty.*" She found Akhmatova remarkable, not only for her poetry, which she had loved since she first read it, but for her readiness to see something extraordinary in the most ordinary person.

When Chukovskaya visited Akhmatova on 27 April 1942, she found Ranevskaya lying in Akhmatova's bed. Both she and Akhmatova had clearly been drinking a great deal. When Ranevskaya began to pester Akhmatova for a book of her poetry, Akhmatova asked Chukovskaya to hand over a copy which she had been given earlier. It was not a very tactful request and, as Chukovskaya noted in her diary, "I felt very hurt."[33] For all this apparent insensitivity to her friend's feelings, it should be said that when Chukovskaya fell ill with typhus in autumn 1942, Akhmatova looked after her most generously.

However, Akhmatova refused to hear a word against Ranevskaya. Sadly, as Chukovskaya records,[34] "From the middle of December 1942, I stopped coming to see Anna Andreevna. And she didn't send any couriers for me." Ranevskaya remarks in her memoirs of this time: "I know that in Tashkent she asked Lydia Chukovskaya not to come because Lydia Korneyevna spoke unfavourably about me."[35] Nadezhda Mandelstam also disapproved of Ranevskaya and wrote to Kuzin that the atmosphere around Akhmatova smelled very strongly of actresses and backstage life.

Ranevskaya was born Fanya Feldman in 1896 in Taganrog, a southern city on the Sea of Azov. Her father, Gersh Khamovich, was the wealthy owner of a paint factory and had several homes. He was one of the synagogue elders. Faina did not advertise her origins but when she first thought of becoming an actress her father told her to look in the mirror first, since actresses were expected to be pretty and charming. She was not unattractive, but when Eisenstein wanted her to act in his film *Ivan the Terrible*, the Minister of Cinema—Bolshakov—said she looked too Jewish.

In spite of this, she became an enormously popular comic actress whose films were famous throughout the Soviet Union. She had an improvisatory, impudent style which led Akhmatova to call her "Charlie," after Chaplin, whom Akhmatova admired very much. People often called out lines from her most famous films in the street: "In Tashkent, Akhmatova often called me to walk with her. We wandered around the market and through the old town. She liked Tashkent. Children ran after me and shouted in chorus 'Mulia, ne nerviruiu menya.' " ("Mulia, stop getting on my nerves," a classic line from her film *Podkidysh*, 1940.)[36]

Some idea of the style of Ranevskaya's wit can be gained from the anecdotes collected together as *F. Ranevskaya Monolog*.[37] Once she replied to a friend who asked her if she was Jewish: "What are you saying? I just have an intelligent face." Shrewd observation underlies some of her amusing one-liners. While recovering from a heart attack, for instance, she said, "If the patient wants to recover, the doctors are powerless." When a temperamental young actress declared she could not perform unless the pearls she was wearing in the first act were real, Ranevskaya assured her that "everything will be real. The pearls in the first act—and the poison in the last." She once said to an actor, "Young man, I can still remember decent people. God, how old that makes me."[38]

Ranevskaya's words were not always ironic. When she remarked, "If you only knew my loneliness. Damn the talent which made me so unhappy," the mixture of pride and bitterness sounds altogether genuine. She was a warm-hearted woman who was touched by Akhmatova and wanted to help her:

The first time I went to visit her in Tashkent, I found her sitting on the bed. It was cold in the room and there were traces of dampness on the walls. It was deep in autumn and I smelt of wine. "I will be your Madame de Lamballe as long as they don't cut my head off. I will light the stove for you," I offered. "I have no firewood," she said cheerfully. "Then I shall steal it." "If you can manage it, it would be kind."[39]

Ranevskaya successfully found a block of wood and a man with an axe who was willing to chop the block into pieces small enough to go into the stove. When she remembered she had no money to pay him, and told him as much, he continued to chop her wood, saying, "But I don't need money, you will be warm, and I will be happy for you, and who needs money?"[40] When the stove was alight, Akhmatova discovered a potato and they boiled and ate it with great relish.

Ranevskaya was an open lesbian and it has been suggested that her close friendship with Akhmatova in Tashkent had an erotic element. There are reports that Ranevskaya liked to tickle her feet, which Akhmatova enjoyed very much. Yevgeny Rein agreed that the quarrel with Chukovskaya had been about Ranevskaya and conjectures: "Probably there was a lesbian element in that friendship. Chukovskaya was a bit puritanical."[41]

Anatoly Nayman thought the lesbian element was unlikely, and I have to say what comes through Ranevskaya's memories of this period is a deep love untouched by the least sensuality. She loved Akhmatova's spirit. And it tells us a good deal about Akhmatova that Ranevskaya remarked after her death that life "is boring without her."[42] When people who knew how close she had been to Akhmatova suggested that she write her memoirs, she answered: "I don't write about her, because I love her very much."[43] "For me, Leningrad without Akhmatova is completely faded. I can't even be bothered to climb a hill to look around at it."[44]

Other members of the intelligentsia in Tashkent included a Polish artist, Joseph Czapski, who had volunteered for the Polish army in 1939 and been arrested by the Soviet authorities following the Nazi-Soviet pact. After nearly two years in Soviet prisons, he was released in September 1941 to serve in General Anders' army of former prisoners of war. In spring 1942, he was working in the propaganda section of Anders' temporary headquarters at Yangiyul, a few miles south-east of Tashkent. On a trip to the city in search of cultured company, he made the acquaintance of Alexey Tolstoy and "on one memorable and emotional evening of poetry and conviviality" he met Akhmatova.[45]

Czapski describes Akhmatova sitting next to a lamp wearing a dress of light material, cut very simply, with greying hair held by a red scarf. She might not have been altogether pleased to read his note on the encounter. "She *must have been* very beautiful," he wrote (author's italics), "with her even features, the classic oval of her face, her grey eyes."[46] He was intrigued by the way she spoke as if she were joking, even about the saddest things. She thought his own ease in speaking came from being "the other side of the mirror," where it was possible to say what was thought without the self-censorship habitual to those who had grown up under Stalin. On that evening, Czapski translated some Polish poetry extempore.

Akhmatova usually read her poems in a quiet voice and, even though Czapski found her reading style a strange sort of chant, he also found her poems about Leningrad the only ones of their kind to move him. The intensity of their encounter, as Akhmatova remembered it, can be made out in a poem from the cycle *Tashkent Pages* written in 1959 as if dreaming of a town that could have been Istanbul or even Baghdad rather than Warsaw and Leningrad, where they each belonged:

> We drove one another out of our minds that night.
> The ominous darkness shone as if for us,
> the canals seemed to be murmuring to themselves
> and all the carnations smelled of Asia.

In the last verse she suggests:

> If perhaps you recall this night, in a life
> whose future shape remains hidden from me,
> then simply think these sacred moments once
> returned to a stranger in a dream.[47]

Akhmatova told Chukovskaya that this poem arose after her meeting with Czapski. In his own memoirs, however, Czapski does not write of walking Akhmatova home, or indeed of spending any time with her alone. His description of Akhmatova as "a rather detached person with whom it was difficult to make contact" hardly suggests intimacy, though he adds, "I should have liked to get to know this poet better, see her tête à tête. But I did not dare to pursue the acquaintance."[48]

A 1998 article by Professor Simon Franklin[49] considers the possibility that in writing this poem Akhmatova might have mingled memories of the composer Alexey Fedorovich Koslovsky, who fell in love with her in Tashkent. Akhmatova, however, remembered confiding in Czapski some time at the beginning of June 1942 how difficult it was to discover what was happening to Lev. "I've kissed the boots of all the important Bolsheviks in order to find out if he's alive or not, and I know nothing."[50] Two months earlier, the sad news had reached her that Valya, the elder son of her neighbours the Smirnovs, had died during a bombing raid:

> *Knock with your little fist—I will open the door—*
> *I always opened the door to you.*[51]

Her health continued to be a matter of grave concern. She fell ill with typhus in 1942 and again with scarlet fever in 1943, and on this last occasion was looked after by local Uzbeks, many of whom evidently regarded her as one who had mysterious wisdom. "It was in Tashkent I found out for the first time what a tree's shadow meant in the scorching heat, and the sound of water."[52]

Many of her best poems of these years are dreamy and coloured with delirium. Later, recalling these days in another fever, she wrote "There are four of us," acknowledging Tsvetaeva's greatness and integrity alongside Mandelstam and Pasternak; indeed she is the only one mentioned by name:

> *Herewith I now renounce all earthly goods,*
> *Whatever worldly property I own,*
> *The spirit that is guardian of this place is*
> *Only an old tree stump standing in water.*
>
> *We are no more than guests upon this earth,*
> *To live, essentially, no more than habit . . .*
> *I overhear two friendly voices now,*
> *Speaking to one another in the air.*

> *Did I say two? . . . Look, by the eastern wall*
> *Where raspberry canes are tangling with each other*
> *There is a fresh, dark elderberry branch,*
> *And that is like a letter from Marina.*[53]

Punin was evacuated from Leningrad with his family on 19 February 1942 along with other members of the Institute of Art History. He was in a very bad shape; "close to death" as Kaminskaya put it. Shortly before his evacuation, Punin observed in his journal the silver-white city under a green sky, and the corpses, wrapped only in sheets, lying in the streets. He went and stood for a long time on the embankment looking at the cupola of St. Isaac's. The gilt had been scraped off the dome, so that it would not serve as a marker for incoming planes.

They left across the frozen Lake Ladoga in a lorry. Kaminskaya was then only a child of three but can still remember her terror when the left wheel of the lorry stuck in the ice. Fortunately, Anna Ahrens recognised they were close to the edge of the lake and she ran across the breaking ice to find help. Kaminskaya recalls they were intermittently raked by machine-gun fire.

When Akhmatova heard that Punin would be passing through Tashkent on his way to Samarkand with Anna Ahrens, Irina and her child Anna, she went to the station to see him. Zoya Tomashevskaya remembers Akhmatova waiting with a bunch of red carnations in her hands. Akhmatova was overjoyed to meet Punin again, though he looked as if he might not be strong enough to reach his destination. Punin could only stay in Tashkent for one day but, on reaching Samarkand, he wrote a very moving letter explaining that he had thought of Akhmatova with particular intensity when close to death, and again when he had some hope of living:

It seems to me that for the first time I understood you so completely and clearly, precisely because it was absolutely unselfishly; that is, I did not count on seeing you ever again; it was really my meeting with you and farewell before death. And it seemed to me then that I knew there was no one whose life could be so whole and so complete as yours. From your first poems of youth (the glove with the left hand) to your prophetic murmuring along with the rumble of your poem.[54]

He mentions in the same letter that he knew people were inclined to judge Akhmatova badly for her treatment of her son. This offers an insight into the cruel gossip that surrounded her, which may even have reached Lev in the camps. Punin encouraged her with the thought that she had always done the best she could in the circumstances in which she found herself, and that Lev's childhood with his grandmother in Bezhetsk had in fact been good for him. In the same letter, he admitted feeling guilty on his own part about the way he had treated Lev.

Punin's main purpose was to describe the peaceful happiness he associated with Akhmatova: "You seem to me then, and now too, to be the highest expression of the Immortal that I had come upon in life."[55] Akhmatova treasured his letter and carried it with her, as a tribute few women can hope to earn. In his diary on 23 September 1942, Punin noted:

> I wrote two letters to An. from the hospital. She was in Tashkent and came to the train when we stopped there. She was kind and tender, as she had never been before, and I remember how I was drawn to her and thought a lot about her, and I forgave everything, and confessed everything, and how all this was connected to that feeling of immortality, which came and stayed with me when I was dying of starvation.[56]

On 4 January 1943, Akhmatova received a cheerful letter from Lev, the first since the war began. A telegram from Akhmatova to Ardov confirms that she was getting news from her son through him.[57] Several letters followed saying that he was healthy. In March 1943 came news that signalled Lev's five-year term of imprisonment was over. Lavrov quotes her writing to Khardzhiev of "a telegram from Lev. He's well and has gone on an expedition," and criticises her for sounding emotionless rather than filled with joy. This was not indifference, of course, but fear. Lavrov does not even mention the risk of saying anything more specific.[58] She wrote nothing about Lev in letters to other friends.

Even in 1943, when Lev's sentence had been served, he was still not allowed to leave the far north, though he was permitted to go on geological expeditions and was even paid a small salary. One of the expeditions he led was responsible for the discovery of a significant layer of iron ore, and as a reward for this he was awarded a week's trip to the Siberian city of Turuhansk. According to Lavrov,[59] he was there able to persuade the local military commissar to let him enlist and send him to the front line: "Unfortunately, I did not end up in the best of batteries. The commander of this battery, the old lieutenant Filshtein, took a dislike to me and denied me all rewards and incentives."[60] However this might be, he enjoyed fighting, displayed great courage—rather as his father had done—and found conditions in the army vastly superior to those in Siberia.

Akhmatova moved into a new house in May 1943, 54 Zhukovskaya Street, where she lived in the former room of Yelena Bulgakova. Her quarters were just above those of Nadezhda Mandelstam, at this time very quiet and compassionate. "She is extremely gentle with me."[61]

At the end of August, Martha Golubeva joined the Punin family in Samarkand. He noted dismally in his diary: "It became clear that I don't love her." Perhaps his love for Akhmatova had revived. As he wrote to his niece, M. A. Punina, on 6 October, he had recovered enough strength to spend eight days with Akhmatova in Tashkent: "She is okay, she's holding up, and is still preparing to fly to Moscow, and yet never does. She was very tender and attentive."[62]

When he returned, he found his wife had fallen ill. Up to that time, she had been healthier than she had ever been in her life; now: "she faded away in a month. On the eve of her death, she was emaciated, like death itself. Perhaps in Leningrad she could have been saved . . . lately in spite of her great activity she gave the impression of someone who was very tired of life."[63] On Saturday, 28 August, Anna Ahrens died. When Akhmatova heard of this by letter, she sobbed. Ranevskaya, who had not often seen her cry, asked her what news had made her so unhappy. Akhmatova shook her head as if hardly believing herself how upset she was at the death of Punin's first wife.

In a diary entry of 24 February 1944, Punin mentions that he saw Akhmatova once more on the journey back to Leningrad, when his train stopped again at Tashkent. Akhmatova came in a car, her greying hair covered by a fur hat, and bearing presents. She gave Irina soap, Anna a little dog, and Punin some cigarettes. However, he was irritated by her calling Garshin "my husband," and perhaps for that reason a little sceptical about her saying how much she had been moved by Ahrens' death: "I would like to know what kind of thoughts accompanied this feeling."[64] As Punin began to brood about his dead wife, and the way she had never abandoned him for all his infidelity, he reflected cogently: "She fell out of love with me just enough to stay with me in the conditions of my life."[65]

It was in Tashkent that Yelena gave Akhmatova a copy of Bulgakov's extraordinary novel *The Master and Margarita*. This is a novel with two layers of time: in twenties Moscow, at the time of Lenin's New Economic Plan, a talking cat and a plausible magician cheat greedy writers trying to wangle *dachas* and other easily corrupted Soviet citizens dazzled by the chance of Western goods. The central character, the Master, is writing a passionate novel about Pontius Pilate's encounter with Christ, which has naturally been banned by the censors. Bulgakov's novel asserts a belief in God by entering the *Walpurgisnacht* of the Devil. Surprisingly, his assertion, through the Master, that "manuscripts don't burn," turned out in post-Soviet Russia to be sometimes true. The NKVD kept with extraordinary care the manuscript they confiscated from him.

Between 1943 and 1944, Akhmatova wrote a play, *E nu ma Elish*. The title is taken from an Assyrian epic poem about Creation and means "When Up Above." It was written in three parts and the last was titled "A dream within a dream." The manuscript was burnt at the time of a new crisis after the war. Akhmatova was never able to reconstitute the play as it had been, but Ranevskaya remembers her trying to do so many years later in Leningrad, and claimed that the play prefigured alarmingly many of the terrible events that were to happen to her in the coming years.

In January 1944, the siege of Leningrad was finally lifted and Akhmatova sought permission to return there, not least to be with Garshin again. All through her time in Tashkent, Akhmatova received letters from him. In one of them, in which he told her how his wife had fallen dead in the streets during the first winter, he claimed that he now thought she had been the most important woman in his life. Akhmatova was rather put out by this. But he also wrote asking her to marry him and, since she was tired of living in other people's houses, as she put it, she agreed, even consenting to take his name.

She was so sure of their future together that she told several friends in Tashkent of her plans. Leaving for Leningrad on 15 May, she stayed over on the way with Nina Olshevskaya in Moscow. She gave a poetry reading there, and several witnesses commented on her youthful radiance though she no longer wore her hair in a fringe and, after typhus, as Ranevskaya put it, had grown "catastrophically fat."[66] Aliger remembers that she had never seen Akhmatova looking so young and happy.

Garshin was waiting for her at the Leningrad railway station when she arrived in mid-June accompanied by her friends the Admonis. He had promised he would find a new apartment for them both, since her old room in the Sheremetev Palace was unfit to live in. The House on the Fontanka had no water, light or gas; the windows were smashed and the ceilings collapsed. Olga Berggolts' husband, Makogonenko, was helping to transform Akhmatova's quarters, but they remained bleakly unwelcoming.

It soon transpired her hopes in Garshin had been misplaced: he was no longer the man she had known. He had endured terrible privations both as a doctor and as a man, and witnessed starvation, even cannibalism, during the long siege. Akhmatova was unsurprised to see darkness in his face but intended to go off with him nevertheless. Humiliatingly, it appeared even in their first conversation that Garshin had changed his mind.

She had made no plans of her own other than to put herself in Garshin's hands and after she and Garshin had walked up and down the platform for about ten minutes, she returned to the Admonis and explained without agitation that the situation had changed and that she would now be staying with her old friends the Rybakovs. She could only bring herself to admit to Moscow friends what had happened in a telegram to Nina Olshevskaya a month and a half after her arrival in Leningrad: "I wish good health to all of you. I'm living alone. Thank you for everything. Akhmatova."[67] This elliptical note was supplemented by another telegram which explained that Garshin was mentally ill.

Garshin's distress is well attested, and some part of it was attributable to his experiences during the siege; he had, for instance, discovered his wife's body in the morgue: rats had eaten her face and he was only able to identify her by her clothes. However, another factor which had contributed to his change of mind was his love affair with a woman doctor, Kapitolina Grigorievna Volkova. New research suggests Garshin took up an old friendship with Volkova after the death of his wife and that his wife had recommended that Garshin should marry Kapitolina if she died. Kapitolina looked after him and made sure he had something to eat.[68] After 1943, he came to visit her every day. She seems to have been a beautiful woman, though without much spark. According to his daughter, N. I. Garshina, there was never any suggestion of psychological illness in Garshin during the siege.

Olga Rybakova has pointed out that he did not marry Volkova during the blockade, as gossips reported, but after his meeting with Akhmatova, and that she was not "a young nurse" as the story had it, but a professor and doctor and was born in 1889,[69] which made her the same age as Akhmatova. This makes the story less banal, but not less hurtful. Kaminskaya suggested to me that a reason for his unwillingness to marry Akhmatova was because his first wife appeared to him in a dream and forbade him to do so. This is confirmed by Rybakova, who explained that Garshin had confided just before Akhmatova's arrival that he was having visions of his dead wife, and that she had forbidden him to marry Akhmatova.

Several voices, including that of Yu. I. Budyko, suggest that Akhmatova came to the hospital to see Garshin after the break-up of their relationship, and behaved hysterically there, even fainting.[70] N. I. Garshina remembers overhearing Garshin describe such an incident angrily to Kapitolina. He continued to feel responsible for her, however, and, no doubt, guilty. While she lived with the Rybakovs, he visited her every day for two weeks to explain his behaviour, until one day he said something that infuriated her. After that, she crossed him out of her life. Part of Akhmatova's *Poem Without a Hero* had been dedicated to Garshin, but after their relationship ended she removed that dedication. Rybakova's mother went to Garshin at Akhmatova's request and collected all her letters and destroyed them, along with letters Garshin had written to her.

Other causes for distress followed. In May 1944, Akhmatova showed Emma Gerstein Lev's latest photograph. His handsome grey eyes were gloomy. Gerstein, still in love with Lev, wanted his address: "I wanted to let him know that I was alive and unharmed, despite the bombing of Moscow . . . but Akhmatova did not give me her son's address . . . I was then guilty of an unworthy deed. She briefly left my room. Immediately I opened her handbag in which she kept her private letters . . . and copied down the address."[71] Once initiated by Gerstein, Lev's correspondence with her confirms a continuing grievance against his mother. In February 1945, he wrote:

> You can hardly imagine how disappointed I was to leave Moscow without seeing you. Only the hope that the war will soon end and that I shall come back "cheerful and by a familiar road" can be of moderate consolation. . . . I do not live badly now. The greatcoat suits me, and we have a real abundance of food, sometimes they even hand out vodka; and travel in Western Europe is much easier than Northern Asia. . . . *Mama is not writing to me and that's sad.* . . . Write, I shall be happy to get a letter from you.[72] [Author's italics.]

On 12 April, he writes with more exuberance but repeats his disappointment at not hearing from his mother: "So far my war has been successful. I was part of an offensive, captured a city, drank ethyl alcohol, ate chickens and geese, and took a particular liking to jam. . . . Mama is not writing to me. I imagine I am once again the victim of her psychological games."[73]

The four months before demobilisation after the end of the war Lev spent near Berlin. His complaints at not hearing from his mother continued. He claimed that she took great care of herself and did not care about him at all, and that his spirits were broken, mainly because of her attitude. Almost every one of these assertions seems unjust, since Akhmatova took very little care of her own well-being and was hardly responsible for his poor health. The form of his interrogation had persuaded him both of Akhmatova's indifference and the ability she would have had to help him if she chose to do so. Akhmatova spoke of his tormentors "destroying his soul" while he was in their hands.

But what of her silence? This might simply have been attributed to failures in the postal service, but Gerstein points out that Akhmatova had more or less stopped corresponding with all her friends in the years since Nikolay Gumilyov's execution. She described Akhmatova's silence as a kind of charm; as if she believed there were superstitious omens in whatever she wrote.

THIRTEEN

Peace

What do they want from me, from me, and from Lyova?

—AKHMATOVA

ith the blackout lifted in Leningrad on 30 April 1945 and the Soviet flag flying over Berlin two days later, the end of the war with Hitler was announced on 8 May. There were celebrations throughout Russia, and Akhmatova too—apart from her bitter disappointment over Garshin—could hope for a better life, though Tashkent had changed her appearance. Several observers, including Emma Gerstein, found her small, regular features in an oval face still beautiful. For the rest of her life she did not speak about her rejection by Garshin except to stress his mental collapse.[1]

The Leningrad she returned to had been nearly destroyed by German bombardment. The collapsing ceilings and broken windows of the House on the Fontanka had been repaired but most objects had been looted during the siege. The accountant billeted in Akhmatova's room when she was evacuated in September 1941 burnt everything he could lay his hands on, including Akhmatova's books, to keep warm. It was fortunate that she was as contemptuous of "things" as Tsvetaeva, who had once written:

There is no thing I ever prized
in this empty world of things.[2]

Punin, with his daughter, granddaughter and Martha Golubeva, had returned to Leningrad by train on 24 July 1944. They brought a cat with them, having heard a rumour that all cats had been eaten, but the gardens of the House on the Fontanka turned out to be filled with them.

Much in the apartment remained disturbingly the same as when they had left. The rope Ahrens had tied over the stove to dry her stockings was still in place. Punin felt her death acutely. Akhmatova, still living with the Rybakovs, came to see him frequently, though she did not return to the House on the Fontanka herself until February 1945. As ever, she was concerned about news, often contradictory, about Lev, who was still on the front line. When Osmyorkin, who had once painted her portrait, came to see her soon after her return, bringing a bottle of champagne and some crab, Akhmatova drank from her Central Asian bowl and became a little drunk. When her visitor had gone, Punin returned to help clear up and found her in tears. Osmyorkin had passed on a rumour that Lev had been placed in a penal battalion, which was equivalent to a death sentence: "What do they want from me, from me, and from Lyova . . . they won't be happy until they kill him and me . . . What did my boy see? He was never a counter-revolutionary . . . He is capable, young, full of strength."[3]

Her room in Punin's flat had always been sparsely furnished. Despite all the destruction during the war, a small table, three or four chairs, a wooden chest and a sofa survived. When Ehrenburg came to see her he was touched to make out the same little mahogany table he remembered from twenty years earlier and observed that all the objects in the room seemed to be full of the year 1913. Her drawing by Modigliani, which she had carried away with her, was once again on her wall.

Even more people than before put pressure on the four rooms of the Punin household. Martha Golubeva was now Nikolay Punin's wife. His daughter Irina Kaminskaya, widowed in the war, also lived there with her small daughter Anna. In spite of the wonderful letter Punin had written to Akhmatova after their meeting in Tashkent, he was now part of another family and often too agitated to be kind.

Many years later Lev recalled that his short experience of front-line warfare and the four months after victory were the happiest period of his life. After demobilisation in November 1945, he returned to Leningrad so that he could complete his degree in the History Faculty of Leningrad University. This he did with distinction in four months, while living in the little space Akhmatova could offer. He was then allowed to enrol as a postgraduate student in April 1946. At this time, relations with Akhmatova were good, though later, reflecting on this very period, Lev remarked in a letter to Emma Gerstein: "I cannot forget how difficult it was in 1945 after returning from the Front. Nor can I forget my incredulity then."[4]

Akhmatova had not yet seen the last of Garshin. Aliger writes how he appeared at Akhmatova's door one day: " 'You have come at just the right moment,' she exclaimed quite genuinely. 'I feel really ill and there is no one here to fetch a doctor. How good that you can at least take my pulse.' Who knows why Garshin called? Maybe with condolence and sympathy, maybe with something more. They never met again."[5]

As Akhmatova knew well, she remained under police surveillance. It was during her first weeks back in Leningrad that she burnt the play she had written in Tashkent, and remained afraid to commit *Poem Without a Hero* to paper. A police report on her for this period is shrewd:

> Akhmatova has many acquaintances. She has no close friends. She is good-natured and does not hesitate to spend her money when she has it. But at heart she is cold and arrogant with a childish egoism. She is helpless when it comes to the practical tasks of everyday life. Mending a stocking poses an insoluble problem for her. Boiling potatoes is an achievement. Despite her great fame, she is very shy. . . .[6]

For all the pressure of people in her domestic environment, and for all the applause with which she had been greeted in the Writers' Union in Moscow, Akhmatova was lonely. The reception of her poetry became even more important to her. In 1944, Akhmatova had been among those to appear at an *Almanakh Muz* performance at the Writers' Union. When Prokofiev brought her to the platform, there was thunderous applause. As she made her way to the platform she was still recognisable to Sophie Kazimirovna Ostrovskaya, a young woman of a Polish aristocratic family, who remembered her from the days when she read her poems in 1921: "She had the same regal, supple gait and her carriage was still very erect, swanning and proud."[7] After the reading she stood for a moment alone: "a tall, dark, regal woman, trailing behind her an invisible mantle of fame, sorrow, great losses, hurts."[8]

Towards the end of 1945, the *Literaturnaya gazeta* published an interview with Akhmatova in which she announced proudly that a large collection of her poems was to be put out in early 1946 by Goslitzdat, the State Literary Publishing House. Even as she took pleasure in her strength as a poet, she lamented the damage to Leningrad and Tsarskoye Selo:

> *They've burnt my little toy town*
> *And now there is no wormhole to the past*
> *It is as if I were a river*
> *Forced by this brutal age to change my path . . .*
>
> *And yet if I had been able to look forward*
> *To see my life as it is shaped today*
> *Then I should have felt what envy is.*[9]

The idea voiced in this first verse is repeated in the third of her *Northern Elegies*, which she finished in September 1945, almost in the same words. That poem, too, concludes with the thought that she would have understood envy if she had been able to look forward from the years of her adolescence to the life she was living in 1945. Is it possible that it was the "bitter glory" of her literary fame that her immature self might have envied?

When Sophie Ostrovskaya came up to Akhmatova after another reading, to thank her for returning, surviving "and for just being alive," she apologised for not having written a letter to tell her how much she and her mother loved Akhmatova's poems. She explained she had not dared to do so, imagining Akhmatova had too wide a circle of acquaintances to be interested. Akhmatova replied sadly: "You are wrong—quite wrong . . . I am quite alone. The town is empty for me. There is no one here."[10]

Ostrovskaya was a woman of culture and charm, who had kept a diary from her earliest years, though much of it was burned by her brother or herself in the thirties, when they were imprisoned. She had lived through the Leningrad siege, looking after her sick mother, in grave doubt that any of her journal would survive. At the time of the entries about Akhmatova, she was a member of the Translators' Section of the Leningrad Writers' Union.

Ostrovskaya developed what amounts to a romantic crush on Akhmatova, but her observations are unsentimental even as she vividly describes Akhmatova's "medieval" beauty. She observed a "bitter, cross and scornful" quality in her smile. She notices that "her room is untidy as a bivouac, that she is badly dressed and that her slippers are falling apart."[11] Ostrovskaya reflects on Akhmatova's life as a woman and her unhappiness because "it is always the man who goes away from her."[12] "She is lonely—very. And on the alert. That is why she casts such a glance from time to time—rapid, sidelong, hostile."[13]

If we are to believe Ostrovskaya's memoirs, Akhmatova not only returned her affections but initiated several meetings by telephone herself. In much of the conversation between them that Ostrovskaya records, Akhmatova's ironic tone resembles sentences in the memoirs of Lydia Chukovskaya, which Ostrovskaya could not have read. For instance, when asked whether she was warm enough in her room, Akhmatova replied, "When they put the heat on, it's fine." Ostrovskaya persuasively records Akhmatova's stories about Punin's irascible behaviour and the characteristic inconsistency which led him to hesitate about inviting Akhmatova to see in the New Year with his family, and to be incensed when she arranged to do so with Ostrovskaya. However, since the claim is made in these pages that lesbian advances were made to Ostrovskaya by Akhmatova, doubt has been thrown on her memoirs by some of Akhmatova's admirers.[14] Unlike Ranevskaya, Akhmatova's later friends could not remember any mention of Ostrovskaya.

Ostrovskaya, Akhmatova and Lev saw in the New Year in 1946, and Akhmatova read *Poem Without a Hero*[15] to her and tried to find out how much she understood. Ostrovskaya guessed correctly that the heroine in the first part is Olga Sudeikina. Ostrovskaya notes that Akhmatova then made several unkind remarks about Vera Inber. Ostrovskaya speculates that this may have been because Inber speaks of her walking through Leningrad with a certain Dr. Garshin. She wonders whether it was reading as much that led Akhmatova to remove the dedication to Garshin from her *Poem Without a Hero*. Ostrovskaya frequently makes sharply observant comments stressing Akhmatova's bisexual tendencies and vanity about her posthumous fame: "She is saucy, egotistical, plays at being the good queen, and has ceased to live her own life, for she lives only biographically with an eye on the gesture and the word 'for the future.' "[16]

On 17 July, Ostrovskaya and Akhmatova spent a whole day together, drinking vodka and eating crab salad for lunch. In this relatively comfortable period of Akhmatova's life, the usual financial pressures had been alleviated, since Akhmatova was now receiving a pension of 500 roubles a month, nearly double a professor's salary. As usual, she gave away her money recklessly to anyone who looked to be in poverty and took no great pleasure in it for herself. She was in far greater need of affection.

Describing Akhmatova's lesbian behaviour, Ostrovskaya presents herself as ignoring it yet is unusually explicit at several points in the diary about Akhmatova's sexual advances. For instance, on 22 September 1946 she kept Ostrovskaya with her until 4 a.m.: ". . . a drunken, lonely woman. Once again there is her dual sexuality. I pretend I am shortsighted in everything. . . . It is distasteful to me, odd and strange. She bares her breast, sighs, kisses me on the lips with her sharp stinging lips—the way she once used to kiss her lovers no doubt. I hasten to depart."[17] Ostrovskaya protests her own heterosexuality, but it is hard to imagine such kisses—if they were given—being received without some consent, and paradoxically it is Ostrovskaya's reticence about her own response which makes the passage questionable. Her evidence of Akhmatova's love for vodka, in spite of a weak heart, however, is borne out by many friends.

❧

Akhmatova, now a woman in her middle fifties, would have one last great love in her life. In 1945 Isaiah Berlin was appointed to the staff of the British Embassy in Moscow. Berlin, a distinguished Oxford historian of great personal charm, had spent most of the war gathering intelligence for Britain in the United States. His mission there had been to bring America into the war, and his ability to make successful contacts and to write entertaining and accurate reports much impressed Winston Churchill. Russian by birth, he had emigrated with his family in 1920 when he was eleven, horrified by the violence he had seen in the streets, which was to colour his response to European history for the rest of his life. He went on to become Master of All Souls College, Oxford and took his place at the heart of the British academy. On this visit to Russia in 1945, he had been deputed by the Foreign Office to prepare a despatch about American–Soviet–British relations. It was a posting he accepted eagerly.

Berlin grasped that he himself was followed everywhere, but viewed the situation with equanimity, imagining that the worst days of oppression were in the past and unafraid of being reunited with his own remaining family, an uncalculating optimism which was to prove sadly unfounded.* In Moscow, he met Korney Chukovsky, and through him Boris Pasternak, who spoke to him with immense candour about his guilty relationship to his own Jewishness and his longing to be a fully Russian writer.

In Leningrad, where bookshops were said to have a wider choice of pre-Revolutionary authors, Berlin stayed at the grand if dilapidated Hotel Astoria. The people he observed in the streets were shabbier and more emaciated than Muscovites, and most of the façades of the grand palaces he remembered were pitted with shell bursts even when they were still standing. At the top of Nevsky Prospekt, only a day after his arrival, Berlin and another member of the Embassy staff, Brenda Tripp, entered the bookshop of Gennady Moseivich Rachlin, who invited them into his inner sanctum. Rachlin was an interesting figure, a balding, red-haired Jew who arranged theatre tickets, lectures and contacts with foreigners, and could number many of the literary intelligentsia among his clients.

In the shop, Berlin struck up a conversation with Vladimir Orlov, the distinguished critic, and asked him about the fate of some of the city's writers. One of the names he mentioned was Mikhail Zoshchenko, whose melancholy *Scenes from a Bathhouse* Berlin had once enjoyed. Zoshchenko was, as it happened, in the bookshop at the time, looking pale, weak and very thin. Berlin also asked what had happened to Akhmatova, though he had no idea she was still alive. When Rachlin asked if he would like to meet her, and went off to telephone, Berlin remembered that it was as if he had been invited

---

* His visit was to be part of charges brought against his cousin, who was subsequently imprisoned.

to meet Christina Rossetti. An appointment was made for 3 p.m. that afternoon.

Akhmatova received him like a queen: stately, grey-haired and with a white shawl around her shoulders. Isaiah knew of her only as the brilliant and beautiful member of the group who frequented the Stray Dog and he had read none of her poems written after 1925. Their conversation was at first constrained, and unfortunately, as they began to talk more freely, Berlin became aware that someone was shouting his name. His friend Randolph Churchill had entered the courtyard below and was calling up for him loudly. It was an absurd episode in itself, but was to have dangerous repercussions. Randolph only wanted to get Isaiah's help with the Russian language to ensure the caviar he had purchased would be put on ice at the Astoria. For Berlin's nervous NKVD "tails," however, the fact that Randolph was Winston's son was politically significant.

Embarrassed and apologetic, Berlin excused himself to Akhmatova and returned to the hotel to deal with the caviar. Then he telephoned Akhmatova again. Her reply was simple: "I shall wait for you at 9 p.m. this evening." With how much eagerness she waited for his return we can tell from several poems whose theme is this encounter. As it happened, when she opened the door to him she was dealing with another visitor, a woman who was an expert on Assyrian antiquities. She and Berlin were not on their own again until midnight.

Alone, their conversation became magical. Berlin was able to tell her about all her most intimate friends who had emigrated: Artur Lurye, whom Berlin had known in New York; Boris Anrep, who was working as an artist in London; Salomea Andronikova, who had married a Russian lawyer, Alexander Halpern. Berlin became a link into her unforgotten past. In that closeness, she opened up her whole life for his inspection: her childhood on the Black Sea coast and her marriage to Gumilyov. When she described Gumilyov's execution in 1921, tears came to her eyes.[18] She also told him about Lev's second arrest, in March 1938, the arrest of Punin and the persecution of Mandelstam. Then she began to recite her own poems—*Requiem* and parts of *Poem Without a Hero*—refusing the while to let him copy any of them out as he asked. Berlin recognised he was in the presence of genius, and she saw as much. Perhaps it was his admiration which excited her most deeply. She confessed her own loneliness and, though they sat upon opposite sides of the room and never touched each other, the erotic charge between the thirty-six-year-old man and this ageing beauty of fifty-six was intense.

It was three in the morning when Lev, only three years younger than Berlin, appeared and offered some freshly cooked potatoes, which was the only food in the house. He struck Berlin as formidably well-read, despite his arrest and imprisonment. All three ate together. Berlin talked to Lev for some time, and formed the impression he had a warm and affectionate relationship with his mother. Then Berlin and Akhmatova were alone again.

Berlin enjoyed the variations in Akhmatova's behaviour: the way her queenly manner was sometimes replaced by something sarcastic and slightly malicious. They talked all through the night. In the morning, he kissed her hand and departed. Brenda Tripp, an organic chemist working for the British Council, clearly remembers when he lay down on his bed later that morning he repeated, "I am in love. I am in love."[19]

In the first poem of *Cinque*, which Akhmatova has carefully dated 26 November 1945, she speaks of her own excitement:

> *As if on the edge of a cloud*
> *I remember all you said*
>
> *And because of my words to you*
> *Night became brighter than day.*
>
> *We were torn away from the earth*
> *And rose up like stars together*
>
> *We felt no despair and no shame*
> *Not then, not now, not later.*
>
> *Listen to the way I am calling*
> *you now. I am fully awake*
>
> *and I don't have the strength*
> *to shut the door you half opened.*[20]

Even by 20 December she could still hear the words of their late-night dialogue and in another lyric of that date, she marvels:

> *For such a long time, I have*
> *hated anyone to pity me.*
> *But one drop of your pity, and*
> *I go about with the sun in my body.*
> *That's the reason there is dawn around me*
>
> *And I have the power to work miracles*
> *—That is why.*[21]

They had a final meeting on 3 January 1946, when Berlin stayed once again at the Astoria before leaving for Helsinki. That afternoon he called on her while she was alone and waiting for him. She gave him a copy of *White Flock,* inscribed "To I.B. to whom I said nothing of Cleopatra," and another of her poetry collections, inscribed with a new poem which subsequently became the second in the cycle *Cinque,* which refers to their night of conversation. He presented her with a copy of Kafka's *The Castle* in English and a collection of the Sitwells' poetry.

Within days of Berlin's departure, secret police arrived while Akhmatova was out. Lev was at home, having chosen not to accompany her to a recital of her poetry, when he heard a knocking above him and the sound of a drill. Then pieces of plaster fell from the ceiling, signalling, as any Soviet citizen would recognise, that a microphone was being installed there. They were once again in danger, although on 28 February 1946 the Moscow Literary Fund gave Akhmatova 3,000 roubles to enable her to enter a sanatorium. She was grateful for the financial help but ironic about the microphone that remained above the ceiling.

By 6 January she was writing in lyric four of *Cinque* of the "bitterness" of her meeting with Berlin, realising that their relationship had no future. All the more important, then, to leave him with a vivid memory of their encounter:

> *What can I leave behind to remind you of me?*
> *My ghost? What use is a ghost to you?*

> *A dedication of my burnt play, perhaps,*
> *Of which not even ash remains.*[22]

Her own erotic response to their meeting remained strong, and on 11 January she speaks of the intoxication with a kind of wonder. "We hadn't breathed in the sleepy fume of poppies," she begins, and concludes:

> *What kind of invisible glow was it*
> *That drove us out of our minds before dawn?*[23]

One of the saddest and most beautiful lyrics from *Sweetbriar in Blossom*, "In a Dream," is dated 15 February 1946 and suggests that her obsession with Isaiah Berlin was sharpened by distance, rather as her longing for Anrep had been:

> *I have to bear as much as you do*
> *The blackness of eternal separation.*
> *Why are you crying? Rather give me your hand.*
> *Promise you will enter my dreams again.*
> *We are like two mountains, you and I . . .*
> *We shall never meet again in this world.*
> *If only at midnight you would greet me*
> *Across the stars, with just a single word.*[24]

For a time her literary reputation remained high. She read at an evening in the Leningrad House of Scholars, introduced by Boris Eikhenbaum; on 19 March there was an evening in Leningrad, in which her reading was followed by more praise from Eikhenbaum. After an April event at the Hall of Columns, Moscow University, the critic V. N. Vilenkin remembers that the hall breathed as one as they listened to her. When Ehrenburg reminded her of the ecstatic reception she had been given, she seemed uneasy: "I don't like it," she replied. "But the main thing is that *they* don't like this here." There she was prescient, though just how prescient was not immediately apparent.

On 11 July, Akhmatova spoke on Leningrad radio and many letters came to the radio station afterwards to thank her for her poems, and on 7 August another ovation followed her announcement that she would read poems about Blok. But two days later Akhmatova's poems were denounced in *Protokol 172.*

That Akhmatova's meeting with Isaiah Berlin led directly to the Cold War, as she often said, seems to verge on megalomania; by March 1946 Churchill had already spoken of an iron curtain coming down over Europe. Clearly, however, her own relations with the regime were now once again fraught with danger. Stalin himself remarked, when he read the police report: "So our nun has been receiving foreign spies."[25]

The executive committee of the Writers' Union were summoned to Moscow urgently for a meeting on 9 August 1946. It was at this meeting that Andrey Zhdanov launched his notorious attack on Akhmatova:

> I come now to the question of Anna Akhmatova's literary work. Her verse has recently appeared in Leningrad journals in print runs of increased size . . . Anna Akhmatova is one of the representatives of a reactionary literary quagmire devoid of ideas . . . one of the standard bearers of a hollow, empty, aristocratic salon poetry which is absolutely foreign to Soviet Literature. . . . The range of her poetry is pitifully limited. This is the poetry of a feral lady from the salons, moving between the boudoir and the prayer stool. It is based on erotic motifs of mourning, melancholy, death, mysticism and isolation . . . half nun, half whore, or rather both nun and whore, with her petty, narrow private life, her trivial experiences, and her religious-mystical eroticism. Akhmatova's poetry is totally foreign to the people.[26]

This declaration was serious not only because the anticipated publication of her poems was no longer likely, but also because such condemnation was bound to lead to the loss of her monthly pension. Her ration card from the Writers' Union was taken away, and once again she had no possibility of finding work. Zoshchenko was another writer condemned in the same decree and he was altogether devastated.

Akhmatova had, earlier the same day, been into the Writers' Union on other business. Everyone moved respectfully to one side and thought her serenity and self-control remarkable. On this occasion, as she observes in her own account with some amusement, her calm was preserved by ignorance: "I knew absolutely nothing whatsoever about it. I had not looked at the morning papers and had not turned on the radio, and apparently no one had dared to phone me."[27] She only learned of Zhdanov's diatribe when unwrapping the newspaper around her purchase of fish that evening and reading her own name there.

Pasternak, who was a member of the board of the Union of Soviet Writers, refused to go to the meeting which denounced Akhmatova and Zoshchenko. For this, he was expelled from the board, but went to see Akhmatova, in spite of the obvious danger to himself, and gave her 1,000 roubles, which was soon to be much needed.

That a link exists between Akhmatova's fall from grace and the visits of Isaiah Berlin seems clear, though the standing ovations she had received in Moscow—of which Stalin famously asked, "Who organised this?"—may have played a part. Stalin's special interest in Akhmatova's case is revealed in the minutes of the Organisation Bureau which dealt with refractory Leningrad journals:

> PROKOFIEV:* As far as the poems are concerned, I don't think it's such a great sin to have published Anna Akhmatova's poems. She is a poet with a quiet voice and it's normal even for Soviet people to express sadness.
> STALIN: Apart from the fact that Akhmatova has a name that has been well-known for some time, what else is there to see in her?
> PROKOFIEV: There are some good poems in her war work.
> STALIN: You can count them on the fingers of one hand.
> PROKOFIEV: She doesn't write many poems on present-day themes, Iosif Vissarionovich . . .
> STALIN: Then she should be published elsewhere. Why in *Zvezda?*
> PROKOFIEV: I have to say that all we have rejected for *Zvezda* have been published by *Znamya* [in Moscow].
> STALIN: We'll sort *Znamya* out too. We'll sort them all out.[28]

Akhmatova endured her new disgrace with apparent composure, saying: "I experienced great fame, I experienced great disgrace and I have come to the conclusion that, in essentials, it is all the same."[29]

---

* Chairman of the Leningrad Union of Writers. A minor poet, not the composer.

She refused to grumble at her expulsion from the Writers' Union, only marvelling at the tactical stupidity of those who thought her fame would be stifled by such a punishment, as she remarked with amusement to Chukovskaya on 26 October 1946: "If they had given me a *dacha* and heaped all sorts of rations on me, while secretly forbidding me to publish . . . everyone would have hated me for my material prosperity."

However, she was not indifferent to the way many critics began once again to attack her poetry, finding fault even with her patriotic verse written during the war. Alexander Fadeev, who had once spoken up for her and was now Secretary of the Writers' Union, deliberately referred to her decadence and pessimism in a speech made in Prague, later published in *Literaturnaya gazeta*. At the end of August, Akhmatova asked sadly: "Tell me, why has my great country, which has driven out Hitler with all his technology, found it necessary to drive over the chest of a sick old woman?"[30]

At the beginning of September, Nina Olshevskaya went to stay with Akhmatova for a few days and then brought her back to the Ordynka in Moscow until Lev returned home from his expedition and he and his mother could set out together for Leningrad. On 26 November, Akhmatova went down with pneumonia and continued to have a high temperature until 23 December, though she was able to walk around. Lev and his mother were on particularly good terms all through the following year, and it is touching to hear that she told I. Lyubimova, "The room is tidy, the stove lit. It is nice. . . . Lev cleared up like a good son."[31]

～

However, the political skies continued to darken. On 12 January 1948 the renowned Yiddish actor, Solomon Mikhoels, was murdered in Minsk on the direct orders of Joseph Stalin. His body was left in the snow on a quiet street and his death was declared to be the result of a traffic accident. Few believed that, and most Jews in the arts, particularly those who had been members of the Jewish Anti-Fascist Committee, saw the death as the signal for a possible pogrom.

The Jewish Anti-Fascist Committee had been established in 1942, and played a significant role in drumming up support against Hitler in the United States of America. Mikhoels had been in Tashkent, where the State Jewish Theatre had been evacuated in 1941, when he was directed to go to America with the poet Itzik Fefer and Ilya Ehrenburg. A national reception committee headed by Albert Einstein was organised to meet them. Support was overwhelming. In New York a mass rally attracted 50,000 people.

Ehrenburg, who had been widely read by Russian soldiers all through the war, had contacts through the literary and artistic circles in the West. After the war, and shattered by his discovery of Nazi atrocities, Ehrenburg began, with the novelist Vasily Grossman, to compile a Black Book, which would show his fellow Russians the enormity of Jewish suffering. Such an expression of anguish was perceived as being dangerously nationalistic at a time when the newly formed state of Israel was attracting emotional support. Mikhoels was one of the few Jews who dared to speak out about the terrible losses of the Jewish people in the Soviet Union and did not conceal his Zionism.

Supporters of the Soviet Union in the West paid little attention to these ominous signs, though Paul Robeson, the black American singer who could read Russian and knew something of what had begun to be the fate of Jewish intellectuals, publicly regretted the death of Mikhoels at a concert in Moscow and even concluded his performance with a famous Jewish partisan song of the Warsaw uprising.

Akhmatova was unprotected by Robeson's international celebrity. And, as so often in Soviet times, punishment fell on those close to her. The first to suffer was Nikolay Punin, though he could be said to have brought trouble on himself. As early as 1947, objections had been made against him because he refused to comment on the "ideological level" of works of art. He proudly resigned from the board of the Leningrad Section of Soviet Authors in protest, a dangerous gesture in the context of the times and his earlier brushes with the State. On 26 August 1949, following a decree two weeks earlier, Punin was arrested, the main charge being hostility to the existing government structure of the Soviet Union. Punin's textbook on the history of western European art was said to contain "major mistakes of a formalistic and cosmopolitan character and is permeated with bourgeois subjectivism."[32] In a year when "rootless cosmopolitanism" was often a coded way of referring to Jews, soon to be weeded out of positions of authority, to have Punin's sympathies for the Modernist movements of western Europe called "cosmopolitan" was a dangerous label, suggesting as it did a lack of interest in what was traditionally Russian and Soviet.

His daughter Irina and granddaughter Anna Kaminskaya were devastated, especially Anna, who frequently called Punin "Papa." In his first interrogation, Punin was reported as commenting on the decline of art under the Soviet system, though in his interrogation on 19 September he was ready to protest that he had always valued the tradition of Russian realist art. Akhmatova was not interrogated as a witness. By September 1950, Punin was in Vologda on his way to the camp at Abez in Siberia and writing to his wife that his health was good. He seems to have begun to love her much more in their separation. She responded with gifts of expensive tea, which he knew she could not have afforded to do without borrowing money. He continued to claim he was perfectly well but his health was evidently far worse than he wanted her to know. By 17 April 1952 he was writing to his granddaughter asking if her mother could obtain penicillin for him. His letters to Anna are very moving. Once in the camp, he seemed to be suffering mainly from boredom, since he had been freed from all work and had so little to do with himself that he was considering taking up painting again.

Lev, too, had immediately suffered from his mother's disgrace. In autumn 1947, Akhmatova was already aware that the authorities were giving Lev difficulties in the postgraduate Academy of Sciences. A year and a half after being enrolled as a postgraduate student in April 1946, he was refused entry to the University premises. Lev's exclusion was almost certainly a result of Zhdanov's statement about Akhmatova.[33] Although he was dismissed as a postgraduate student altogether in 1947, he was allowed to defend his dissertation but Akhmatova did not dare go to hear him in case her presence drew undue attention to their connection. One of the people present at Lev's defence of his thesis recollects that, when his biographical details were read out—father Nikolay Gumilyov, mother Akhmatova—every point sounded like an indictment. Nevertheless, on 28 December, Irina Punina remembers a celebratory dinner in honour of Lev's defence of his dissertation for which she cooked a bird and baked pies with cabbage.

On 26 January 1948, Akhmatova suffered an attack of angina pectoris, the medical term for chest pain or discomfort due to coronary heart disease. Angina is a symptom of a condition called myocardial ischemia. It occurs when the heart muscle (myocardium) does not get as much blood (hence as much oxygen) as it needs. This usually happens because one or more of the heart's arteries is narrowed or blocked. It is a sign that the patient is at risk of a heart attack, but is not in itself a heart attack. In May Akhmatova had a temperature of 37.8°C and a violent cough, and it is worth noting that Lev, who had begun to work at the Ethnography Museum, came home every day on his lunch break to look after her.

On 23 June 1949, Akhmatova reached sixty, and remarked, "I never thought I would get this far."[34] The difficulties of her journey, however, were far from over. Lev was arrested on 6 November. Akhmatova was so overcome with shock when the officers came to the door that she found it impossible to move from the bed, and it was Irina Punina who helped Lev to pack. For some time afterwards Irina and Anna sat by Akhmatova's bed. Nobody spoke. Akhmatova's temperature rose and she remained feverish for several days, getting out of bed only to burn all her papers with great urgency.

An unnamed acquaintance of Emma Gerstein happened to be at a reception of the town Public Prosecutor. He mentioned that he had seen a tall woman with a proud head, whose whole manner expressed a self-contained suffering, who had appeared in the town hall. It was Akhmatova, there to discover what was happening to Lev. On this first visit, she discovered he had been sent to Moscow, so she set out for the capital once again to hand all she could collect through the little window of the Lefortovo prison.[35]

Lev was held for a time and, as long as he was there awaiting his fate, Akhmatova sent him 100 roubles a month: a gift of the poet Maria Petrovykh. The Diploma of Historical Sciences was signed on 31 December 1949 but by then Lev had already been sent to the Omsk prison camp in Siberia.[36] In September 1950 Lev's sentence was handed down: ten years to be served in a strict prison camp. Correspondence was to be limited, and parcels of provisions were not allowed to weigh more than eight kilos including the box. Akhmatova must have doubted that she would ever see her son again.

Akhmatova's own life was difficult enough. She now had no pension and was reduced to handouts of flour instead of bread from the

Writers' Union. Nevertheless, every month she sent Lev a parcel and in 1950 she decided that a gesture of compromise and repentance might appease Stalin. She therefore wrote several poems "In Praise of Peace," which by implication praised Stalin, hoping they would do something to soften that fierce heart, but he was entering the last and most paranoid phase of his life. The poems, dated May–July 1950, appeared in *Ogonyok*, though without her name; they were not remarkable. If Stalin was pleased with them, he gave no sign and at this stage of his monstrous career he was unlikely to be moved by any poetic tribute.

By November 1950, as Punin explained to Irina when he had already spent a month and a half in hospital:

> I wasn't judged by a tribunal, since there wasn't any material for a trial, but by a special meeting. My case is based on 1935 and cosmopolitanism . . . Gumilyev [Lev] damaged me without wanting to; they connected me to his case . . . Akuma hung by a thread. Probably her poems in "Ogonek" saved her.[37]

Convinced that it was unwise to plead for her son's freedom in her own name, Akhmatova from this time onward decided to act through well-known authors such as Ilya Ehrenburg. The future Nobel Prize winner Mikhail Sholokhov also wrote a letter on Lev's behalf. Both were unsuccessful. Well-known scientists, too, bravely attempted to help. One academician—Conrad—was willing to look over a manuscript of Lev's which had been smuggled to him out of prison; another academician, Oklinikov, wrote to ask for a review of Lev's case.

On 22 May 1951, after sending a loving birthday telegram to Anna Kaminskaya, Akhmatova suffered a further cardiac crisis and on 28 May, while trying to get together some money for food parcels for Lev, she was taken to hospital. The ambulance brought her to the 5th Soviet hospital with the diagnosis "pre-heart attack condition." The next day, a Sunday, Emma Gerstein found her completely alone: "She lay on her back, stretched out and silent with a terrible pain in her chest. She hardly recognised me. . . . She was at that very moment having a myocardial heart attack."[38] By the beginning of June, however, she had recovered enough for Emma to ask her about the organisation and financing of parcels to her son. On

19 July there was a letter from Lev: "Dear Mama, I confirm receipt of the parcels of post no. 277 and thank you, only in future instead of sending pies send more fat and tobacco; cheaper and better. I embrace you."[39]

On 28 July, Akhmatova came out of hospital and planned to stay on the Ordynka with the Ardovs. The staircase to their flat presented a problem for her. Nikolay Khardzhiev, who was escorting her, suggested a series of absurd options which might lessen the strain on her heart of climbing the stairs. She was so amused that she happily—though very slowly—managed to mount to the Ardov flat.

Lev knew nothing about either her illness or the efforts she had made on his behalf, and stubbornly continued to press his mother to plead for his release in her own name. One reason for this may well lie in the form his interrogations had taken. His tormentors frequently told him that his mother could easily be of help if only she could be bothered. This was cruelly unjust. Akhmatova knew that the impact on what would happen to Lev of anything she said or did was quite unpredictable. Her caution was entirely justified at a time when Stalin had begun to initiate purges which had an ominous similarity to those of 1937. Her stress levels were intolerable.

At the beginning of the 1950s, the only remaining point of stability in Akhmatova's life was removed when the Arctic Institute laid claim to the flat in the House on the Fontanka. She then began an itinerant existence, initially at 20 Krasnaya Konnitsa Street, an apartment with a long, dark corridor and very little furniture; she remained stoical, though Makogonenko, Olga Berggolts' husband, reported that she looked sterner.

In 1952, however, an old friend came back into her life: Lydia Chukovskaya, whom she had not seen since their quarrel in Tashkent ten years earlier, made tentative contact by telephone on 13 June. Akhmatova was eager to renew their friendship. Chukovskaya had heard of Akhmatova's troubles and hesitated before pulling the bell to her room. When she entered, she was struck by Akhmatova's silver hairs and unexpected corpulence. She seemed an altogether different person at first, only wanting to talk about Lev, and repeating several passages from his letters, which she knew by heart. Then they spoke about Gogol's *The Overcoat*, in which Akhmatova saw allusions to Russia under Tsar Nicholas I. But she was not yet ready to read her own poems to Chukovskaya. On

31 August the two women met again—in the company this time of Nina Ardova, who had returned from the Crimea happy, energetic and well-tanned. Akhmatova seemed to be in much better spirits. By 4 May 1953, their evenings together had begun to approach their old closeness. Akhmatova read Chukovskaya several poems, including the poems she had written for Isaiah Berlin, and made her a present of *Poem Without a Hero*.

Akhmatova's financial situation started to improve surprisingly in 1953. She had begun to be given a good deal of translation work, which earned her substantial sums. With feckless generosity, she gave presents to the actor Alexey Batalov, whom she remembered as a small child at the Ardovs', bought a car for Emma Gerstein, and a hat, gloves and shoes for Nina Olshevskaya.

Her health was not good, but when she did go into hospital she was now at least receiving good treatment. On 1 July she wrote to Lev about the separate room she had been allocated at a sanatorium and how good and fresh it was. She sounds almost sprightly when she is able to correct a reference of Lev's to an author he was interested in, and who he had mistakenly thought was a Hun. She points out that he was instead a Turk of the Kitan tribe. Contrary to her son's suspicion, she was always acutely aware of the conditions he was living in: "Yesterday I heard on the radio that it was minus 22 degrees in Omsk. Poor Lyovka." She also asks him to write back politely to Natalya Vasilyevna[40] because the girl had made an unsuccessful marriage, and "repairs my dressing gown, which is coming apart at the seams."[41]

～

During the first weeks of January 1953, the world heard the first news of the so-called Doctors' Plot to murder Soviet leaders. *Pravda* announced the arrests of several physicians, all Jewish, who were declared to be clandestine assassins. Signatures on a petition demanding their punishment began to be collected. Ilya Ehrenburg was among a handful of individuals who bravely refused to sign, and indeed took the additional step of writing to Stalin to explain how badly this would harm Soviet prestige in the West. Stalin hesitated. The full-scale pogrom he had undoubtedly intended to launch was put on hold. His health was failing and he died in March 1953. For many Russians, his death was an occasion of genuine grief. To prisoners and their relatives, however, it brought the hope of release.

For some prisoners freedom came swiftly, but Lev remained in Norilsk. On 2 February 1953 Chukovskaya observed that Akhmatova had written to Kliment Voroshilov, an ardent supporter of Stalin, and had his secretary on the phone. ("Who would she not have gone to see to help Lev?" Chukovskaya reflected.) Lev remained in the Gulag even so though many other prisoners were being released. Punin was never to see home again, but died in Abez in August. Now Akhmatova wrote in a poem to him:

> Your heart always responded to my voice
> Whether in joy or anger, but will do so no more.
> Everything is over. My song drifts
> Into the empty night, where you exist no longer.[42]

Anatoly Nayman comments in *Sir* that Punin is the only man she loved who didn't leave her but who walked the whole way with her from being in love to being no more than a friend right up to his own death.

Conscious that any rash word could damage Lev, Akhmatova answered very cautiously when a group of students asked to see her in 1954. She imagined they might have come from Isaiah Berlin, but in fact none were from Oxford, and it was largely ignorance of her situation that led them to question both Akhmatova and Zoshchenko about their attitude to the Zhdanov declaration. Instead of protesting the injustice of the accusation, as they naïvely hoped she would, she replied submissively that she accepted the Writers' Union decree. Some news of this must have reached Lev, who was incensed by further evidence of her importance, and her failure to act on his behalf.

Parents, children and wives had the right to a visit, so Akhmatova could visit him. On 29 April 1954, Lev wrote a very sad letter to Emma Gerstein, insisting that his mother neither understood nor wanted to understand what he needed and demanding an explanation of why she could not come. The train journey to Omsk, Lev had written earlier, is no more arduous than that to Leningrad from Moscow. It would, however, have been an exhausting journey and no doctor would have recommended it. Ill as she was, Akhmatova

began to prepare for a journey to see Lev with Gerstein as her companion. Lev treated the news that his mother was planning to visit
him in the far north with bitter irony: "I very much want to know
whether Mama has decided to come and see me or is still wavering.
Stanley spent less time preparing to search for Livingstone than
Mama to visit me."[43]

When Lev heard that Akhmatova indeed planned to make the
trip, he was conscience-stricken: "But to get Mama to travel that distance, without a night in Omsk, and for a two-hour meeting, is
impossible. Apart from which, my appearance will only distress
her."[44] In the end, Irina and Anna opposed the trip with such vehemence that Akhmatova changed her mind. One of their arguments
referred to cases when prisoners had suddenly died due to the emotional stress of such meetings.

On 26 May, Lev wrote to Emma Gerstein that he was not particularly surprised at the change of mind, but that he had decided to
write to his mother no longer since, "she either did not understand
or pretended not to understand." To Gerstein, he confided that he
knew the problem: "Her poetic nature makes her horribly egotistic,
in spite of her extravagance. She can't be bothered to think about
unpleasant things, and that she must make an effort."[45] Lev, who was
now beginning to believe he would only be rehabilitated posthumously, was particularly tart about Irina: "You ask my opinion of
Irina Punina. Nina [Ardova] is better, more sincere. Irina is a leech
who will cling to Mama for as long as there's something to suck.
That's the base Punin nature for you."[46]

At the beginning of June, Gerstein wrote to Lev about Akhmatova's unhappiness as a result of this break. With some pathos,
Akhmatova said to Gerstein, "After all, we always used to understand
one another with half a word." Akhmatova wrote three postcards to
Lev nevertheless, which he could not answer for a long time "as they
upset me so much," not because of anything unkind in them but for
what they did not say. He described them as like those written by
people holidaying on the south coast of the Crimea.

He often complained that Akhmatova had not sent the books he
wanted, for instance the second volume of *The Three Kingdoms*, a historical novel of a fourteenth-century Chinese writer, Lo Guanchun.
She hastened to write back and explain that this volume was not yet
published. She was able to send it to him in November 1954.

Lev was now forty-two years old. His health had deteriorated so much that he was recognised as disabled, which was very rare for prisoners. This label had some advantages, since it gave him more time for his scientific studies, and his workload became lighter. According to his own letters, he was even given permission to write, although in the camp all written work was usually forbidden.[47]

Letters from Lev to Emma Gerstein are some of his most bitter. On 25 March 1955, for instance, he wrote:

> You write that Mama is not to blame for my fate. Who else then? If I were not her son, but the son of an ordinary woman, I would have been before anything else a blossoming Soviet professor, a non-party specialist, a great many of them are like that . . . Mama knows . . . that the only cause of my difficulties is my kinship with her. I understand that she was afraid even to breathe in the first few months but now it is her duty to save me, to prove my innocence. To neglect that duty is a crime.[48]

On 27 March, Akhmatova responded with dignity to a letter Lev had written to her directly:

> On 19 March I received your letter which contained a hail of grudges against me. Ever since I have been writing you my reply in my mind. . . . No students came to see me or were interested in my health. A year ago indeed at a meeting at the Writers' Union some kind of English footballers, semi-fascists, asked me quite a tactless question, but my categorical answer cut short any further discussion . . . I did not appear at the Writers' Conference, my name was only pronounced once by Pavel Antokolsky in connection with translations . . . I sent you a very long and detailed letter with the historical information you need (about the period 90 years before our era). . . .[49]

His letters continue to suggest that Akhmatova was not doing much to help him. On 3 April he wrote to Gerstein, reassuring her that he had not written anything unpleasant to his mother: "But it is strange . . . she has absolutely no imagination or concern for me, therefore she considers herself an angel, but to me it seems her attitude is more than cruel. I ask Mama questions . . . she answers irrelevantly."[50]

On 14 April, he wrote a letter to his mother that perhaps goes to the heart of his unhappiness: "All I want from you is a little attention so that, for example, you at least answer my questions to you regarding my personal affairs."[51] In responding to this letter on 29 April, Akhmatova wrote: "I have only just received your letter of 14 April. . . . Believe me, I do write to you myself, daily. . . . You forget that I am 66 years old, that I am carrying three fatal diseases, and that all my friends and contemporaries are dead. My life is dark and lonely . . . all this does not facilitate a flowing epistolary style."[52]

Other prisoners were being released daily, but not Lev. Several of those who had died were being given posthumous rehabilitation, including the theatre director Vsevolod Meyerhold.

Akhmatova herself had nowhere permanent to live and continued to move like a gypsy from one friend to another. Her greatest solace was to keep her mind open to literature. She was reading Hemingway, for instance, though she was less filled with admiration for his *The Old Man and the Sea* than *A Farewell to Arms,* and *The Snows of Kilimanjaro.* Not all her reading gave her such pleasure. On Freud, she declared to Chukovskaya: "He is my personal enemy. I hate him. And everything he has written is false."[53]

She was working on Pushkin again, too, notably *The Stone Guest,* from which she teases out several aspects of Pushkin's biography. While writing about the last years of his life, disputing the likelihood of his sexual involvement with his sister-in-law Alexandrina, Akhmatova correctly guessed that D'Anthès had a homosexual involvement with the Dutch Ambassador. Letters recently discovered by Professor Serena Vitale from d'Anthès to his protector make this last intuition abundantly clear.

The quarrel between mother and son continued. Akhmatova replied to Lev's grudges point by point, particularly denying that she had given Lev's address to Natalya Vasilyevna, and insisting: "How and why was I supposed to think that she loved you?"[54]

The process of releasing Lev seemed to have come to a halt. But in February 1956, at the Twentieth Party Congress—held in secret but soon promulgated all over Russia—Khrushchev spoke openly and for the first time of the full scale of Stalin's crimes against his own people. Inquiries were begun into those of his victims who survived. On 20 March, Akhmatova heard from Emma Gerstein that the case against Lev was going to be reviewed. Akhmatova was radiantly happy as she prepared for Lev to come home, and tried to find out where she could buy him a decent suit.

At last, on 15 May 1956, Lev returned home through Moscow. He had chosen to stay with the Ardovs, not realising that his mother was there. Akhmatova was revivified by happiness at seeing him. Her little room at the Ardovs' was soon filled with cigarette smoke, since Lev now smoked like a chimney. He had returned home with two suitcases stuffed with books rather than clothes. Mikhail Ardov remembers it well: "And I remember Akhmatova sitting with her son in our home, and the faces of both shining. . . . I was nineteen and Akhmatova gave money to me and asked me to help Lev buy some clothes because he hadn't any normal clothes after the camp. So we went and bought some for him."[55]

Akhmatova's relief at having him safe was soon muted by his black resentment, which made itself manifest almost at once.

FOURTEEN

The Thaw

Long ago your horoscope was cast.

—AKHMATOVA

*I*n the summer of 1956, while she was staying with the Ardovs in Moscow, Akhmatova had a telephone call from Isaiah Berlin, who was on a brief visit to Russia. He wanted to meet her, but she refused, terrified that any meeting with a foreigner might lead to the rearrest of her son. Another factor led to her refusal, however. Pasternak alerted her to the fact that Berlin had married on 7 February that year and was travelling with his new wife, Aline Halban (née Gunzbourg), with whom he was deeply happy. Although Akhmatova refused to see him, Berlin's voice stirred memories of her passionate feelings, which came to be expressed in a cycle of poems, *Sweetbriar in Blossom*, dedicated to him.

Akhmatova gave an interesting subtitle to that cycle: "From a burnt notebook." It is possible this refers to a real notebook which once included poems to Vladimir Garshin which Akhmatova had burned. Amanda Haight writes about these poems in relation to others composed for Anrep in *White Flock*, and those for Czapski in Tashkent. Akhmatova was now sixty-seven, but she went on writing love poetry to the very end of her life.

In this period of the brief and seemingly miraculous "Thaw," Alexander Tvardovsky was the editor of *Novy mir* and many writers were published who had been suppressed under Stalin. A new generation of writers from Yevtushenko to Solzhenitsyn were finding a wide readership. Akhmatova was also being rehabilitated. She appeared in two Moscow anthologies in 1956, and had begun to be referred to favourably in the press. When asked about the possibilities of staging the play she had written and then burned in Tashkent, she could not remember it and nor could friends she consulted. The framework was a satire set in World War Two with an author as the heroine who undergoes interrogation and trial and finds a tragic death.

On 6 April 1957, Akhmatova was excited and pleased to be asked by the Writers' Union to become one of the members of the commission charged with the literary heritage of Osip Mandelstam. That year, the distinguished critic and editor, Vladimir Orlov, took the whole of *Poem Without a Hero* for publication in a Leningrad almanac, and Margarita Aliger took six other poems for *Literaturnaya Moskva*. However, Akhmatova was not entirely easy about her new situation and on 11 May 1957 she grumbled to Chukovskaya about the risks *Literaturnaya Moskva* were taking in their rash publication of two or three poems of Tsvetaeva. Nor was her health good.

Akhmatova wrote *Poem Without a Hero* from 1940 to 1945, and continued to work on it until the end of her life. It is one of her few long poems: complex, many-layered and allusive; not a series of linked lyrics like *Requiem*, but imagined and invented as a whole.

The poem opens with a prose passage in place of a foreword, as *Requiem* had, describing how the poem had come to her, unsummoned, on 27 December 1940. She dedicates the poem to friends and fellow citizens who died during the siege of Leningrad the following year. This foreword has an epigraph, "Deus conservat omnia" (God preserves everything), which is the motto on the coat of arms of the Sheremetev family. It is appropriate partly because the action starts in the House on the Fontanka, partly because Akhmatova began to write the poem there, but also because beneath its shifting, allusive surface the central theme of the poem is an evocation of a world seemingly lost for ever. In November 1944, aware of the difficulties of the poem and some readers' wish for clarification of it, Akhmatova added a defiant refusal either to change or explain it. In the words of Pontius Pilate she wrote: "What I have written—I have written." This said, between 1940 and 1961 she added several passages and altered others.

The first section has an initial dedication to "Vs.K.," usually taken to be Vsevolod Knyazev, the young man whose jealous love for Olga Sudeikina led him to kill himself in 1913.[1] Perhaps, as Roman Timenchik has suggested, Knyazev is a cover for another young man, Mikhail Lindeberg, who committed suicide after Akhmatova rejected him.[2] In either case, it is the waste of young life that makes him an appropriate figure; and that this continues in another form in the evil world of Stalinist Russia is pointed up by her use of the date of Mandelstam's death, rather than that of Knyazev.

The second dedication is to Olga Sudeikina; she is an apparition with a fluttering black and white fan, in the person of "Confusion Psyche," one of the parts Sudeikina played to so much applause. It is written in May 1945 and Akhmatova is dreaming of their shared youth. The lyric ends movingly with a description of a cup, perhaps of life, that has passed the young man by:

> *If you like, I'll give it to you*
> *for a souvenir. A flame in a clay dish*
> *or a snowdrop in an open grave.*[3]

In the third dedication, she quoted Zhukovsky's phrase, "Once, on Epiphany Eve," since it is indeed written on 5 January. To the sound of a Bach chaconne, a man enters:

> *who will never be my beloved husband*
> *but what we do together here*
> *will shake the Twentieth Century.*[4]

He arrives late at the House on the Fontanka. It is a foggy night. What he brings is not the first branch of lilac, or a ring or sweet prayers, but the knowledge of death. This section of the poem was written in 1956, and probably refers to Isaiah Berlin.

In a further introductory poem, already written in the odd, stepped form which characterises the first section, Akhmatova lays out her central intention for the whole poem:

> *From the year 1940*
> *as if from a tower, I take a last look*
> *at everything and say goodbye to it.*[5]

The first part of *Poem Without a Hero* is titled "The Year 1913: A Petersburg Tale." The story opens on New Year's Eve in the House on the Fontanka with holy candles. Instead of the guest she is expecting, ghosts from the year 1913 enter her room in the masks of mummers. Then, in a hallucinatory flash, the walls divide and the room in which she is writing is transformed into the White Hall of mirrors in the Sheremetev Palace. People she once knew return to frighten her disguised as Don Juan, Faust or Dapertutto. Her portrait of the Actress on her wall steps out of its frame. The Devil himself, usually taken to be Mikhail Kuzmin, appears, and she guesses at a tail under his evening dress. She wonders:

> *How did it come to pass*
> *That I am the last of us alive?*[6]

It is a hallucinatory, Hoffmannesque landscape, at once intriguing and alarming, especially when the torches go out and the ceiling descends. In an interlude, snatches of conversation arise from the Venice of Casanova and habitués of the Stray Dog.

In the second chapter of "A Petersburg Tale," we return to the heroine's bedroom with three portraits of Olga, the first as the goat-legged nymph, the second as "Confusion Psyche" and the third a shadowed painting that may be Columbine or perhaps Donna Anna from *Don Giovanni*. There are verses unmistakably addressed to Olga:

> *. . . Oh, my flaxen-haired wonder,*
> *You came to Russia from nowhere*
> *The Columbine of the 1910s—*
> *Why do you look at me so sharply?*
> *You are one of my doubles.*[7]

The central figure is afraid that among the masked guests she will identify her past self:

> *I don't want to meet again*
> *The woman I once was*
> *With a necklace of black agate.*[8]

Poem Without a Hero uses quotations from other poets, and allusions to their work, rather as T. S. Eliot had, and there are several echoes of *Four Quartets* themselves, which she had been given as a present by Pasternak and responded to deeply. Eliot's "In my beginning is my end" is transformed in several lines throughout the poem, notably her description of "The future ripening into the past."

Everything is already fixed and fated as the second chapter closes: "Long ago your horoscope was cast." The poem moves through Akhmatova's own memories with loving ease; Olga Sudeikina in the second section of "A Petersburg Tale" is described as living in an apartment furnished in the style of Olga's own home.

Not all the references are literary. The title of the whole poem recalls the opening of Byron's *Don Juan*, but da Ponte's line "You will stop laughing before it is dawn," addressed to Don Giovanni by the Commendatore in Mozart's opera, is closer to the mood of the poem. Two lines of Mandelstam, written in 1920, are also used as a sinister epigraph to the third chapter of "A Petersburg Tale."

The fourth chapter begins in a nineteenth-century house which will receive a direct hit in the bombing of 1942. We are led back to the beauty returning, not alone, and the dead cornet with a bullet in his chest and concludes:

> *I am your old conscience*
> *Who discovered this burned story.*[9]

The sins that must be expiated are those which arose from the commonly accepted belief that Nietzsche had been right to claim that if God was dead, "everything was permitted." Akhmatova herself had never lost her faith in God, but she was altogether a part of the same licentious world. Now she judged her behaviour and those of her friends harshly, holding on only to the possibility of atonement.

Part Two—"The Other Side of the Coin"—had been dedicated to Vladimir Garshin, but after his rejection of her Akhmatova removed his name. One of the epigraphs to this part, taken from a comic poem of Pushkin, suggests it is necessary to drink the waters of

Lethe, since "his doctor has forbidden despondency." Akhmatova admires Pushkin, but she quotes him here ironically, believing that human beings have a duty to remember rather than forget.

This section, however, has a lighter, humorous tone. The heroine imagines an editor's likely objections to what she has written:

> *[. . .] Three themes at once?*
> *After reading the last sentence*
> *You still don't know who loves whom*
> *Who met whom, and when or who*
> *died or who survived.*
> *And who is the author, who is the hero*
> *And what need do we have today*
> *for a conversation between a poet*
> *and a swarm of ghosts?*[10]

This chapter includes a number of stanzas represented only by asterisks. In some editions these blanked-out verses are replaced by verses which appear in Chukovskaya's diaries and refer to the horrors of the Great Terror, notably:

> *All my contemporaries—*
> *hundred-and-fivers or convicts—*
> *will tell you how we lived*
> *in barely sentient fear, raising*
> *children for the executioner,*
> *prison, or the torture chamber.*[11]

In the last section of the triptych, we are once again in the House on the Fontanka, but in 1942 with the city in ruins. Scenes collapse into one another: the River Kama, where Tsvetaeva took her own life, the harsh road trodden by her son in Siberia. From behind barbed wire in the depths of the Taiga, another double is interrogated, as she hears, in her own voice:

> *In cash I paid for you, and*
> *lived under the gun for ten years,*
> *looked neither left nor right*
> *with disgrace rustling after me!*[12]

The poem concludes with lines of terrifying resonance:

> *Then Russia lowered her dry eyes,*
> *Because the hour of vengeance had arrived*
> *And clutching her own hands, fled far away*
> *Ahead of me to the East.*[13]

Although the drama of her own life was far from over, Akhmatova's relationship with Boris Pasternak became surprisingly uneasy. She had never been as close to him as she had to Mandelstam. They had not grown up together in the same city and, though he had helped her on several occasions, she was not sure how much he admired her poetry. In 1956 she told Chukovskaya that she wondered if Pasternak had read any of her poems before 1940; and it still rankled a little that when he wrote *Safe Conduct* he had only praised her simplicity and sense of reality in a few paragraphs, while giving up many pages to describing the genius of Marina Tsvetaeva.[14] Nevertheless, on several occasions, as we have seen, he took great risks to help Akhmatova in times of need. She often stayed at his Moscow flat and, when he quarrelled with his wife, he would sometimes travel to Leningrad and sleep on the floor of her apartment.

Akhmatova regarded Pasternak as a very great poet, even a genius, and Yevgeny Rein agreed that Pasternak probably had asked her to marry him: "She used to joke about it." There was no erotic relationship between them, however, which she said was because of Pasternak's wife Zinaida. Not that she liked Zinaida: "She didn't like Zinaida's attitude. Zinaida thought there was less interest in Akhmatova than Pasternak, and that he had grown into a far more important poet."[15]

In fact, Akhmatova did not like either of Pasternak's wives. She thought Yevgenia, his first wife, was gentle and well-educated but made the mistake of thinking herself a great artist. Zinaida she found a "dragon on eight feet." She particularly disliked Pasternak's last mistress, Olga Ivinskaya, who in 1946 had been working on the Moscow journal *Novy mir.* She was blonde, voluptuous and more than twenty years younger than Pasternak—she was only thirty-four when they became lovers. Pasternak adored her to the end of his life, though he chose not to leave his second wife, but divided his time between his mistress and his family.

Olga was taken away to the camps in 1949, in the same year as Lev. It was then that Chukovskaya, who knew Ivinskaya when they worked together on *Novy mir* in 1946–7, began to send packets of food, clothes and books for her friend the writer Nadezhda Adolf-Nadezhdina, who was in the same camp. When Nadezhdina returned from the camps in 1956, it appeared that she had not received a single one of these parcels. The implication of this story is that Olga had been robbing a friend who was dying of hunger.[16] For that reason, Akhmatova was reluctant to extend friendship to her when she was released, though she insisted that Pasternak should not be disturbed with the story.

On 20 January 1954, when Chukovskaya asked about Akhmatova's relations with Pasternak, whom she had not seen for some time, Akhmatova responded with ironic affection: "Well, he's unbearable. He rushed in yesterday to explain to me that he's a nonentity. And what did that mean? I said to him, 'Dear friend, calm down, even if you have not written anything for the past ten years, you are still one of the greatest poets in the twentieth century in Europe.' "[17] Akhmatova nevertheless showed some impatience when Pasternak expressed his need to write poems to earn money for Olga. On one occasion, she even shrieked at him, "in the voice of an old peasant," that it was a great fortune for Russian culture that he needed extra money. Pasternak continued to write many love poems to Ivinskaya, and often begged Akhmatova to let Olga visit her, but she refused, never telling him why she was doing so because she did not want to hurt him.

What Akhmatova shared with Pasternak often drove them further apart. Pasternak was renowned for his translations of Shakespeare, which were radical, original and deliberately free. Akhmatova was able to read the plays in English* and was able to see the risks he had taken. She admired his versions as poetry but was saddened because her good friend Lozinsky, who had produced translations much more faithful to the original and well-known before Pasternak, had been displaced. In 1957, she declared impatiently that she could not go along with the popular preference for Pasternak over Lozinsky:

---

* Although, to judge from Isaiah Berlin's comments on his conversation with her, her spoken English was hard to understand.

I have often heard that actors prefer Pasternak's translation as more lively, more natural than Lozinsky's. It's true that when spoken by Hamlet himself, the verses of Boris Leonidovich are easier to pronounce. Lozinsky, who achieved a miracle of freedom and lightness in his translation of the Spaniards, is solemn and grand in *Hamlet*, which is more faithful and corresponds better to the spirit of Shakespeare. . . . In attempting to free the text from rhetoric and bombast, Boris Leonidovich purposely simplifies and brings the vocabulary down to earth. . . . But is the text of *Hamlet* not characterized by a hypertrophy of metaphors, ornamentation, even mannerism—is it not this that one can call the gift of the baroque?[18]

Apart from translation, Pasternak continued to work on *Dr. Zhivago*, the novel he had been writing since 1945, and he began to read sections from it to close friends. In 1954, ten of the poems at the end of the book had been published in *Znamya*. On 4 December 1957, Akhmatova told Chukovskaya that she had read *Dr. Zhivago*, and found some pages so bad that she thought they must have been written by Ivinskaya. She particularly disliked what she thought was a preaching tone in the narrative. Nevertheless, she praised the landscapes in the novel: "I sincerely assure you there's nothing in Russian literature to equal them. Not in Turgenev or Tolstoy or in anyone else. They're brilliant." Not all of Pasternak's other friends approved of *Dr. Zhivago*. Yevtushenko, for instance, found it too much like a nineteenth-century novel.[19]

All seemed to be set fair. In 1956 the novel was completed and Pasternak signed a contract for its publication with Goslitizdat. Pasternak gave a copy of the manuscript to Sergio Angelo, a member of the Italian Communist Party, who passed it to Giangiacomo Feltrinelli, the owner of a Milan publishing house, who decided to publish the novel in an Italian translation. Pasternak agreed to this, though he stressed that the Russian version had to appear first. Even with that caveat, his decision to publish abroad was rash. In *Dr. Zhivago*, Pasternak is not only critical of Stalin, as Ehrenburg had been in *The Thaw*, but goes much further in suggesting that the Terror had risen inevitably from the very nature of Bolshevik ideology.[20] And the level of tolerance for such opinions was uncertain.

In 1956, in the wake of the uprisings in Hungary and Poland, there was growing unease in the Party about how far relaxation of censorship could be allowed to go. Accordingly, in September 1956 *Novy mir* decided not to publish an abridged version of *Dr. Zhivago*. Although he had a contract with Goslitizdat, Pasternak began to worry about whether his novel would be published in the Soviet Union at all. His anxiety was well-founded. His book was due to be released in Italy in September 1957, and the Soviet authorities asked Pasternak to intervene. This Pasternak was unwilling to do, and only contacted his Italian publishers when it was too late to stop publication. *Dr. Zhivago* appeared in the West to huge press coverage, but in the Soviet Union Pasternak was vilified as a traitor.

Ironically, a year later, on 23 October 1958, Pasternak received a telegram informing him he had won the Nobel Prize, an award made for his poetry rather than for *Dr. Zhivago*; however, many members of the Writers' Union felt that anti-Bolshevik views in the novel had influenced the decision. Although he was the first Slav writer to be so honoured, it was not long before Soviet displeasure was made known. On 29 October, Pasternak, seeing what must happen next, sent a cable to the Swedish Academy refusing the Prize in the light of the interpretation given to his winning it in his own country. When this news reached the world press, the Writers' Union had to face exactly the criticism of the Soviet Union they had feared. His refusal of the Prize was not enough to placate the Writers' Union, who voted that he ought to be expelled, thus making it impossible for him to earn his living. By the end of October, the Writers' Union had voted that Pasternak be sent into exile.

This last threat drew an anguished letter from Pasternak to Khrushchev, pointing out that he was tied to Russia by birth, life and work and could not imagine a fate outside her borders. Perhaps Khrushchev was moved. At any rate, Pasternak was allowed to remain in Russia and to continue work on translations, but the stress had begun to tell on his health.

As it happens, Chukovskaya had not been at the Writers' Union meeting when the decision to expel Pasternak was taken because she was looking after her father, and she felt guilty that she had been unable to speak up for him. It was she who brought Pasternak the news of his expulsion. She wept when Akhmatova tried to comfort her with the thought that no one else would have had the courage to visit him at such a time. From April 1958, Chukovskaya's diary began to give more news about Pasternak than about Akhmatova.

For her part, Akhmatova disapproved of the wish she sensed in Pasternak for the crown of the Nobel. To Chukovskaya she repeated her belief that in comparison to what had been done to herself and Zoshchenko, what had happened to Pasternak was "a battle of butterflies," a phrase she was to repeat in other contexts. Rebelliously, Chukovskaya noted in her diary that in her opinion, in comparison with what had been done to Mandelstam, Akhmatova's story was also "a battle of butterflies," though she admitted that Akhmatova's torment was impossible to compare, since her son had been sent to a camp. Pasternak, the while, was dying.

In the last years of Pasternak's life, Akhmatova often spoke unkindly of him, though Nayman remembers she always acknowledged his genius after his death even while she was ironic about his helplessness, his treatment of his wives and his choice of women. Shortly before Pasternak's death, Akhmatova, despite her own illness, visited him in Peredelkino. Cancer had been diagnosed and he was weak and in pain. Although Akhmatova was not allowed into his sickroom, Pasternak was told of her presence and she felt some kind of reconciliation between them.

On 22 May 1960, Akhmatova herself was taken to hospital in an ambulance, then transferred to the Botkin hospital in Moscow where she could be looked after by a leading cardiologist. When Chukovskaya arrived at the Ardovs' she found that Akhmatova had been suffering from serious chest pains all day and it had all the air of an infarct. By this time Pasternak only had a few days to live. It was not Chukovskaya who broke the news of his death to Akhmatova on 30 May, but Maria Petrovykh. She reported that Akhmatova, who rarely cried, was moved to tears.

A month later, however, Akhmatova was speaking to Chukovskaya once again about the inappropriateness of talking about Pasternak as a martyr, since he had always been an unusually happy man. Implicitly, she is contrasting her own fate when she points out: "Everything was always published, if not here—then abroad . . . There was always money . . . If you compare his with other fates: Mandelstam's . . . Tsvetaeva's—whomever you take, Pasternak's fate was happy."[21]

The poems she wrote in hospital on 11 June are altogether more generous:

> Yesterday, a voice no one could imitate
> Fell silent; he who spoke to forests has abandoned us.
> He has become a life-giving grain of wheat,
> Or the first rain of which he loved to sing.
> All the flowers in the world will greet his death.
> But suddenly it has become very quiet here
> On this humble planet we call . . . Earth.[22]

Akhmatova was not immune from petty emotions. She had been annoyed when Pasternak did not come to see her. She disliked Zinaida's making clear that she thought Pasternak surpassed her. And Anatoly Nayman acknowledges that in the fifties she felt a rivalry between herself and Tsvetaeva. At the time when Yevgeny Rein got to know Akhmatova in 1958, Tsvetaeva was hugely popular. There was great interest in her life and tragic death and many poets dedicated poems to her. About Tsvetaeva's poetry, Rein said that Akhmatova liked the long poems, *Poem of the End, Poem of the Mountain* and the *Ratcatcher* more than the early lyrics.[23] Nevertheless, she put photographs of Mandelstam and Tsvetaeva on display and pointed out to Chukovskaya eagerly that in one of them Tsvetaeva was wearing a brooch which she later gave to Akhmatova.

∾

In 1958, a slim volume of Akhmatova's poems, the first since Stalin's death, was published in an edition of 25,000 copies. In *Literaturnaya gazeta*, the critic Lev Ozerov described her lyrics as representing a conquest of loneliness, "confessions of a daughter of this century who understood that solitude and isolation force the writer into an impossibly difficult role."[24]

Her poems had never been forgotten, despite all the attempts to suppress them, and the movement in Akhmatova's life from disgrace to recognition and acclaim had begun. As she remarked to Nadezhda Mandelstam in the sixties, seeing with astonishment the publication of Tsvetaeva and Osip Mandelstam, "I am easier in my mind now. We have seen how durable poetry is." And her fame was spreading abroad. In 1958 she was praised by an Italian journal as a model of Soviet womanhood. Reading it, she reflected wryly,

"Where are you, Zhdanov?"[25] On 4 April 1959, Chukovskaya visited Akhmatova in Moscow at the Ardovs'. Akhmatova was lying down, as so often, and she also looked ill. She showed Chukovskaya a little book of her own poems translated into Italian, but was evidently anguished by several glaring mistranslations.

In Leningrad, she continued to live in the same flat as Irina Punina and Anna Kaminskaya until 1961 when they all moved together to Lenin Street. Akhmatova was extremely fond of Anna and kept her photograph above her bed, perhaps showing her some of the love she could have given a daughter. She had no such easy relationship with her own son.

On 26 March 1958, soon after Lev's release from the camps, Chukovskaya records her own first encounter with him in Akhmatova's flat. He had deep lines round his eyes and on his forehead and she did not at first recognise him. The last time she had seen him was in 1932, and then he was a young man of twenty. She observed that he no longer resembled his father and that something in his temples and head shape resembled Akhmatova. He was with his mother for a short time, before leaving for another appointment.

Akhmatova was cultivating a coolness in relation to her son. According to Chukovskaya in her journal on 17 September 1956, Akhmatova mentioned that Lev had been thinking of getting married and had now decided against it. She did not give the name of this possible future wife and shrugged away Chukovskaya's inquiry about how she felt, saying that she did not mind one way or another.

It is understandable that Lev felt he was entitled to his own life, but it was Akhmatova rather than Lev who thought that until they had a chance of a larger flat they should not move in together. Joseph Brodsky recalls: "At this, Lev Gumilyov was beside himself and he flew into a rage ... In the last years before Akhmatova's death they didn't see each other."[26] This is not quite so. Rumours abound that Akhmatova cut Lev out of her life completely. When they did meet, they often quarrelled bitterly, but the break was not complete. Brodsky, who knew her well in those years, rebuts the charge of Akhmatova's indifference to Lev. However, he repeats a terrible story: "Lev did blame her and he said something to her that tormented Akhmatova greatly. I think it may have been the cause of a heart attack. .... This isn't an exact quotation, but the sense of Gumilyov's words was 'For you it would have been even better if I had died in the camps.' He meant 'for you as a poet.' "[27] No doubt Lev had *Requiem* in mind: he was outraged to have his mother grieve for him as if his life were ended on the Cross.

Brodsky concedes that some of Lev's indignation was just. In describing her "hardened heart" as part of the natural splitting between sufferer and writer, he is perhaps describing himself. But his observation that her genuine pain was transmuted once she came to write poems is an insight into what may well have infuriated her son. As a poet "submits to the demands of the muse, the language . . . it is a greater truth than the truth of experience . . . inadvertently you sin against the ordinary truth, against your own pain."[28]

However, Lev's words were certainly hurtful. He felt that, because he had endured so much, he ought to be forgiven whatever he did or said, according to Brodsky. Akhmatova continued to care about her son and on 11 March 1960, Akhmatova spoke to Chukovskaya with particular unhappiness about the slow progress his book on Asian history was making: "His book is getting on, but they don't pay him. He thinks that is my fault. Indeed, according to him, everything is my fault. His health? I don't understand anything about it. He refuses to go to a doctor but he is convinced he has an ulcer."[29]

About Lev's very complex personality, Yevgeny Rein commented: "He had experienced a difficult life in the camp. Maybe I don't know everything . . . because his problems existed before I met him. The problem was that Akhmatova had to live with Punin's family. Both his daughter and his granddaughter."[30] According to Rein, when Lev realised that his mother was unwilling to go through the law courts to obtain a permanent address for him in the Punins' flat:

> Lev said, in that case he does not want to see her, and would never come back to visit her again . . . he went away from Leningrad to Pskov. For the rest of Akhmatova's life, they didn't see each other, and he only came to see her when she was dying. And this situation gave birth to many intrigues. Some people tried to make them friends again, others tried to drive them further apart.[31]

Chukovskaya often tried to explain Lev's attitude to his mother by his sense of abandonment in childhood, when both of his parents seemed so much more interested in their own lives than in him. But Akhmatova guessed gloomily at other factors. On 1 January 1962, when Chukovskaya congratulated Akhmatova on Lev's successful defence of his thesis, Akhmatova responded miserably. She had been in hospital on several occasions, and he had not once come to see her: "He is a sick person. They destroyed his soul there in the camps. They suggested to him—your mother is so famous. She just has to say the word and you will be home. And he won't admit I'm sick. 'You were always sick even when you were young. It's all pretending.' "[32]

In the midst of this domestic turmoil, the Literary Fund allocated Akhmatova a *dacha* in Komarovo: a small, weather-boarded house with a single, rather dark room and a tiny kitchen. It gave her the first sense of her own living space she had enjoyed since before the First World War. It was furnished largely with gifts from friends: there were old chairs with beautifully carved legs, whose upholstery was torn, and a narrow table evidently made from a door. She worked at a long, narrow desk on which stood porcelain candlesticks and a porcelain inkwell. Beneath the desk was a shelf where she kept all kinds of folders and papers. She was in the habit of rifling blindly through this shelf, Brodsky recalled, and would sometimes find a forgotten poem among the papers, often from many years previously. She would say the poem had "surfaced" and then append the correct date beneath it. There were always flowers everywhere, standing in pitchers and jars if not vases.

In these last years, Akhmatova rarely found herself alone. There was always someone to look after her, sometimes other writers from Komarovo, sometimes visitors. In June 1961, Anna Kaminskaya was living in Komarovo with her. But when her mother, Irina Punina, fell ill, Anna had to go home to look after her in Leningrad. For a few days Akhmatova lived with the scholar Vladimir Admoni and his wife, who were old friends. Then Lev appeared and took her to stay with the Ardovs in Moscow—a welcome sign that the break between them was not absolute. Yet for all his help in taking her to Moscow, Akhmatova remarked sadly, "Lev does not take account of how ill I am."[33]

In 1963, Lev Ahrens, the brother of Punin's first wife and his wife Sarra, came to help her. Silvia Gitovich, the wife of the poet and translator, lived in a *dacha* next door, and often prepared great dinners in Akhmatova's "cabin," as she called it.

Akhmatova's poems, which had sustained her through so many terrible years, now attracted to her a group of young, talented poets. The one we know best in the West is Joseph Brodsky, who was thrown out of Russia after a memorably dramatic trial (see pp. 265–7), but Anatoly Nayman, a poet who became Akhmatova's unpaid literary secretary, Dmitry Bobyshev, who went to live in the United States, and Yevgeny Rein, whom Brodsky regarded as his mentor and who was awarded the prestigious Pushkin Prize for poetry in Moscow in 2003, were all friends at that time. Aside from Bobyshev, who was a pure Russian, they were all Jewish. Asked why she was surrounded by so many Jewish friends, Rein raised his bushy eyebrows and insisted, "She was absolutely part of the old intelligentsia where such questions of nationality did not matter in the least."

Rein himself maintained that in his lifetime he had felt no ill effects from being Jewish. Indeed, he did not think of himself as Jewish. His family were not observant, and he did not know the Hebrew or Yiddish language. He had no memory of the fears engendered by the Doctors' Plot because he was born in 1935 and so was too young; or so he said. (He would have been eighteen, however.) His father was an architect and his mother a specialist in German language and literature. "My father died during the war. My stepfather was a Russian of noble blood." He learnt that he was Jewish only from his grandparents.

Rein met Akhmatova first through his aunt, a doctor who had known Akhmatova in Tashkent. After the war ended, she invited Rein, then a young boy, to a grand party at the Astoria Hotel in Leningrad, to which Akhmatova had also been asked. Although there must have been other beautiful women present, something in Akhmatova's presence impressed him deeply.

In 1958, when he was still in his early twenties and had begun to write poems of his own, he learnt that Akhmatova was living somewhere in Leningrad. He very much wanted to meet her again. For the sum of 15 kopeks, the Department of Leningrad Inquiries—which existed for that purpose—gave him Akhmatova's address. Rein remembered she was then living in Flat 4, Krasnaya Konnitsa Street, on the first floor. This was in the Smolny district of the city—not far from Tauride Street, where Ivanov used to hold his salon in the pre-war period. "Some woman opened the door who turned out to be the ex-wife of Akhmatova's brother. When I asked whether I could see Akhmatova, she said there was no problem."[34]

In those years Akhmatova was visited by many young poets, to whom she always responded politely. In June 1961 renovations of the building on Krasnaya Konnitsa Street meant that Irina Punina, Anna Kaminskaya and Akhmatova had to move out. In this move, Akhmatova was helped by Yevgeny Rein, as he explained: "She asked me about other young poets, and what I was doing myself. Then she explained she was moving house and had a problem with her books. She wondered if I had a friend who could help her to pack them."

Rein had a friend—Dmitry Bobyshev, who recalls the occasion— and together they helped her pack. Bobyshev remembers buying string and wrapping paper from a stationery shop before entering the flat on Krasnaya Konnitsa Street. Once inside, he recognised Akhmatova though she was by now portly and grey: she had an unmistakable profile. The young men began to pack books in preparation for moving house. They packed very slowly, commenting on each book as it was taken from the shelves. Many were inscribed. Akhmatova commented particularly proudly on offprints of ethnographic papers written by her son Lev. Gradually the packing slowed altogether and became a conversation about literature.

On Bobyshev's second visit, it was Anna Kaminskaya who answered the door. He thought she looked rather like a young Akhmatova; which is odd since there was no genetic relationship. On this occasion, talking about the drawing by Modigliani on the wall, Akhmatova explained that it was one of a series of twenty which were stored at one time in Tsarskoye Selo but which had now disappeared. Asked what had happened to them, Akhmatova answered: "I don't know—they must have been rolled up into cigarettes and smoked by the Red Army." Bobyshev, though quite convinced that Akhmatova had had an affair with Modigliani, was a little shocked in later years at the sensational discovery made by Modigliani's doctor, Polya Alexander, of Akhmatova portraits in the nude.

Rein continued to visit her, though not frequently, until he made the acquaintance of Joseph Brodsky and introduced him to Akhmatova. Brodsky at the time was far more interested in the poetry of

Osip Mandelstam or the technical virtuosity of Marina Tsvetaeva and had thought Akhmatova was dead, but he wanted to meet her. In 1961 Brodsky had a job in the Crystallography Department of Leningrad University, which gave him access to a library and from this he drew out books such as Mandelstam's *Stone*, which he found overwhelmingly impressive.

Bobyshev remembers Brodsky, Rein and Nayman reading their poems to Akhmatova and she, too, reading her latest poems to them. Sometimes they discussed poetry and once, talking about Tsvetaeva, she recommended that they read Tsvetaeva's extremely difficult "Poem of the Air." What Bobyshev most sharply recalls is sitting round a table with vodka and snacks and feeling wonderfully happy.

By 1961, Akhmatova much preferred to live in her *dacha* in Komarovo in winter as well as summer. It gave her more space than her room in Leningrad, and a measure of independence, though she always needed someone to look after her. When Rein and Brodsky arrived, she had a visitor already with her. Rein observed:

> I realised afterwards that she didn't really like mixing different groups of people together. She told us, "Would you two guys mind going for a walk for a couple of hours?" So we went off and looked at the lake there, and Joseph, who was the son of a cameraman, had a camera with him and took many photographs. When we came back, she gave us each a glass and brought out a bottle of wine.[35]

With Brodsky, Rein began to visit Akhmatova more often.

In Komarovo there were several *dacha*s of writers and scientists as well. Rein remembered: "There was a very nice woman, a biologist, and she suggested we could live in her *dacha* when it was unoccupied. Brodsky was at the time involved in a love affair, and very much needed a place to stay. So he and his girlfriend lived there for a while before returning to Leningrad. After that, Brodsky began to see Akhmatova two or three times a week." Brodsky gives a very telling account of how and why that came about. He was only twenty-one, but was already famous and quite used to receiving praise for his poetry. But in her presence he had an instant awareness of her *goodness*: "In conversation with her, or simply drinking tea or vodka, you became a Christian, a human being in the Christian sense of the word."[36] Some time after his first few visits, when he was returning home in a commuter train, he suddenly realised "who—or rather what—he was dealing with. By this, he undoubtedly meant the force of her genius."[37]

Although Brodsky continued to the end of his life to be more interested in Tsvetaeva as a poet than Akhmatova, he had the most profound respect for Akhmatova's spirit. And he saw what she needed and tried to provide it. For instance, Akhmatova has many references to music in her later poetry, particularly Bach and Vivaldi. Whether or not he gave her a record player at her *dacha* is unclear but he brought her discs, including Purcell, and also spoke a great deal about Mozart.

Akhmatova read her poems to the group of young poets, and was always interested in their opinions, or at least—as Brodsky put it— "We would say what specifically, in our opinion, didn't work. Not often, but it did happen."[38] Brodsky, in the same conversation with Volkov, reported:

> She was a terrific drinker. If anyone knew how to drink, it was Akhmatova and Auden. I remember a winter spent in Komarovo. Every evening she would tell either me or someone else off over a bottle of vodka. Of course, there were people around who could not bear this. Lydia Chukovskaya, for example. At the first sign of her appearance, the vodka was tucked away. . . . After the non-drinker's departure, the vodka was pulled out again from under the table.[39]

Chukovskaya was well aware of Akhmatova's vulnerable heart, and it was not only Puritanism that made her reluctant to encourage Akhmatova's drinking. Nayman agreed that Akhmatova liked to drink, and thought Chukovskaya would in any case, and apart from concerns for her health, have preferred her to remain "like a heroine on the barricades."[40]

When I asked Rein to comment on Brodsky's description of Akhmatova "telling people off," he was oblique: "She was a woman who never hid what she was feeling, what she liked or didn't like." Brodsky was an abrasive character himself in later life but, as Boby-shev pointed out, "with Akhmatova he [Brodsky] was always like silk."[41]

In 1959, Zoya Tomashevskaya, with whom Akhmatova had lived for a time during the war in Leningrad, introduced Anatoly Nayman to Akhmatova. They became close friends, and Nayman helped her in many aspects of her life, though he did not go shopping for her, except perhaps for alcohol. Tomashevskaya knew Nayman's wife, who worked as an art historian at the Hermitage. According to Tomashevskaya, Nayman was constantly begging her to let him meet Akhmatova and one day, when she was driving to Komarovo to bring fruit and flowers to Akhmatova, she agreed he could come with her. He then sat out in the car until Akhmatova peered out, saw him, and invited him in.

Anatoly Nayman left school in 1953, just three months after Stalin's death. His father was an engineer, his mother a doctor. He had had an open heart operation ten months before I met him but still looked spruce and attractive. Where Yevgeny Rein has a heavy face with big features, Nayman's is more Italianate. When he first went to meet Akhmatova, in the autumn of 1959, he was only twenty-three and already had a sense of her as a legend. He was not disappointed. He left "stunned by the fact that I had been in the presence of someone with whom no one on earth could have any-thing in common."[42] When she was living in Leningrad in Krasnaya Konnitsa Street, he remembers being let into the flat and being offered a saucer on which lay a single boiled carrot, not scrupulously peeled.

In his memoirs,[43] Nayman gives us a sense not only of her appear-ance, but even the tone of her voice and the quality of her spirit. She was genuinely disinterested in material things, and once wondered to him why Picasso liked to be photographed with so many expen-sive objects around him: "like a banker," as she put it contemptu-ously.[44]

Nayman came not only to act as her literary secretary, but also to collaborate with her on translations of the melancholy Italian poet Leopardi. At this time Nayman's main source of income came from translating. As they worked together, she became very close to him. Far from exploiting Nayman's willingness to help her, she would proclaim majestically, "We will only do one job a day," and often preferred to postpone necessary chores. When Volkov asked Brod-sky about rumours of a romantic relationship between Nayman and Akhmatova, Brodsky agreed he had heard the rumours many times but dismissed them.

Nayman has the dark, handsome features of Modigliani, which

was why, no doubt, Akhmatova found him very attractive. He, too, was drawn to her. He had recently left his wife and soon began to spend much of his time with Akhmatova. A woman in her late sixties with an unpredictable heart condition, she continued to exert an amazing attraction over young men. Nayman knew about the rumours of a love affair and confesses that he loved her but insists that, although he saw her every day, there was no erotic element in their attachment. He offered help because it was his pleasure to do something useful for her. For instance, he remembers typing the *Northern Elegies* with joy. But their relationship was such that he never used the familiar form of "you"—"ty."

In addition to the reasons often adduced for Lev's bitterness against his mother, Rein added another: "He was jealous of Nayman, who he felt took up too much space in her life, perhaps the space that would normally be filled by a son."[45] Mikhail Ardov disputes this possibility, saying that: "All the young friends around Akhmatova appeared during the five years when Lev didn't see Akhmatova. At all. Five years. From 1961 until her death."[46]

Nevertheless Nayman said he had met Lev on several occasions. He pointed out that he knew many who had spent time in the camps and "none of their reactions were like ours—you could not survive if you didn't change your soul." Nayman agreed that Lev had said something like the words Brodsky attributes to him, but doubted that he would have said them directly to his mother.[47] For all the pain Lev caused her, Nayman remembers that when someone in her hearing suggested that Lev was a difficult person, Akhmatova spoke up sharply to defend him: "Don't forget that from the age of nine he was not allowed to enrol at any library because his father had been executed as an enemy of the people."

Akhmatova was writing about Nikolay Gumilyov when she was close to Nayman. It struck him that she was aware of a string of anniversaries—1962 was fifty years from the first publication of *Evening,* for instance, and 25 August memorable for the execution of Nikolay Gumilyov. Nayman understood her unhappiness that Gumilyov had not lived to enjoy his own fame, but could not himself see anything comparable to Mandelstam in Gumilyov. He pointed out that Akhmatova herself remembered listening, faintly bored, to many other poets reading long ago until Mandelstam began to read.

History placed these four young men around Akhmatova, but Nayman assessed their importance to Akhmatova very differently. He said that she loved Brodsky because she understood the importance of his poetry; and she was fond of Bobyshev also. But he claims she didn't love Rein and wasn't interested in his poetry.[48] This suggests some ill feeling between Nayman and Rein, and other remarks confirm an element of competitiveness. Nayman pointed out to me that Akhmatova wrote thirty letters or telegrams to him and only three to Rein, that he saw her seven times more often than Rein and that this, rather than any interference on his part, led to the fact that in an index to her books there are seventy references to Nayman. It seems Rein suspected Nayman of having some influence on that index.

For all her interest in young poets, Akhmatova was not impressed by those most popular at this time. Of Yevtushenko, then at the height of his reputation, Akhmatova often spoke unkindly though, as she admitted to Nayman, she had hardly read him. She simply distrusted the spiritual and moral life of those who had made their reputation by public readings. Referring to a poet Chukovskaya calls V (presumably Voznesensky), whose popularity also rose during the sixties, Akhmatova said categorically: "I tell you as my considered judgement not a single word of his poems has passed through his heart."[49] Nor was she kind about Bella Akhmadulina, telling Chukovskaya that she had liked a translation of hers very much, but did not then enjoy any of her poems.

Akhmadulina told me a wonderful story about a personal encounter. Akhmadulina had offered to drive Akhmatova to a wedding party in her car, which unfortunately was not very reliable. It broke down in the middle of Moscow. Akhmadulina did everything she could to bring the engine to life, using the cranking-handle and finding people to help her by investigating under the bonnet. Nothing succeeded. When she was at her wits' end, a friend drove up and at once offered the two women a lift to wherever they wanted to go. Akhmatova, however, refused the offer grandly, saying: "I never make the same mistake twice."[50]

Akhmatova was incensed at this time by many of the memoirs that began to be published in the West in the émigré press by people who had never known her intimately. Some of their conjectures were certainly wide of the mark: for instance, they found evidence to support the view that Nikolay Gumilyov discouraged his wife's poetry in a famous poem of hers in which the central figure meets a lover on the embankment and is told that it is absurd for a woman to think of being a poet.[51] As we have already noted, Akhmatova disproved this assertion with her usual wit, pointing out that as she saw Gumilyov at breakfast she had no need to meet him on an embankment.

Akhmatova's life continued to be nomadic. She changed her place of residence many times a year between Moscow, Leningrad and Komarovo. In Moscow, she often took refuge in the Ardovs' flat, particularly when she came out of hospital. With Lev continuing to be angry and far from supportive, Akhmatova became more and more dependent on Irina Punina and Anna Kaminskaya for affection, domestic assistance and for hospital visiting. They were good-hearted and affectionate, as Dmitry Bobyshev could see,[52] but there are many friends who thought they were not disinterested in their attentions.

Akhmatova continued to believe in God, and always had the Church calendar in her head, but in her later years only went to church in order to cross herself and say a prayer. As Brodsky points out, it would have been physically impossible for her to go to church very often.[53] It was indeed difficult for her to travel without help, partly because of her heart trouble. She needed young people to carry her baggage, and someone to make themselves responsible for her having her nitroglycerine tablets. She had to walk to her carriage slowly and leaning on someone's arm. She remained superstitious, taking delight in being born on Midsummer Night, and the conviction that she had assimilated the magic powers associated with that day.

Mikhail Meylach, a noted scholar and editor of Akhmatova's poems, remembers that at fifteen years old he took a copy of her slim volume *From Six Books* with a bunch of lilac and presented it to her at Komarovo, where he was living with his father, also a literary scholar.[54] This was an amazing act of daring from a boy who was at that time painfully shy. She inscribed the book to him. After this, he brought her flowers, fruit and gramophone records to the end of her life, and sometimes helped her with the chores of travelling. Several years later, he and Nayman went to visit Brodsky in his northern exile. Sadly, Nayman and Meylach are now literary enemies rather than friends. They seem to have been held together mainly by their love for Akhmatova.

Many have commented on how interested Akhmatova had become in being remembered after her death, and certainly she did not want to be forgotten. This was more than vanity. The affections of her four young poets, too, represented a kind of posterity.

FIFTEEN

Last Years

You will write about us on a slant. *

—JOSEPH BRODSKY

t the Twenty-second Congress of the Communist Party in October 1961, Khrushchev denounced Stalin as a murderer and ordered his remains to be removed from Lenin's tomb. In 1956 he had only spoken of Stalin's tyranny to a carefully selected audience; now he laid out publicly the full extent of Stalin's crimes. Optimism flooded the Soviet publishing world. Among many signs of the new freedoms, Solzhenitsyn's *One Day in the Life of Ivan Denisovich* was published in 1962 in *Novy mir* and Alexander Tvardovsky was actually considering publishing a section of *Poem Without a Hero*. It was no longer dangerous for Akhmatova to recite *Requiem* to friends and she did so to Lev Kopelev and his wife Raisa at the Ardovs' in May 1962. The Kopelevs became good friends and Akhmatova hoped that Raisa could help Emma Gerstein, who had come under attack in *Oktyabr* for an article about Pushkin's death.

* This may either refer to the slope of her handwriting, or her characteristically oblique style.

In the summer of 1962, Solzhenitsyn came to the Kopelevs' *dacha* and, finding they had a manuscript there of *Poem Without a Hero*, he copied it out with great excitement. At the end of October in the same year, Chukovskaya records a meeting between him and Akhmatova, who had been impressed by the power of Solzhenitsyn's prose though less certain about his poetry and his way of reading it. Akhmatova repeated their conversation to Chukovskaya, beginning with her own remark:

> "You know that in a month you will be the most famous person on earth?"
> "I know. But this will not be for long."
> "Can you endure fame?"
> "I have very strong nerves. I endured the Stalin camps."
> "Pasternak could not endure fame. It is very difficult to endure fame, especially late fame."[1]

After Akhmatova's generous, if oblique, expression of admiration, it was a little curmudgeonly of Solzhenitsyn to express reservations about *Requiem*, which he thought represented personal grief rather than the suffering of a whole nation. Thereafter he sensed a certain coolness in Akhmatova. "Perhaps she didn't like this. She is used to praise and flattery." He underestimated her. Reporting his comment to Chukovskaya, Akhmatova shrugged off the criticism, pointing out that *Ivan Denisovich* too was only about a single man's experience which nevertheless encapsulated a whole people's suffering.

In one respect, however, Solzhenitsyn was right: Akhmatova was now enjoying more adulation than at any time in her life. Letters flooded in from all over Russia. She received many young poets—including Natalya Gorbanevskaya, whose poems she admired—and was surrounded by young men who were willing to go to any trouble to help her. So much was this so, that Rein declared Nadezhda Mandelstam's criticism[2] of Akhmatova in the second volume of her memoirs arose from her own envy: "Akhmatova always had many men and poets around her, like a court; notably Nayman, Bobyshev, and Brodsky. Nadezhda Mandelstam was perhaps a little jealous."[3] Nayman remarked there was another hidden rivalry: Nadezhda thought Akhmatova received more from life than she deserved because she didn't suffer like Osip Mandelstam.

Lev had been made a senior researcher at the Hermitage, where he worked so desperately that his health deteriorated and for a time he had to be hospitalised. In 1957 he was given, for the first time in his life, a room of his own in a communal flat. His financial situation remained precarious, though in 1959 Akhmatova, at the time earning a great deal of money from her translation work, was able to help him. He became a Doctor of Science in 1961, and in 1963 was made a Senior Researcher of the Research Institute of Leningrad University.

At Komarovo, one of her neighbours was Viktor Maksimovich Zhirmunsky,[4] who had known Akhmatova since the first decade of the century, and was now an academician. Sarra Yosifovna Ahrens acted as her housekeeper: a little old lady of nearly seventy who wore a pinafore from morning till night. Doctors told Akhmatova to take a walk several times a day, but she usually only managed to do so once.

Nayman observed how readily Akhmatova changed her style according to the company she kept. "When she was with Chukovskaya, Akhmatova was entirely different from when she was with Ranevskaya, for instance."[5] Nayman did not disapprove of Ranevskaya. When he spoke of her to me, he called her "a hooligan—a free spirit." With Nayman, Akhmatova often showed a wry, sardonic wit and was particularly amused by practical difficulties. For instance, she liked to speak of the "Akhmatova Hour." "This was her name for the lunch break at official institutions which always started, for some inexplicable reason, at the very moment when her taxi was approaching the door."[6]

Humour is a rarity in her poetry, but she often joked in conversation and liked to exaggerate the details of a story to bring out its comic effect. Once, in Komarovo, Nayman looked at a letter that had taken almost two months to reach them and remarked that "it had walked every step of the way." Akhmatova commented, "And we don't know who's been holding its hand."

Akhmatova had come to admire several contemporary foreign poets. In 1963 a collection of poems by Gabriel Mistral, the Chilean Nobel Prize winner who had recently been translated into Russian, particularly moved her. Akhmatova found Mistral's tone strikingly similar to her own early poetry; and even recognised identical phrases. Nayman reported that she was delighted by this, and perhaps surprisingly untouched by competitiveness when she remarked, "That Redskin's overtaken me."[7] Her own translation work, notably of the Yiddish poet Peretz Markish, enabled her to read an even wider range of poets. Akhmatova read Chukovskaya poems of Markish which she had translated, and together they grieved for so much talent destroyed. One image she particularly loved: a dried-up leaf blown in the wind which resembled a golden mouse.

All four of the young poets surrounding Akhmatova wrote poems for her. In 1962, after Dmitry Bobyshev had brought a bouquet of five beautiful roses, she wrote poems to each of her young admirers. For Brodsky she wrote "The Last Rose," in which she begs God for a simple life rather than the heroic fate of famous women in history such as Joan of Arc. The last verse runs:

> *Dear Lord, you see how tired I am*
> *Of dying, resurrection, life itself.*
> *Take everything away, but let me still*
> *Savour the freshness of this scarlet rose.*[8]

Many of the short lyrics written in the early sixties reflect dreamily on her past relationships. Perhaps she was thinking of Boris Anrep when she wrote in 1961:

> *In spite of all the promises you made*
> *when you took the ring from my hand,*
> *in your deepest being you forgot me*
> *and could give me no help at all.*
> *So why, once again, are you sending*
> *your spectre to haunt me tonight?*
> *He is young, red-haired and handsome*
> *with a woman's good looks, and whispers*
> *about Rome and Paris and wails*
> *like a hired mourner, claiming*
> *how indifferent to prison or disgrace he is*
> *and couldn't bear to live without me . . .*
>
> *I found I could manage without him.*[9]

She shifts to the third person when she describes her encounter with her lover's spirit in a dream, as if mocking herself for the invention. The shrug in the last line has something of the amused tone which so commonly enters her speech as her friends recalled it, and never more so than in these last years when she had Ranevskaya to share a joke and young men ready to laugh with her.

Sometimes her still-living lovers from earlier days made contact with her. She received a letter from Artur Lurye, for instance, on 25 March 1963, in which he gave an account of the way his own fame had been "lying in a ditch" since he arrived in the United States. Sometimes she heard from her only surviving sibling, her young brother Viktor, once thought dead, but now in America. She usually spoke of him with a kind of mockery, because he understood so little about contemporary Russian life. He sent inappropriate presents— a scarf, for instance, but no coat to wear with it. He was a midshipman who found himself in the Far East at the end of the Civil War in 1921. On leaving his wife Khanna, he began to travel through China and Japan. He then became a merchant seaman, and when he ended up in the United States after the Second World War, he became a security guard. In this capacity he was hired to guard the composer Shostakovich on a visit to America. It was through Shostakovich that Akhmatova learned that her brother was alive.

In her seventies, Akhmatova remained interested in everything, even poets she disapproved of such as Yevtushenko and Voznesensky. In September 1963, she received the American poet Robert Frost, whose importance was such that Soviet bureaucrats would not allow him into Akhmatova's "kennel." She was taken to the academician Mikhail Alekseev's large *dacha,* where a magnificent white tablecloth had been set with silver and crystal. With her hair elegantly combed, and simply dressed, Akhmatova welcomed Frost with her usual dignity, though she could not help contrasting their fates. At the same time, she reflected, "A single end awaits us. And perhaps the real difference is actually not so great."

She was not entirely free from rivalry, however, for all her habitual calm. Chukovskaya observed on several occasions that Akhmatova seemed to dislike any comparison being made between herself and Tsvetaeva, once noting that Tsvetaeva was far closer to Mayakovsky than herself. She criticised Tsvetaeva for being a pessimist from birth. "She didn't feel comfortable abroad, but she wasn't happy in Russia either." Speaking of Tsvetaeva, Nayman remarked intriguingly: "She was a poet who had no paradise. Akhmatova had paradise and Joseph Brodsky was on the side of those who had no paradise."[10]

In 1963, Khrushchev became concerned that the intelligentsia were beginning to forget the importance of continuing to praise Communism in their writing. Perhaps one of the first signs that the Thaw had its limitations was the rebuke given to Ehrenburg for his memoirs *People, Years, Life*. Then, as part of a campaign to keep the artists of Leningrad in check, Brodsky found himself in the firing line. The campaign began with an article in *Vecherniy Leningrad* in November 1963, written by A. Ionin, Yakov Lerner and M. Medvedev, titled "Subliterary Drone." This led directly and unfairly to formal charges against him. The three authors of this article quoted poems they attributed to Brodsky which he had never written. They also alleged that he met an American in Samarkand to whom he wanted to give a manuscript for publication abroad. He was supposed to be going to steal a plane with his friend O. Shakhmatov and fly it out of the country. In the seventies, Brodsky admitted that this last contained a grain of truth,[11] since he had once considered the possibility while knowing there was little chance of success. Brodsky's attempt to rebut the other charges was never published. Akhmatova did what she could. She spoke to Shostakovich, then Deputy to the Supreme Soviet for the District of Leningrad, but he said nothing could be done for Brodsky because he had been meeting foreigners. Akhmatova's friend Vladimir Admoni, and Efim Etkind, a distinguished scholar at the Herzen Pedagogical Institute, protested out of admiration for Brodsky's poetry.

Sensibly, Brodsky left Leningrad and went to live in Moscow at the suggestion of Mikhail Ardov, who thought he could arrange a safe hiding place in a psychiatric clinic. This Brodsky found intolerable and when he heard that the woman he loved was having an affair with Bobyshev, he rashly returned to Leningrad. On 13 February 1964, he was arrested in the street. Three men seized him, bundled him into a car and took him to a police station where he was put in solitary confinement.

On 18 February, Brodsky's trial began. Several witnesses dared to become formal witnesses for the defence: Akhmatova's friend Admoni, Efim Etkind and Natalya Grudinina, who had once taught a seminar which Brodsky had attended. Distinguished writers such as Konstantin Paustovsky, Alexander Tvardovsky and Samuel Marshak also spoke for the defence. Nothing of this kind could have happened under Stalin.

News of his trial excited wide interest, particularly among the young. At the court on Vosstanya Street, students filled the corridors in support. Brodsky sat on a bench close to his parents. His face showed a strange, innocent calm as the judge ranted at him. Frida Vigdorova took down the words said at this trial. Neither she nor Chukovskaya were able to obtain a formal press pass. (Yevtushenko, Akhmadulina and Voznesensky also asked for press passes and were refused.) Nevertheless, the Vigdorova transcript was successfully disseminated as *samizdat* (typed material copied and circulated) across Russia and was soon published in the West.

The judge began by asking what Brodsky did for a living. He replied, "I write poetry. I translate." The judge then asked him what *regular* work he had, and he replied, "I thought that was regular work." When the judge asked him who it was who had recognised him as a poet, Brodsky replied: "No one . . . Who was it decided I was a member of the human race?" The judge wanted to know where Brodsky had learned to be a poet and he replied, "I didn't think you learnt that. I think it is from God."

These questions and Brodsky's responses coursed round the Soviet Union like a surge of electricity. Brodsky's lawyer then proved that he did indeed earn money from his translations, and that he lived at home and had few expenses, which destroyed the whole basis of the charge of "parasitism." Nevertheless, Brodsky was sent to a psychiatric clinic for the next three weeks to see if he was fit enough to go into exile. Like many others, he found those three weeks the worst of his life. On 13 March he was brought to face a second trial. Chukovskaya and Vigdorova had worked in the interim to gather signatures and by this time many distinguished people had written letters of support for Brodsky. Scholars, writers, journalists and others protested. Yevtushenko, using his fame abroad rather as Ehrenburg had done in another era, returned from Italy and reported that the Brodsky affair was damaging the reputation of the Soviet Union.

Akhmatova and Shostakovich sent telegrams. However, a number of workers and pensioners were suborned to stand up and testify against Brodsky at his trial. He was sentenced to five years' compulsory labour in the far north.

No doubt, as Akhmatova had said about Pasternak's problems, in comparison with the Terrors of 1937 the Brodsky trial was a "battle of butterflies." In the event, his exile meant poetry and fame for him, and Akhmatova, while doing what she could to help him, spoke with ironic approval of the biography "they were making for our ginger-haired boy."

He had to work a twelve-hour day in the fields but the conditions were otherwise not too bad. He had a house in the village and people treated him well. Nayman, who went to Archangelskoye to visit him, found his hut quite cosy with enough to eat and wood to burn. He was even able to listen to the BBC and the Voice of America.

Requiem began to circulate at about the same time as Vigdorova's transcript of the trial. On 15 October 1964 Khrushchev stepped down from power, giving ill health as his reason. The leadership of the Party passed to Brezhnev. Admoni seized the moment to write a petition to the Supreme Court, and a letter from Jean-Paul Sartre to Mikoyan, a key figure in the Soviet leadership, was decisive. In September 1965 the Supreme Court reviewed the case and, though the verdict was not repealed, Brodsky was freed. Nayman received a telegram of rejoicing from Akhmatova and Sarra Ahrens.

Akhmatova knew she was entering the last years of her life. Several of her poems show a preoccupation with death. There are evocative fragments in which she describes lifting the receiver, saying her own name and hearing a voice answer as if from another world. The dead she has loved return to her. Once, while snuffing candles, she remembered 1940. A ghost—probably of Punin—calls her name, "Anna," from the other side of death. Sometimes the sense of being the sole survivor of another age dispirits her. She does not only remember lovers. A short lyric written on 9 September 1964 recalls the death of her childhood friend Sreznevskaya which she finds almost impossible to believe, since:

> You were always at my side
> in the shade of lindens, or the siege, or the hospital.
> In prison cells, or the place of evil birds.[12]

Sreznevskaya's voice calls out from beyond the grave, not to tempt her to die but urging her to wait for the miracle of death to arrive in its own time. The last short line of this poem is once again very colloquial and has a similar ironic shrug in the voice:

Well, all right then! I'll try.[13]

To Nayman, who often protested about this obsession with her own death, she wrote a very beautiful letter on 31 March 1964: "I am now finally convinced that all conversations on this subject are destructive and I promise never to begin one again. We shall simply live like Lear and Cordelia in a cage, translate Leopardi and Tagore, and trust each other."[14]

She only felt truly independent in Komarovo. In 1965, Lydia Chukovskaya gave a troubling verdict on Akhmatova's situation in the Lenin Street flat: "Despite the fact that the Union of Soviet Writers gave the flat to Akhmatova, not the Punins, they did not consider themselves obliged to follow a routine which would correspond to her work, her illness, her writing, her habits. They have tried to portray themselves everywhere as 'Akhmatova's family' but it is a lie: they are not her family."[15]

Brodsky told Solomon Volkov the story of how it was perhaps his own words—discussing the fate of Pasternak's archive—that decided Akhmatova to make a will which named Irina Punina as her heir. But this would put the decision some time after Lev had been released from the camps in May 1956 and it seems likely that her first will, leaving everything to the Punins, was made when Lev was far away and she was afraid that after her death, as she put it, "the residents' management committee would come round for the jumble."[16]

She went to some trouble to change this will, by writing a memorandum in one of her notebooks which would automatically revoke her previous will and mean that Lev, as her son, became the sole heir. This memorandum, however, since it was not witnessed by a notary, had no legal effect. Nayman advised her that a notary was essential and, though she shouted at him for the suggestion, she took it on board. On 29 April 1965—that is, a little under a year before her death—she suddenly decided they must call a taxi and go to the notary's office.

The office, in Moisenko Street, turned out to be up three flights of steep stairs. Nayman, who knew that the doctors had advised her against any such climb, thought they should return home and that the notary could easily visit her there. Akhmatova slowly and stubbornly insisted on climbing the stairs, but was too exhausted to write when they at last reached the notary's office. It was Nayman who wrote, at the notary's direction, and she managed to sign. When they were once again in the street, she muttered: "What inheritance to speak of? Tuck Modi's drawing of me under your arm, and go."[17]

Sadly, she and her son were hardly seeing one another, partly because Lev was putting most of his energy into his work. He had set himself the task of understanding the history of Asia and Siberia in such a way as to acknowledge the greatness of the Mongol Empire, the importance of Genghis Khan and of the Huns who had held back the advance of the Chinese. The book, which gave this Eurasian version of history, was published in 1961. It was immediately savaged by an article in *Vestnik drevney istorii*, which accused Lev of not knowing the original sources he was quoting and having no acquaintance with modern scientific literature on the topic in Chinese and Japanese. Fortunately, the Head Librarian of the Hermitage, Matvey Gukovsky, and the Director of the Hermitage, Professor Adamonov, objected both to the tone of this review and its conclusions. Nevertheless, Lev continued to have many opponents. His second book, *Ancient Turks*, was not published until 1967, a year after Akhmatova's death.

In these last years of her life, unexpectedly and fortunately, Akhmatova began to enjoy worldwide fame. On 30 May 1964, a special ceremony at the Mayakovsky Museum celebrated the fiftieth anniversary of the publication of *Rosary* and in 1965 a collection of Akhmatova's poetry, over four hundred pages long, was at last published in the Soviet Union. Heinrich Böll, who had read her work in translation, came to visit her in Komarovo and declared himself proud to have met her.

She was translated into many languages, and awarded prestigious honours, of which the most important were the Etna-Taormina Prize and an Honorary Doctorate at the University of Oxford. The Italian literary prize was awarded by the Comunità Europea degli Scrittori. Both Jean-Paul Sartre and Simone de Beauvoir, then two of the most famous writers in the world, telephoned to congratulate her. When she replied to accept this honour, she described it as coming from "a country I have loved tenderly all my life, which has shed a ray of sunshine on my work." As was customary for Soviet citizens at this period, it took several months for her travel documents to be processed. She was amused at the delay: "What do they think—that I won't come back? That I stayed here when everyone was leaving, that I've lived my whole life in this country—and what a life!—in order to change everything now!"[18]

If we remember the precarious state of her health, and the constant help she needed to get about in Moscow and Leningrad, her courage in planning travel to Sicily to collect her award in person is remarkable. She intended that her old friend Nina Olshevskaya should accompany her, but sadly Olshevskaya had a stroke while performing in Minsk. Irina Punina took her place as travelling companion. Akhmatova was very upset by her friend's unexpected illness, and asked Nayman to fly to Minsk immediately to find out what was happening to her. He telephoned from Minsk to report that Nina continued to be ill.

Akhmatova and Irina travelled to Italy by train. In general she liked travelling by train, partly because railways had changed very little since the beginning of the century. Nevertheless, moving from place to place by any form of transport was difficult for her. Supportive friends had to arrive at the station long before the train came in. A young person would be put in charge of Akhmatova's luggage, and another had to be at her side with her nitroglycerine tablets for her heart. She could only walk to her carriage slowly, leaning on a companion's arm and stopping to rest from time to time.

Akhmatova and Irina travelled first to Rome, and she sent a postcard to Anatoly Nayman from the Piazza di Spagna which read: "This is what it is like, this Rome. Like this, or even better. Very warm. Latterly came through a pink and scarlet autumn, but beyond Minsk there were snowstorms dancing and I thought of Nina. . . ."[19] Two days later, she wrote again, describing a visit to the Trevi Fountain and how moving she had found it to drive down the Via Appia, and see Raphael's tomb in the Pantheon. Her own health was not reliable, however. A postcard from Rome to Nayman dated 9 December 1964 reports that she is waiting for the Embassy doctor to confirm whether she was well enough to go on to Taormina.[20]

She and Irina set out for Sicily by train and then by ship. On the morning of 10 December they arrived in Sicily and Akhmatova dozed for the rest of the day, though it is not clear whether this was exhaustion or a side-effect of her medication. They found Taormina filled with flowers and stayed in a charming old monastery. On 12 December she wrote Nayman a letter rather than a postcard, describing the arrangements:

> Poetry concert in the hotel this evening. Everyone will read in their own language. . . . Tomorrow the award of the prize in a solemn ceremony—in Catania—then Rome again and home. . . . It's all like a dream. For some reason writing letters is not at all difficult. . . . The doctor has given me some wonderful medicine and I felt better straightaway. How is my Nina? What would comfort her?[21]

In the same letter she sent a message to Anna Kaminskaya reassuring her that she and Irina were getting on very well, which suggests there might have been some anxiety about that when the arrangements had to be changed. Akhmatova still had difficulty walking, but was nevertheless determined to see as much as she could of the island and even went to look at an ancient Graeco-Roman theatre at the top of a hill.

The ceremony itself took place in Catania, and Akhmatova and Irina were driven there from Taormina on 12 December, by a winding road alongside the Ionian Sea, at a hundred miles an hour, as Irina remembers it, adding that the driver often took both hands off the steering wheel. Akhmatova, though alarmed at the time, turned her experience of these hairpin bends into a favourite story when they returned to Russia.

In Catania they stayed at the Hotel Excelsior, a skyscraper packed with reporters and photographers, though since they found they had been assigned a single room with a double bed, some adjustments were necessary. The ceremony itself was very grand and, after a reading by Akhmatova, Arseny Tarkovsky, the poet, and Alexander Tvardovsky, the editor of *Novy mir,* among others, read poems dedicated to her. The Italian film director Paolo Pasolini was able to give a showing of his latest film, *The Gospel According to St. Matthew.* On Saturday evening many people came to her hotel room to offer their congratulations. With true Russian largesse, Akhmatova then produced many characteristically Russian foods from her trunk: caviar, jam, black bread and a bottle of Stolichnaya vodka. The party went on long into the night.[22]

In 1965 Akhmatova travelled to Oxford to receive her honorary degree. She knew that Isaiah Berlin, still happily married, was living in Oxford, which gave the occasion a strange frisson. She hoped she would also meet many of her émigré friends whom she had not seen for fifty years, notably Boris Anrep. She arrived, exhausted, at Victoria Station on 2 June. Most London newspapers carried photographs and articles about her. On this occasion, Irina Punina was not well enough to accompany Akhmatova so Anna Kaminskaya was at her side. Amanda Haight, who had written her Oxford D.Phil. about Akhmatova, was also in attendance.

Akhmatova was right to conclude that Isaiah Berlin had been influential in her being offered a Doctorate,[23] and part of the excitement of this visit to Oxford derived from her knowledge that they would meet again. It did not make her well-disposed towards his wife, Aline.

Aline was half Russian and half French, born into a wealthy Jewish family; her father was the Russian banker Baron Pierre de Gunzbourg, who had settled in Paris after the Revolution. Aline grew up in a large family mansion in the Avenue d'Ilena in the 16th *arrondissement*. She had been married twice before and had purchased Headington House, a three-storey Georgian mansion near Oxford, so that she and her second husband, Hans Halban, a physicist, their family and a son from her first marriage could live there together. She did not speak Russian, since her father had not encouraged her to learn the language, and it was for this reason that she did not visit Akhmatova at her hotel with Isaiah when she first arrived.

Following a party for Akhmatova at New College with several members of the Russian Department, the Berlins invited her to dinner, as Lady Berlin recalls: "which was a mistake . . . she more or less ignored me. . . . She didn't talk to me at all, really. And she was so regal, I was very intimidated. . . . She didn't smile or laugh. . . . Luckily we had not asked her to stay with us, it would not have been a good idea."[24]

Akhmatova herself might have felt a little intimidated. Headington House is a huge stone building with twenty-four windows on its front façade. The house, with pillars at the front door and a curved staircase leading out of the hall to the upper floors, is surrounded by gardens and approached by a drive. The drawing room, where the guests sat, is enormous, with chandeliers and oil paintings. A grand piano tucks easily into one of the corners. The dining room has an oval curve of three windows overlooking a long garden.

The contrast between this splendour and Akhmatova's two-room "kennel" in Komarovo or her single room in Lenin Street could hardly have been more pronounced. As far as Lady Berlin remembers, Akhmatova was wearing a black dress with a big shawl round her on this occasion. Prepared for a legendary beauty, Lady Berlin thought she looked rather fat, and old. Even so, once dressed in black under the ceremonial scarlet robes the following day, she was still able to impress with her imperial bearing. The rumours of Isaiah's attachment to Akhmatova were well-known to Lady Berlin. When we spoke in 2004, she repeated her confidence that when Isaiah said to Brenda Tripp, "I'm in love," it was only a way of signalling how overwhelmed with admiration he was "because he thought she was so marvellous—but there was no question of being in love in the ordinary sense. When he said 'I'm in love,' it just meant he was so enthusiastic about what a marvellous woman she was."[25]

On her visit to Oxford, Akhmatova described to Isaiah Berlin some of the young poets she knew as her friends, particularly Brodsky, who she declared would soon eclipse her own generation, in which she included Tsvetaeva, Mandelstam and Pasternak. In later years, when Brodsky was sent into exile abroad, Berlin remembered Akhmatova's words and was ready to help.

Mikhail Ardov recalls being told by Akhmatova that in Oxford she refused to meet the Metropolitan Bishop: "She said, 'As a Russian Orthodox Church believer, I would have to tell him the whole truth about reality in Soviet Russia, and I can't.' This was because she felt that as a member of a Russian Orthodox Church which did everything the Soviet Government required, what she said would get back to the Soviet authorities."[26]

Akhmatova received her honorary degree on 4 June alongside the English poet Siegfried Sassoon. Before she left Oxford, the scholar Peter Norman, her official interpreter, made a tape recording of her reading her own poems. The following two days she spent in Stratford-upon-Avon, an excursion which took courage and determination. She visited the house where Shakespeare is said to have been born, and Trinity Church, where there is a gravestone and a famous bust of him. Akhmatova did not think the face looked like the great spirit whose plays she so much admired, and was sceptical throughout her visit about "the actor" being the true author of them.

On 17 June, thirteen days after the ceremony, Akhmatova and Anna Kaminskaya were invited by Peter Norman to a meal at his home in Golders Green. She had met him before, in the summer of 1964 at Komarovo. Norman's wife, Natasha, though hospitable, was a little shy. Nor did Akhmatova talk a great deal. When Kaminskaya brought her a glass containing the medicine for her heart, Akhmatova asked wistfully if it was vodka.[27]

Akhmatova met Princess Salomea Halpern, her old friend from the days of the Stray Dog, in London before travelling to Paris, where she stayed at the Hôtel Napoléon. There she was able to see many of her friends from St. Petersburg in the Silver Age including the critic Georgy Adamovich, who wrote:

> Among the comments made by Tolstoy . . . how true that all the changes are noticed the first minute. . . . But later amazement abates and it sometimes seems as if the person has always been this way. That's what happened with me. In the armchair sat a portly old woman, beautiful and grand, smiling pleasantly . . . it was only by this smile that I was able to recognise Akhmatova. Yet . . . in a moment or two before me was Akhmatova, only more talkative, more sure of herself.[28]

The person Akhmatova most wanted to see was Boris Anrep, who she had hoped would travel to Oxford to watch her receive her degree. She was hurt that he did not. Anrep, for his part, was apprehensive about meeting her, partly because he had lost the black ring which she had given him and perhaps because he wanted to preserve the memory of her as young and beautiful; perhaps because he was also older and fatter. When she reached Paris, she boldly telephoned him, even though she must have felt some timidity about the encounter herself, and invited him to come and see her at the hotel that evening. By his own account, Anrep was nervous for the whole day beforehand, wondering what he should say if she asked about the ring. He had been wearing the ring on a chain, but when the chain broke he put the ring in a box where he kept objects of sentimental value. This box was lost during a Nazi air raid on Paris.

Akhmatova's disappointment when she met him was intense. It is not clear what she expected. At this period he was a portly old man, courteous and considered witty by an English acquaintance[29] but no longer the young officer who had left her in 1917. Akhmatova may have hoped for some confession of Anrep's regret at having abandoned her all those years ago. When she read part of *Requiem* to him, he was overwhelmed by its tragic power. There were other, more intimate poems. Many listeners have noted that her customary kind, mocking smile disappeared when she read her poems aloud, and how they seemed to come from within her. When he left her in her hotel room he walked about Paris quoting her lovely lines: "He went away and in my soul / everything became empty and clear." Nayman saw those lines as a kind of victory. "Her life was painful, very painful, but it doesn't mean she was a victim."[30] Even in defeat her spirit was clear as a sunny day, when everything is visible.

Akhmatova also met Yury Annenkov, who had made two portraits of her in her youth, and Nikita Struve, nephew of Gleb Struve, who made a remarkable tape of her reading poetry.

On her return to Russia, she lived as she always had, sitting at home for many days without going out. Visitors arrived in a constant stream, usually bringing flowers; some of them knew only her poems and reputation. Most were in awe of her. She liked to laugh at jokes, though her well-known sympathies for Jews meant many anti-Semitic jokes then current were not told in her presence.

She liked to be driven round Moscow, and Nayman remembers that the last time they did so was only twelve days before her death:

> It was frosty and the sun was setting. . . . We asked the driver to take us to the Saviour Andronikov monastery. . . . The street leading to the monastery turned out to be strewn with large chunks of ice which apparently chipped from the road and the taxi began to jolt. Akhmatova frowned and clutched her heart with her hand. I told the driver to go to Ordynka Street. She sucked a little nitro-glycerine and the driver began to drive round alongside the white wall of the monastery.[31]

They came back beside the three huge blocks of flats built for Government favourites near the Stakhanovite cinema. Many of the original residents of those flats had been shot during the Terror. Passing them, Akhmatova reflected sardonically that the architect should also have been shot.

Her days out of Russia were an unexpected, glorious finale to her seventy-six years, but no doubt the strenuous travels took a toll. In November 1965 she suffered another heart attack and was taken to the Botkin hospital, where she had to remain for three months, until 18 February 1966 when she was allowed to return home to the Ardovs. She hated hospital, finding, as she wrote in her diary, that "after a lengthy stay all hospitals turn into a prison," though Nayman observed on earlier occasions that: "In conversation she was always herself. She spoke in a tranquil tone, extremely clearly, and laconically, was not afraid of silences, and did not, as is the custom, make meaningless remarks to put visitors at ease."[32]

Margarita Aliger remembered that her friends set up a strict timetable for visitors so that Akhmatova should not be tired. Sadly, when Lev arrived at the hospital to see his mother, he was refused entrance because his name was not on the list. He sent in a note and when Akhmatova received it she was profoundly grieved and angry that her friends could not understand that "this is my only son, the person closest to me, my only heir."

Aliger's account is sad, but not hostile to the group of friends who were trying to safeguard Akhmatova's tranquillity. According to Joseph Brodsky, it was Anna Kaminskaya who brought the message from Akhmatova to Lev. After this exclusion, Lev never went to see Akhmatova in the hospital.

On 3 March 1966, Akhmatova, Nayman, Kaminskaya and Olshevskaya, accompanied by a nurse, set off to the sanatorium at Domodedovo in two taxis. The sanatorium was for the privileged and had carpets, a conservatory and wide semicircular steps leading up to the main yellow building. When she saw as much, Akhmatova murmured, "L'année dernière à Marienbad." "Robbe Grillet's book was more or less the last book she read."[33] She was, whether as a result of medication or illness, constantly dozing. She had come across Yeats' poem in Nayman's hand and was fond of repeating the line, "When you are old and grey and full of sleep." She found her new home "enchantingly quiet" and was able to read about the discovery of the Qumran scrolls with alert fascination.

When Nayman said goodbye to Akhmatova on 3 March, he arranged to make a fair copy of her memoirs of Lozinsky before they were sent to a journal. On 5 March he set out for Domodedovo with a bunch of narcissi. A woman in a white coat met him in the corridor but he could not make out what she was saying. When he went into Akhmatova's room, he was astonished to find Nina Olshevskaya lying in Akhmatova's bed and breathing with difficulty. She had been given a sedative. Anna Kaminskaya stood by her side in tears. Akhmatova had died two hours earlier, and was now lying in the next ward covered by a sheet.

SIXTEEN

Aftermaths

Akhmatova's orphans.

—DMITRY BOBYSHEV

A nna Akhmatova's death was announced on the radio and her body was brought to the Sklifosovsky Institute in Moscow, where it remained while the funeral was arranged. The Punins attended to the necessary paperwork for the issue of a death certificate, and then gave it to Brodsky, asking him to find a cemetery.[1] Three Leningrad authorities offered a plot in one of the municipal cemeteries, but Brodsky and Mikhail Ardov decided a grave in Komarovo would be more appropriate "since Akhmatova had walked the ground there."[2] Zoya Tomashevskaya used her connections with distinguished architects to help Brodsky organise a burial in Komarovo, where the authorities had at first been opposed to this idea.

Anna Kaminskaya arranged for the coffin to be flown from Moscow to Leningrad on 9 March. The Moscow Writers' Union, who were afraid of a demonstration[3]—rather as the bureaucrats in Pushkin's time had been at his death—were mainly eager to have everything over as soon as possible. They asked Tarkovsky, Ozerov and Viktor Ardov to accompany the coffin on the flight. This made it difficult for friends to arrange a memorial gathering before the funeral, since 8 March was Women's Day and workers involved in moving the coffin were all women and were entitled to a day off. Nevertheless, they were persuaded. In a small grey room at the morgue, her friends came to kiss Akhmatova's hand and say goodbye.

On 10 March the funeral took place in St. Nicholas' Cathedral, a blue and white baroque building where Akhmatova lay in an open coffin, her head covered by black lace which had been given to her in London by Princess Salomea Halpern. "Akhmatova's orphans," as Bobyshev dubbed them in a poem—Brodsky, Rein, Nayman and himself—were all present, though Brodsky arrived at the tail end of the Requiem Mass after making arrangements with the gravediggers in Komarovo. Photographers and film cameras arrived in force, and police cordons surrounded the cathedral. Brodsky observed that, "Lev Gumilyov rushed about pulling the film out of the cameras taking pictures."[4] According to Mikhail Ardov, Lev took a much greater part in organising the funeral than Brodsky's account suggests. Ardov also remembers poignantly that on the day of her death, 5 March 1966, Lev said, "It would be better if I were dead, not my mother."[5]

After the ceremony, a procession left in buses and cars for Komarovo. There, priests scattered soil on Akhmatova's body, closed the coffin and lowered her into her grave. Lev and her closest friends went back to her "kennel" for another service. Later the Writers' Union held a civil memorial for Akhmatova, which Lev and Anna Kaminskaya both attended.

The question now arose of what should be done with Akhmatova's archive. Yevgeny Rein recalls that consideration along these lines had been in several people's minds long before Akhmatova's death. According to Sergey Lavrov, before Lev and his mother quarrelled, they had agreed that her manuscripts should go to Pushkinsky Dom, where all the most precious manuscripts of Russian literature—including Pushkin's manuscripts—are stored. Mikhail Ardov, a close friend of Lev, recollects that Lev did not address the question of what should be done with the archive for some months. Kaminskaya recalled[6] that in the aftermath of her death Lev refused to take anything belonging to Akhmatova, "neither her papers nor possessions." He also asked that none of her friends should be given access to her archive.

Nayman told me these papers were kept in two fibre-board suitcases, which Akhmatova carried with her on trips to Moscow, and in a wooden chest in her room in Leningrad, along with a few other precious objects. He reported that after Akhmatova's death a car from the sanatorium where she was being treated took him to Moscow, and he brought the two suitcases with him to the apartment of Maria Petrovykh.

Kaminskaya describes the suitcases as artificial leather rather than fibre-board, and explained that one contained material about Blok which Akhmatova was preparing for a TV interview, as well as clothes. Of the second suitcase, given to Akhmatova by Punin in 1936, Kaminskaya remembered Akhmatova often remarking as a joke: "Don't sit on the museum exhibits." In this suitcase, she kept current translations and MSS on which she was working continually, such as *Poem Without a Hero*. According to Kaminskaya this suitcase was given to the Akhmatova Museum on Fontanny Dom in July 1994.[7]

As to the bulk of Akhmatova's archive which remained in Fontanny Dom, Kaminskaya claims that much of this was given by Irina Punina to RGALI (Russian State Literary Archive), obeying a directive of Akhmatova herself in a notebook of 1958. Other parts of the archive were sold to the State Public Library in Leningrad.

In September 1966, Lev received the documents about his rights as the heir of his mother from the notary. Lev made a written declaration that all Akhmatova's papers should be sold to Pushkinsky Dom for the nominal price of 100 roubles.

A literary Commission was arranged to look into the matter in December 1966, and as Nayman explained: "Then there was a court hearing. I don't remember the date. It was within a year and a half of her death.

"I found myself—I am describing my feelings, my situation—I found myself on Lev's side. I didn't like him. He didn't like me. I think in some way he hated me because, first, I occupied something like his place near his mother, and then he was anti-Semitic. But I wound up on his side."

The court case acquitted Punina of any wrongdoing but control of Akhmatova's estate passed to Lev. The estate is now administered by his widow.

Certainly Akhmatova's manuscripts are now widely dispersed, and some may have been lost altogether. Nayman was characteristically wry about the fate of the archive. "It was a customary fate for Akhmatova. And we lost almost nothing, because we know all we are destined to know."[8]

As for Lev's inaction, Nayman explained that: "He didn't need money. He worked. He was a professor.* He didn't want to be involved. I don't know. I can only describe what I was a witness to."[9] There were other reasons for his emotional detachment. In 1966, Lev was allowed to go to Prague to attend an ethnographic congress, and there he met Savitsky, one of the most distinguished Eurasian thinkers, for the first time. It was then, too, that he met his future wife, Natalya Viktorova, and they were married in 1967, the year after his mother's death. A friend considered that this marriage gave Lev Gumilyov an extra ten or fifteen years of life.[10]

Rein saw Akhmatova needed to be part of a family. For him, what was important was not the archive but how Akhmatova had been treated when she was alive. Akhmatova had known Anna Kaminskaya from birth, and regarded her almost as a daughter. But he felt that Irina Punina did not accord her sufficient respect. "The two women did not behave as if Akhmatova was a great poet . . . they gave her the worst room, and they used her income."[11] However, Dmitry Bobyshev thought they looked after Akhmatova well enough, as far as he could see.

After Akhmatova's death, she came in for some unexpected criticism from her long-standing friend Nadezhda Mandelstam. In the second volume of her memoirs, Nadezhda accused her of vanity, and of being incomparably more selfish than Tsvetaeva. These were thoughts she would not have expressed while Akhmatova was alive. This did not make them altogether false. Nayman, too, acknowledges that Akhmatova was: "sometimes capricious, despotic, and unjust to people; she behaved selfishly at times and she collected, as if for show, her readers' latest raptures. . . . Consciously or unconsciously she encouraged people to see in her an exceptional figure of greater stature than themselves."[12]

But Nayman understood that her vanity had its source in the pains of her own life, and that this was why she often tried to triumph over

---

* In a recent email Kaminskaya pointed out that her mother was at that time a Professor of Fine Arts herself.

earlier rivals. He remembers how once she summoned the actress
Olga Vysotskaya, whose son by Gumilyov was close to Lev in age,
wanting to consult her on some fact in the history of pre–First
World War society. Ardov and Nayman brought Vysotskaya to
Ordynka Street by taxi. Akhmatova sat in majesty, with her hair
carefully combed, "while her former rival was feeble, old and
broken."[13]

Lev Gumilyov went on to become a distinguished anthropologist,
one of the founding fathers of the modern anthropological theory of
Russian Eurasianism, which rejects any attempt to incorporate western European values into so-called Eurasian states such as Russia.
The ideology was first articulated by Count Nikolay Trubetskoi in
the 1920s and then developed by Lev in the 1960s; its central postu-
late is that there is an irreconcilable difference between Eurasian
states and those of the West which can only be overcome by the victory of one side or the other. During Soviet times, Eurasianism
attracted supporters within the military and the KGB. In the early
1980s, one of the leaders of the movement, Alexander Dugin, began
his public career as an activist in Dmitry Vasiliev's rabidly anti-
Semitic Pamyat organisation.

Between 1970 and 1975, Lev wrote more than forty articles, many
of which were translated abroad, and a sequence of his lectures was
broadcast on Leningrad TV. Two books were published in 1987 and
1988. Also in 1988, after many years of promises, the first significant
collection of his father's poems was published in Tbilisi, Georgia.
Towards the end of his life, Lev reflected on the saying that to live
happily one should live a long time. He had reached seventy, to his
own surprise, for all the hardships of his life. By the late 1980s, Lev
had become something of a celebrity in Gorbachev's Russia. Writing
for the press and speaking on television, he broadcast his views
about Huns and Khazars, and also talked about his famous parents.[14]

UNESCO named 1989, the centenary of her birth, as the year of
Anna Akhmatova. This was celebrated all over the world. Rather as
Pushkin was claimed by all political factions in Russian society after
his death, Akhmatova was praised on every side. To the mass reader,
her simplicity made her poems easy to understand and memorise.
The liberals saw her as an opponent of Stalinism, religious people
recognised her love of God, patriots saw she was deeply Russian.

Even Communists observed that she had never been outspokenly anti-Soviet.

During that Jubilee year, Lev's thoughts frequently turned to his mother and he often repeated, "It would have been better if I had died before her." This, it will be recognised, is a significant variation on what Brodsky reports him saying when he returned from the camps and it suggests the deep sadness he continued to endure. Two years later, in 1991, Lev had a serious stroke, and died the following year. In 1994, correspondence between Lev and Akhmatova was published for the first time, selected and edited by his widow Natalya, who was helped by the literary specialist Alexander Panchenko, a close friend of Lev. Unfortunately, both in his introductory article and his commentary on the letters, Panchenko entirely followed Lev's version of events. The ten letters from Akhmatova which had been kept by her son seemed to perpetuate the image of Akhmatova as an unfeeling mother. Unlike her son, Akhmatova had kept *all* her son's letters but in this selection only five of his numerous angry and hurtful letters were included.[15]

Provoked by the injustice of the picture of Akhmatova that began to emerge, Emma Gerstein, who had already published two early memoirs abroad as *A New Look at Mandelstam*, was prompted to begin writing her lifelong account of her attachment to Akhmatova and her son in the section "Unwanted Love," now included in *Moscow Memoirs*. This was published in 1998, when Gerstein was ninety-five. Gerstein had known Akhmatova intimately, and was the recipient of many letters from Lev. In the last years of his imprisonment he wrote to her at least three times a month. Other sections of *Moscow Memoirs* threw uncomfortable light on Nadezhda Mandelstam, notably her lesbian proclivities. Contemporary Moscow found the book deeply shocking.

Akhmatova enjoyed fame worldwide in her own lifetime, particularly after *Requiem* appeared; and the success of Nadezhda Mandelstam's first book of memoirs, titled in English *Hope Against Hope*, confirmed her heroic place among a small band of poets who could trust one another, even in a vicious world.

EPILOGUE

*A*khmatova was born as the curtain began to fall on Imperial Russia and survived through the worst horrors of
the Soviet regime. Since she came to stand as a symbol
of heroic resistance to the State, it might have been expected that,
with the collapse of Communism, her importance would diminish.

Not so. Thirty years after her death, Akhmatova's achievement is
honoured in St. Petersburg by a museum, set up in the Sheremetev
Palace on the Fontanka, where she once had to live in a single bed-
sitter. Other buildings associated with her life have been restored.
The bronze chandelier which hung from the ceiling of the Stray
Dog, for instance, now hangs there again, and a single glove lies
across it to remind visitors of Akhmatova's early lyric in which a
woman in emotional turmoil tries to pull her right glove on to her
left hand.

Sales of poetry have declined almost to Western levels in post-
Soviet Russia. A 1960 edition of Akhmatova had a print run of
1,700,000, while only 15,000 copies of the recent six-volume edition from Ellis-Lak (1998–2001) were published. These figures,
however, are misleading as a guide to her popularity. The Ellis-Lak
edition was aimed at a specialist readership; there are many other
books of Akhmatova's poems available, including school editions,
and it should be noted that these days most other poets have print
runs of 3,000 to 5,000.

There is another important factor: her poems can now be downloaded from the Internet as readily as Westerners download CDs, as
Dr. Jana Howlett pointed out to me:

In Soviet times books by "unapproved" authors were a sign of "culture," and everyone wanted to have them in their *stenka,* the fitted glass-fronted cupboard which was part of every well-appointed flat. And a book priced at a rouble often changed hands for ten. But the fact that the classics are now all available on the Internet means that lovers of poetry (myself included) can download the works for nothing.[1]

Akhmatova remains an iconic figure, not of dissidence and resistance alone but as a poet of womanly feeling in a brutal world. As Isaiah Berlin exclaimed to a friend after her death, her courage was exemplary: "an uncontaminated, unbroken and morally impeccable reproach to . . . [all those] . . . who believed individuals could never stand up to the march of history."[2]

At Akhmatova's memorial gathering on 8 March 1966, two days before her funeral, Efim Etkind—a key witness for the defence at the trial of Joseph Brodsky—quoted Akhmatova's own resonant words about the way Pushkin's name had outlived those of seemingly more influential members of his society:

> All the beauties, ladies in waiting, mistresses of the salons, Dames of the Order of St. Catherine, members of the Imperial Court, ministers, aides-de-camp, gradually began to be referred to as contemporaries of Pushkin, and at length have been simply laid to rest (with their dates of birth and death garbled) in the indexes to editions of Pushkin's works.[3]

Etkind predicted Akhmatova would enjoy the same triumph and so she has, even in Putin's Russia. Poems are written to her by a new generation of poets. Memoirs, tributes, academic articles and critical books pour out every year. Visitors stream round her museum. Stalin himself will not be quickly forgotten but the names of many of his henchmen are by now fading from the popular mind, while Akhmatova's genius and stoic endurance continue to be honoured by her countrymen.

ELAINE FEINSTEIN, *October 2004*

MARINA IVANOVNA TSVETAEVA

*B*oth Akhmatova and Tsvetaeva must be counted among the greatest European poets of the twentieth century and continue to fascinate readers worldwide long after their deaths. Their temperaments were altogether different, however. Akhmatova kept her dignity even in the face of tragedy; Tsvetaeva showed her emotions nakedly. Akhmatova's poetry was marked by a classic restraint; Tsvetaeva's by a constant pressure to invent new forms. Akhmatova always refused to leave her native Russia; Tsvetaeva followed her husband into exile. Both women had lives of tormenting unhappiness as a result of their choices.

The sound of their poetry is equally different. Tsvetaeva has many voices but most of her poems use difficult syntax, enjambment and leaps over what can be assumed; her pages are filled with dashes and spattered with exclamation marks. Akhmatova, though often allusive, is literal, bare, bony and precise.

Marina Ivanovna Tsvetaeva was born in Moscow in 1892, to Professor Ivan Tsvetaev and Maria (née Mein). Marina's early years were dominated by her mother, a clever woman of many talents who spoke French and German. While Akhmatova's mother lived in a gentle dream, Tsvetaeva's mother burned with passionate intensity. She was a gifted pianist, who had been compelled to give up any hope of a musical career by her father. Her involvement with a married man separated from his wife was also forbidden and she was forced to settle for a widower still in love with his first wife and totally devoted to his world of art history.

Tsvetaeva's mother was a lonely and frustrated woman, who knew herself to be less beautiful than her predecessor. All her energies were directed towards the education of her first child. She had hoped for a son, but soon recognised the precocity of her daughter and was determined she should fulfil her own ambitions as a concert pianist. In the process she was despotic, demanding and often cruel. Where Akhmatova was carelessly allowed to be as indolent or adventurous as she chose every summer in the south of Russia, Tsvetaeva was treated with oppressive attention. She was forced to learn the piano for four hours a day, and then, as her love of literature became apparent, she was denied writing paper and had her early attempts at poetry ridiculed. It was a Spartan childhood. Tsvetaeva inherited her mother's fiery nature and although, after her mother's death, she gave up the piano altogether, her need to excel remained ferocious. As Tsvetaeva put it: "After a mother like that, I had no alternative but to become a poet."[1]

In 1912 she married Sergey Efron, a beautiful young man whom she had met as a child. The initiative was taken by Tsvetaeva. Efron, only seventeen, was a year younger and for most of their life together he was perceived by their friends as the weaker figure. He was an orphan whose parents had been early revolutionaries; an aspirant writer and actor. He and Tsvetaeva remained together for the rest of their lives, although she had a number of love affairs, notably one with the lesbian poet Sophia Parnok, and another with a Russian émigré, Konstantin Rodzevich, in Prague which inspired her two greatest long poems: *Poem of the Mountain* and *Poem of the End*.[2]

A biographer would pinpoint one contrast between Akhmatova and Tsvetaeva as particularly significant: Akhmatova's beauty and presence led men to fall in love with her even in old age, while Tsvetaeva once declared that, although she knew she would be the most important person in the memoirs of men who knew her, she had never counted in the masculine present.

Akhmatova's capacity for calm endurance—or perhaps her phlegmatic disposition, as Joseph Brodsky describes it—could not be further removed from Tsvetaeva's febrile energies, yet they had much in common, too. Brodsky, speaking about Sergey Efron, and impatient with his changing political allegiances and his inability to find work, concedes that "to be married to a major woman poet is not a bed of roses."[3]

NOTES

ACKNOWLEDGEMENTS

1. L. A. Zykov, *N. Punin; Sostavlenie, predislovie, primechaniya* (Moscow, 2000).

CHAPTER ONE · ST. PETERSBURG 1913

1. Anna Akhmatova, *Sobranie sochinenii, v shesti tomakh*, ed. A. M. Smirnova et al., Vol. 3, p. 185.
2. Solomon Volkov, *St. Petersburg* (London, 1996), p. 147.
3. Orlando Figes, *A People's Tragedy* (London, 1996), p. 18.
4. *Poem Without a Hero*, Akhmatova, *Sobranie*, Vol. 3, p. 185.
5. Among the most respected voices of Russian Futurism was Nikolay Nikolaevich Punin, who was to become Akhmatova's third "husband."
6. Volkov, *St. Petersburg*, p. 187.
7. Akhmatova, *Sobranie*, Vol. 4, p. 44.
8. Konstantin Polivanov, *Anna Akhmatova and Her Circle* (Fayetteville, 1994), p. 65, "George Adamovich, Meetings with Anna Akhmatova."
9. Polivanov, p. 64.
10. Polivanov, p. 130.
11. Akhmatova, *Sobranie*, Vol. 3, p. 184.
12. Nadezhda Mandelstam, *Hope Abandoned* (London, 1974), Vol. 2, p. 453.
13. Volkov, *St. Petersburg*, p. 194.
14. Polivanov, p. 232.
15. Conversation with E.F., Frankfurt, 2003.
16. Elaine Feinstein, *Selected Poems of Marina Tsvetaeva* (Manchester, 1999), p. 4.
17. Ibid.

CHAPTER TWO · BECOMING AKHMATOVA

1. Akhmatova, *Sobranie*, Vol. 1, p. 10.
2. Lydia Chukovskaya, *The Akhmatova Journals, 1938–41*, Vol. 1 (London, 1994), p. 119.
3. Anatoly Nayman, *Remembering Anna Akhmatova* (London, 1991).
4. Anna Akhmatova, *My Half Century: Selected Prose,* trans. and ed. Ronald Meyer (Ann Arbor, 1992), p. 7.
5. Akhmatova, *My Half Century*, p. 6.
6. Jessie Davies, *Anna of All the Russias* (Liverpool, 1989), p. 3.
7. Interview with E.F., Frankfurt, 2003.
8. Akhmatova, *Sobranie*, Vol. 4, p. 295.
9. Interview with E.F.
10. Akhmatova, *Sobranie*, Vol. 4, p. 8.
11. Akhmatova, *Sobranie*, Vol. 3, p. 9.
12. Much of this material can be found in Roberta Reeder, *Anna Akhmatova: Poet & Prophet* (London, 1994).
13. See Appendix.
14. Polivanov, p. 52.
15. Davies, p. 1.
16. Vadim Chernykh, *Letopis zhizni i tvorchestva Anny Akhmatovoi, 1889–1917*, 4 vols. (Moscow, 1996–2003), Vol. 1, p. 21.
17. Chernykh, Vol. 1, p. 23.
18. However, conditions in Tsarist prisons were in general better than might have been expected, since prisoners had access to books and writing paper, as a former inmate, the Communist Ilya Ehrenburg, attests.
19. Figes, *A People's Tragedy*, p. 96.
20. Davies, p. 5.
21. *Novy mir* 1986, No. 9, pp. 196–206. Yevgeny Rein confirmed that Akhmatova spoke of him as her first lover.
22. Akhmatova, *My Half Century*, p. 278.
23. Chernykh, Vol. 1, p. 27.
24. Chernykh, Vol. 1, p. 26.
25. *Nilokay Gumilyov v vospominanyakh sovremennikov,* ed. Vadim Kreid, pp. 33–4, quoted in Frances Laird, *Swan Songs: Akhmatova & Gumilyov* (1st Books, 2002).
26. Akhmatova, *My Half Century*, p. 275.
27. Akhmatova, *My Half Century*, p. 278.
28. On 13 March 1907.
29. Akhmatova, *Sobranie*, Vol. 1, p. 10.

30. Laird, p. 70.
31. Chernykh, Vol. 1, p. 32.
32. Roberta Reeder's suggested date.
33. Akhmatova, *Sobranie*, Vol. 2(a), p. 172.
34. Chernykh, Vol. 1, p. 34.
35. E.F. conversation with Nayman, October 2003.
36. Akhmatova, *My Half Century*, p. 277.
37. Anna Akhmatova, *Stikhi, perepiska, vospominaniya, ikonografiya*, comp. A. Proffer (Ann Arbor, 1977), Vol. 3, p. 324.
38. Interview with E.F., 2003.

CHAPTER THREE · MARRIAGE TO GUMILYOV

1. Nadezhda Mandelstam says that this was because both parents disapproved of the match.
2. Irina Odoevtseva, *Na bergakh nevy* (Moscow, 1967), p. 464.
3. Chukovskaya, *Akhmatova Journals 1938–41*, p. 148.
4. Odoevtseva, pp. 463–4.
5. Chernykh, Vol. 1, p. 38.
6. Laird, p. 147.
7. Laird, p. 139.
8. Akhmatova, *Sobranie*, Vol. 4, p. 47.
9. Akhmatova, *Sobranie*, Vol. 4, p. 31.
10. Chernykh, Vol. 1, p. 45.
11. Chernykh, Vol. 1, p. 37.
12. Akhmatova, *Sobranie*, Vol. 4, p. 12.
13. Ibid.
14. Akhmatova, *Sobranie*, Vol. 4, p. 14.
15. Chukovskaya, *Akhmatova Journals 1938–41*, p. 109.
16. Pavel Luknitsky, *Vstrechi s Annoi Akhmatovoi, 1924–1925*, Vol. 1 (Paris, 1991), p. 141.
17. Akhmatova, *Sobranie*, Vol. 4, p. 29.
18. I am indebted to Frances Laird, *Swan Songs*, for this insight.
19. Chernykh, Vol. 1, p. 43.
20. Several others have since been discovered. See above, p. 252.
21. Nikolay Gumilyov, *On Russian Poetry*, ed. and trans. David Lapeza (Ann Arbor, 1977), p. 142.
22. Akhmatova, *My Half Century*, p. 76.
23. Osip Mandelstam, *The Complete Critical Prose and Letters*, ed. Jane Gary Harris (London, 1991), p. 178.
24. Akhmatova, *Sobranie*, Vol. 4, p. 10.

25. Akhmatova, *Sobranie*, Vol. 4, p. 19.
26. As Catriona Kelly suggests in *A History of Russian Women's Writing, 1820–1992* (Oxford, 1994), *passim*.
27. Interview with E.F.
28. Chernykh, Vol. 1, p. 61.
29. Chernykh, Vol. 1, p. 66.
30. Chernykh, Vol. 1, p. 55.
31. Akhmatova, *Sobranie*, Vol. 4, p. 44.
32. John Malmstad and Nikolay Bogomolov, *Mikhail Kuzmin: A Life in Art* (Boston, 1999), p. 174.
33. Interview with E.F., 2003.
34. Akhmatova, *Sobranie*, Vol. 4, p. 50.
35. Ibid.
36. Chukovskaya, *Akhmatova Journals 1938–41*, p. 147.
37. Akhmatova, *Sobranie*, Vol. 4, p. 74.
38. Chernykh, Vol. 1, p. 71.
39. Chernykh, Vol. 1, p. 67.
40. Akhmatova, *Sobranie*, Vol. 1, p. 197.
41. Ibid.
42. Akhmatova, *Sobranie*, Vol. 4, p. 50.
43. Akhmatova, *Sobranie*, Vol. 4, p. 73.
44. He was to be her third husband.
45. V. M. Zhirmunsky, *Tvorchestvo Anny Akhmatovoi* (Leningrad, 1973), p. 198.
46. Akhmatova, *Sobranie*, Vol. 4, pp. 106–7.

CHAPTER FOUR · PETROGRAD

1. Akhmatova, *Sobranie*, Vol. 4, p. 118.
2. Chernykh, Vol. 1, p. 76.
3. Chernykh, Vol. 1, p. 77.
4. Reeder, p. 83.
5. Laird, p. 252.
6. Akhmatova, *Sobranie*, Vol. 4, pp. 108–9.
7. Figes, *A People's Tragedy*, p. 253.
8. *Listen! Early Poems of Mayakovsky 1913–1918*, trans. Maria Enzensberger (London, 1987).
9. Chernykh, Vol. 1, p. 81.
10. At least 1,700,000 men, though the figures are unreliable and the total may well exceed 2,000,000.
11. Akhmatova, *Sobranie*, Vol. 4, p. 41.
12. Akhmatova, *Sobranie*, Vol. 4, p. 79.

13. Chernykh, Vol. 1, p. 86.
14. Akhmatova, *Sobranie*, Vol. 4, p. 110.
15. Chernykh, Vol. 1, p. 86.
16. Feinstein, *Selected Poems of Marina Tsvetaeva*, p. 25.
17. Reeder, p. 93.
18. Ibid.
19. Reeder, p. 85.
20. Lazar Fleischman, "Izakhmatovskikh materialov v arkhive Guverovskogo instituta," in *Akhmatovskii sbornik*, ed. Serge Deduline and Gabriel Superfin. Bibliothèque Russe de l'Institut d'Études slaves, Vol. LXXXV (Paris, 1989), p. 174.
21. Akhmatova, *Sobranie*, Vol. 4, p. 116.
22. Chernykh, Vol. 1, p. 93.
23. N. V. Nedobrovo, "Anna Akhmatova," in *Russkaya mysl*, 1915, Book 7, p. 639.
24. Chukovskaya, *Akhmatova Journals 1938–41*, p. 99.
25. See Angelica Garnett, *Among the Bohemians: Experiments in Living 1900–1930* (London, 2002); *Deceived with Kindness: A Bloomsbury Childhood* (London, 1984), *passim*.
26. Akhmatova, *Sobranie*, Vol. 4, p. 123.
27. Garnett, *Among the Bohemians*, *passim*.
28. Reeder, p. 96.
29. Akhmatova, *Sobranie*, Vol. 4, p. 117.
30. Laird, p. 285.

CHAPTER FIVE · REVOLUTION

1. Marina Tsvetaeva, *A Captive Spirit: Selected Prose*, ed. and trans. J. Marin King (Ann Arbor, 1980), p. 174.
2. Figes, *A People's Tragedy*, p. 283.
3. Figes, *A People's Tragedy*, p. 300.
4. Figes, *A People's Tragedy*, p. 351.
5. Figes, *A People's Tragedy*, p. 369.
6. Figes, *A People's Tragedy*, p. 400.
7. Akhmatova, *Sobranie*, Vol. 4, p. 166.
8. Akhmatova, *Sobranie*, Vol. 4, p. 153.
9. Akhmatova, *Sobranie*, Vol. 4, p. 154.
10. Akhmatova, *Sobranie*, Vol. 4, pp. 145–6.
11. Nayman, p. 79.
12. Akhmatova, *Sobranie*, Vol. 4, p. 148.
13. Amanda Haight, *Anna Akhmatova, A Poetic Pilgrimage* (New York and London, 1976), p. 51.

14. Interview with E.F.
15. Lois Oliver, *Boris Anrep: The National Gallery Mosaics* (London, 2004), p. 52.
16. Akhmatova, *Sobranie*, Vol. 4, p. 107.
17. Akhmatova, *Sobranie*, Vol. 4, p. 98.
18. Boris Anrep, "About a Black Ring," in Polivanov, p. 85.
19. Roberta Reeder, in conversation with E.F., 2004, suggested that, even if he had, it would not have affected her.
20. Akhmatova, *Sobranie*, Vol. 4, p. 124.
21. Telephone conversation with E.F., June 2004.
22. Osip Mandelstam, *Selected Poems*, trans. Clarence Brown and W. S. Merwin (New York, 1983), p. 44.
23. Ibid.
24. Reeder, p. 112.
25. Tsvetaeva, *Selected Prose*, p. 90.
26. Alexander Blok, *Selected Poems*, trans. Jon Stallworthy and Peter France (Oxford, 1970), p. 153.
27. Blok, *Selected Poems*, p. 160.
28. Reeder, p. 119.

CHAPTER SIX · IN A TIME OF FAMINE

1. Akhmatova, *Sobranie*, Vol. 4, p. 79.
2. Conversation with E.F.
3. See above, p. 70.
4. Chernykh, Vol. 2, p. 14.
5. See above, pp. 83–84.
6. E-mail from Rein to E.F.
7. Haight, p. 55.
8. Akhmatova, *Sobranie*, Vol. 4, p. 151.
9. Akhmatova, *Sobranie*, Vol. 4, p. 152.
10. Chernykh, Vol. 2, p. 17.
11. Interview with E.F.
12. Akhmatova, *Sobranie*, Vol. 4, p. 177.
13. Reeder, p. 126.
14. Elaine Feinstein, *A Captive Lion* (London, 1987), p. 61.
15. Chukovsky, Vol. 1, p. 143.
16. Chernykh, Vol. 2, p. 20.
17. Akhmatova, *My Half Century*, p. 91.
18. Polivanov, p. 93.
19. Writing about this period in March 1925.

20. Chernykh, Vol. 2, p. 19.
21. Laird, p. 376.
22. Chukovsky, Vol. 1, p. 157.
23. Akhmatova, *Sobranie*, Vol. 4, p. 188.
24. A letter to Marina Tsvetaeva from Anna Akhmatova, quoted in Chernykh, Vol. 2, p. 25.
25. Akhmatova, *Sobranie*, Vol. 4, p. 124.
26. Chukovskaya, *Akhmatova Journals 1938–41*, p. 74.
27. Akhmatova, *Sobranie*, Vol. 4, p. 110.
28. Akhmatova, *Sobranie*, Vol. 4, p. 199.
29. Sergey Lavrov, *Sudba i idei* (Moscow, 2003), p. 43.
30. Akhmatova, *Sobranie*, Vol. 4, pp. 184–5.
31. Akhmatova, *Sobranie*, Vol. 4, p. 189.
32. Akhmatova, *Sobranie*, Vol. 4, p. 190.
33. As Nayman recalled in an interview with E.F., Frankfurt, September 2003.
34. Ibid.
35. Zhirmunsky, *Tvorchestvo Anny Akhmatovoi*, p. 182.
36. Akhmatova, *Sobranie*, Vol. 4, p. 205.
37. Akhmatova, *Sobranie*, Vol. 1, p. 329.
38. A. O. Belousov, *Vospominaniia uchitelia*, manuscripts published on www.tstu.ru/koi/tambov/kirsanov/source/belous/belous.html.
39. Laird, p. 399.
40. Laird, pp. 442–6.
41. Akhmatova, *Sobranie*, Vol. 4, p. 187.
42. Lavrov, p. 39.
43. Akhmatova, *Sobranie*, Vol. 4, p. 193.
44. Reeder, p. 154.
45. Akhmatova, *Sobranie*, Vol. 4, p. 177.
46. Akhmatova, *Sobranie*, Vol. 4, p. 175.
47. I remember remaining reluctant to accept this when Isaiah Berlin explained as much to me in Rome in 1987.
48. An account of these is given in Figes, *A People's Tragedy*, p. 646.

CHAPTER SEVEN · INFIDELITIES

1. S. Monas and J. Green Krupala (eds.), *The Diaries of Nikolay Punin 1904–1953* (Austin, Texas, 1999); L. Zykov (ed.), *N. Punin. Mir svetel liuboyu. Dnevniki. Pisma* (Moscow, 2000).
2. Monas and Krupala, p. 60.
3. Monas and Krupala, p. 66.

4. Ibid.

5. Monas and Krupala, p. 64.

6. Monas and Krupala, p. 43.

7. Monas and Krupala, p. 48.

8. Monas and Krupala, p. 53.

9. Monas and Krupala, p. 73.

10. Monas and Krupala, p. 79.

11. Monas and Krupala, p. 82.

12. Ibid.

13. Ibid.

14. Monas and Krupala, p. 93.

15. Monas and Krupala, p. 88.

16. Monas and Krupala, p. 87.

17. Monas and Krupala, p. 86.

18. Monas and Krupala, p. 88.

19. Ibid.

20. Monas and Krupala, p. 87.

21. Ibid.

22. The first two lines are quoted in *Poem Without a Hero*. The last toast is usually taken to refer to the "Guest from the Future" from that poem. Zykov believes it refers to Punin.

23. Monas and Krupala, p. 89.

24. Ibid.

25. Monas and Krupala, p. 90.

26. Monas and Krupala, p. 94.

27. Monas and Krupala, p. 91.

28. Monas and Krupala, p. 103.

29. Monas and Krupala, p. 91.

30. Akhmatova, *Sobranie*, Vol. 4, p. 182.

31. Monas and Krupala, p. 108.

32. Monas and Krupala, p. 103.

33. Monas and Krupala, p. 110.

34. Monas and Krupala, p. 111.

35. Monas and Krupala, p. 114.

36. Monas and Krupala, p. 116.

37. Reeder, p. 169.

38. Reeder, p. 172.

39. Ibid.

40. Reeder, p. 174.

41. Reeder, p. 171.

42. Monas and Krupala, p. 99.

43. Monas and Krupala, p. 98.

44. Monas and Krupala, p. 126. However, this nickname is given as *Katon* in M. Kralin and I. Slobozhan (eds.), *Ob Anne Akhmatovoi* (Leningrad, 1990).

45. Monas and Krupala, p. 135.

46. Akhmatova, *Sobranie*, Vol. 4, p. 219.

47. Chernykh, Vol. 2, p. 77.

48. Chernykh, Vol. 2, p. 79.

49. Akhmatova, *Sobranie*, Vol. 4, p. 174.

50. Korney Chukovsky, "Akhmatova and Mayakovsky," *Dom isskustvo I* (1920), pp. 23–42; trans. John Pearson in Edward J. Brown (ed.), *Major Soviet Writers: Essays in Criticism* (London, 1973), pp. 33–53.

51. They can now be seen in the Akhmatova Museum in the House on the Fontanka, St. Petersburg.

52. Monas and Krupala, p. 145.

53. Many people deny this but there is some corroboration for it in a memoir written by Lev Gumilyov's wife Natalya, published in Lavrov, p. 483.

54. Chernykh, Vol. 2, p. 96.

55. Monas and Krupala, p. 161.

56. Monas and Krupala, p. 167.

57. Chernykh, Vol. 2, p. 93.

58. Monas and Krupala, p. 87.

59. Interview with E.F., St. Petersburg, 2003.

CHAPTER EIGHT · THE HOUSE ON THE FONTANKA

1. Note in Akhmatova Museum, St. Petersburg.

2. Ibid.

3. Chernykh, Vol. 2, p. 77.

4. Ibid.

5. Akhmatova, *Sobranie*, p. 402.

6. Ibid.

7. Osip Mandelstam, *Selected Poems*, p. 69.

8. Monas and Krupala, p. 97.

9. Chernykh, Vol. 2, p. 77.

10. Monas and Krupala, p. 163.

11. Monas and Krupala, p. 160.

12. Yevgeny Zamyatin was the author of several key satirical novels, notably *We*.

13. This prediction long pre-dates the honour Akhmatova received from Oxford University, and is inexplicable.

14. This is recorded by Luknitsky. Chernykh, Vol. 2, p. 94.
15. Chernykh, Vol. 2, p. 96.
16. Monas and Krupala, p. 162.
17. Monas and Krupala, p. 174.
18. Chernykh, Vol. 2, p. 76.
19. Monas and Krupala, p. 175.
20. Monas and Krupala, p. 175.
21. Ibid.
22. Monas and Krupala, p. 176.
23. Reeder, p. 192.
24. According to Amanda Haight.

CHAPTER NINE • THE VEGETARIAN YEARS 1928–1933

1. Haight, p. 91.
2. Polivanov, p. 142.
3. Polivanov, p. 130.
4. Chernykh, Vol. 2, p. 80.
5. Polivanov, pp. 133–4.
6. See Feinstein, *Pushkin* (London, 1998) and Serena Vitale, *Pushkin's Button* (1998).
7. Chernykh, Vol. 2, p. 96.
8. Chernykh, Vol. 2, p. 107.
9. Chernykh, Vol. 2, p. 115.
10. Chernykh, Vol. 2, p. 124.
11. Lev Gumilyov, "Avtobiographiya. Vospominaniya o roditeliakh." Transcript of a tape recording made in September 1986, pp. 7–17 in Lavrov.
12. Lavrov, p. 94.
13. Article by Nikolay Punin, *Isskustvo kommuny*, No. 1, Dec. 1918.
14. Yevgeny Rein interview with E.F., Moscow, September 2003.
15. Recorded in Akhmatova Museum.
16. Lev Gumilyov, cited in Lavrov, p. 9.
17. Interview with E.F., St. Petersburg, September 2003.
18. Ibid.
19. It is not an opinion you would find in present-day consumerist Russia.
20. E.F. interview with Yevgeny Rein, September 2003.
21. Lev Gumilyov, cited in Lavrov, p. 10.
22. See above, pp. 204–5.
23. Interview with E.F., St. Petersburg, 2003.
24. See above, p. 223.

25. Simon Sebag Montefiore, *Stalin: The Court of the Red Tsar* (London, 2003), p. 79.
26. Reeder, p. 180.
27. Reeder, p. 189.
28. Interview with E.F., Frankfurt, September 2003.
29. See above, p. 117.
30. Polivanov, p. 144.
31. Akhmatova, *Sobranie*, Vol. 4, p. 210.
32. Ibid.
33. Emma Gerstein, *Moscow Memoirs* (London, 2004), p. 56.
34. Ibid.
35. Interview with E.F., St. Petersburg, 2003.
36. Gerstein, p. 183.

CHAPTER TEN · THE TERROR 1933–1938

1. Interviews with E.F., September 2003.
2. Reeder, p. 202.
3. Nadezhda Mandelstam, *Hope Against Hope* (London, 1975), p. 84.
4. Gerstein, p. 62.
5. Gerstein, p. 56.
6. Gerstein, p. 203.
7. Nadezhda Mandelstam, *Hope Against Hope*, p. 8.
8. Nadezhda Mandelstam, *Hope Against Hope*, p. 16.
9. Vitaly Shentalinsky, *The KGB's Literary Archive* (London, 1995), Case No. 4108, p. 178.
10. Sebag Montefiore, p. 134.
11. Lavrov, p. 65.
12. She claimed that evidence for this could be found in NKVD files which she had seen, but to which she could give us no access.
13. Lavrov, p. 64.
14. Pasternak is referring to Stalin's telephone call in response to his letter about the arrest of Mandelstam.
15. Lavrov, p. 65.
16. Ibid.
17. Quoted in Lavrov, p. 57.
18. Gerstein, p. 188.
19. Gerstein, p. 219.
20. Lavrov, pp. 55–6.
21. Gerstein, p. 191.
22. Interview with E.F., 2003.

23. Sebag Montefiore, p. 166.
24. Gerstein, p. 205.
25. Akhmatova, *Sobranie*, Vol. 4, p. 212.
26. Monas and Krupala, p. 178.
27. Akhmatova, *Sobranie*, Vol. 4, p. 230.
28. Gerstein, p. 217.
29. Akhmatova, *My Half Century*, p. 108.
30. Gerstein, p. 230.
31. Lavrov, p. 66.
32. Lavrov, pp. 65–6.
33. Gerstein, p. 231.
34. P. S. Pozdnyakova (ed.), *V. G. Garshin* (Moscow, 2002), p. 22.
35. Ibid.
36. Pozdnyakova, p. 24. Recollections of E. M. Kirschenbaum.
37. Pozdnyakova, p. 25.
38. Pozdnyakova, p. 18.
39. Lavrov, p. 56.
40. According to Kaminskaya that was why he had asked Akhmatova to move to the small children's room.
41. Haight, p. 94.

CHAPTER ELEVEN · THE LAMB

1. Chukovskaya, *Akhmatova Journals 1938–41*, p. 16.
2. Chukovskaya, *Akhmatova Journals 1938–41*, p. 27.
3. Quoted in Lavrov, p. 20.
4. Lavrov, p. 69.
5. Akhmatova, *My Half Century*, a variant of *Pages from a Diary*, dated 1957.
6. Lavrov, p. 70.
7. Chukovskaya, *Akhmatova Journals 1938–41*, p. 32.
8. Ibid.
9. Akhmatova, *Sobranie*, Vol. 3, p. 21.
10. *Istochnik*, 1999, No. 1, p. 80.
11. Chernykh, Vol. 3, p. 36.
12. Chukovskaya, *Akhmatova Journals 1938–41*, p. 31.
13. Ibid.
14. Lavrov, p. 72.
15. As Jana Howlett demonstrated to me.
16. Part of which was played to me by Professor Valentina Polukhina.
17. Akhmatova, *Sobranie*, Vol. 3, p. 23.
18. Akhmatova, *Sobranie*, Vol. 3, p. 25.
19. Akhmatova, *Sobranie*, Vol. 3, p. 24.

20. Ibid.
21. Akhmatova, *Sobranie*, Vol. 3, p. 26.
22. Ibid.
23. Akhmatova, *Sobranie*, Vol. 3, p. 28.
24. Akhmatova, *Sobranie*, Vol. 3, p. 30.
25. Chukovskaya, *Akhmatova Journals 1938—41*, p. 25.
26. See Punin, p. 178.
27. Chukovskaya, *Akhmatova Journals 1938—41*, p. 48.
28. *Zvezda*, 1999, No. 8, p. 228.
29. Babichenko, quoted in Chernykh, Vol. 3, p. 39.
30. Chukovskaya, *Akhmatova Journals 1938—41*, p. 69.
31. Chukovskaya, *Akhmatova Journals 1938—41*, p. 76.
32. Chukovskaya, *Akhmatova Journals 1938—41*, p. 78.
33. Akhmatova, *Sobranie*, Vol. 4, p. 184.
34. Akhmatova, *Sobranie*, Vol. 4, p. 175.
35. Akhmatova, *Sobranie*, Vol. 4, p. 295.
36. Chukovskaya, *Akhmatova Journals 1938—41*, p. 164.
37. Chukovskaya, *Akhmatova Journals 1938—41*, p. 175.
38. Irma Kudrova, *The Death of a Poet* (New York, 2004).
39. Kudrova, p. 72.
40. Kudrova, p. 76.
41. Haight, p. 109.
42. Chernykh, Vol. 3, p. 55.
43. Ibid.
44. Akhmatova, *Sobranie*, Vol. 4, p. 340.

CHAPTER TWELVE · WAR

1. Akhmatova, *Sobranie*, Vol. 4, p. 266.
2. Sebag Montefiore, p. 268.
3. Chukovskaya, *Akhmatova Journals 1938—41*, p. 35.
4. An art dealer; the graphic artist of the same name was by this time living in France.
5. See above, p. 177.
6. Akhmatova, *Sobranie*, Vol. 4, p. 244.
7. Akhmatova, *Sobranie*, Vol. 4, p. 245.
8. If his memory is correct, Akhmatova must have been in Leningrad when the war began.
9. Haight, p. 122.
10. Ibid.
11. Monas and Krupala, p. 184.
12. Monas and Krupala, p. 185.

13. Vera Inber, *Leningrad Diary* (London, 1971), p. 19.
14. Monas and Krupala, p. 186.
15. Inber, p. 8.
16. Interview with E.F., St. Petersburg, 2003.
17. Monas and Krupala, p. 187.
18. Chernykh, Vol. 3, p. 58.
19. E. Schwartz, *Living Unquietly*, pp. 655–7. Quoted in Chernykh, p. 60.
20. Monas and Krupala, p. 187.
21. Presumably bought in a privileged shop for the *nomenklatura* still operating at this stage in the siege.
22. Akhmatova, *Sobranie*, Vol. 4, p. 266.
23. Annual magazine of Pushkinsky Dom, 1974, pp. 70–71.
24. Monas and Krupala, p. 190.
25. Kudrova, p. 162.
26. Kudrova, p. 154.
27. Kudrova, p. 180.
28. Akhmatova, *Sobranie*, Vol. 4, p. 223.
29. Sophie Ostrovskaya, *Memoirs of Anna Akhmatova's Years, 1944–1950* (Liverpool, 1988), p. 75.
30. Akhmatova, *Sobranie*, Vol. 4, p. 251.
31. Akhmatova, *Sobranie*, Vol. 4, p. 252.
32. Chernykh, Vol. 3, p. 70.
33. Chernykh, Vol. 3, p. 72.
34. Chukovskaya, *Entretiens*, pp. 21–5.
35. Dmitry Sheglov, *F. Ranevskaya Monolog* (Smolensk, 1998), p. 52.
36. Sheglov, p. 46.
37. Sheglov, p. 46.
38. Sheglov, p. 19.
39. Faina Ranevskaya, *Dnevnik na klochkakh Sudba-Shlokha*, ed. D. Sheglov (Moscow, 2003), p. 46.
40. Faina Ranevskaya, *Dnevnik na klochkakh* (St. Petersburg, 2002), p. 46.
41. Interview with E.F., St. Petersburg, September 2003.
42. Sheglov, p. 43.
43. Sheglov, p. 49.
44. Sheglov, p. 47.
45. Simon Franklin, "New Light on a Poem by Anna Akhmatova? Notes on the Textology of Recollection," *Oxford Slavonic Papers:* New Series, Vol. XXXI (1998), p. 96.
46. Reeder, p. 326.
47. Akhmatova, *Sobranie*, Vol. 4, p. 346.
48. Franklin, p. 98.

49. Ibid.
50. Haight, p. 30.
51. Akhmatova, *Sobranie*, Vol. 4, p. 268.
52. Reeder, p. 269.
53. Akhmatova, *Sobranie*, Vol. 4, p. 325.
54. Monas and Krupala, p. 192.
55. Monas and Krupala, p. 193.
56. Monas and Krupala, p. 194.
57. RGALI (Russian State Literary Archive), f. 13.
58. *Zvezda*, 1994, 1, p. 104.
59. Lavrov, p. 70.
60. Lavrov, p. 21.
61. Reeder, p. 272.
62. Monas and Krupala, p. 201.
63. Ibid.
64. Monas and Krupala, p. 202.
65. Monas and Krupala, p. 209.
66. See above, p. 117n.
67. Reeder, p. 280.
68. Pozdnyakova, p. 62.
69. O. I. Rybakova, "Grustnaya Pravda," *Ob Anne Akhmatovoi*, pp. 225–8, quoted in Chernykh, p. 101.
70. Pozdnyakova, p. 66.
71. Gerstein, p. 160.
72. Gerstein, p. 163.
73. Gerstein, p. 164.

CHAPTER THIRTEEN · PEACE

1. Bobyshev to E.F., August 2003.
2. Feinstein, *Selected Poems of Marina Tsvetaeva*, p. 82.
3. Monas and Krupala, p. 209.
4. Gerstein, p. 457.
5. Ostrovskaya, Appendix Margarita Aliger, p. 78.
6. Georgy Dalos, *The Guest from the Future: Anna Akhmatova and Isaiah Berlin* (London, 2000), p. 28.
7. Ostrovskaya, p. 1.
8. Ibid.
9. Akhmatova, *Sobranie*, Vol. 4, p. 299.
10. Ostrovskaya, p. 6.
11. Ostrovskaya, p. 27.

12. Ostrovskaya, p. 47.
13. Ostrovskaya, p. 44.
14. Notably Richard McKane. Anatoly Nayman did not remember Ostrovskaya being mentioned to him.
15. See above, pp. 213–14.
16. Ostrovskaya, p. 48.
17. Ostrovskaya, p. 49.
18. Michael Ignatieff, *Isaiah Berlin* (London, 1998), p. 157.
19. Ignatieff, p. 161.
20. Akhmatova, *Sobranie*, Vol. 4, p. 300.
21. Akhmatova, *Sobranie*, Vol. 4, p. 301.
22. Akhmatova, *Sobranie*, Vol. 4, p. 301.
23. Akhmatova, *Sobranie*, Vol. 4, p. 302.
24. Akhmatova, *Sobranie*, Vol. 4, p. 302.
25. Dalos, p. 66.
26. Dalos, p. 56.
27. Dalos, p. 76.
28. Dalos, p. 70.
29. Lavrov, p. 76.
30. Ranevskaya, *Dnevnik na klochkakh*, p. 48.
31. Chernykh, Vol. 4, p. 59.
32. KGB records concerning N735–49.
33. Lavrov, p. 76.
34. Liubimova, L., quoted in Chernykh, Vol. 4, p. 61.
35. *Horizon*, 1989, No. 6, p. 56.
36. Lavrov, p. 89.
37. Monas and Krupala, p. 223.
38. Punin, p. 223.
39. Chernykh, Vol. 4, p. 79.
40. A girl who had been introduced to Emma Gerstein as Lev's fiancée.
41. Gerstein, p. 452.
42. Akhmatova, *Sobranie*, Vol. 4, p. 329.
43. Gerstein, p. 463.
44. Chernykh, Vol. 4, p. 110.
45. Gerstein, p. 457.
46. Gerstein, p. 464.
47. Lavrov, p. 98.
48. Gerstein, p. 456.
49. Gerstein, p. 459.
50. Gerstein, p. 456.
51. Gerstein, p. 461.
52. *Zvezda*, 1994, No. 4, p. 182.

53. Chukovskaya, *Zapiski ob Anne Akhmatovoi,* Vol. 3: *1963–1966* (Moscow, 1997), p. 248.
54. Gerstein, p. 459.
55. Interview with E.F.

CHAPTER FOURTEEN · THE THAW

1. Akhmatova, *Sobranie,* Vol. 3, p. 187.
2. Reeder, p. 384.
3. Akhmatova, *Sobranie,* Vol. 3, p. 168.
4. Akhmatova, *Sobranie,* Vol. 3, p. 169.
5. Akhmatova, *Sobranie,* Vol. 3, p. 170.
6. Akhmatova, *Sobranie,* Vol. 3, p. 173.
7. Akhmatova, *Sobranie,* Vol. 3, p. 183.
8. Akhmatova, *Sobranie,* Vol. 3, p. 174.
9. Akhmatova, *Sobranie,* Vol. 3, p. 188.
10. Akhmatova, *Sobranie,* Vol. 3, p. 191.
11. Akhmatova, *Sobranie,* Vol. 3, p. 198.
12. Akhmatova, *Sobranie,* Vol. 3, p. 200.
13. Akhmatova, *Sobranie,* Vol. 3, p. 202.
14. When I mentioned this to his son, Yevgeny, in 2003, he attributed this greater warmth in part to the passionate letters he had exchanged with Tsvetaeva in 1926.
15. Interview with E.F., Moscow, September 2003.
16. This story was told to me in the 1970s by Vera Traill, and is confirmed in Chukovskaya and Reeder.
17. Reeder, p. 361.
18. Reeder, p. 354.
19. As he told me when we visited Pasternak's grave in 1978.
20. Isaiah Berlin made a point about the historical truth of this when I met him in Rome.
21. Reeder, p. 367.
22. Akhmatova, *Sobranie,* Vol. 4, p. 328.
23. Interview with E.F., September 2003.
24. Haight, p. 173.
25. Chukovskaya, *Entretiens,* p. 388.
26. Solomon Volkov, *Conversations with Joseph Brodsky* (New York and London, 1998), p. 237.
27. Volkov, *Conversations,* p. 228.
28. Volkov, *Conversations,* pp. 227–8.
29. Chukovskaya, *Entretiens,* p. 388.
30. Interview with E.F.

31. Ibid.
32. Reeder, p. 488.
33. Chukovskaya, *Entretiens*, p. 445.
34. Interview with E.F., September 2003.
35. Ibid.
36. Volkov, *Conversations*, p. 207.
37. Volkov, *Conversations*, p. 209.
38. Volkov, *Conversations*, p. 216.
39. Volkov, *Conversations*, p. 220.
40. Interview with E.F.
41. E-mail to E.F., 2003.
42. Conversation with E.F.
43. See Anatoly Nayman, *Remembering Anna Akhmatova* (London, 1991).
44. Nayman, p. 5.
45. Interview with E.F., 2003.
46. Ibid.
47. Ibid.
48. Or so he remarked in our 2003 conversation.
49. Gerstein, p. 459.
50. Interview with E.F., 1978.
51. See above, p. 48.
52. E-mail to E.F.
53. Volkov, *Conversations*, p. 92.
54. Interview with E.F.

CHAPTER FIFTEEN · LAST YEARS

1. Reeder, p. 372.
2. See above, p. 281.
3. Interview with E.F.
4. He became the editor of the Library of Poets edition of her poems.
5. Nayman, p. 163.
6. Nayman, p. 182.
7. Nayman, p. 168.
8. Akhmatova, *Sobranie*, Vol. 4, p. 367.
9. Akhmatova, *Sobranie*, Vol. 4, p. 364.
10. Interview with E.F.
11. Conversation with E.F., New York, 1978.
12. Akhmatova, *Sobranie*, Vol. 2 (2), p. 213.
13. Nayman, p. 151.
14. Reeder, p. 502.
15. Lavrov, pp. 227–8.

16. Nayman, p. 4.
17. Nayman, p. 5.
18. Reeder, p. 493.
19. Nayman, p. 174.
20. Nayman, p. 175.
21. Nayman, p. 177.
22. Reeder, p. 496.
23. Or so Lady Berlin confirmed to me.
24. E.F., interview with Lady Berlin, March 2004.
25. Ibid.
26. Ibid.
27. Marialina Frasini, "Il viaggio in Inghilterra di Anna Akhmatova" (Tesi di Laurea, Università Degli Studi di Macerata).
28. Polivanov, p. 70.
29. Anne Wollheim in conversation with E.F.
30. Interview with E.F., 2004.
31. Nayman, p. 184.
32. Nayman, p. 187.
33. Nayman, p. 184.

CHAPTER SIXTEEN · AFTERMATHS

1. Volkov, *Conversations*, p. 236.
2. Mikhail Ardov, *Monografiya o grafomane* (Moscow, 2004), p. 194.
3. Reeder, p. 503.
4. Volkov, *Conversations*, p. 239.
5. Interview with E.F.
6. In an e-mail to E.F., January 2005.
7. Ibid.
8. Interview with E.F., Frankfurt, 2003.
9. Ibid.
10. Lavrov, p. 225.
11. Interview with E.F., Frankfurt, 2003.
12. Nayman, p. 211.
13. Nayman, p. 215.
14. Gerstein, p. xvii.
15. The collection is held at the National Library in Moscow.

EPILOGUE

1. E-mail from Dr. Jana Howlett, Fellow of Jesus College and University lecturer, University of Cambridge, October 2004.

2. Michael Ignatieff, "The Day a Sexual Ingenue Met Russia's Fabled Seductress," *The Times*, 10.10.98. Cited in Frasini, p. 107.
3. Feinstein, *Pushkin*, p. 283.

APPENDIX

1. Tsvetaeva, *Selected Prose*, p. 276.
2. Feinstein, *Selected Poems of Marina Tsvetaeva*.
3. Volkov, *Conversations*, p. 46.

SELECT BIBLIOGRAPHY

Akhmatova, Anna: *Sobranie sochinenii, v shesti tomakh*, ed. A. M. Smirnova et al., 6 vols. (Moscow, 1998–2001)

The Complete Poems, trans. Judith Hemschemeyer, ed. and with introd. by Roberta Reeder, bilingual edn. 2 vols. (Somerville, MA, 1990)

My Half Century: Selected Prose, trans. and ed. Ronald Meyer (Ann Arbor, 1992)

Poslednie gody, ed. Viktor Krivulin, Vladimir Muravyev, Tomas Venclova (St. Petersburg, 2001)

Stikhi, perepiska, vospominaniya, ikonografiya, comp. A. Proffer (Ann Arbor, 1977), Vol. 3

Twenty Poems, trans. Jane Kenyon with Vera Sandomirsky Dunham (St. Paul, MN, 1985)

Way of All the Earth, trans. D. M. Thomas (London, 1979)

Annensky, Innokenty: *The Cypress Chest*, trans. R. H. Morrison, bilingual edn. (Ann Arbor, 1982)

Ardov, Mikhail: "Legendarnaya Ordynka," *Russkaya mysl*, No. 3982 (4–10 June, 1993, p. 8; 11–17 June, p. 10)

Monografiya o grafomane (Moscow, 2004)

Barnes, Christopher: *Boris Pasternak: A Literary Biography*, Vol. 1 (Cambridge, 1989)

Beevor, Antony: *Stalingrad* (London, 1998)

Berlin, Isaiah: "Anna Akhmatova: A Memoir," in *The Complete Poems of Anna Akhmatova*, ed. Hemschemeyer and Reeder, Vol. 2

Blok, Alexander: *An Anthology of Essays and Memoirs*, ed. and trans. Lucy Vogel (Ann Arbor, 1982)

Selected Poems, trans. Jon Stallworthy and Peter France (Oxford, 1970)

Bobyshev, Dmitry: "Akhmatovskie siroty," *Russkaya mysl*, No. 3507 (8 March 1984)

Ya zdes (Moscow, 2003)

Brodsky, Joseph: "The Keening Muse," in *Less Than One: Selected Essays* (New York, 1986)

On Grief and Reason (New York, 1995)

Carlisle, Olga: "A Woman in Touch with Her Feelings," *Vogue* (August 1973)

Chernykh, Vadim: *Letopis zhizni i tvorchestva Anny Akhmatovoi, 1889–1917*, 4 vols. (Moscow, 1996–2003)

Chukovskaya, Lydia: *The Akhmatova Journals, 1938–41*, trans. Milena Michalski, Sylva Rubashova and Peter Norman, Vol. 1 (London, 1994)

Entretiens avec Anna Akhmatova (Paris, 1980)

Zapiski ob Anne Akhmatovoi, Vol. 1: 1924–25 (Paris, 1991)

Coffin, Lyn: *Anna Akhmatova: Poems* (New York and London, 1983)

Curtis, J. A. E.: *Manuscripts Don't Burn: Mikhail Bulgakov, A Life in Letters and Diaries* (London, 1991)

Czapski, Joseph: *The Inhuman Land*, trans. Gerard Hopkins (London, 1951)

Dalos, Georgy: *The Guest from the Future: Anna Akhmatova and Isaiah Berlin*, trans. Antony Wood (London, 2000)

Davidson, Pamela: "Akhmatova's Dante," in *The Speech of Unknown Eyes: Akhmatova's Readers on Her Poetry*, ed. Wendy Rosslyn, Vol. II (Nottingham, 1990)

Davie, Donald, and Livingstone, Angela (eds.): *Pasternak: Modern Judgements* (London, 1969)

Davies, Jessie: *Anna of All the Russias* (Liverpool, 1989)

Ehrenburg, Ilya: *Eve of War, 1933–1944: Men, Years, Life*, Vol. 4, trans. Tatiana Shebunina with Yvonne Kapp (London, 1963)

Post-war Years, 1945–1954: Men, Years, Life, Vol. 5, trans. Tatiana Shebunina with Yvonne Kapp (London, 1966)

Eikhenbaum, Boris: *Anna Akhmatova: opyt analiza* (Paris, 1980)

Etkind, Yefim: *Notes of a Non-Conspirator*, trans. Peter France (Oxford, 1978)

Feinstein, Elaine: *A Captive Lion* (London, 1987)

Pushkin (London, 1998)

Selected Poems of Marina Tsvetaeva (Manchester, 1999)

Figes, Orlando: *Natasha's Dance: A Cultural History of Russia* (London, 2003)

A People's Tragedy (London, 1996)

Fleishman, Lazar: "Iz akhmatovskikh materialov v arkhive Guverovskogo instituta," in *Akhmatovskii sbornik*, ed. Serge Deduline and Gabriel Superfin, Bibliothèque Russe de l'Institut d'Éudes Slaves, Vol. LXXXV (Paris, 1989)

Forrester, Sibelan: "Wooing the Other Woman. Gender in Women's Love Poetry in the Silver Age," in *Engendering Slavic Literatures*, ed. Pamela Chester and Sibelan Forrester (Bloomington, 1996)

France, Peter: *Poets of Modern Russia*. Cambridge Studies in Russian Literature (Cambridge, 1982)

"Reading Akhmatova," *Forum for Modern Language Studies*, No. 3, 13 (July 1977)

Franklin, Simon: "New Light on a Poem by Anna Akhmatova? Notes on the Textology of Recollection," *Oxford Slavonic Papers: New Series*, Vol. 31 (1998), p. 96.

Frasini, Marialina: "Il viaggio in Inghilterra di Anna Akhmatova" (Tesi di Laurea, Università Degli Studi di Macerata)

Garnett, Angelica: *Deceived with Kindness: A Bloomsbury Childhood* (London, 1984)

Garshin, Vladimir Georgievich: *Peterburg Akhmatovoi* (St. Petersburg, 2002)

Gerstein, Emma: *Moscow Memoirs*, trans. John Crowfoot (London, 2004)

Gifford, Henry: "Akhmatova i 1940," in *The Speech of Unknown Eyes: Akhmatova's Readers on Her Poetry*, ed. Wendy Rosslyn, Vol. 2 (Nottingham, 1990)

Ginzburg, Lydia: "Akhmatova: Neskolko stranits vospominanii," in *Literature v poiskakh realnosti* (Leningrad, 1987)

Goldberg, Anatol: *Ilya Ehrenburg* (London, 1984)

Gorbanevskaya, Natalya: "Yeyo golos," in *Akhmatovskii sbornik*, ed. Serge Deduline and Gabriel Superfin, Bibliothèque Russe de l'Institut d'Études slaves, Vol. 85 (Paris, 1989)

Gorenko, Viktor: "An Interview," in Akhmatova, *Stikhi, perepiska, vospominaniya, ikonografiya*, comp. Proffer

Gumilyov, Lev: "Avtobiographiya. Vospominaniya o roditeliakh," in Lavrov, *Sudba i idei*

"Korni nashego rodstva," *Sputnik*, No. 5 (1989)

Gumilyov, Nikolay: *Neizdannoye i nesobrannoe* (Paris, 1986)

Neizdannoye stikhi i pisma (Paris, 1980)

On Russian Poetry, ed. and trans. David Lapeza (Ann Arbor, 1977)

The Pillar of Fire, trans. Richard McKane (London, 1999)

"Review of Akhmatova's *Beads*," trans. Robert Whittaker, Jr., *Russian Literature Triquarterly*, No. 1 (Fall 1971)

Haight, Amanda: *Anna Akhmatova, A Poetic Pilgrimage* (New York and London, 1976)

Hayward, Max (ed.): *Writers in Russia, 1917–1978*, ed. and with introd. by Patricia Blake (New York, 1983)

Hingley, Ronald: *Nightingale Fever: Russian Poets in Revolution* (New York, 1981)

Ignatieff, Michael: *Isaiah Berlin* (London, 1998)

Inber, Vera: *Leningrad Diary*, trans. Serge M. Wolff and Rachel Grieve (London, 1971)

Karlinsky, Simon: *Marina Tsvetaeva* (Cambridge, 1986)

Kelly, Catriona: *A History of Russian Women's Writing, 1820–1992* (Oxford, 1994)

Kenyon, Jane: *A Hundred White Daffodils* (St. Paul, MN, 1999)

Ketchian, Sonia I. (ed.): *Anna Akhmatova: 1889–1989: Modern Russian Literature and Culture* (Berkeley Slavic Specialities, 1993)

Kovalenko, S. A.: "Poemy i teatr Anny Akhmatovoi Svershivsheesia i nedovoploshchennoe," in Akhmatova, *Sobranie Sochinenii v shesti tomakh*, ed. A. M. Smirnova et al.

Kralin, Michael: "Anna Akhmatova i Sergey Yesenina," *Nash sovremennik 10* (1990)

"Nekrasovskaya traditsiya u Anny Akhmatovoi," *Nekrasovskii sbornik 8* (Leningrad, 1990)

Kralin, Michael, and Slobozhan, I. I. (eds.): *Ob Anne Akhmatovoi* (Leningrad, 1990)

Kudrova, Irma: *The Death of a Poet*, trans. Mary Ann Szporluk (New York, 2004)

Kunitz, Stanley and Hayward, Max: *Selected Poems of Anna Akhmatova* (New York, 1967)

Kushner, A.: "Poeticheskoe vospriyatie mira," *Literaturnaya gazeta* (21 June 1989)

Kuzin, Boris: *Vospominaniya Perepiska Nadezhda Mandelstam; 192 pisma k B.S Kuzinu* (St. Petersburg, 1999)

Laird, Frances: *Swan Songs: Akhmatova & Gumilyov* (First Books, 2002)

Lavrov, Sergey: *Sudba i idei* (Moscow, 2003)

Ledkovsky, Marina; Rosenthal, Charlotte; and Zirin, Mary (eds.): *Dictionary of Russian Women Writers* (Westport, CT, 1994)

Leiter, Sharon: *Akhmatova's Petersburg* (Philadelphia, 1983)

Lekmanov, Oleg: *Kniga ob akmeizme* (Moscow, 1998)

Lisnyanskaya, Inna: "Taina muzyki 'Poemy bez geroya,'" *Druzhba narodov* 7 (1991)

Loseff, Lev: "Who Is the Hero of the Poem Without One," *Essays in Poetics* 11, No. 2 (1986)

Loseff, Lev and Scherr, Barry: *A Sense of Place: Tsarskoye Selo and Its Poets: Papers from the 1989 Dartmouth Conference Dedicated to the Centennial of Anna Akhmatova* (Columbus, OH, 1994)

Losievskii, Igor: *Anna vseya Rusi. Zhizneopisanie Anny Akhmatovoi* (Kharkov, 1996)

Losskaya, Veronika: *Marina Tsvetaeva v zhizni* (Tenafly, NJ, 1989)

Luknitskaya, Vera: *Nikolay Gumilyov: zhizn poeta po materialam domashnego arkhiva syemi Luknitskikh* (Leningrad, 1990)

Luknitsky, Pavel: *Vstrechi s Annoi Akhmatovoi: 1924–1925*, Vol. 1 (Paris, 1991)

Lurye, Artur: "Olga Afanasevna Glebova-Sudeikina," in *Poema bez geroya*, ed. R. D. Timenchik with V. Ya. Morderer (Moscow, 1989) (orig. *Vozdushnye puti*, No. 5, New York, 1963)

Makovsky, Sergey: "Nikolay Gumilyov (1886–1921)" and "Nikolay Gumilyov po lichnym vospominaniyam," in *Nikolay Gumilyov: Vo vospominaniyakh sovremennikov,* ed. Vadim Kreid (Paris and New York, 1989)

Malmstad, John and Bogomolov, Nikolay: *Mikhail Kuzmin: A Life in Art* (Boston, 1999)

Mandelstam, Nadezhda: *Hope Abandoned,* trans. Max Hayward (London, 1989)

   Hope Against Hope, trans. Max Hayward (London, 1975)

Mandelstam, Osip: *The Complete Critical Prose and Letters,* ed. Jane Gary Harris, trans. Jane Gary Harris and Constance Link (London, 1991)

   Selected Poems, trans. Clarence Brown and W. S. Merwin (New York, 1983)

McDuff, David: "Anna Akhmatova," *Parnassus* (Fall–Winter 1983 and Spring–Summer 1984)

McKane, Richard: *Selected Poems of Anna Akhmatova* (London, 1969)

   Selected Poems of Anna Akhmatova (Newcastle on Tyne, 1989, reprint)

Medaric, Magdalena: "Avtobiografiya i Avtobiografizm," *Russian Literature,* 40 (1996)

Meylach, Mikhail: "Anna Akhmatova's poem Zaklinanie," in *The Speech of Unknown Eyes: Akhmatova's Readers on Her Poetry,* ed. Wendy Rosslyn, Vol. 1 (Nottingham, 1990)

Molok, Jury: "Kameya no oblozhke. (K istorii odnoi mistifikazii)," *Opyty* I (1996)

Monas, S., and Krupala, J. Green (eds.): *The Diaries of Nikolay Punin 1904–1953* (Austin, 1999)

Nayman, Anatoly: "Akhmatova and World Culture," trans. Galina Kmetyuk, *Soviet Literature,* No. 6 (1989)

   Rasskazy ob Anne Akhmatovoi (Moscow, 1989; also in *Novy mir,* Jan., Feb., Mar. 1989)

   Remembering Anna Akhmatova, trans. Wendy Rosslyn (London, 1991)

Nedobrovo, N. V.: "Anna Akhmatova," *Russkaya mysl,* Book 7 (1915)

Nicholson, Virginia: *Among the Bohemians: Experiments in Living 1900–1930* (London, 2002)

Odoevtseva, Irina: *Na bergakh nevy* (Moscow, 1967)

Oliver, Lois: *Boris Anrep: The National Gallery Mosaics* (London, 2004)

Olshevsky, M: "Anna Akhmatova: otnoshenie k moei Rodine," in *Anna Akhmatova: Desiatye gody,* ed. R. D. Timenchik and K. M. Polivanov

Ostrovskaya, Sophie: *Memoirs of Anna Akhmatova's Years, 1944–1950,* trans. Jessie Davies (Liverpool, 1988)

Pasternak, Boris: "A Safe Conduct," *Selected Writings and Letters,* trans. Catherine Judelson, comp. Galina Dzubenko (Moscow, 1989)

Pasternak, Boris: "Boris Pasternak ob Anne Akhmatovoi," ed. Ye. O. Babaev, *Russkaya rech* 4 (July–August, 1989)

Pasternak, Yevgeny: *The Tragic Years 1930–1960*, trans. Michael Duncan (London, 1996)

Pavlovsky, A. I.: "Bulgakov i Akhmatova," *Russkaya literatura*, No. 4 (1989)

Petrov, Vsevolod: "Fontannyi Dom," introd. L. S. Lukyanova and E. V. Tversky, *Nashe nasledie* 4 (1988)

Polivanov, Konstantin: *Anna Akhmatova and Her Circle*, trans. Patricia Beriozkina (Fayetteville, 1994)

Polukhina, Valentina: "Akhmatova i Brodsky (K probleme pritiazhenii i ottalkivanii)," in *Akhmatovskii sbornik*, ed. Serge Deduline and Gabriel Superfin, Bibliothèque Russe de l'Institut d'Études slaves, Vol. 85 (Paris, 1989)

Popova, N., and Rubinchik, O. E.: *Anna Akhmatova i Fontannyi Dom* (St. Petersburg, 2000)

Porter, Cathy: *Larissa Reisner* (London, 1988)

Pozdnyakova, P. S. (ed.): *V. G. Garshin*, introd. essay by Nina Popova (Moscow, 2002)

Punin, N. N.: "Dnevnik," ed. Irina Punina, *Zvezda*, No. 1 (1994)

"Iz pisma k A. A. Akhmatovoi [14 April 1942]," in *Posle vsego*, ed. R. D. Timenchik and K. M. Polivanov (Moscow, 1989)

Radzinsky, Edvard: *Stalin* (London, 1996)

Ranevskaya, Faina: *Dnevnik na klochkakh*, ed. Dmitry Sheglov (St. Petersburg, 2002)

Slushai, shutki, aforizmi (Moscow, 2003)

Reed, John: *Ten Days That Shook the World* (New York, 1919)

Reeder, Roberta: *Anna Akhmatova: Poet & Prophet* (London, 1994)

Reisner, Larisa: "Iz pisma k A. A. Akhmatovoi," in *Posle vsego*, ed. R. D. Timenchik and K. M. Polivanov (Moscow, 1989)

Rosslyn, Wendy: "A propos of Anna Akhmatova. Boris Vasilevich Anrep (1883–1969)," *New Zealand Slavonic Journal*, No. 1 (1989)

Rubenstein, Joshua: *Tangled Loyalties: The Life and Times of Ilya Ehrenburg* (1996)

Rubenstein, Joshua and Naumov, Vladimir: *Stalin's Secret Pogrom* (New Haven and London, 2001)

Rudenko, M.: "Religionoznye motivy v poezii Anny Achmatovoi," *Vestnik Moskovskogo universiteta. Seriya 9. Filologiya.* 4 (1995)

Rusinko, Elaine: "Gumilev in London: An Unknown Interview" (appendix, C. B. Bechhofer, "Interviews"), *Russian Literature Triquarterly*, No. 16 (1979)

Rybakova, O. I.: "Grustnaya pravda," in *Ob Anne Akhmatovoi*, ed. M. M. Kralin and I. I. Slobozhan

Schwartz, E: *Living Unquietly* (1990)

Sebag Montefiore, Simon: *Stalin: The Court of the Red Tsar* (London, 2003)

Sheglov, Dmitry: *F. Ranevskaya Monolog* (Smolensk, 1998)

Faina Ranevskaya: Sudba-plocha (Moscow, 2003)

Shentalinsky, Vitaly: *The KGB's Literary Archive,* trans. John Crowfoot (London, 1995)

Slonim, Mark: *Soviet Russian Literature: Writers and Problems, 1917–1967* (Oxford, 1964)

Sreznevskaya, Valeriya: "Iz vospominanii," in *Anna Akhmatova: Desiatye gody,* ed. R. D. Timenchik and K. M. Polivanov

Stazekalach, V.: "Obraz Anny Akhmatovoi v russkoi poezii (Anthologiya)," in Igor Losievskii, *Anna vseya Rusi* (Kharkov, 1996)

Struve, Gleb: "Akhmatova i Nikolay Nedobrovo," in *Anna Akhmatova, Sochineniya,* ed. G. P. Struve and B. A. Filipoff, Vol. 1, 2nd edn. (Munich, 1967)

Taubman, Jane Andelman: "Tsvetaeva and Akhmatova: Two Female Voices in a Poetic Quartet," *Russian Literature Triquarterly,* No. 9 (1974)

Thomas, D. M.: *Anna Akhmatova, Selected Poems* (London, 1979)

Timenchik, R. D.: "K analizu 'Poemy bez geroya,'" *Materialy 22 nauchnoi studencheskoi konferentsii* (Tartu, 1973)

"Neizvestnoe stikhotvorenie Anny Akhmatovoi," *Oktyabr,* No. 10 (1989)

"Verses from *A Burnt Notebook,*" *Soviet Literature,* No. 6 (1989)

Timenchik, R. D., and Lavrov, A. V.: "Materialy A. A. Akhmatovoi v rukopisnom otdele Pushkinskogo Doma," *Ezhegodnik rukopisnogo otdela Pushkinskogo Doma za 1974,* ed. Alekseev et al.

Timenchik, R. D., and Polivanov, K. M. (eds.): *Anna Akhmatova: Desiatye gody* (Moscow, 1989)

Tomashevskaya, Z. B.: "Ya—kak peterburgskaya tumba," in *Ob Anne Akhmatovoi,* ed. M. M. Kralin and I. I. Slobozhan

Tsvetaeva, Marina: *A Captive Spirit: Selected Prose,* ed. and trans. J. Marin King (Ann Arbor, 1980)

Earthly Signs: Moscow Diaries, 1917–1922, trans. Jamey Gambrell (New Haven, 2002)

"Pismo k Akhmatovoi" (April 1921), in *Poema bez geroya,* ed. R. D. Timenchik with V. Ya. Morderer (Moscow, 1989)

"Pismo k Akhmatovoi" (August 1921), in *Requiem,* ed. R. D. Timenchik and K. M. Polivanov (Moscow, 1989)

"Pismo k Akhmatovoi" (12 November 1926), in *Requiem*

Sobranie Sochinenii v semi tomakh (Moscow, 1994)

Vilenkin, Vitaly: *Vospominaniya s kommentariyami* (Moscow, 1991)

Vilenkin, V. Ya., and Chernykh, V. A. (eds.): *Vospominaniya ob Anne Akhmatovoi,* commentary A. V. Kurt and K. M. Polivanov (Moscow, 1991)

Volkov, Solomon: *Brodsky: Vospominaniya Akhmatovu* (Moscow, 1992). Also in *Svoyu mezh vas yescho ostaviv ten . . . ,* Akhmatovskiye chteniya, ed. N. V. Korolyova and S. A. Kovalenko (Moscow, 1992)

Conversations with Joseph Brodsky (New York and London, 1998)

St. Petersburg (London, 1996)

Shostakovich and Stalin (London, 2004)

Weissbort, Daniel: "Translating Anna Akhmatova: A Conversation with Stanley Kunitz," in Daniel Weissbort (ed.), *Translating Poetry: The Double Labyrinth* (Iowa City, 1989)

Wells, David: *Anna Akhmatova: Her Poetry* (Oxford, 1996)

"Akhmatova and Pushkin: A Study of Literary Relationship," D. Phil. dissertation, Oxford University, 1998

Willk, Mariusz: *Journals of a White Sea Wolf* (London, 2003)

Zhirmunsky, V. M.: "Symbolism's Successors," trans. Stanley Rabinowitz, in *The Noise of Change: Russian Literature and the Critics, 1891–1917* (Ann Arbor, 1986)

Tvorchestvo Anny Akhmatovoi (Leningrad, 1973)

Zholkovsky, Aleksandr: "Anna Akhmatova, Scripts, Not Scriptures," *Slavic and East European Journal* 40, 1 (1996).

Zykov, L. (ed.): *N. Punin. Mir svetel liuboyu. Dnevniki. Pisma* (Moscow, 2000)

N. Punin; Sostavlenie, predislovie, primechaniya (Moscow, 2000)

RECENT ARTICLES IN RUSSIAN

Golobnikova, O. V. and Tarkhova, N. C.: "Istoriografiya, istochnikovedenie, metodika istoricheskogo isledovannya," *Otechestvennaya istoriya,* Vol. 2 (2001)

"I vsyo-taki ya budu istorikom," *Zvezda* 8 (2002)

Ivanovna, Natalya: "Boris Pasternak i Anna Akhmatova," *Znamya,* No. 9 (2001)

Koroleva, Nina: "Anna Akhmatova—sovremenny mir," *Innostrannaya literatura,* No. 4 (2003)

Kudrova, Irma: "Russkie vstrechi Pitera Normana," *Zvezda* 3 (1999)

Kushner, Alexander: "Anna Adreevna i Anna Arkadyevna," *Novy mir,* No. 2 (2000)

Zykov, Leonid: "Nikolai Punin—Adresat i geroi lyriki Anny Akhmatovoi" (given to E.F. by Anna Kaminskaya, 2003), *Nashi Publikatsii*

PERIODICALS

Annual Magazine of Pushkinsky Dom, 1974, pp. 70–71

Horizon, 1989, No. 6, p. 56

Istochnik, 1999, No. 1, p. 80

Novy mir, 1986, No. 9

Zvezda, 1994, No. 4, p. 182

Zvezda, 1999, No. 8, p. 228

INDEX

Printed in the United States
by Baker & Taylor Publisher Services